CHANGE366

A Daily Guide to Organizational Change Management

Al Lee-Bourke

Al-Lee Bourke is a veteran at shaking things up at work, with a career that spans almost 40 years. Al didn't always know it, but he had a knack for guiding companies through big changes, learning through tough times, hard work, and lots of mistakes. It clicked for him around the year 2000 — that's when he really got the hang of it. Since 2011, for eleven years, Al travelled the globe with Microsoft, helping businesses in 196 cities and 29 countries handle change. In 2017, he hit a career milestone and became a Prosci Certified Advanced Instructor. For the last year, Al's been teaching Prosci, consulting, writing…and riding his motorcycle.

This is Al's third book on Change Management.

ALSO BY AL LEE-BOURKE

This book is one of a three-part series.

For a look at the discipline of Organizational Change Management, see...

> *Change Management Field Notes—How it Works & Tips for Doing it. (2022)*

For the how-tos of Organizational Change Management, see...

> *What They Don't Teach You at Change Management School—From Theory to Practice, and Everything in Between. (2023)*

All my books are on Amazon, in print and Kindle format.

CHANGE366

A Daily Guide to
Organizational Change Management

AL LEE-BOURKE

This book covers various topics on disease, medicine, and health. Remember, this content is not a substitute for professional medical advice. Always seek the guidance of a licensed healthcare expert for health issues, particularly if you have pre-existing conditions. Before you alter any treatments or medication dosages recommended by a healthcare provider, get their approval. Only you are accountable for the health choices you make.

CHANGE366—A Daily Guide to Organizational Change Management.

Copyright © 2023 Al Lee-Bourke All rights reserved. This book may not be reproduced in whole or in part, except for the inclusion of brief quotations in a review, without permission in writing from the author or publisher.

For Information, please contact:

al@554north.scot
www.554north.scot

LinkedIn: www.linkedin.com/alleebourke

Book production by: Kyra Lee-Bourke

Legal Notice:

While all attempts have been made to verify information provided in this publication, the publisher and the author do not assume any responsibility for errors, omissions, or contrary interpretation of the subject matter herein. Further, readers should be aware that the information in this book, including URL and other Internet Website references, is subject to change without notice.

Neither the publisher nor the author assumes any responsibility or liability whatsoever on behalf of any purchaser or reader of these materials.

The purchaser or reader of this publication assumes responsibility for the use of these materials and information. Please remember that each individual's success depends on their background, dedication, and motivation. There is no sure guarantee that you will get specific results.

This work constitutes a fair use/fair dealing of any copyrighted material as provided in section 107 of the US copyright law and the UK Copyright, Designs and Patent Act 1988 (as amended).

Disclaimer: The opinions expressed in this book are the author's own. The hyperlinks are correct at the time of writing.

This book is dedicated to all the great people I've worked with and those close to my heart. You are the giants on whose shoulders I stand. Thanks for raising me up with your wisdom, support, friendship, and love.

You know who you are.

Do you think that I count the days?
There is only one day left, always starting over: it is
given to us at dawn and taken away from us at dusk.

—Jean-Paul Sartre, *The Words*

So…

Carpe Diem

CONTENTS

INTRODUCTION

Oscar Wilde once said, "Most people are other people. Their thoughts are someone else's opinions, their lives a mimicry, their passions a quotation." Issac Newton countered, "If I see further, it is by standing on the shoulders of giants."

In my work in organizational change management, a good quote often clears the fog. I've mulled this over since starting the book. What does a strong quote do for stirring things in the workplace?

About my book: it's a daily thing—366 quotes, one for each day of 2024, leap year and all. Open it to any page for a quick thought. No need to remember the past pages. It can be your daily mental bite for a year.

Each quote, I take apart. I give you my view, the key point, and the 'foundational concepts' it hits—from psychology to economics and more. Then, I distill it to one simple idea, ending with a line that ties it up.

In the back, there's an analysis of the major ideas that kept showing up. I tracked them all as I wrote.

You might not agree with everything. Some advice might even clash. That's fine. It's meant to provoke thought.

Read it your way. Day by day or skipping about, I hope you find value in the quotes and the wisdom they hold.

Enjoy the journey!

Notes on Quotations

In old quotes, you'll find 'he,' 'man,' and 'men.' I kept these words to stay true to the original. In Change366, these quotes mean everyone, every pronoun and gender. In my own words, I use 'they,' 'people,' or what fits best.

At times, I've unpacked long articles, laying out my take on their key messages, the academic ones especially. I point to the original articles or books. I suggest you read them yourself.

JANUARY — CHANGE

Organizational change management is like a symphony where each person's role is important. Lombardi reminds us that a collective win stems from many 'I's' working together. Fuller urges us to innovate, not oppose, making the old ways obsolete by creating new models. Socrates echoes this by advising us to pour our energy into building anew.

Heraclitus tells us that change is the universe's rhythm, Darwin points to adaptability as survival's key, and Einstein says new results need new thinking. These thoughts converge into a principle: to move an organization, start with moving a person, as stated by Prosci.

Bridges tells us that for change to last, we must shift our mindset. de Saint-Exupéry believes in inspiring the dream so that the task will follow, while Bach encourages us to learn today to shape tomorrow. Lao Tzu's wisdom speaks to changing our path to alter our destination, with Carroll adding that without a goal, any path is a detour.

Nietzsche's advises having an open mind for change and managing the journey rather than the destination, as Bridges puts it, the process is as critical as the end. Rodgers shows us that a few ignited minds can fuel many, while Prosci states that changing work habits unlocks value. Thompson sees commitment as essential, and Sinek insists on starting with 'why.'

Change, as Obama and Twain show, is a personal and collective journey that waits for no one and often turns resisted knowledge into embraced wisdom. Mridha and Nietzsche offer a look inward for change, while Tolkien and Pirsig encourage stepping out with caution and reflection. Change366 emphasizes the clarity in goals and understanding the complexity of change, stating that real change is an internal process that requires belief and role commitment.

Aurelius and Alighieri remind us that the universe and our memories are in constant flux, encouraging us to embrace and direct this change rather than be passively molded by it.

Mastering change is about understanding and guiding these principles to orchestrate a future that is robust and dynamic, just as the ever-changing tide of the world around us.

January 1st

TEAM EFFORT TURNS MANY 'I'S' INTO A COLLECTIVE WIN

"The Achievements of an organization are the results of the combined effort of each individual."

—VINCE LOMBARDI, *What it Takes to Be Number One.* [1]

Success is a team game. In any organization, you'll find that truth. No one does it alone. Every goal met, every milestone reached, comes from teamwork. Each person plays a part. From the intern to the CEO, everyone contributes. Don't underestimate anyone. Each task, each project, needs many hands. When all these hands work in sync, magic happens. Achievements roll in. Remember, every 'I' in the team is a pillar of the whole building. Keep every pillar strong and valued.

Takeaways. Achievements come from group effort; Each person matters; Teamwork makes the dream work.

Fundamental Concepts. Teams win games. That's Social Identity Theory. We act based on our group. But don't forget Self-Determination Theory. People need choices. They want to feel valued. That's where Collective Efficacy kicks in. When the team believes, each member works harder. Last is Equity Theory. Treat all as equals. From the intern to the CEO, each hand makes the plan stand.

Bottom Line. Winning depends on teamwork. Every team member's effort matters, from the intern to the CEO. Great teamwork leads to swift success. Support and treat everyone fairly to excel as a team. Share goals, share efforts, and celebrate victories together.

January 2nd

BUILD ANEW TO MAKE THE OLD OBSOLETE

"You never change things by fighting the existing reality. To change something, build a new model that makes the existing model obsolete."

—R Buckminster Fuller, *Critical Path.* [2]

You can't fix a car by hitting it with a hammer. The same goes for an organization. Don't waste time fighting what's already there. Instead, build something better. Make a new model. This new way should be so good that it makes the old one look bad. People will flock to it. They will leave the old ways behind. When the new replaces the old, you win.

Takeaways. Fighting what exists won't work; Create a better model; Make the old way irrelevant.

Fundamental Concepts. Smash the old? No good. That's Cognitive Dissonance. People want peace, not pieces. Build new? Yes! That's Self-Determination Theory. People like control. They'll pick the new path if it's better. How to make it better? Operant Conditioning says reward them. Make the new model a treat, not a trick. And don't forget Social Proof. If many move, more will follow.

Bottom Line. Don't waste time fighting old habits. Build something better. People prefer calm and control. Make a superior model and prove its value. Lead the change, reward new practices, and the old ways will disappear.

January 3rd

FOCUS ON BUILDING NEW, AND THE OLD WILL FADE AWAY

"The secret of change is to focus all of your energy not on fighting the old but on building the new."

—SOCRATES. [3]

Focus changes everything. Don't use your energy to fight old systems. It's a waste. Instead, pour that energy into building new ones. A new system attracts people. It makes them curious. They want to use it. And slowly, the old ways fade out. When you build better, people naturally follow. They move towards the new. So, remember, your energy has a place. Make sure it's in building the future, not wrestling the past.

Takeaways. Focus is key; Don't battle the old ways; Invest in the new.

Fundamental Concepts. Don't scatter your focus. That's Attentional Control. Focus attention precisely on new ideas. Why? Self-Determination Theory says people like freedom. Give them a new, better way, and they'll choose it. Positive Reinforcement plays a part, too. Make the new way rewarding, and people will flock. Don't forget Social Learning. Success breeds copycats. Show that the new works and others will follow.

Bottom Line. Change comes from creating better alternatives, not resisting the old. Focus on building the future and invest your energy there. Make new methods attractive and proven to drive change effectively.

January 4th

CHANGE KEEPS FLOWING—NEVER THE SAME RIVER, NEVER THE SAME YOU

"No man steps in the same river twice. For it is not the same river, and he's not the same man."

—HERACLITUS. [4]

Change is like a river. Always moving. You can't step into the same situation twice. Why? Because things shift. Teams change. Projects evolve. You learn. Next time you face a challenge, remember this. It's a new chance. You're different. The setting is different. So, approach it fresh. Don't get stuck in the past. The river of change keeps flowing. Swim with it.

Takeaways. Change is constant; People evolve; Every interaction is unique.

Fundamental Concepts. Your view changes. That's Personal Construct Theory. You don't see the world like you used to. Self-Concept kicks in too. [5] You're not the old you. You've grown. Then there's Cognitive Flexibility. It helps you adapt. You can't step in the same river twice, right? Finally, Temporal Self-Appraisal. Your past self is different from your future self. Keep that in mind.

Bottom Line. Change is constant. You and situations evolve. Each moment brings a chance to learn and grow. Meet challenges with new thinking. You're different every day. Tomorrow is not today. Flow with change.

January 5th

ADAPTABILITY, NOT STRENGTH, IS THE KEY TO SURVIVAL

"It is not the strongest of the species that survive, nor the most intelligent, but the one most responsive to change."

—CHARLES DARWIN. [6]

Strength is good. So is being smart. But they won't keep your organization ahead. What will? Being quick to change. Markets shift. Customers want new things. Technologies update. To stay in the game, you need to adapt. Fast. Don't hold on to old ways. Open your mind. Welcome change; don't fear it. Being quick to adapt is your secret weapon. Use it.

Takeaways. Strength and smarts aren't enough; Adaptability is key; Being open to change leads to survival.

Fundamental Concepts. Adaptability is your friend. It helps you adjust when things shift. That's the core of Cognitive Flexibility. Change your mindset, change your path. But what fuels this? Self-Determination Theory. Inner drive propels change. Then, there's Resilience. It helps you bounce back. It's your cushion when change gets tough.

Bottom Line. Adaptability is key to success. React fast to market shifts, customer demands, and tech changes. Adopt new methods to remain on top. Be flexible and ready for change. It helps with recovery from setbacks. Your ability to adapt is your best strength. Use it wisely.

January 6th

NEW RESULTS REQUIRE NEW THINKING

"The world as we have created it is a process of our thinking. It cannot be changed without changing our thinking."

—ALBERT EINSTEIN, *The World as I See it.* [7]

We build our world with our thoughts. Your company is no different. It's a result of how you and your team think. Want to change things? Start with your mindset. Old thinking brings old results. New thinking brings new possibilities. Challenge the status quo. Question old habits. Foster a culture that loves fresh ideas. Change begins in your head. Make sure it's the kind of change you want.

Takeaways. Our world is shaped by our thoughts; Change starts in the mind; New thinking brings new results.

Fundamental Concepts. Your mind is a tool. It shapes your world. This is a tenet of Cognitive Psychology. Your thoughts can either limit you or free you. What about the company? It's the same. The whole team's thinking sets the culture. That's Social Constructivism at work. [8] So, want to change the company? Change your thoughts first. But sometimes, it's hard. You feel stuck. That's Cognitive Dissonance. It's a sign. A sign you need new thoughts. Tap into your inner drive. That's where Self-Determination Theory kicks in. Want change? Think change.

Bottom Line. Change your mind to change your outcomes. Your mindset mirrors your world and business. Innovate by accepting new and questioning old habits. Your thinking shapes your team's environment. Stuck? Think anew. Change begins with desire and mindset first. Start there to make an impact.

January 7th

TO MOVE A COMPANY, FIRST MOVE A PERSON

"If we can't manage change with one person, how can we expect to manage change with an entire organization?"

—PROSCI. *ADKAR™*. [9]

Change is personal. Each person must decide to adapt. And each choice matters. Why? Because all those choices add up. Together, they make the company move. Think about how to help one person decide to change. What fears must they face? What hopes can inspire them? When you figure that out, use it. Help others make the same decision. Soon, you'll have a team that's eager to adapt. And a company ready to grow.

Takeaways. Individual decisions matter; Personal change leads to organizational change; The sum of individual changes equals company-wide transformation.

Fundamental Concepts. Change starts small. One person decides to adapt. That's Micro-Level Change. What makes them decide? Self-Determination Theory tells us it's inner drive. That one decision can spark more. It's Social Influence in action. Now, think big. Think company-wide. What happens when everyone changes? The whole system shifts. That's Systems Theory. Every small change adds up. So, focus on each person. Help them want to change. That's how the whole company moves forward.

Bottom Line. Company-wide change starts with individuals. Inspire personal desire for change, and it will spread throughout the organization, driving growth and transformation.

January 8th

FOR CHANGE TO STICK, MINDS MUST MAKE THE SHIFT

> "Change is just moving furniture; transition is building a new room in your mind. Without transition, change won't stick."
>
> —WILLIAM BRIDGES, *Transitions.* [10]

Transition isn't just moving pieces around. It's deeper. It's about how people think and feel. You can change a process. But does your team believe in it? That's the transition. It's the inner shift. It makes change real. It makes it last. So don't just focus on new rules or tools. Focus on mindset. Help your team see the 'why.' Make them part of the journey. When their minds move, the change sticks.

Takeaways. Change is external; transition is internal; Mindset matters in making change stick; Without transition, change is superficial.

Fundamental Concepts. Change is more than a new plan. It's a new mindset. Cognitive Dissonance shows us why. Old ways clash with new rules. The mind seeks balance. That's where Identity Theory kicks in. People ask, 'Is this me?' If the answer's yes, they adapt. That's the transition. It's fueled by Motivation Theory. People need to know the 'why.' When they do, they act. They adapt. That's the Adaptation-Level Phenomenon. [11] Change becomes the new normal. Without this mental shift, change fails.

Bottom Line. To ensure lasting change, foster a shift in mindset within your team. Make them see the purpose behind the change. When they understand and embrace it, the change becomes an integral part of their identity and operations, ensuring its lasting impact.

January 9th

INSPIRE THE VOYAGE, AND THE SHIP WILL BUILD ITSELF

"If you want to build a ship, don't drum up people to collect wood, and don't assign them tasks and work. But rather teach them to long for the endless immensity of the sea."

—ANTOINE DE SAINT-EXUPERY, *Citadelle.* [12]

A big, bold dream. Not just tasks. Tasks are empty without meaning. A shared dream fuels the work. It gives it life. People do more when they see more. Show them the endless sea. Make them want to sail. Tasks will follow. First, make them long for the voyage.

Takeaways. Inspire, don't just instruct; Vision fuels action; The 'why' matters more than the 'how.'

Fundamental Concepts. Don't just give tasks. Give dreams. That's Intrinsic Motivation. People work best when they love the work. Self-Determination Theory backs this. Choice boosts drive. Then comes Expectancy-Value Theory. [13] Show the team the 'big why.' Make them see the value. They will act. Finally, Visionary Leadership ties it all. A clear dream can move mountains. Or build ships.

Bottom Line. Inspire with a vision, not just tasks. Show people the big dream and the 'why' behind the work. When they long for the goal, they'll find the drive to do the tasks themselves. This love for the dream leads to better work and greater commitment.

January 10th

LEARN TODAY TO CHANGE YOUR WORLD TOMORROW

"We choose our next world through what we learn in this one. Learn nothing, and the next world is the same as this one, all the same limitations and lead weights to overcome."

—RICHARD BACH, *Johathan Livingston Seagull.* [14]

A better future? Learn today. Learning is the path to change. It beats limits, breaks barriers. It turns today's lesson into tomorrow's win. Ignore it, and you're stuck. The same problems will follow you. So learn. Adapt. Change. Then, watch the world change around you.

Takeaways. Learning shapes our future; Stagnation keeps us in place; Adapt or stay stuck.

Fundamental Concepts. Learning paves the way. That's Learning Theory. What you learn sets what you do. Next is Self-Efficacy. Believe you can change. Then you will. Growth Mindset comes in. Think skills can grow? They will. Finally, Future Orientation. Long-term goals steer your now. Learn today, lift tomorrow.

Bottom Line. To shape a brighter tomorrow, start learning today. Learning is the path to overcoming limitations and achieving change. Without learning, you'll remain stagnant. Believe in your ability to grow and set long-term goals. This mindset and action will transform your world.

January 11th

CHANGE YOUR STEPS TO CHANGE YOUR DESTINATION

"If you don't change direction, you may end up where you are heading."

—LAO TZU, *Tao Te Ching.* [15]

Be alert. Know where you're going. It's easy to drift. Drifting can lead you off track. Off-track means missed goals. Want to hit the mark? Change your steps. Change your path. Only then will you change your end point. Act now. Adjust your course.

Takeaways. Actions predict outcomes; Change to change your destination; Be mindful of your course.

Fundamental Concepts. Goals set the course. That's Goal-Setting Theory. Know what you want. Then aim for it. Self-Regulation comes next. Control your steps. Make them count. Last is Mindfulness. Be aware now. Know each step. Then you can shift.

Bottom Line. Change your steps to reach new goals. Actions lead to outcomes. Set clear goals and control your steps towards them. Stay aware and adjust as needed to avoid drifting off course. Mindful changes to your actions change your destination.

January 12th

WITHOUT A CLEAR GOAL, EVERY PATH IS A DETOUR

"Would you tell me, please, which way I ought to go from here?" "That depends a good deal on where you want to get to," said the Cat. "I don't much care where," — said Alice. "Then it doesn't matter which way you go," said the Cat. "So long as I get SOMEWHERE," Alice added as an explanation. "Oh, you're sure to do that," said the Cat, "if you only walk long enough. If you don't know where you are going, any road will get you there."

—LEWIS CARROLL, *Alice's Adventures in Wonderland.* [16]

Know your goal. Be clear. A foggy goal leads nowhere good. You end up lost. It's like driving with no map. You may enjoy the ride. But you'll miss your spot. You'll wander. Plan well. Pick the right road. Reach your goal.

Takeaways. Clarity matters; Know your goals; Unclear plans lead to random results.

Fundamental Concepts. Clear goals work. That's Goal-Setting Theory. They set your pace. They guide your race. Next is Cognitive Clarity. Be clear in your mind. It helps you find the way. Lastly, Self-Determination Theory. Inner drive guides. It provides the tide for your ride.

Bottom Line. Have a clear goal. Without one, you'll get lost. Clear goals lead to real progress. Know your aim to stay motivated. Goals set the pace and direction of your journey.

January 13th

OPEN MINDS BREED CHANGE—CLOSED MINDS SEAL FATE

"The snake which cannot cast its skin has to die. As well, the minds which are prevented from changing their opinions; they cease to be minds."

—FRIEDRICH NIETZSCHE, *Human all too Human.* [17]

Change is life. It's not an option; it's a must. Like a snake shedding skin, companies must evolve. If they don't, they die. Same goes for thinking. Lock your thoughts? Then, your growth stops. In an organization, keep an open mind. Listen to new ideas. They're your new skin. They keep you alive. They make you thrive.

Takeaways. Be adaptable; Do not stagnate, it leads to decline; Be open to new ideas.

Fundamental Concepts. Change is key. That's Self-Determination Theory. People want freedom to choose. So if you manage, let them. Next, avoid the slump. That's Behavioral Stagnation. Stick to old ways, and you fail. Finally, be open. That's Social Psychology. New ideas are your friend. They help you adapt and win.

Bottom Line. Embrace change, shed old ways, and stay open to new ideas. Success comes from adapting and evolving, not stagnating.

January 14th

MANAGE THE JOURNEY, NOT JUST THE GOAL

"Change comes more from managing the journey than from announcing the destination."

—William Bridges, *Managing Transitions.* [18]

Goals are good. But they're just the start. The real work? The journey. That's where change happens. As a manager, your job isn't just to set targets. You guide the team. You manage the road to get there. Steps matter. Each one. Don't just talk about the end. Make the path clear. Help people move. Solve problems. Adapt. The goal isn't the only win. The journey is full of them.

Takeaways. The journey matters, not just the goal; Steps count; guide each one; Adapt and solve problems along the way.

Fundamental Concepts. Focus on the journey. That's Process-Oriented Thinking. Goals aren't the only wins. Then, manage fear. That's Change Resistance. Clear steps make change easy. Last, adjust and fix. That's Adaptive Problem-Solving. It keeps the team on track. What to remember: Each step counts. Guide them all.

Bottom Line. Manage the journey, not just the goal. Each step in change is crucial. Guide your team's every move. Help them see progress and solve problems. Adjust as needed. Remember, real change happens on the way, not just at the destination.

January 15th

SPARK THE FEW, FUEL THE MANY

"Once an idea hits around 20% adoption, it's unstoppable. It spreads like wildfire, fueled by the power of word-of-mouth in our social circles."

—EVERETT M RODGERS, *Diffusion of Innovations.* [19]

Catch them early. That's the game. Hit 10 to 20 percent adoption, and you're golden. You break a barrier. The change spreads. It's like a snowball rolling down a hill. First slow, then unstoppable. Peer networks fuel this. People talk. Word spreads. Opinions form. The curve takes off. Change becomes the new normal.

Takeaways. Aim for 10 to 20 percent early adoption; Peer networks are your ally; Once you hit the mark, change is unstoppable.

Fundamental Concepts. People act in groups. It's Social Network Theory at work. Your idea? It's not just yours. Share it. Get a few on board. Reach that magic 10 to 20 percent. Then, change takes off. It's 'Diffusion of Innovations' in action. Early adopters speak up. Their words carry weight. Others listen. They join in. The change spreads. Before you know it, it's the norm. Social proof seals the deal. That's when change sticks.

Bottom Line. Get early adopters on board, use peer networks to spread the word, and share your ideas. When it gains popularity, it becomes the norm. Early support from a few can influence many.

January 16th

CHANGE THE WORK, UNLOCK THE WORTH

"Value is only realized when people change the way they work."

—PROSCI, *Unified Value Proposition.* [20]

Talk is cheap. Real value shows up in action. Say your team has a new tool. But no one uses it. Does it add value? No. So, your task isn't just to introduce new things. You have to change habits. Make sure people do things differently. Then, and only then, will your efforts pay off. The real win is in the doing, not just the having.

Takeaways. Introducing change isn't enough; Changing habits is where value appears; Success is in the action, not just ownership.

Fundamental Concepts. Action over words. That's the gist. It's based on Operant Conditioning. Rewards follow actions, not intentions. You got a new tool? Great. But it's useless until used. That's where Behavioral Change steps in. Habits must shift for value to show. The end goal isn't having a new system. It's using it effectively. That aligns with Self-Determination Theory. People need to feel competent and autonomous to make a change stick.

Bottom Line. Change habits to create value. Tools need users to work. Real benefits come from new practices. Use systems well to add value. Action-based changes bring success.

January 17th

COMMIT TO THE RIDE, NOT JUST THE TICKET

"Buy the Ticket, Take the Ride."

—Hunter S Thompson, *Fear and Loathing in Las Vegas.* [21]

In change management, commitment is king. Buying the ticket isn't enough. You must take the ride. What does that mean? Fully dive into the change process. Don't just plan. Act. Don't just talk. Do. A bought ticket is wasted if you don't board the train.

Takeaways. Commitment goes beyond initial buy-in; Action turns plans into reality; Full engagement is non-negotiable.

Fundamental Concepts. Commit, then act. That's Self-Determination Theory. People need to feel in control. So when you commit, you take charge. Next comes action. That's Behavioral Activation. Saying yes isn't enough. You need to go for it. Fully engage. That's Cognitive Dissonance. Your actions must match your words. Or else, it's just talk. No ride.

Bottom Line. Commit with action, not just words. True commitment is active, not passive. Dive in, engage, and act. Align actions with plans for real change.

January 18th

KNOW THE 'WHY', NAVIGATE THE 'HOW'

"Start with the 'why'".

—SIMON SINEK, *Start with the Why.* [22]

Change is coming. You feel it. Your team feels it. But why? Don't skip that question. It's the first one to ask. Why are we changing? The answer powers everything. It fuels the team. It aligns the goals. It's your compass in the chaos. Know it. Share it. Make the 'why' your rallying cry.

Takeaways. 'Why' drives change and team buy-in; 'Why' aligns the change with goals; 'Why' sets the stage for success.

Fundamental Concepts. Start with 'why.' That's Self-Determination Theory. People need meaning. When you know the why, you're in charge. Next, share it. That's Social Cohesion. Alone doesn't cut it. You must loop in the team. Keep the goal in sight. That's Intrinsic Motivation. A clear why fuels the drive. Without it, you're lost. No map.

Bottom Line. Know and share why change matters. The 'why' drives and directs the team. Make sure all grasp and accept it. It motivates and guides when uncertain. The 'why' unites and commits the team. Without it, direction and drive may waver.

January 19th

DIVERSE 'WHYS' DRIVE CHANGE, NOT NARROW VIEWS

"For 'why change?' two answers—profit and culture. Blend both for strength, top-down, tech & culture, plan surprises, empower all for success."

—CHANGE366.[23]

Two paths guide the 'why' of change. One, eyes the prize-money. Shareholders cheer. The other cares for culture. It enhances skills. Employees grow. But why pick just one? Blend both for the best change recipe. Leaders, you start the fire. But everyone fans the flames. Technical needs matter. So does the team vibe. Don't just plan for sunny days. Pack an umbrella for surprise rain. Reward those who adapt.

Takeaways. Mix the 'why' for effective change; Leadership starts it, everyone else drives it; Plan for the unplanned; Reward adaptability; Empower staff, don't just solve problems.

Fundamental Concepts. Two 'whys,' one goal. That's Cognitive Dissonance. People resist mixed methods. Blending the 'why' fixes this. Leaders spark change. That's Social Proof. People follow examples. A leader's role is crucial. Team involvement is key. That's Self-Determination Theory. People engage when they have a role. They stay invested. Unexpected events shake us. That's Loss Aversion. We dislike losing more than we like winning. Planning helps. So do rewards. They boost motivation. That's Operant Conditioning. Rewards guide behavior. Consultants as coaches? That's Social Learning Theory. We learn by example. A coach provides that example. People learn, adapt, grow. Blend, lead, involve, plan, and empower. That's Behavioral Complexity. Multiple needs met, multiple wins scored.

Bottom Line. Mix profit and culture for effective change. Balance pleasing shareholders with nurturing employees. Leaders lead, everyone pushes. Reward adaptability. Empower and value staff. Combine goals with readiness for the unexpected.

January 20th

DIG IN TO CHANGE, DIG OUT THE TRUTH

"If you truly want to understand something, try to change it."

—KURT LEWIN. [24]

True grasp comes from change. It's easy to talk about a system or a process. Trying to alter it? That's where you learn. You uncover weaknesses. You see hidden strengths. Change isn't just a new path. It's a mirror. It shows you what's working. It shows what's not. It's the best teacher you'll ever have.

Takeaways. Change reveals hidden flaws and strengths; Understanding deepens when you attempt to make changes; Change is both a path and a mirror for assessment.

Fundamental Concepts. Dig in by doing. That's Action Research. Change teaches you. Next, watch the pushback. That's System Resistance. Weak spots show. Strengths too. Adjust your views. That's Cognitive Dissonance. What you think meets what is. Lastly, choose to change. That's Self-Determination Theory. You're in control. More motivated. You learn better.

Bottom Line. Change reveals what works and what doesn't. It's a path to improvement and deeper insight. When you encounter resistance, it shows where to make improvements. Taking action aligns your thoughts with reality. Change empowers you with control, motivation, and valuable learning.

January 21st

CHANGE WAITS FOR NONE, SO WHY WAIT?

"Change will not come if we wait for some other person or some other time. We are the ones we've been waiting for. We are the change that we seek."

—Barack Obama, *Speech.* [25]

Change starts now. It starts with you. You're the driver. No waiting. Be proactive. Own it.

Takeaways. You are the driver of change; Don't wait for the 'right time'; Own the change.

Fundamental Concepts. You're the key. That's Self-Efficacy. Change starts now. That's Temporal Motivation Theory. [26] No waiting. That's Locus of Control. Be proactive. That's Proactivity. Own it. That's Ownership. Be the change. That's Identity Theory. Own your fate. That's Autonomy. Make your stage. That's Role Theory. No delay. That's Present Bias. Change starts with self. That's Intrinsic Motivation.

Bottom Line. Change begins with you, immediately. You lead the change. Don't delay for others or timing. Believe in your impact. Act now, take charge, and craft your role. Change is about starting, not waiting.

January 22nd

RESISTED CHANGE TODAY IS TOMORROW'S WISDOM

"When I was 17, my father was so stupid, I didn't want to be seen with him in public. When I was 24, I was amazed at how much the old man had learned in just 7 years."

—MARK TWAIN. [27]

Change isn't just about systems or strategies. It's about people. Think of your team like a growing child. They may not see the wisdom in change at first. Later, they realize its value. This is the journey of maturity in an organization. Lead them with patience. Educate continuously. Soon, they'll see the wisdom in what felt like a burden.

Takeaways. People often resist change due to lack of understanding; Patience and continuous education can foster acceptance; The journey to embracing change is a mark of organizational maturity.

Fundamental Concepts. Narrative shift. That's Cognitive Reappraisal. Old views make way for new. People learn. That's Continuous Reinforcement. Lead patiently. That's Delayed Gratification. Wisdom shared repeatedly. That's the Spiral Curriculum in play. [28] Change matures the team. That's Psychological Growth. Team trust builds. Leadership strengthens. That's Social Capital.

Bottom Line. Change is initially resisted but later valued. Teams grow to appreciate it. Patience and teaching are key. Understanding deepens; trust in leadership grows.

January 23rd

CLOCKS DON'T TICK FOR CHANGE—YOU DO

"Time never changes—only we change. We measure the changes of our lives and think that we are measuring time. We are just measuring the movement of the earth."

—DEBASISH MRIDHA, *Verses of Happiness.* [29]

Time doesn't shift; we do. In a company, don't blame time for lack of progress. Look inward. Change comes from us, not the clock. We make moves, not minutes. Set goals. Take action. Make the earth under your company move.

Takeaways. Time remains constant; change is in our hands. Progress depends on our actions, not the passing minutes. Set clear objectives and act to bring about change.

Fundamental Concepts. Time as scapegoat. That's External Attribution. We shift blame. Self-control missing. That's Locus of Control skewed. Goals set. Focus sharpens. That's Goal-Setting Theory. Action follows. That's Self-Determination Theory at work. Making earth move. Personal Agency triggered. Company changes. That's Organizational Behavior Modification. Time, just a metric. We are the equation. That's Agency Theory.

Bottom Line. Change comes from doing, not waiting. Time passes—we must act. Set goals and move toward them. Act to control change, not just watch time. Actions drive change, not the clock.

January 24th

LOOK INSIDE, THEN DECIDE

"For some natures, changing their opinions is just as much a requirement of cleanliness as changing their clothes; for others, however, it is merely a requirement of vanity."

—FRIEDRICH NIETZSCHE, *Twilight of the Idols.* [30]

Change is personal. For some, it's like a fresh shirt—needed and refreshing. For others, it's about showing off. In a company, know why you change. Is it a deep need? Or just to look good? Get real. Make change meaningful.

Takeaways. Change is different for each person; Know the real reason behind organizational changes; Vanity-driven changes don't last. Genuine changes stick.

Fundamental Concepts. Change varies. That's Individual Differences. Some need it. That's Internal Motivation. Others show off. That's External Validation. Uncover the real reason? Must know? That's Self-Reflection. Vanity short-lived. That's Temporal Discounting. Genuine lasts. That's Enduring Change. People differ. Recognize it. That's Emotional Intelligence. Aim true. Skip the show. Real change grows.

Bottom Line. Change hinges on honest intent, not vanity. It must be deeply needed for lasting effect. Know the true reason for change and aim for real, enduring transformation, acknowledging personal differences.

January 25th

STEP OUT, BUT STAY STEADY

"It's a dangerous business, Frodo, going out your door. You step onto the road, and if you don't keep your feet, there's no knowing where you might be swept off to."

—J.R.R. Tolkien, *The Lord of the Rings.* [31]

Change is like stepping out the door. It's risky but needed. You don't control all outcomes. Stay steady. Keep your focus. You'll manage where the change sweeps you.

Takeaways. Change comes with risk; Stability helps navigate the unknown. Keep focused to control where change takes you.

Fundamental Concepts. Change is risky. That's Uncertainty Avoidance. Need for stability? That's Psychological Safety. Focus helps. That's Goal Orientation. Don't drift off. That's Self-Regulation. Unknowns abound. That's External Locus of Control. Steer where you can. That's Internal Locus of Control. Take the leap. Know the stakes. Walk the road with care. That's Risk Management.

Bottom Line. Embrace change's risks with stability and focus to steer its course. Stay grounded to manage the unpredictable journey of change.

January 26th

FORGE AHEAD, PATTERNS EMERGE

"You look at where you're going and where you are, and it never makes sense, but then you look back at where you've been, and a pattern seems to emerge."

—Robert M. Pirsig, *Zen and the Art of Motorcycle Maintenance.* [32]

The future looks fuzzy. But look back. Patterns appear. Change is like that. It feels random now. Later, it makes sense. Stay the course.

Takeaways. Future is uncertain; Past reveals patterns; Change only makes sense in hindsight.

Fundamental Concepts. Future unclear? That's Uncertainty Tolerance. Past shows patterns? That's Retrospective Sense-making. Change feels random? That's Complexity Theory. [33] Sense comes later? That's Temporal Construal. Stay on path? That's Sustained Motivation. Understand the past. Grasp the future. Sense in change comes late. That's Delayed Gratification.

Bottom Line. Change seems random until past patterns bring clarity. Keep going to make sense of change over time.

January 27th

CLARITY IN GOALS LIGHTS CHANGE'S WAY

"Change is a tough journey; determination, a roadmap, and support are vital. Avoid juggling many changes; even one shift brings challenges. Familiarity is comforting, but stepping out takes courage. Clarity is crucial for vague goals. Persistence matters; quick wins are rare. Real change begins within."

—CHANGE366.[34]

Change is everywhere. We often say it's hard and believe it. Trying to change many things confuses us. A single change can affect many areas. Being in a comfort zone stops us. It's easy to talk about change, but acting is tougher. Sometimes, we can't see why change is good. If we can't see a better future, motivation drops. Vague goals are confusing. We need clear goals. Giving up early stops change. Change takes time and has challenges. Being strong helps us push through. Trying to change others is tough. Changing ourselves is where real power is.

Takeaways. Changing many aspects at once can scatter focus; Every change brings ripple effects; The familiar comfort zone can be a trap; The allure of change needs clarity.

Fundamental Concepts. Humans crave stability. That's Status-Quo Bias. Uncertainty unnerves us. That's Ambiguity Aversion. Broad goals daze. Call it Choice Overload. We're impatient by nature. It's Temporal Discounting. We struggle to influence others. A tale of External Locus of Control. Want true change? Dive within. That's Self-Determination. Transform self, not others. It's the Intrinsic Motivation key. Every action, every thought, governed by our psychology. Understanding it? First step to mastering change.

Bottom Line. Change requires clear goals, focus, and inner drive. Don't shift too much at once; start internally. Overcome comfort for clear progress. Patience and persistence are key as change unfolds from within.

January 28th

NATURE'S DANCE NEEDS CHANGE'S BEAT

"Every part of me then will be reduced by change into some part of the universe, and that again will change into another part of the universe, and so on forever...what can take place without change? And can anything else that is useful be accomplished without change? Do you not see then that for yourself also to change is just the same and equally necessary for the universal nature?"

—MARCUS AURELIUS, *Correspondence.* [35]

Change is constant. We're part of that endless cycle. Everything transforms, from us to the universe. Embrace it. Fear of change? It's natural. Yet, everything needs it. Bathing, eating, working. Change fuels all. Understand this. You and change? Allies in nature's dance.

Takeaways. Change is a universal process; Daily actions require transformation; Embracing change aligns with nature; Fear is a barrier, not a stop.

Fundamental Concepts. Change is unending. That's Cyclical Evolution. Nature's law? Embrace transformation. That's Intrinsic Adaptation. Daily routines thrive on change. Clear Behavioral Dynamics at play. Fear stifles progress. That's Avoidance Behavior. Overcome and sync with nature. That's Alignment Principle. Change isn't just external. It's deeply Internalized Conditioning. Every action, every choice? Driven by change. That's Behavioral Adaptation. Join nature's rhythm. Success will follow. This is Flow State Realization. [36] Understanding the need to adapt? It's Cognitive Assimilation. To resist is against nature. That's Dissonance Creation. Embrace the inevitable. Flourish in life's dance. This is Adaptive Mastery.

Bottom Line. Embrace change as nature does. From eating to creating to working, it's necessary. Fear not, for change is nature's ally. Sync with it and thrive.

January 29th

COMPLEXITY IN CHANGE? FIND BELIEF OR BIND ROLES

"Win the change game? Know the forces. It's not just money and people. Watch for seven game-changers. Critical mass. Social vibes. Group logic. Common woes. Network perks. Mind hacks. Change heroes. Ignore them, you lose."

—CHANGE366. [37]

Change isn't just a numbers game. It's more complex. It has many faces. Influence matters more than sheer numbers. People need cues. They look for leaders. Watch group dynamics too. Groups can either push or pull change. Don't forget the shared concerns. They bring people together. Use networks to your advantage. Networks spread change faster. And above all, be the change you wish to see. Be the hero. Lead from the front.

Takeaways. Influence is stronger than numbers; People seek leaders for cues; Group dynamics can make or break change; Networks can amplify or squelch change.

Fundamental Concepts. Influence rules, that's Social Proof. Leader cues play a role linked to role modeling. Leaders shape behavior; their actions speak. Group dynamics matter, touching on Groupthink and Social Identity Theory. Groups sway individual choices; a group's mood impacts its actions. Shared concerns are about Social Cohesion; common issues bind people, creating a Shared Mission. Network effects are vital, hinging on Viral Spread. More users add value, magnifying the change.

Bottom Line. Drive change by leading with influence, uniting groups over common issues, and using networks to spread progress. Be a proactive change agent.

January 30th

MEMORY MARKS CHANGE—USE IT WELL

"In that book which is my memory, On the first page of the chapter that is the day when I first met you, Appear the words, 'Here begins a new life.'"

—DANTE ALIGHIERI, *Vita Nuova.* [38]

Think of your organizational memory as a valuable book. Each significant meeting, each transformative encounter, marks a new chapter. Like meeting a pivotal person, change in organizations requires recognition. Here begins a new life—these words are powerful. They signal a departure from the old, embracing the new. Leaders need to capture these moments, celebrate them. They need to guide their teams through transformation. Recognizing change helps in creating a culture of renewal. So, start a new chapter together. Embrace change and transformation.

Takeaways. Use organizational memory as a resource for change; Mark and celebrate significant moments of transformation; Embrace change as a start of a new life; Lead teams through change, fostering a culture of renewal.

Fundamental Concepts. The book of memory opens. That's Cognitive Encoding. A pivotal meeting starts a chapter. That's Event Segmentation. Words mark a new life. That's Positive Reinforcement. Change becomes a celebrated event. That's Social Validation. The narrative embraces transformation. That's Growth Mindset. Leaders guide the change. That's Transformational Leadership. They create a culture of renewal. That's Organizational Culture Change. Embracing change, we renew. That's the essence of Adaptability. Recognize, celebrate, and lead through change. Watch the organization thrive.

Bottom Line. Mark change as a fresh start in your organization's memory. Celebrate growth milestones to foster a culture of adaptation. Lead with vision as each change begins a new chapter.

January 31st

CHANGE, OR BE CHANGED BY CHANGE'S SWIFT TIDE

"In the tapestry of enterprise, strategic weaves of change stitch the future's robust fabric."

—CHANGE366.[39]

Imagine a thriving forest. It's not static. Trees grow, seasons change, and animals adapt. Similarly, a business thrives in a changing environment by evolving. When the market shifts, a company must sprout new strategies and shed outdated practices. Change management is not a single event but a continuous journey that requires foresight and reactivity.

Takeaways. Enterprises are akin to living systems, complex and ever evolving; Strategic shifts are essential to remain competitive and profitable; Approaches to change vary: some are gradual, others are swift and sweeping; Anticipating and managing change requires a blend of flexibility and structure.

Fundamental Concepts. Behavioral Inertia leads to resistance, and Comfort Zone Bias keeps employees in known routines. Leadership faces Autonomy Struggle, while top-down changes cause Controlled Motivation. Anxiety and uncertainty grow, causing Motivational Deficit and Intrinsic Motivation Absence. Community Disconnect and Sociocultural Adjustment follow. Autonomy Support, Involvement Engagement, and Competence Building lead to Integrated Regulation and Congruence Creation. Collaborative Transformation unites teams, breaking the cycle for Organizational Rebirth. Involve, inspire, and empower for transformation.

Bottom Line. Organizations thrive by evolving with change. Adapting strategies and dropping old ways are key to staying competitive. Managing change combines planning with the ability to adapt.

Organizational change management is an art and science, requiring skilled navigation through the complexities of human behavior. Nadella compares well-managed change to transformed behavior, emphasizing the difficult but vital nature of behavioral change. It's akin to coaching a team to victory, as Prosci puts it, it's driving project benefits by ensuring people adopt new solutions.

Inaction and delay hinder progress. 'Yes, Minister' humorously captures the stages of denial and procrastination that hinder change, while Bridges reminds us that incomplete tasks today create challenges tomorrow. Berra's words, distinguishing theory from practice, underline the unpredictability of real-world application. Rodgers' mention of diffusion reflects on time's essence in change management—delay, and opportunities slip away.

de Rubens on LinkedIn advocates for agile's true meaning—incremental improvement, not rushed outcomes. Lincoln's approach to preparation teaches us that thorough groundwork leads to success. Meadows encourages a model open to scrutiny and evolution, embracing adaptive change.

A Scottish proverb reminds us that small incremental changes lead to significant results. Russell's teapot analogy prompts us to trust in data over unfounded beliefs, and systems thinking, as described in Change366, encourages seeing the broader picture in change efforts.

Change366 suggests starting with the desired impact and working backward, while innovation's clarity can facilitate adoption. Aligning perceptions with the proposed change makes the transition smoother. Change managers must simplify their models, and adapt strategies to align with organizational goals.

Frameworks and models are tools to enable change, as Phillips notes, while the 'DICE' framework helps predict the success of change initiatives. A journey of change is marked by purpose and people, as Change366 frames it, with choices and leadership being pivotal to guiding this process. Gaps in understanding must be appropriately labeled to guide actions effectively.

Clear communication, effective training, and unified efforts lead to successful change, as highlighted by Change366. Lencioni teaches us that unity is key for long-term success, and the alignment of personal values with organizational change efforts can amplify the impact.

Popper reminds us to remain open-minded, never settling on a single perspective as the 'truth.' Change366 notes the importance of addressing individual needs like mastery, choice, and connection for fostering well-being and motivation, which are essential for enduring change. Newell's perspective on heuristics reinforces that discovery is a journey, not a destination.

Managing change is managing a portfolio—prioritizing, assigning roles, and maintaining momentum are crucial for finishing strong. This collective wisdom forms the backbone of effective change management practices.

February 1st

CHANGE WELL-MANAGED IS BEHAVIOR TRANSFORMED

"It is behavior change which is always hard. That's why change management is everything…I want us to get good at, position, pitch, evangelize the fact that this is a very different thing."

—Satya Nadella, *Microsoft Inspire.* [40]

Changing habits is hard. This is a fact we all know. In a company, it's even harder. We're not just dealing with one person's habits, but many. So, what do we do? We manage change. But it's not just about new tech or systems. It's about how people act and think. We need to manage this change in behavior. How? By showing everyone it's not just the usual stuff. It's different. It's something we all need to 'get.' To do this, we don't just tell people. We sell it. We make it so appealing that people want to change. We put it in the spotlight. We cheer for it. We make it the star of the show.

Takeaways. Behavior change is tough; Change management is vital; You must make others see the unique aspects of change.

Fundamental Concepts. Change is tough. That's Behavioral Inertia. Old habits die hard. How to shift? Use Self-Determination Theory. Give people choices. Make them part of the plan. Then, use Social Proof. If peers cheer, others join in. But beware of Cognitive Dissonance. Old ways will fight back. That's tension. Clear it by showing the new way is better. That's Persuasion Principles. Make the change appealing. Make it the star.

Bottom Line. Transform behaviors with 'excellent' change management. Involve and convince people to adopt new actions and thinking. Celebrate the benefits to ensure they embrace the change.

February 2nd

CHANGE MANAGEMENT IS THE COACH, NOT THE TROPHY

"Change Management is not an end in itself; it is designed to drive project benefit realization and adoption and is necessary wherever a project's result and outcomes depend on individuals adopting and using a solution."

—PROSCI, *Definition of Change Management.* [41]

Change Management isn't the trophy; it's the coach. You don't do it for its own sake. You do it to win the game—that game being business benefits. The aim is to make sure your project brings real benefits. More than that, it's about getting people on board. Imagine a new software tool. If no one uses it, what's the point? You spend money and time on something that sits idle. So, getting your team to adopt and use a solution is critical. That's where Change Management comes in. It guides your team. It makes the new normal easier to accept. And it ensures your project doesn't just end; it transforms.

Takeaways. Change Management is a means to an end; The goal is real, tangible project benefits; Human buy-in is critical for success.

Fundamental Concepts. Change is a tool, not the goal. That's Instrumental Motivation. It helps you win the project game. Want it to stick? Use Self-Determination Theory. Let people take the wheel. Make them feel skilled. Next, weigh the scales. That's Cost-Benefit Analysis. Show the gains, beat the pains. Team spirit counts too. That's Social Proof. If the crew moves, the stray follows.

Bottom Line. Use change management to guide teams and gain benefits from projects. Ensure success by leading the team to adopt and apply new solutions effectively.

February 3rd

INACTION IS THE MOTHER OF MISSED CHANCES

"Then we follow the four-stage strategy. In stage one, we say nothing is going to happen. In stage two, we say something may be going to happen, but we should do nothing about it. In stage three, we say that maybe we should do something about it, but there's nothing we can do. In stage four, we say maybe there was something we could have done, but it's too late now."

—'YES, MINISTER,' *The Skeleton in the Cupboard.* [42]

Don't fall into the four-stage trap. It's a loop of denial, inaction, regret. Sound familiar? You've seen it in companies. Maybe even your own team. First, they ignore change. Next, they downplay it. Then, they claim powerlessness. Last, they regret the missed chance. Break the cycle. Acknowledge change. Act fast. Or be left behind.

Takeaways. Denial and inaction make you miss opportunities; The four-stage trap ends in regret and failure; Be alert to change; act before it's too late.

Fundamental Concepts. Skip denial; it's a lie. That's Cognitive Dissonance. Your brain's fooling you. Don't buy in. See the risk? Act. That's Counterfactual Thinking. [43] You dodge regret by making a bet. Feel stuck? Break free. That's Learned Helplessness. Shift your mindset. No more regret. Missed the boat? Learn. That's Hindsight Bias. It fools you. But you can school you.

Bottom Line. Act against denial and address change promptly to avoid missed chances and failure. Acknowledge and move on change quickly to outpace regret.

February 4th

UNFINISHED TASKS ARE FUTURE BURDENS

"Every phase of life has…a task and failing to complete it satisfactorily means that you make the transition into the next phase accompanied by unfinished business."

—William Bridges, *Transitions: Making Sense Of Life's Changes.* [44]

Completing tasks thoroughly is crucial in change management. Each stage in organizational change presents unique tasks. If tasks remain unfinished, they become burdens in subsequent stages, hindering progress and growth. As change managers, we must ensure that every task is addressed and completed before moving on to avoid the drag of 'unfinished business' that can compromise the success of future initiatives.

Takeaways. Finish current tasks fully before transitioning to new stages; Unfinished tasks can hinder transformation; Diligent completion is essential for unburdened progress.

Fundamental Concepts. Incomplete tasks linger. That's the Zeigarnik Effect in action. [45] Remembered until finished. That's Cognitive Persistence. Unfinished business creates drag. That's Task Residue impacting progress. Closed tasks satisfy. That's Psychological Completion at play. Task significance motivates. That's work's Meaningful Impact. Completion breeds competence. That's Self-Determination Theory speaking. Clear each stage; set for the next. That's Progressive Clarity. Avoid task carry-over. It burdens your mental journey. That's Clean Transition Logic. [46]

Bottom Line. Ensure each task in change management is complete to prevent future complications. Unfinished tasks can become barriers to progress, so clear completion is necessary for maintaining momentum and preventing the accumulation of 'future burdens.'

February 5th

PLANS ARE PENCILS—REALITY'S THE ERASER

"In theory, there is no difference between practice and theory. In practice, there is."

—YOGI BERRA. [47]

Think it's all mapped out? Think again. Plans look great on paper. Reality? Not so neat. Change management is messy. Twists and turns. Unseen snags. Your team must adapt. Adjust the course but keep the core. Learn as you go. Make theory meet practice. That's the art of change.

Takeaways. Plans are just a starting point; adaptability is key; The unexpected will happen; be prepared to adjust; Use real-world feedback to make theory practical.

Fundamental Concepts. Plans in place? Great. That's Cognitive Theory—it's your mental map. When a curveball comes? Don't freeze. That's Expectancy Violation Theory. It shocks, but you can adapt. Feel stuck in theory? Flex. That's Cognitive Flexibility. It lets you rewrite the plan, not toss it. Who decides? You do. That's Self-Determination Theory. You're the captain, not a passenger.

Bottom Line. Treat plans as flexible guides. Adapt to reality with agility and use feedback to evolve. Lead changes actively, adjusting strategies as needed.

February 6th

TIME TICKS, CHANGE PICKS, DELAY, AND IT SLIPS AWAY

"Diffusion is the process by which an innovation is communicated over time among the participants in a social system."

—EVERETT M. RODGERS, *Diffusion of Innovations.* [48]

Change needs talk. Not just any talk. Smart talk. Spreading a new idea? You need everyone on board. All hands. You must share the vision. Time matters. So does the network. Who says what to whom? It can make or break your change plan. Be strategic. Make your message stick. Keep it alive in the social loop.

Takeaways. Communication is key to spreading change; Time and network matter; they shape the diffusion process; A strong message gains traction and outlasts the noise.

Fundamental Concepts. Change spreads by talk. That's Social Influence. The way we shape others' choices. But not just any talk works. That's Persuasion Theory. Craft your message. Make it hit home. Why? The brain prefers easy over hard. That's Cognitive Ease. Time? It's more than ticks on a clock. That's Temporal Psychology. Quick or slow, time shapes how change spreads. Networks matter. Who talks to whom? That's Social Network Theory. It's the web of who knows who. It sets the path for change. Make your plan smart. Be strategic. That's Game Theory. Predict moves. Plan your plays.

Bottom Line. Communicate change clearly and quickly through your networks. Make messages resonate to accelerate change and overcome obstacles. Use time and social connections strategically for impactful change management.

February 7th

AGILE RIGHT, NOT AGILE LIGHT

> "ADKAR is always applicable, including iteratively. That said, my Prosci practice (despite best efforts) often feels one step behind. In a world (tech) where projects barely have a charter, it is a constant game of supporting basic PjM activities that CM relies upon. My emerging belief is that PjM is struggling with "agile" and CM by extension. And the word 'agile' is being used (especially by leaders) to mean 'faster than reasonable' when it really is supposed to mean incremental release or fix forward. Sometimes I just hear the word, it's hard not to groan because of what it's come to mean."
>
> —SHANNON DE RUBENS, *LinkedIn.* [49]

Change is agile. Yet, agile isn't about haste. It's about smart steps. Make sure 'agile' keeps its true meaning. Be ready. Stay one step ahead. Keep your change model flexible.

Takeaways. Agile is misunderstood; Flexibility is key in Change Management. Keep pace with Project Management—and vice versa.

Fundamental Concepts. Agile twisted. That's Conceptual Drift. Flexibility matters. That's Adaptability. One step behind? That's Reactive Management. Keeping pace is crucial. That's Synchronization. Takeaways laid out. That's Cognitive Structuring. Agile gets clarity. That's Operational Definition. Flexibility built in. That's Resilience Strategy. Keep pace, keep face. That's Organizational Alignment. Guide the change. That's Proactive Leadership. Stay a step ahead. That's Predictive Modeling.

Bottom Line. Practice agile OCM by planning and adapting, not rushing. Anticipate project demands to guide change effectively and stay ahead in project management.

February 8th

PREPARE TO PREVAIL

"If I had eight hours to chop down a tree. I'd spend six hours sharpening my ax."

—Abraham Lincoln. [50]

Prep matters. Sharp tools, smooth work. Six hours make the other two count. Don't rush into change. Get your ax sharp—your plan, your team, your skills. Then chop. Time spent in preparation isn't wasted—it's invested.

Takeaways. Preparation is key; Sharp tools make for easy work; Invest time to save time later.

Fundamental Concepts. Prep matters. That's Planning Efficacy. Sharp tools, smooth work. That's Resource Optimization. Six hours shape two. That's Time Management. Don't rush. That's Impulse Control. Invested, not wasted. That's Delayed Gratification. Takeaways give guide. That's Cognitive Framing. Sharp plan wins. That's Strategic Anticipation. Time's a friend. That's Temporal Perspective. No rush, only plan. That's Behavioral Self-Regulation.

Bottom Line. Prioritize preparation in OCM for effective execution. Sharpen planning, team skills, and execution strategy to transform time spent into successful change outcomes.

February 9th

ADAPT, DON'T JUST ADOPT

> "Remember, always, that everything you know, and everything everyone knows, is only a model. Get your model out there where it can be viewed. Invite others to challenge your assumptions and add their own."
>
> —DONELLA H. MEADOWS, *The Limits to Growth.* [51]

All you think you know about change management is just a model. Show it. Let others see. Welcome their thoughts. Adapt the model—change is teamwork.

Takeaways. Knowledge is a model; Share your views openly; Welcome challenges; Adapt and improve.

Fundamental Concepts. Model thinking? That's Mental Schemata. Show it off? That's Transparent Communication. Others can see? That's Social Verification. Invite input? That's Collaborative Inquiry. Adapt model? That's Cognitive Flexibility. Team effort? That's Collective Intelligence. Transparency rules. That's Open Culture. Be open to change. That's Adaptive Leadership. A shared vision grows. That's Social Constructivism.

Bottom Line. OCM evolves through collaboration. Share your change strategy, seek input, and use collective insight for continual improvement.

February 10th

SMALL WINS WIN BIG

"Mony a mickle maks a muckle."

—SCOTTISH PROVERB. [52]

Small actions seem trivial, right? Wrong. In the world of organizational change, the little stuff matters. A tweak here. A new process there. These small changes add up. They shape culture, drive adoption, and inspire transformation. Stop waiting for a grand plan, start with a small step. Show others the value of steady progress. Before you know it, you've got real change.

Takeaways. Small changes matter; Accumulate steps for progress; Lead by example; Steady gains spark change.

Fundamental Concepts. Small seems trivial? That's Cognitive Discounting. Small matters? That's Incremental Theory. Leading by doing is Behavioral Modeling. Steady gains matter? That's Continuous Reinforcement. Cognitive Discounting gets in the way. Incremental Theory changes minds. Behavioral Modeling shows the way. Continuous Reinforcement keeps it alive. Real change starts small. Steady gains fuel it. Modeling leads. Reinforcement sustains. That's the psychology of Cumulative Change.

Bottom Line. OCM succeeds through consistent, small steps. Initiate minor changes and showcase their compound effect to drive organizational transformation.

February 11th

TRUST DATA, DOUBT DOGMA

> "'Russell's Teapot' is an argument that the burden of proof for a claim lies with the person making it rather than shifting the burden of disproof to others. It uses a hypothetical teapot orbiting the Sun, too small to detect, to demonstrate that just because a claim can't be disproven, it isn't automatically valid."
>
> —BERTRAND RUSSELL, *The Collected Papers.* [53]

Change thrives on evidence. Not just on tradition. Methodologies come and go. But evidence stays. In managing change, question methods. Seek proof. Because what's popular isn't always right. Don't adopt a method blindly. Scrutinize it. Validate before you act. Ancient doesn't always mean accurate. New doesn't always mean better. Seek evidence, always.

Takeaways. Evidence is vital in change management; Challenge traditional methods; Validate new approaches with data; Avoid blind adoption of any methodology.

Fundamental Concepts. Evidence drives decisions. That's Rational Verification. Traditions bind. But can blind. That's Orthodoxy Inertia. Validate to navigate change. That's Methodological Scrutiny. Blind faith? Risky in business. That's Dogmatic Pitfall. Embrace data. Avoid untested myths. That's Empirical Emphasis. Real leaders question the known—seek the provable. It's the heart of Evidenced Change. Dive deep into methods. Challenge the status quo. Lead with insight. Success follows when you prioritize the evidence.

Bottom Line. In OCM, prioritize evidence over traditional methods. Scrutinize and validate approaches with data to drive successful change. Avoid unquestioned adoption of any practice.

February 12th

SEE THE WHOLE, NOT JUST PARTS

"In organizational change, systems thinking has six key themes: interconnectedness, synthesis, emergence, feed-back loops, causality, and systems mapping. They reveal hidden connections and guide adaptation."

—CHANGE366. [54]

Systems thinking helps understand an organization's big picture by showing how different parts connect and impact each other. It's crucial for effective change management, recognizing that organizations are complex and changes in one area can ripple through the entire system. Change managers must predict and manage these outcomes.

Takeaways. Systems thinking is seeing the big picture; Organizations are interconnected. A change in one part affects others; Change managers must use systems thinking to manage change effectively.

Fundamental Concepts. Systems thinking ties to our human need for order. It's rooted in Cognitive Complexity. We seek patterns. We yearn to make sense of chaos. That's Pattern Recognition. Our brain desires to connect dots. That's Neural Networking. When change happens, we resist. It's our natural Fear of the Unknown. But systems thinking eases this. It gives us a roadmap. It lights up our neural paths. Understanding the whole helps us cope. That's Cognitive Coherence. Clarity reduces resistance. That's the power of Holistic Vision.

Bottom Line. Managers must understand the entire organizational system to handle change effectively. They should link all parts of the company to understand their combined effect. This big-picture view prepares managers to predict the impact of changes and manage their ripple effects efficiently.

February 13th

IMPACT IS NOT JUST THE END BUT THE ASPIRATION

"Start with outcomes to stir the change; track, act, and impact—the change-maker's range. Preconditions plant, interventions bind, rationales and assumptions refine the mind."

—CHANGE366. [55]

Understanding change means grasping the framework of outcomes and pathways. These models guide policy shifts, behaviors, and even attitudes. Both short-term and long-term changes are part of this. 'Impact' is the zenith. Yet, it's like a distant star, not always visible. Organizations aim high, setting their sights on measurable goals. And like building a house; foundations matter. These foundations? Preconditions.

Takeaways. Change is a journey with short and long stops; Impact is the pinnacle, but it's elusive; Foundations are vital; never overlook them.

Fundamental Concepts. Understanding leads to action, a reflection of Cognitive Processing. Behavior has its roadmap, stemming from Pathway Orientation. Goals steer us, a testament to Goal-Setting Theory. [56] Foundations are laid through Structural Framing. Ambitions rise when we aim high, an echo of Aspiration Psychology. Clarity comes from indicators, and their success measurement is the Feedback Loop. Misaligned actions hint at Cognitive Dissonance. Delving into the 'why' reveals Rationale Comprehension. When we question beliefs, we engage in Reflective Thought. By clearing doubts, we lessen risks, embodying Risk Management Psychology.

Bottom Line. Change starts with setting goals and measuring progress. Short-term and long-term goals guide us. Impact is our goal, but it's hard to measure. We need to set the right conditions before we see results. Actions must link clearly to goals to understand what works. We must think about why things are connected and check if our beliefs are true to avoid mistakes.

February 14th

CLARITY IN INNOVATION SPEEDS ADOPTION

"Innovation has five attributes that drive adoption: Advantage, Compatibility, Complexity, Trialability, and Observability. Adoption rate depends on these factors. Speed of adoption is influenced by decision-making, communication, social systems, and change agents."

—CHANGE366. [57]

Innovation thrives on perception. How people view an innovation steers its adoption. An innovation isn't just new. It's how well it fits, how it improves, how clear it is. It's how easy one can test it and how visible its results are. Recognize these attributes for successful change. Value them. Drive adoption by ensuring these boxes are ticked.

Takeaways. Perception drives innovation adoption; Adoption is about fit, improvement, clarity, testability, and visibility; Successful change managers understand and leverage these attributes.

Fundamental Concepts. Attributes steer innovation through Behavioral Anchoring. Perceptions mold our actions due to Cognitive Appraisal. Self-Determination Theory highlights the importance of fit and values. Visibility, backed by Social Proof, accelerates adoption. If it's complex, adoption lags because of increased Cognitive Load. The importance of testability? It's real-time Risk Mitigation. Catalysts, or change agents, drive adoption forward. Understanding your innovation boosts its progress, embodying strategic Change Management. Ultimately, everything hinges on the might of perception.

Bottom Line. Change managers boost innovation adoption by valuing its fit, clarity, and visibility. They use clear communication and social proof to make innovation attractive. Managers must guide teams to test and showcase the benefits of innovations, simplifying complex ideas for quicker adoption.

February 15th

ALIGNMENT IN PERCEPTION PAVES THE PATH FOR CHANGE

"Shape the view, align the story, pinpoint the problem, present a fix, fuel the fire for change. Frame it. Make it fit, make it familiar, make it timely—that's how you move mountains."

—CHANGE366. [58]

Frame analysis is about how people interpret situations. [59] It's based on their background and beliefs. It's like using different filters to view change. Frames are powerful. They shape our view of change. When these individual frames line up, they resonate. This resonance guides groups to shift their perspectives. But it's not always easy. The success of framing depends on its robustness and how well it's understood.

Takeaways. Frames must be relevant to the larger organizational belief system; Frames must be credible and fit organizational cultural narratives; Proper framing can achieve big changes.

Fundamental Concepts. Frames guide. That's Cognitive Structuring. Alignment means congruence. That's Behavioral Coherence. Recognize problems, plan solutions. That's Organizational Diagnosis. [60] Fire up for action. That's Motivational Priming. Values in focus? That's Cultural Resonance. Relevant frames matter. That's Narrative Validity. Frame's history plays a role. That's Societal Echoing. Aligned frames, societal shift. That's the Sociocultural Metamorphosis. Change needs proper framing. That's Constructive Blueprinting.

Bottom Line. Align how people see things to enable change. Clearly explain problems and provide practical solutions to motivate action. Match these explanations to what people already believe and their experiences. Timing is crucial. Strong, understandable frames can lead to big changes. They must ring true to people's values and history to really work.

February 16th

SIMPLIFY, REFLECT, SUCCEED

"Change Managers simplify change models. Adapt advice, as one size doesn't fit all. Reflect and experiment. Align goals. Effective change balances opportunity and security but consider employee expectations. Build trust, don't rush."

—CHANGE366. [61]

Change isn't one-size-fits-all. Adapt models. Simplify them. Reflect and experiment. Align goals. Test approaches. Ensure stakeholder needs align. Employee expectations matter. Trust is key. Slow and steady works, quality over speed.

Takeaways. Adapt change models to specific situations; Align goals: individual, group, and organization; Balance stakeholder needs with employee expectations; Prioritize effective change over quick change.

Fundamental Concepts. Adaptability is king. That's Cognitive Flexibility. Flexible methodology. That's avoiding the Einstellung Effect. [62] Simplification aids understanding. That's Cognitive Load Reduction. Reflection fosters growth. That's Introspective Insight. Experimentation fuels learning. That's Behavioral Adaptation. Aligned goals? That's Motivational Synergy. Stakeholders need guide actions. That's Societal Feedback Loop. Employees' voices matter. That's Social Validation. Trust is the glue. That's Relational Bonding. Speed can mislead, slow, deliberate action prevails. That's Quality Over Quantity. Effective change understands needs. Adjusts accordingly. Wins hearts. Achieves goals. That's the essence of Informed Change Management. Understanding, adjusting, and thriving lead to success.

Bottom Line. Change managers must customize change models to suit specific situations, aligning individual, team, and organizational goals. Prioritize understanding stakeholder and employee needs, build trust, and prefer effective change over quick fixes.

February 17th

KNOWLEDGE IGNITES, READINESS RULES, DREAMS DRIVE, GOALS GROW, STEPS STRIDE, VALUES NURTURE

"Fact-finding fuels change, readiness rules, evidence evolves, leadership leads, visions voice, networks navigate, goals grow greatness, small steps sprint, progress pulses, culture cradles change."

—CHANGE366. [63]

Lay the groundwork with facts. Know your readiness. Evidence shapes evolution. Leadership? Essential. Craft a vision. Use networks. Clear goals. Fairness is crucial. Small wins matter. Regularly check progress. Blend change with culture.

Takeaways. Build with facts, gauge readiness; Lead with trust, communicate vision; Utilize networks, ensure fairness; Embrace micro-moments, embed cultural change.

Fundamental Concepts. Foundation built on facts. That's Cognitive Anchoring. Readiness gauged. That's Situational Awareness. Evidence leads evolution. That's Empirical Decision-Making. Leadership's trust? That's Social Validation. Vision communicated. That's Motivational Framing. Networks navigated. That's Social Capital Utilization. Fairness ensures commitment. That's Distributive Justice. Small wins celebrated. That's Incremental Reinforcement. Progress checked. That's Feedback Loop Activation. Change respecting culture. That's Sociocultural Integration. Proper planning, trusted leadership, and regular feedback. The crux of Change Mastery. Understand, adapt, integrate.

Bottom Line. Argue for change using facts. Check readiness and learn from past experiences. Develop and empower leaders. Implement evidence-based solutions. Communicate a clear plan. Use networks for broader influence. Set distinct goals, educate, involve, and maintain fairness. Celebrate small victories and encourage innovation. Monitor progress with specific metrics. Embed change in culture while preserving core values.

February 18th

FRAMEWORKS DREAM, MODELS DELIVER

> "Whereas frameworks may identify variables or theories required to promote change, models focus on the specific processes that lead to change."

—Jeffrey Phillips, *Change Management from Theory to Practice.* [64]

Frameworks outline the theory. Models show the way. Theory points, processes guide. Understand the difference. Use both. Maximize change outcomes.

Takeaways. Frameworks highlight variables and theories; Models detail change processes; Theory informs, processes direct; Use both for effective change.

Fundamental Concepts. Frameworks define. That's Cognitive Structuring. Models direct. That's Behavioral Pathfinding. Theory informs. That's Abstract Reasoning. Processes drive change. That's Procedural Execution. Merging both? That's Synergistic Integration. Frameworks provide insight. Models give direction. Two tools, one mission: successful change. Grasp the abstract, execute the tangible. Change becomes reality.

Bottom Line. Change managers should use frameworks to grasp theories and models to follow specific steps. Both are essential for effective change.

February 19th

CHANGE'S PATH CASTS DICE'S PREDICTIVE SHADOW

"To gauge change success, use the DICE framework: Duration, Integrity, Commitment, Effort. Score them. Win Zone, Worry Zone, Woe Zone. Focus on Integrity and Commitment; they carry more weight."

—CHANGE366. [65]

Change is tough and unpredictable. The DICE framework simplifies it with four elements: Duration, Integrity, Commitment, and Effort. Regular reviews track progress. Team strength depends on leadership and commitment. Senior management's engagement and employees' extra effort are crucial. The DICE score, combining these factors, predicts and guides successful change.

Takeaways. DICE: A predictor of change program success; Four pillars: Duration, Integrity, Commitment, Effort; Scoring gives clarity: Win, Worry, or Woe Zone; Weighted emphasis on Integrity and Commitment.

Fundamental Concepts. Framework in place. That's Cognitive Structuring. Predictability calms minds, it eases Anxiety. DICE gives a roadmap. That's Navigational Certainty. Regular checks? Boosts Environmental Mastery. Team's strength and commitment? Social Cohesion displayed. Senior management's voice? Sign of Hierarchical Structuring. Score guides destiny. Represents Operational Control. Commitment and effort? Showcases Internal Locus. DICE doubles down. Enhanced Predictive Validity. Navigate change with clarity. DICE provides that lens.

Bottom Line. Use the DICE framework to predict success in change management. Focus more on Integrity and Commitment. Score the factors to identify if your change project is likely to win, cause worry, or face woe.

February 20th

PURPOSE IS THE COMPASS—PEOPLE ARE THE JOURNEY

> "Change involves the 'who' and 'why, not just the 'what'. Start by defining the project, then focus on the purpose, serving as the compass. Detail the specifics in a roadmap. The key players, the drivers of action, are crucial. Consider how many are needed for success. The challenge lies in aligning all these elements, the blueprint for change. Connecting these dots leads to transformation."
>
> —CHANGE366. [66]

Know the game. Define the shift. Plot the path. Remember, people drive change. Numbers fuel us. Align and transform.

Takeaways. 'Who' and 'Why' frame change; Purpose is the compass; Roadmap: details the shift; People and numbers: Heart and fuel.

Fundamental Concepts. Know your goal. That's Purpose Recognition. Define reasons for change. That's Intrinsic Motivation. Navigate the change terrain. That's Cognitive Mapping. People are key. That's Social Capital. How many join matters. That's Quantitative Value. Blend purpose, plan, people. That's Holistic Integration. Alignment makes transformation. That's Synchronous Action. Change's heart beats with purpose and people. That's Collective Drive. Blueprint of success? Purpose, plan, people, and metrics. That's Comprehensive Transformation Strategy.

Bottom Line. In change management, clearly define the project and its purpose to set the direction. Detail the changes needed. Focus on people, the drivers of change, and the required number for success. Align all elements for transformation.

February 21st

CHOICES SHAPE CHANGE—LEADERSHIP GUIDES IT

"Change arises from individual decisions, influencing organizational transformation. IT isn't sufficient; 84% need adoption guidance. Change Management combines technical and human aspects, boosting adoption and efficiency. Leadership, particularly executives, is key to change success. A solid change program markedly increases success, reliant on executive support. Lack of this support commonly causes failure."

—CHANGE366. [67]

Change is a personal choice. Together, choices form organizational shifts. Most seek guidance. Tech doesn't drive change alone. Leadership is key. Executive support? Essential.

Takeaways. Personal choices shape organizational change; Change Management connects tech and people; Leadership catalyzes change; Active executive support: critical success factor.

Fundamental Concepts. Change is a choice. That's Individual Agency. Many seek guidance. That's Extrinsic Motivation. Tech isn't the driver. That's Tool Limitation. Leadership's role: undeniable. That's Social Influence. Executive support shines. That's Leadership Endorsement. Change's strength: Leadership. That's Directive Power. Guidance leads to action. That's Behavioral Prompt. Change Management's role? Bridging gaps. That's Mediating Function. A strong leader? Change's best friend. That's Inspirational Motivation. Lack leadership? Change stumbles. That's Leadership Vacuum.

Bottom Line. Change hinges on individual choices and requires effective leadership. Many need assistance to adopt new changes. Effective Change Management blends technology with people's needs. Active, visible leadership greatly increases project success chances. Without it, change efforts frequently fail.

February 22nd

MISLABELING 'GAPS' CAN MISGUIDE ACTIONS

"Know your destination and measure your journey. Only then can change be not just an act but a culture."

—CHANGE366. [68]

In organizational change management, recognizing the gap is vital. This gap shows the distance between our current state and our goal. However, just seeing a gap isn't enough. We must understand it. Mistakenly labeling every gap as a 'need' can mislead us. It might make us focus on the tools (means) rather than the goals (ends). Clear vision and proper understanding prevent derailment.

Takeaways. Recognize and understand the 'gap'; Avoid mislabeling gaps to prevent confusion; Focus on goals (ends) over tools (means); Proper clarity ensures successful planning.

Fundamental Concepts. Gaps evoke discomfort. That's Cognitive Dissonance. We naturally seek balance. That's Equilibrium. Recognizing gaps? It's vital for growth. But mislabeling? It causes confusion. That's Misattribution. A clear understanding? It combats Ambiguity Aversion. Focusing on ends? Aligns with Goal Theory. Ensuring clarity? It's fundamental for Self-Determination. Clarity in change? Anchors our Behavioral Drive. Proper vision? That's Cognitive Clarity. Successful planning? Relies on Effective Heuristics.

Bottom Line. Know where you're going and track progress to make change part of the culture. Understanding gaps between now and your goals is crucial. Don't confuse every gap for a need; it may cause wrong focus. Aim for clear goals over just using tools. Clear vision and understanding are essential for success.

February 23rd

TALK CLEARLY, TRAIN WELL, WIN CHANGE

"In the symphony of digital transformation, technology sets the tempo, but it's the human elements that hit the high notes. Master the ensemble of culture, motivation, communication, and task design, and your change strategy will sing."

—CHANGE366. [69]

Change is unceasing, with technology and markets constantly shifting. People are crucial in this; their buy-in is essential. Effective communication and training are key. Motivation leads to success. New tech tools bring change but carry risks. Prepare your team for role shifts and clarify tasks. Monitor time and emotions. Learn from previous successes to refine processes. Aim to make change seamless, not contentious.

Takeaways. People are central to successful change; Good communication and training are vital; Tech tools are double-edged swords—beneficial but risky; Measure time and emotion for an accurate change impact.

Fundamental Concepts. People are the core. That's Social Influence. They sway the change. Drive or derail. Team spirit helps. That's Group Cohesion. It fuels motivation. Good talk flows. That's Open Communication. It wipes out fear. Training equips. That's Skill Acquisition. It builds task mastery. Tech changes the field. Brings Opportunity and Risk. That's the Dual Nature of Technology. Time counts. So do feelings. They set the pace. That's Emotional State and Time Management. Learning from past wins? That's Experiential Learning. It carves a safer path. Tech and people mesh. Change works. That's Organizational Synergy.

Bottom Line. Talk well, train right, and manage change. Keep people first; they drive change. Good communication and training are key. Use tech carefully; it can help or harm. Track time and emotions to see how change really hits. Learn from success to improve. Make change smooth, not hard.

February 24th

SPEED SPRINTS, UNITY ENDURES

"If you want to go fast, go alone. If you want to go far, go together."

—Patrick Lencioni, *The Five Dysfunctions of a Team.* [70]

In organizational change, understanding the balance between speed and sustainability is vital. While a single individual or small group might achieve quick results, it's the collective effort that ensures long-term success. Teamwork transcends the limitations of individual efforts, opening doors to boundless possibilities. Unity in an organization is necessary for enduring success.

Takeaways. Balance speed with sustainability for lasting change; Teamwork breaks the bounds of individual limitations; For long-term success, collaboration is key; Unity in a team ensures strength and endurance.

Fundamental Concepts. Speed shows autonomy. That's Individual Mastery. It brings quick results. That's Rapid Achievement. Alone, you control the pace. That's Personal Agency. But it's short-lived. That's Temporal Success. Sustainability needs more. That's Long-term Investment. Collaboration brings depth. That's Team Synergy. It ensures enduring success. That's Sustainable Achievement. Shared goals guide us. That's Common Purpose. Together, we go far. That's Collective Strength. It turns efforts into legacies. That's Lasting Impact.

Bottom Line. Going alone means going fast, but going together means going far. During change, a team's effort lasts longer than what one person does alone. Quick wins from solo work won't last without a team. For success over time, work together. Teamwork is necessary for long-term results and turns short-term wins into lasting success.

February 25th

ALIGNED VALUES, AMPLIFIED CHANGE EFFORTS

"Autonomy, aligned with personal values, is the cornerstone of sustainable change in any organization."

—CHANGE366. [71]

Embrace the day by aligning personal values with daily tasks. When tasks at work echo our own beliefs, we dig deeper, push further, and climb higher. It's about connecting the dots between personal purpose and daily grind. This nexus becomes the powerhouse of change within an organization.

Takeaways. Match personal beliefs with work goals for deeper engagement; Personal value in tasks leads to increased motivation; Autonomy supports motivation and enhances task performance; Recognizing individual motivations is vital in managing change.

Fundamental Concepts. We start with Tool Underuse. This echoes lack of Autonomy Support. Employees need freedom to use tools effectively. That's Autonomy Support Deficit. Without leaders, chaos reigns. That's Leadership Void. Managers must act, not observe. We call this Active Engagement. Teams need skill, not just tools. That's Competence Support. Autonomy, Competence, Relatedness—they're Self-Determination Theory's pillars. Offer these, change thrives. Ignoring them invites failure. Leadership's task? Align these elements. That's the mantra for Organizational Change.

Bottom Line. Believe in your work. It boosts effort and success. Share values with your job, and you'll excel. Choices at work improve performance. Personal drive matters in change. Align jobs with values for better change management. Decision freedom increases happiness and change coping. Personal fit eases change. Positive workspaces lift motivation.

February 26th

ONE KEY NEVER FITS ALL LOCKS IN CHANGE

"Whenever a theory appears to you as the only possible one, take this as a sign that you have neither understood the theory nor the problem which it was intended to solve."

—KARL POPPER, *The Poverty of Historicism.* [72]

Imagine this—a single key opens every lock. Impossible, right? So why do we treat complex change in organizations with one-size-fits-all solutions? To understand change, we must dig deeper. Only then can we see the full landscape of solutions. As change managers, we break the mold, challenge the norm, and innovate.

Takeaways. Doubt the 'only one right way' to manage change; Dive deep to truly understand the organizational challenges; Encourage exploring a variety of solutions; Innovation blooms from questioning the status quo.

Fundamental Concepts. Single solutions deceive. That's Solution Bias. Depth lacks. That's Shallow Comprehension. Challenges multiply. That's Complexity Underestimation. Question, explore. That's Solution Diversification. Innovation flourishes. That's Creativity Cultivation. Understand deep. That's Problem Exploration. Change thrives on variety. That's Diversity Dependence.

Bottom Line. Don't rely on just one way to handle change. Look closer at the problem. Use many ways to find solutions. This helps change work better. Innovation thrives when we explore beyond the norm. Understand the problem deeply. This leads to more options for successful change.

February 27th

MASTER, CHOOSE, CONNECT—CHANGE'S POTENT TRIO

"Needs are central. Mastery, choice, and connection matter most. They build well-being. Workplaces that meet these needs boost motivation and success. Focus on these for lasting change."

—CHANGE366. [73]

True growth needs more than just skill. It craves competence, the feel of mastery. Change asks for autonomy; control over our actions. It seeks relatedness; connections that matter. Together, they are the core of change. They fuel our drive at work. When met, we find more than success. We find meaning.

Takeaways. Champion competence for mastery in skills; Foster autonomy for control in change; Cultivate relatedness for meaningful connections; Meeting these needs drives well-being and effective change.

Fundamental Concepts. Needs form the core. That's Universal Necessity. Mastery defines skill. That's Competence Essence. Choice drives ownership. That's Autonomy Affirmation. Connection fuels spirits. That's Relatedness Relevance. Satisfying these builds well-being. That's Psychological Wellness. Organizations thrive when needs are met. That's Climate Cultivation. Champion autonomy, competence and relatedness. Watch motivation, well-being, and innovation grow.

Bottom Line. Master skills, choose freely, and connect well. These three lead to change. They make work meaningful and help us do well. When businesses help us feel skilled, free, and connected, they thrive. This way, change lasts and brings success and joy. Focus on skill, freedom, and connection for strong change at work.

February 28th

CHART NEW COURSES, PROOF IS IN THE JOURNEY

"The essence of a heuristic is that it is an aid to discovery. It is not a method of proof."

—ALLEN NEWELL, *The Logic Theory Machine.* [74]

A heuristic (a guess) is like a compass on a ship—it points you where you need to go to explore uncharted waters. It's not about having all the answers but about finding new ways to solve problems. This concept is vital in organizational change management, where innovation comes from the willingness to venture into the unknown.

Takeaways. Use heuristics as tools to explore new strategies in change management; Focus on discovery and innovation, not just verification; Embrace the journey of finding new solutions to challenges; Understand that proof may follow, but discovery leads.

Fundamental Concepts. Heuristics pave new roads. That's Cognitive Shortcutting. They inspire trials. That's Exploratory Behavior. Risk-taking guides. That's Affective Engagement. Discovery beats rote learning. That's Cognitive Creativity. Heuristics are hunches turned habits. That's Adaptive Learning. They spark questions. That's Inquiry-Based Stress Reduction. Discovery validates change. That's Constructivist Learning. Exploration over proof. That's Openness to Experience. Heuristics evolve with use. That's Dynamic Learning Processes.

Bottom Line. Guessing opens new doors. It urges us to explore, not just confirm known facts. Guessing initiates problem-solving. It sparks learning and fresh ideas. The search matters more than immediate proof. Guessing adds excitement to change. It broadens our thinking and actions.

February 29th

STEER CHANGE WITH A SOLID PORTFOLIO

> "Prioritize with precision, distribute roles with care, and pace your change to sustain momentum. In the art of managing multiple change programs, it's not just about starting strong—it's about finishing stronger."
>
> —CHANGE366. [75]

Change is a marathon, not a sprint. It's managing long-term transformations by prioritizing tasks, defining roles, and maintaining a steady pace. As a change manager, your job isn't only to kick off projects but to see them through to successful completion. Careful planning and role assignment are the cornerstones of effective change management. It's the art of balancing urgent tasks with important ones and ensuring that every change initiative gains from this balance.

Takeaways. Portfolio change management is a compass; Plan each stage of change with focused priorities; Assign roles clearly and thoughtfully for effective execution; Maintain a pace that ensures lasting change.

Fundamental Concepts. Portfolio guides change. That's Cognitive Anchoring. Autonomy drives change. That's Self-Determination Theory. It fuels engagement and lasting commitment. That's Enduring Involvement. Clear roles build competence. That's Role Efficacy. Steady paces foster relatedness. That's Sustainable Progress. Planned actions predict success. That's the Theory of Planned Behavior. Personal buy-in brings change home. That's Internalization. Effective planning meets psychological need. That's Cognitive Harmony. Change isn't just action; it's psychological readiness. That's Behavioral Preparedness.

Bottom Line. Effective change demands strategic planning, clear goals, and paced execution. It's a process that goes beyond starting; it's about maintaining direction and finishing with impact. Goals and governance drive successful change.

MARCH — TECHNOLOGY

In digital transformation, a multitude of voices guide us through the intricate dance of change. Levitt emphasizes focusing on outcomes over processes. It's not about the tools we use, but the results they yield. Change366 echoes this, underscoring that beliefs and systems are both sculptors of change. As Jung wisely points out, acceptance is the precursor to transformation. This journey through change is riddled with uncertainty, a crucible forging true transformation, as van Gennep illustrates.

Campbell's insight into the hero's journey resonates deeply in this context. It's a team's collective march towards change, guided but not dictated by a leader. Joyce's reflection on personal struggles and resistance mirrors the challenges organizations face during digital shifts. Kierkegaard and Twain remind us that while understanding the past is crucial, navigating change requires forward-looking actions and an appreciation of the fluid nature of facts.

Change366 highlights the unseen aspects of change, the hidden costs that often go unnoticed. Carey's notion of conceptual change being a creation within a cognitive system is pivotal. It's not just about adopting new technologies but transforming our mindsets. Change366 also emphasizes the role of Organizational Change Management as the driver of digital transformation, turning the key in the engine of growth and innovation.

Westerman's analogy of digital transformation being a metamorphosis, not merely a speed race, is particularly striking. It's about aligning strategy, leadership, and a culture of innovation. Sagan encourages us to keep questioning, to fuel innovation. Rogers and Change366 urge us to view digital transformation as a continual journey, not a one-time event.

O'Neil's caution about algorithms and ethics is a vital reminder in our tech-driven world. Change366, Hitchens, and Crowley all emphasize the importance of anticipation, informed decision-making, and finding balance. Good warns against manipulating data, while Russell speaks to the wisdom in knowing when to embrace change and when to let go.

Aristotle's words on excellence being a result of wise choices resonate with the need for strategic alignment in tech decisions. Drucker's perspective on the paramount importance of continual learning echoes throughout this digital transformation journey.

In essence, these voices converge to form a chorus, each emphasizing different aspects of the digital transformation narrative: focus on outcomes, embrace change, lead with wisdom, and never stop learning. This journey is less about the tools and more about the minds wielding them, a dance of innovation and human insight, steering towards a future shaped by collective wisdom and shared purpose.

March 1st

TECH FOR SHOW FAILS—OUTCOMES MAKE THE GLORY

"People don't want to buy a quarter-inch drill. They want a quarter-inch hole."

—Theodore Levitt, *Marketing Myopia.* [76]

Levitt's insight is a beacon for change managers navigating the choppy waters of technology change. It reminds us that the value of technology is not in its existence but in its utility. When managing organizational change, we focus on outcomes, not tools. For technology to be more than just a shiny new object, it must create meaningful work, simplify tasks, and solve problems. This mindset shift from features to benefits is the essence of technology adoption in change management.

Takeaways. Focus on technology's outcomes, not its features; Ensure technology solves problems and simplifies work; Guide teams to see technology as a means to an end, not the end itself.

Fundamental Concepts. Technology gathers dust when it doesn't meet needs. That's Tool Irrelevance. A guiding vision is missing; we call this Leadership Gap. Without involvement, there's no commitment. That's Engagement Deficit. Understanding lags behind tech; we name this Knowledge Gap. Change stalls without purpose or clarity. That's Change Paralysis. Tech's potential shines with direction and instruction. That's Effective Enablement. Teach the use, spell out benefits, watch teams transform.

Bottom Line. Aim for results, not the tech to get there. Sell the benefit, not the tech. Show how tech change creates gains. People buy into reasons and results. Make the payoff clear to get support. Focus on what people want: the outcome, not the tool.

March 2nd

BELIEFS SCULPT ACTION, SYSTEMS SHAPE POSSIBILITY

"Change: Two Views—'Attitude Shift' or 'System Realignment.' One says beliefs drive behavior, the other, interactions within systems. Change means adjusting attitudes or roles; both tackle complexity, personal beliefs, or the system."

—CHANGE366. [77]

Beliefs and systems intertwine to define our approach to technology change. Beliefs motivate action, providing the 'why' for change. Meanwhile, systems construct the realm of what's possible. A successful technology change manager harnesses both: shifting mindsets to propel action and redesigning systems to enable possibility.

Takeaways. Beliefs motivate actions necessary for embracing technology; Systems define the boundaries of technological possibility; Aligning beliefs with systems facilitates effective change.

Fundamental Concepts. Belief fuels the fire for change. That's Intrinsic Motivation. Systems provide the playground. That's Environmental Structuring. When tech sits unused, it's not a tech issue—it's a Utilization Failure, a gap in aligning tools with intrinsic goals, and a sign of Environmental Misalignment. Effective change stitches belief into the fabric of systems, driving Utilization Uptake.

Bottom Line. In technology change, focus on aligning individual beliefs with organizational systems, driving action, and creating possibilities. Reinforce change by shaping attitudes and environments conducive to the desired transformation.

March 3rd

ACCEPTANCE FIRST, TRANSFORMATION NEXT

"We cannot change anything until we accept it."

—Carl Jung, *Modern Man in Search of a Soul.* [78]

Acceptance is the first step in the technology change journey. People must first acknowledge the current state before transforming it. It's about understanding where the organization stands with its technology and people's readiness for change. Acceptance paves the way for genuine transformation, creating a roadmap that reflects where you are and where you need to go.

Takeaways. Acknowledge current tech use and limitations; Understand employee readiness and resistance to change; Acceptance leads to a clear transformation roadmap; Start change with acceptance for effective transition.

Fundamental Concepts. Acceptance is crucial for change. That's the Acceptance Precept. Recognizing your current position, that's Status Awareness. Refusal to acknowledge facts. That's Denial. Understanding current technology. That's Baseline Mapping. Fluctuating willingness to change. That's Readiness Variability. The difference between current and desired states. That's Resistance Gap. Transition Planning develops from acceptance. Starting change with acceptance. That's Change Initiation. Acknowledging the truth. That's Reality Acceptance and Transformation Foundation. Leaders accepting reality and motivating teams. That's Leadership Activation leading to Visionary Progression. Change involves considering the human aspect, readiness, and culture, termed Human Factor Focus.

Bottom Line. To drive change, start by accepting current technology and practices. This acknowledgment is a prerequisite to successful change management. It lays the groundwork for a smooth transition, preparing everyone for the shifts ahead.

March 4th

UNCERTAINTY IS WHERE CHANGE TAKES SHAPE

"Liminality is the quality of ambiguity or disorientation that occurs in the middle stage of rituals when participants no longer hold their pre-ritual status but have not yet begun the transition to the status they will hold when the ritual is complete. During a ritual's liminal stage, participants 'stand at the threshold' between their previous way of structuring their identity, time or community, and a new way, which the ritual establishes."

—Arnold van Gennep, *The Rites of Passage.* [79]

Tech changes bring chaos and a liminal phase, like being in transit. This stage can cause anxiety and resistance. Managers must navigate their teams through this uncertainty, helping them envision future benefits. Keeping focus and easing fears is key. Though challenging, liminal stages are crucial for meaningful transformation.

Takeaways. The middle stage of change is full of uncertainty; This liminal stage can cause resistance and fear; As a manager, guide your team through this stage.

Fundamental Concepts. Change is messy and uncertain, that's Uncertainty Avoidance. In the middle lies Liminality, an uncertain transition phase. Resistance comes from Status Quo Bias. Guide using Self-Determination Theory. Maintain focus, mirroring Cognitive Dissonance. Ease anxiety, addressing Resistance to Change. Liminality is tough and entwined with Cultural Rituals.

Bottom Line. Change management involves leading through the uncertainty of a technical transition from the old to the new. The liminal stage can be chaotic, sparking fear and resistance. Managers must navigate their team through this stage, easing fears and focusing on the transformation ahead.

March 5th

THE GUIDE LIGHTS THE PATH, BUT THE TEAM WALKS IT

> "The Hero's Journey always begins with the call. One way or another, a guide must come to say, 'look you're in sleepy land, Wake, come on a trip. There is a whole aspect of your consciousness, your being, that's not been touched. So, you're at home here? Well, there's not enough of you there.' And so it starts."
>
> —JOSEPH CAMPBELL, *The Hero with a Thousand Faces.* [80]

Technical shake-up? Staying comfy won't cut it. Someone needs to light the fire. Be that guide. Your team's full potential? Not reached yet. Step out. Make waves. Ignite the hidden skills in your team. Lead them on a journey of change. Be the guide who says, 'let's go!'

Takeaways. The call to change needs a guide. Be that leader; Comfort zones limit potential. Break free; A new journey taps into untapped skills.

Fundamental Concepts. Change rings. Will you answer? That's the Hero's Journey. [81] The call needs a guide. That's the Role of Leadership. Comfort is a trap. It dulls your edge. That's the risk of Stasis. The untapped part of you? It's a gold mine. That's Unrevealed Potential. When a leader says, 'let's go,' new doors open. That's Activating Agency.

Bottom Line. Managers lead change by guiding teams out of comfort zones. They unlock new skills and potential. They encourage progress and act as guides.

March 6th

TECH CHANGE RESHAPES MINDS, NOT JUST TOOLS

> "I done me best when I was let. Thinking always if I go all goes. A hundred cares, a tithe of troubles and is there one who understands me? One in a thousand of years of the nights? All me life I have been lived among them but now they are becoming lothed to me. And I am lothing their little warm tricks. And lothing their mean cosy turns."
>
> —JAMES JOYCE, *Finnegan's Wake.* [82]

In technology change management, constraints often hinder our full potential. Many feel their efforts are curtailed. This breeds a sense of indispensability, yet also isolation. Teams feel misunderstood, craving a leader who truly gets the intricacies of technology and its impact. There's disillusionment with shallow solutions and a yearning for deeper, more meaningful change. Authentic transformation beats superficial adjustments.

Takeaways. Constraints hinder tech potential; Tech leadership needs deep understanding; Superficial solutions in tech are ineffective; Deep, meaningful tech change is essential; Empathy is crucial in tech leadership.

Fundamental Concepts. Constraints bind. That's Learned Helplessness in tech; Leadership missing. That's Absence of Autonomy Support; Effort fades; That's Social Loafing in group dynamics; Skills lacking. That's Competence Frustration; Unclear vision. That's Lack of Relatedness; Active leadership thrives. That's Self-Determination Theory in action.

Bottom Line. Technology change is more than just tools; it's about leadership and understanding. Constraints limit tech potential. Teams need leaders who really get technology. Superficial fixes don't work. Empathy is key in tech leadership. Understanding these aspects is vital for successful tech transformation.

March 7th

LESSONS LOOK BACKWARD, ACTIONS FORWARD

"Life must be understood backward. But it must be lived forward."

—Søren Kierkegaard, *Philosopher of the Heart.* [83]

Change, it's constant. Look back. Learn lessons. But keep moving. Life's rearview mirror? Clarity. The windshield? Vision. Change management mirrors this. Reflect on past projects. Inform future actions. It's the balance. Understand. Then advance.

Takeaways. Learn from past change efforts; Reflection aids future strategy; Balance understanding and action; Look back, move forward.

Fundamental Concepts. Life's rhythm. Intrinsic Motivation. Understanding past? Reflective Analysis. Living forward? Autonomous Action. Change anchored in history. Behavioral Insight. Lessons offer growth. Knowledge Accumulation. Balance is key. Equilibrium Attainment. Reflect, not dwell. Constructive Contemplation. Act with purpose. Directed Determination. Future beckons. Progressive Orientation leads. Remember the past. Historical Anchoring. Navigate forward. That's Change Mastery.

Bottom Line. Learn from the past. Improve future strategies. Keep a balance: reflect, then act. Progress purposefully in change management.

March 8th

CHANGE IS AN ART, NOT JUST ACTION

"Facts are stubborn things, but statistics are pliable."

—MARK TWAIN. [84]

Changing habits is hard. This is a fact we all know. In a company, it's even harder. We're not just dealing with one person's habits, but many. So, what do we do? We manage change. But it's not just about new tech or systems. It's about how people act and think. We need to manage this change in behavior. How? By showing everyone it's not just the usual stuff. It's different. It's something we all need to 'get.' To do this, we don't just tell people. We sell it. We make it so appealing that people want to change. We put it in the spotlight. We cheer for it. We make it the star of the show.

Takeaways. Behavior change is tough; Change management is vital; You must help others see the unique aspects of change.

Fundamental Concepts. Change is tough. That's Behavioral Inertia. Old habits die hard. How to shift? Use Self-Determination Theory. Give people choices. Make them part of the plan. Then, use Social Proof. If peers cheer, others join in. But beware of Cognitive Dissonance. Old ways will fight back. That's tension. Clear it by showing the new way is better. That's Persuasion Principles. Make the change appealing. Make it the star.

Bottom Line. Guide behavior change. Make it appealing. Engage people. Show benefits. Motivate action.

March 9th

CHANGE NEEDS WIDE, OPEN EYES

"Every man takes the limits of his own field of vision for the limits of the word."

—ARTHUR SCHOPENHAUER. *Studies in Pessimism.* [85]

In change management, it's easy to get tunnel vision. People tend to believe their view is the whole truth. But this is a trap! We must seek diverse perspectives. Different angles bring clarity. They show us what we miss. To manage change well, we need to break boundaries. Our personal limitations can blind us. Let's strive to see beyond. Expanding our vision is key. It leads to better decisions. Embrace diversity and broaden your view. This is the path to successful change.

Takeaways. Avoid tunnel vision in change management; Seek diverse perspectives for clarity; Break personal boundaries to succeed; Broaden your vision for better decisions.

Fundamental Concepts. Vision's limited. That's Perception Bias. People stick to their views. That's Confirmation Bias. Embracing diversity breaks biases. That's Perspective Taking. Expanding vision aids decisions. That's Cognitive Flexibility. In change, be open. That's Mindful Leadership. Avoid the tunnel; seek clarity. That's Inclusive Leadership. Change thrives on diverse views. That's the essence of Adaptive Leadership. Embrace all perspectives, broaden your view. Watch the change succeed.

Bottom Line. Seek diverse viewpoints. Overcome biases. Make informed decisions. Open your eyes to different perspectives for successful digital change.

March 10th

SEE BEYOND THE BREAK, GAUGE CHANGE'S COST

"True wisdom in change lies in discerning the unseen, weighing the cost of our actions not just by the immediate repairs but by the opportunities we forfeit, and understanding that sometimes the pieces left unbroken hold more value."

—CHANGE366. [86]

In 'The Broken Window,' Frédéric Bastiat challenges us to think critically about change. [87] The story is about a shopkeeper's broken window. A child breaks it. People think this is good for the economy. They believe it creates work for the glazier. Bastiat disagrees. He urges us to see the unseen. We must consider opportunity costs. What else could the shopkeeper have spent money on? This idea applies to organizational change management. Change is not always beneficial. We must evaluate its true cost. Leaders must look beyond the surface. They need to think strategically. What are we giving up? Is the change worth it? These are critical questions.

Takeaways. Don't just look at the immediate effects of change; Think about the long-term and unseen impacts; Evaluate the true cost of change; Be strategic and thoughtful in managing change.

Fundamental Concepts. People see only the broken window. That's Confirmation Bias. They ignore unseen opportunities. That's Opportunity Neglect. Leaders must think deeper. That's Holistic Analysis. Evaluate change critically. That's Smart Decision-making. Beyond the surface, find true costs. That's Comprehensive Evaluation. Change requires thoughtful choices. That's the crux of Adaptive Leadership. Think wider, evaluate deeper. Watch your decisions improve.

Bottom Line. Assess costs, consider sacrifices. Think long-term and opportunity costs. Guide strategic decisions. Understand change's full value.

March 11th

RISK WEIGHS HEAVY ON THE DECISION MAKER'S MIND

"Navigate digital change with wisdom—weigh risks, listen to your gut, speak clearly, honor culture."

—CHANGE366. [88]

In change, we often fear regret and weigh risks. Our body's reactions guide us—they're signals to listen to. But beware of trusting predictions about how we'll feel. Words and culture also steer our choices. Choose paths with less regret and balanced risks.

Takeaways. Emotions like regret shape choices in change management; Risk assessment is crucial in decision-making; Bodily reactions can guide leaders in decision processes; Predicting future emotions can be unreliable; Language and culture impact organizational decisions.

Fundamental Concepts. Emotions dictate choices. That's Affective Influence. Risks loom large. That's Risk Perception. Gut reactions lead. That's Somatic Guidance. [89] Future feelings fail us. That's Affective Forecasting. Words wield power. That's Linguistic Pragmatics. Culture curates decisions. That's Cultural Context. Decision-making dances with emotion, risk, language, culture. Understand these for informed choices. They're the fabric of Organizational Behavior.

Bottom Line. In Digital Transformation, understand how emotions, risk, language, and culture impact decisions. Trust your gut, assess risks, communicate clearly, and make balanced choices.

March 12th

TECH SHIFTS, MINDS SHIFT—SO MUST OUR METHODS

"Conceptual change is the creation of new representational resources within a cognitive system."

—SUSAN CAREY, *The Origin of Concepts.* [90]

Imagine a person's mind like a toolbox. It needs new tools for new jobs. Similarly, an organization's mind needs new ideas to grow and adapt. We don't just add tools; we create them. This is conceptual change. It's the craft of shaping new mental models to meet the shifting demands of our workplace. This is essential in guiding a team through change.

Takeaways. Update thinking to manage change effectively; Create, not just add, new ideas for growth; Shape new mental models for workplace demands; Guide teams with fresh, adaptive strategies.

Fundamental Concepts. Minds hold patterns. That's Cognitive Mapping. Change comes; we need new maps. That's Conceptual Innovation. Teams use old ways. That's Habit Persistence. Change scares us; we cling to the known. That's Fear of Uncertainty. Leaders must craft new paths. That's Visionary Guidance. Create fresh mental tools. That's Cognitive Crafting. Introduce novel concepts. That's Idea Generation. We steer the cognitive shift. That's Mental Navigation. Teach the team new ways. That's Knowledge Transfer. Adopt, adapt, improve. That's the cycle of Change Mastery.

Bottom Line. Update thinking and methods in change management. Create new ideas, not just add to old ones. Shape fresh mental models. Guide teams to adapt to new workplace realities. Encourage learning and innovation to keep pace with tech shifts.

March 13th

TECH WITHOUT OCM IS LIKE A CAR WITHOUT A DRIVER

> "OCM turns the key in the engine of digital transformation, powering growth, driving innovation, and ensuring that technological change translates into corporate success."
>
> —CHANGE366. [91]

Digital transformation is not just a tech upgrade—it's a company-wide evolution. Effective organizational change management (OCM) is essential to guide this evolution. It makes sure that people not only adopt new tech but also use it efficiently. It's about asking the right questions to manage the transformation. OCM is a beacon, steering the company towards innovation, market competitiveness, and satisfied customers. It's about understanding that without the human element, technology alone may not suffice.

Takeaways. OCM bridges the gap between new tech and people; It steers the company's project from chaos to innovation; It ensures talent sticks around by providing clarity and direction; OCM transforms resistance into acceptance, making operations more efficient.

Fundamental Concepts. Change calls for action. That's Self-Determination Theory at play. A quote inspires change. That's Cognitive Awakening. Minds ponder the message. That's Reflective Deliberation. Questions spark discussion. That's the Socratic Method. Learning grows from inquiry. That's Constructivism. Daily quotes fuel growth. That's Incremental Conditioning. Wisdom becomes action. That's Praxis. [92] The book turns pages; so does the mind. That's Cognitive Turnover.

Bottom Line. OCM is crucial for effective tech upgrades. It guides adoption and boosts efficiency. It navigates company change. OCM turns tech potential into performance. It focuses on people, securing a competitive advantage and customer satisfaction.

March 14th

SPOT TROUBLE EARLY, ADAPT SWIFTLY

"Embrace 'system accidents' as feedback; pilot change with ADKAR, steer to success."

—CHANGE366. [93]

Digital transformation can be tricky. Like a juggler at a circus, leaders must keep many balls in the air. Some balls may drop. We call these drops 'system accidents.' [94] These accidents happen when we change too much, too fast. The ADKAR model helps us keep all balls in the air. It shows us how to juggle Awareness, Desire, Knowledge, Ability, and Reinforcement all at once.

Takeaways. Spot trouble early, adapt swiftly; Make staff crave the digital leap; Knowledge beats fear, hands down; Skills turn users into champions; Constant push makes change stick.

Fundamental Concepts. Tech sits unused. That's Opportunity Wastage. Awareness brings insight. That's Cognitive Spark. Desire drives pursuit. That's Motivational Fuel. Knowledge builds expertise. That's Informational Power-Up. Skills enhance capability. That's Functional Upgrade. Accidents become lessons. That's Learning Leverage. Reinforcement cements habits. That's Behavioral Solidification. ADKAR is not static. It's a behavioral framework in motion; it's the Innovation-Decision Process. That's Dynamic Utilization. The cycle of adaptation continues. That's Progressive Transformation. Understanding meets application. That's Operational Synthesis. Tech and teams unite. That's Digital Integration.

Bottom Line. Effective digital transformation uses ADKAR to foresee and adapt to adoption issues promptly. Learning from mishaps and systematically fostering awareness, desire, knowledge, ability, and reinforcement turns potential setbacks into successful adaptation and sustained improvement.

March 15th

TECH'S VALUE—IT'S UNLOCKED BY MINDS

"Value in technology is a harvest of human insight, not a feature."

—CHANGE366. [95]

The true value of tech lies in our actions. Critical thinking prevents waste. People are the key to unlocking tech's potential. Training and adaptability are vital. Responsible use of tech protects society. Integrating tech with purpose solves real problems. These steps guide organizations through digital transformation effectively.

Takeaways. Critical investment evaluation prevents wasteful spending on tech; Human creativity unlocks tech potential, demanding skill development; Adaptability ensures tech serves evolving organizational needs; Ethical tech use guards against harmful societal effects; Purposeful integration aligns technology with problem-solving.

Fundamental Concepts. 'Tech's value? It's unlocked by minds.' That's Cognitive Engagement. Belief shifts gear. That's Belief Revision. Training leads the tech race. That's Skill Acquisition. Adapt or fail. That's Behavioral Flexibility. Tech reflects values when used wisely. That's Applied Ethics. Human touch turns tech gold. That's Human-Centered Design. Wisdom in tech use beats tech news. That's Practical Judgment. Ready for change? You've planned well. That's Proactive Adaptation. Align tech to needs, not greed. That's Value-Driven Deployment.

Bottom Line. Effective change management involves critical thinking about tech investments, skill development, adaptation, responsible tech use, and purposeful integration. It prevents waste, fosters innovation, ensures ethics, and addresses digital transformation issues.

March 16th

DIGITAL SHIFT DANCES TO THE TUNE OF HUMAN RHYTHM

"In digital transformation, lead with technology, dance with humanity."

—CHANGE366. [96]

The journey to the cloud is a dance. Tech teams lead with strong execution steps. Change managers follow closely, guiding each stride with strategy and support. Like in tango, both must sync for grace and impact. Change managers shine by understanding the rhythm of tech and choreographing the organization's movement towards innovation. This balance is the key to transformation.

Takeaways. Sync tech execution with change strategies; Guide teams through the digital dance; Balance tech and human factors in transition; Monitor and adjust to perfect the organizational tango.

Fundamental Concepts. Tech leads. Change follows. That's Role Clarity. Strategies meet execution. That's Synchronized Effort. Change managers guide, tech executes. That's Dual Leadership. Human factors balance tech. That's Human-Technology Integration. Transition dances with technology. That's Organizational Rhythm. Measuring adaptation effectiveness. That's Reinforcement Evaluation. Teams learn new steps. That's Competence Mastery. Each side learns, adapts. That's Relatedness and Growth.

Bottom Line. Effective change management aligns tech progress with human needs, crafting strategies for successful digital transformation.

March 17th

TRANSFORMATION WITHOUT CHANGE IS MERE MOTION

"When digital transformation is done right, it's like a caterpillar turning into a butterfly, but when done wrong, all you have is a really fast caterpillar."

—George Westerman, *Leading Digital.* [97]

True digital change is more than speed. It's a complete change like a caterpillar becoming a butterfly. True change means making new systems. It uses technology to create big improvements through adoption. If we only focus on speed, we miss the chance to truly change. Good change transforms how we work. It makes us better, not just faster.

Takeaways. Reimagine processes, don't just speed them up; Align technology with new, efficient workflows; Seek evolution in business, akin to a butterfly's metamorphosis; Make technology a tool for revolution, not just rapid motion.

Fundamental Concepts. Tech makeover, not speed chase. That's true Digital Transformation. Tech must alter tasks. That's Functional Reassessment. Evolve workflows, don't rush. That's Process Redesign. Tech is wings for change. That's Evolutionary Advancement. A butterfly of business, not a caterpillar on steroids. That's Organizational Metamorphosis. Understanding drives adoption. That's Cognitive Engagement. Evolution beats haste. That's Efficiency over Speed.

Bottom Line. Change management transforms tech use from mere speed to significant progress by evolving workflows and promoting deep, efficient business changes.

March 18th

DIGITAL WIN—STRATEGY, INSIDERS, CUSTOMER FOCUS

"Digital Transformation is not about technology—it's about change. And it's a change journey that requires vision, leadership, and a culture of innovation."

—GEORGE WESTERMAN, *DT is Not About Technology.* [98]

Digital transformation should align with company goals. Leverage employee insights and customer feedback for better experiences. Assure job security with new tech. Adopt a start-up approach for quicker changes. Focus on process improvements, not just tools. Success relies on strategic planning, active listening, and a committed team.

Takeaways. Align tech with your company's mission; Prioritize insider knowledge and customer needs; Alleviate employee concerns to encourage new tech adoption; Adopt start-up culture for efficient change.

Fundamental Concepts. Tech tools sit like unused treasures. That's Tool Neglect. Leaders look away. That's Guidance Deficit. Staff know the day's truth; leaders often miss. That's Insight Loss. Listen to the users; their voices lead. That's Customer Anchoring. Fear grips the crew; assure them, they'll sail through. That's Job Security. Change is a tide; let the insiders ride. That's Empowerment. Make the team quick, adaptable, small. That's Agile Structuring. Success is trying, failing, refining. That's Experimental Learning. Sell it like a game; watch engagement flame. That's Gamification. Involve all hands; the ship lands. That's Cross-Functional Teamwork.

Bottom Line. Achieve digital success by aligning tech with goals, tapping into staff insights, and prioritizing customer feedback. Secure team buy-in through addressing job concerns and promoting agility. Victory comes from aligning strategy, fostering internal guidance, and continuously innovating.

March 19th

INQUIRE MORE, INNOVATE OFTEN

"There are naïve questions, tedious questions, ill-phrased questions, questions put after inadequate self-criticism. But every question is a cry to understand the world. There is no such thing as a dumb question".

—CARL SAGAN, *The Demon-Haunted World.* [99]

In digital transformation, questions fuel growth. They show a hunger to learn and adapt. When a team member asks, it's a chance to guide. It's how we find gaps in our digital strategy. It's our signal to teach and explain. Even a question that seems silly can lead to breakthroughs. In this digital journey, every query is valuable.

Takeaways. Questions show a desire to understand and improve; Each query is an opportunity to strengthen digital strategy; No question is dumb; all can lead to innovation; Questions help identify and close knowledge gaps.

Fundamental Concepts. Questions emerge. That's Curiosity in Action. Confusion surfaces. That's Knowledge Gap. Inquiry invites answers; it's a Learning Opportunity. Innovation starts. That's Creative Inquiry. Knowledge builds. That's Cognitive Construction. Every question matters. That's the Premise of Constructivism. Fearless asking is key. That's Psychological Safety. Understanding grows. That's Information Integration. Transformation thrives on this. That's Organizational Learning. Embrace curiosity. Drive change. Ignite digital evolution.

Bottom Line. Foster constant questioning to drive digital innovation. Welcome all questions to sharpen strategies and fill in knowledge gaps. Simple queries can lead to big breakthroughs. Promote a culture of curiosity for sustained transformation.

March 20th

LEAD TO ADAPT, NOT JUST TO ACCOMPLISH

"Digital transformation is a journey, not a destination."

—DAVID L ROGERS, *The Digital Transformation Playbook.* [100]

Digital change is a path with no end. It is a cycle of learning, adapting, and growing. Good leaders guide their teams on this path every day. They turn change into a habit, not just a finish line. Teams that adapt together, grow together. They keep moving, keep learning. This is the heart of digital transformation.

Takeaways. Treat digital transformation as a continuous journey; Adapt to new technology as part of regular work; See learning as an ongoing process; Guide teams to embrace change as normal.

Fundamental Concepts. Change rolls on. That's Continuous Growth. Tech evolves. That's Innovation's March. Constant Adaptation. That's Change Mastery. Leaders lead. That's Directive Support. Teams learn. That's Collective Competence. Growth mindset in place. That's Psychological Empowerment. Walking the transformation road, we find our rhythm. That's Process Internalization. Empower change, ease fears, champion tech, make the journey together.

Bottom Line. View digital transformation as a perpetual process. Leaders must foster a culture of constant learning and adaptation. Team growth comes from daily change, embedding technology use into everyday activities. Encourage a collective embrace of ongoing change.

March 21st

TRANSFORM OR TRAIL IN THE DIGITAL RACE

"Right tech, right skills, right lead, right change—digital transformation's creed."

—CHANGE366 [101]

Digital transformation shapes our business' future. But it's tough. You need the right tech, skills, strategy, change, and leaders. Here's how to make it work. Get the best tools. Teach your team. Create a clear plan. Lead with vision. This journey is about more than just new software. It's about changing your company's mindset. Every step matters.

Takeaways. Equip with the right digital tools; Train employees in digital skills; Develop an effective digital transformation strategy; Lead transformation with clear vision and purpose.

Fundamental Concepts. Tech overflows, we need a filter. That's Choice Overload. Strategy lacks, chaos backs. That's Plan Scarcity. Skills match tools. That's Competence Support. Vision leads, success breeds. That's Autonomy Boost. Businesses bend, trends extend. That's Market Resilience. Study past, grasp the fast. That's Historic Insight. Aim research, gain perch. That's Knowledge Targeting.

Bottom Line. To succeed in digital transformation, take action. Choose the right technology and train your team effectively. Craft a clear digital strategy and lead with a distinct purpose to reshape your company's approach. Remember, a change in mindset is crucial for successful transformation, so approach each step with diligence and dedication.

March 22nd

EVERY HAND STEERS THE DIGITAL SHIP

> "In the digital era, transformation isn't static—it's a dance of agile innovation where every person steps in tune with technology."
>
> —CHANGE366.[102]

Digital transformation redefines roles beyond IT. Organizational change management leads, with change leaders emerging company-wide, focusing on strategy. Management practices evolve, emphasizing cross-functional teams for diverse expertise. Technology, now pivotal in leading change, redefines collaboration. Change management fosters flexibility, equipping companies for ongoing digital innovation and success in change.

Takeaways. In digital transformation, every hand steers the digital ship; Agility in governance trumps old IT scripts; Leaders spark change, not just CIO sages; Governance sails on tech's transformative tides; Platforms don't just connect—they command and guide.

Fundamental Concepts. Collaboration reigns in digital transformation's domain. It's about value, not just tech's gain. Business and IT align or miss the mark. That's Collaborative Integration. Culture must shift, making innovation its craft. That's Cultural Transformation. Leaders must champion, not just delegate. That's Participative Governance. Digital transformation is a mix: structures, processes, and people's flex. That's Governance Fusion. Tech guides and governs, a new kind of helm. That's Technological Stewardship. A company's pulse quickens with digital health. That's Strategic Agility.

Bottom Line. Master digital transformation by involving everyone in steering the company's course, not just IT. Use technology to lead, not just to do daily jobs. Create flexible management and cross-functional teams for innovation. This makes companies ready for continuous change and keeps them competitive.

March 23rd

SHARE THE VISION, MULTIPLY INNOVATION

"In digital transformation, wise leadership is not just about shifting gears but steering minds towards a future crafted by collective wisdom and shared purpose."

—CHANGE366.[103]

True leadership in digital transformation is more about managing change than just spearheading projects. Leaders who excel in digital shifts understand that it's about guiding people through the change. They create a vision that's clear and a culture ripe for innovation. They act as custodians of change, advocating for a process that's inclusive and sustainable.

Takeaways. Effective leaders guide change, fostering a culture of innovation; They prioritize clear communication and shared understanding in transformations; Wisdom in leadership blends ethical decision-making with practical action; Creating learning spaces and encouraging critical thinking are vital for adaptation.

Fundamental Concepts. Good leaders guide change. That's Change Mastery. They spread vision, make innovation routine. That's Cultural Engineering. Understanding big and small, they balance all. That's Holistic Strategy. Storytelling simplifies complexity. That's Conceptual Communication. Power in their palm, they bring calm. That's Influence Management. Encouraging smart risks, they craft future progress. That's Creative Governance. They sow seeds of wisdom, growing company acumen. That's Educational Leadership. Transforming not just tech, but team spirit. That's Organizational Renewal.

Bottom Line. Good leaders in digital transformation manage change by setting a shared vision and encouraging innovation. They communicate effectively, make decisions wisely, and build a culture open to learning and critical thinking. They nurture their teams to adapt, take smart risks, and grow together, ensuring sustainable transformation.

March 24th

QUICK TECH, SLOW CHANGE, LEADS THE DANCE ASTRAY

"Fast tech meets slow change; transformational leadership ignites the exchange."

—CHANGE366.[104]

Leaders need to address the slow pace of organizational change to match fast-moving technology. They play a key role in shaping the culture and building trust in new systems. Transformational leadership is essential in overcoming the challenges of adapting to digital transformation. Leaders who communicate well and involve their teams can drive successful change. The ultimate success in digital transformation lies not in the technology itself but in the people and culture ready to embrace it.

Takeaways. Speed in tech demands swift organizational pace; Leaders must focus on culture, not just the tech race; Building trust in tech is a significant leadership task; Transformational leadership can pave the way for staff to unmask.

Fundamental Concepts. Tech outpaces change. That's Change Lag. Leaders with vision? They're rare. That's Leadership Deficit. Trust is scarce where myths about tech flare. That's Mistrust Phenomenon. People behind, tech ahead. That's Adaptation Lag. Leaders as coaches, not bosses, they're Change Catalysts. Culture shifts slow; transformational leadership knows. That's Cultural Momentum. Change management is a leader's true exam. That's Leadership Challenge. Trust builds, tech blooms, change zooms. That's Trust Amplification.

Bottom Line. Leaders must speed up organizational change to match technology's pace. They should foster a culture built on trust, adopt transformational leadership, and engage teams in navigating digital shifts. Success depends on people and culture, not solely on tech adoption.

March 25th

ETHICS GUIDE ALGORITHMS, NOT VICE VERSA

> "Big Data processes codify the past. They do not invent the future. Doing that requires moral imagination, and that's something only humans can provide. We have to explicitly embed better values into our algorithms, creating Big Data models that follow our ethical lead. Sometimes that will mean putting fairness ahead of profit."
>
> —CATHY O'NEIL, *Weapons of Math Destruction.* [105]

Big Data looks at the past. It does not see the future. In changing organizations through digital transformation, we use this data to learn. Our values must lead the way in tech changes. Fair choices should come before profit. We must build fair algorithms. These algorithms should do good first, then make money. In managing change, this is how we make tech better.

Takeaways. Use data to inform, not dictate, future strategies; Embed ethical considerations in technology development; Prioritize fairness in algorithmic decisions; Change to think beyond profit to what's fair and right.

Fundamental Concepts. Data tells history. That's Retrospective Coherence. Humans dream of futures. That's Proactive Creation. Morals guide tech. That's Ethical Shaping. Algorithms need values. That's Virtue Coding. Profit chases fairness. That's Justice Over Revenue. Teach tech the good. That's Moral Programming. Fair algorithms reflect us. That's Ethical Reflection.

Bottom Line. Set the path for change management by putting ethics first in technology. Teach algorithms to prioritize fairness over profit. Use Big Data to guide but not dictate the future. Ensure tech development reflects human values.

March 26th

ANTICIPATE TO SUCCEED—HESITATION LEADS ASTRAY

"The only way to be sure of catching a train is to miss the one before it."

—CHRISTOPHER HITCHENS. [106]

To catch the train of digital change, be early at the station of innovation. If you miss one opportunity, don't despair. Prepare for the next. Know the timetable—understand technology trends. Keep your ticket ready—change management. And watch the tracks, monitor progress.

Takeaways. Learn from missed chances to grasp future opportunities in digital tech; Anticipate technology trends to stay ahead; Invest in learning change management for readiness; Monitor progress to adapt swiftly to new changes.

Fundamental Concepts. Choices guide tech's course is Self-Regulation. Learning from loss is about Growth Mindset. Anticipation beats haste. That's Future Orientation. Preparation trumps regret is Competence Assurance. Insight fueling foresight is about Informed Proactivity. Training turns to triumph. That's Capability Building. Monitoring merges with mastery is Reflective Adaptation. Tech trepidation to tech triumph is described by Transformational Resilience. Readiness reaps results is Proactive Competence. Learn, anticipate, prepare, adapt. That's Change Acumen.

Bottom Line. Be proactive in digital change and learn from missed opportunities. Stay informed about tech trends and practice change management to prepare. Keep monitoring and adapting for success.

March 27th

TRANSFORM, DON'T JUST INFORM—BALANCE PERFORMS

"Balance every thought with its opposition. Because the marriage of them is the destruction of illusion."

—Alester Crowley, *The Book of Lies.* [107]

In digital change, balance is the ticket, innovation the track. Wise managers watch both. They know when to hold fast, when to leap ahead. Marrying old and new breaks illusions, opening eyes to progress. Change isn't just arrival—it's the journey of thinking anew. It's readiness, not speed, that defines success. It's thoughtful balance that outpaces blind rush. It's unity in diversity that charts the true course of change.

Takeaways. Balance breeds clarity in digital change; New meets old to create the gold; Change, not chance, forges tech's advance; Balanced decisions make stable visions; Transform, don't just inform; balance performs.

Fundamental Concepts. Change chases change is Evolutionary Drive. Balancing acts in management is about Equilibrium Seeking. Managers mixing new and old is Integration. Tech's edge meets tested methods is the Balance of Innovation. Beliefs clash, insights emerge. That's Dialectical Method. [108] Staff split on tech causes Division of Adoption. Visionaries rushing, traditionalists resisting is Pace Disparity. Digital transformation needs clear vision creating Organizational Clarity. Managers guiding, not just deciding, is Democratic Leadership. The balanced approach prevails. That's the Art of Change Management. In marrying tech and tradition, illusions shatter. Progress takes shape.

Bottom Line. In digital transformation, balance innovation with tradition. Mix the new with the old for progress. Seek clarity, not speed. Embrace diverse ideas to navigate change effectively.

March 28th

TWIST DATA, LOSE TRUTH

"Torture the data, and it will confess to anything."

—IRVING J GOOD, *The American Statistician.* [109]

Data tells stories. But like any good tale, the truth depends on how you tell it. In digital change, we sift through data to guide decisions. Sometimes, we push data until it fits our needs. But that's risky. Real insight comes from clear, honest data analysis—not from forcing it to support our biases. Data can illuminate the path of change if we treat it with respect.

Takeaways. Look at data objectively to see the real story; Avoid manipulating data to fit preconceived ideas; Use data to inform decisions, not to dictate them; Recognize the power of data in shaping digital change.

Fundamental Concepts. Data confesses under pressure. That's Confirmation Bias. Analysts hunt for patterns. That's Patternicity. Change hangs on interpretation. That's Attribution Theory. Bias blinds, truth enlightens. That's Cognitive Dissonance. Wise managers seek truth, not comfort. That's Informed Decision-Making. Data guides, not decides. That's Rational Emotive Behavior. Clarity in data, clarity in strategy. That's Action-Oriented Management. Understanding data improves outcomes. That's Evidence-Based Practice. Seek facts, not fiction. That's Intellectual Integrity.

Bottom Line. Handle data carefully in digital transformation. Look for truth, not just patterns that fit our ideas. Honest data analysis lights the way for informed decisions and successful change.

March 29th

WISDOM IGNITES CHANGE, BURNS OLD PATHS

"The hardest thing in life is to know which bridge to cross and which to burn."

—DAVID RUSSELL, *Last Dance.* [110]

In the journey of digital transformation, managers act as the navigators of change. They stand at the crossroads, making pivotal decisions about when to adopt new technologies and when to retire the old. This choice, like deciding which bridge to cross or burn, is fundamental to success. It requires a deep understanding of both the current organizational landscape and the horizon of technological possibilities. The essence of successful change management is in these decisions that shape the future path of an organization.

Takeaways. Evaluate technology with a clear understanding of organizational goals; Discard systems that hinder agility and adaptability; Embrace innovations that align with strategic vision; Balance technological advancement with team readiness and culture.

Fundamental Concepts. Choices challenge managers. That's Decision Conflict. Tech adaptation shapes cultures. That's Cultural Integration. Overcoming old habits demands skill. That's Habit Discontinuation. Adoption takes courage and strategy. That's Strategic Innovation. Rejecting outdated tech requires discernment. That's Discriminative Assessment. Marrying new tech with culture secures advancement. That's Congruence Achievement. Forward-thinking leads to action. That's Proactive Innovation. Manage change, manage future success. That's Future-Focused Leadership.

Bottom Line. Change management thrives on wise choices. Know when to embrace new tech and when to let go of the old. Align technology with goals and readiness for successful digital transformation.

March 30th

ALIGN TECH CHOICE WITH STRATEGIC VOICE

"Excellence is never an accident. It is always the result of high intention, sincere effort, and intelligent execution; it represents the wise choice of many alternatives—choice, not chance, determines your destiny."

—ARISTOTLE.[111]

Technology change is a strategic choice leading to excellence, not a random event. It requires a vision, effort, and smart decisions. Effective technology management aligns tools with the company's goals, demanding continuous learning and adaptation. Success in digital transformation is a measure of deliberate action and intelligent execution.

Takeaways. Tech excellence by choice, not by chance; Vision, plan, execute: the tech change mantra; Align tech choice with strategic voice; Sincere effort in tech paves the path to success; Execute tech changes with change intent.

Fundamental Concepts. Tech adoption is strategy's game. That's Behavioral Commitment. Choices shape tech's use. That's Intentional Strategy. Effort meets tech. That's Competence Building. Execution defines success. That's Outcome Realization. Clear goals, clear outcomes. That's Objective Clarity. Smart tech reflects vision. That's Cognitive Alignment. Consistent tech choices make destiny. That's Determined Progression. Effort in learning tech pays off. That's Skill Mastery. Decisions over chance for tech gains. That's Deliberate Action.

Bottom Line. Excellence in technology transformation emerges from deliberate choices and efforts, not accidents or chance. Leaders must choose wisely among alternatives. They must plan and execute with precision, to steer their organizations toward the intended destiny with 'excellent' organizational change management.

March 31st

SKILL TODAY, HISTORY TOMORROW, LEARN AGAIN

"The only skill that will be important in the 21st century is the skill of learning new skills. Everything else will become obsolete over time."

—PETER DRUCKER. [112]

In the fast-evolving landscape of technology, learning is the only constant. For change managers, the ability to learn and adapt is the most critical skill. As technology advances, yesterday's expertise can quickly become today's history. The key to enduring success in organizational change management is fostering a culture where continuous learning is valued and new skills are pursued relentlessly.

Takeaways. Value continuous learning in a changing world; Prioritize learning over knowing; Teach adaptability in organizations; Update skills to avoid obsolescence.

Fundamental Concepts. Learning drives change. That's Behavioral Activation. Skills outdated? Learn anew. That's Skill Refresh. Open minds grow. That's Cognitive Expansion. Flexibility overcomes obsolescence. That's Adaptability Triumph. Continuous learning outlives tech. That's Sustained Relevance. Share knowledge freely. That's Collaborative Learning. Learn, evolve, excel. That's Organizational Agility. Learning today arms for tomorrow. That's Proactive Development.

Bottom Line. Master new skills fast to thrive amid change. Learning beats knowing. Update skills to stay relevant. Teach teams constant learning for company strength.

APRIL — CULTURE

Culture is the silent force behind every organizational change, and as we venture into digital transformation, its influence becomes more evident. Kotter warns that neglecting culture can doom even the most well-planned projects, for culture is the undercurrent that guides the collective action of an organization. Drucker famously stated that culture trumps strategy, reminding us that for technology to shine, it must align with the cultural fabric of an organization.

Harari teaches us that culture is a narrative we craft and believe in, akin to an author writing a script. Change the narrative, and you change the direction of the organization. The culture of an organization, as Science Direct articulates, is its heritage and compass, defining what is and isn't possible within its realms.
Cultural readiness is a deciding factor in the success of change management, as Prosci highlights. Understanding culture's dimensions allows change managers to tailor their strategies

effectively. Culture is not just an aspect of business, as McKinsey points out, but it's foundational to an organization's operation and its approach to change.

Plutarch's ship of Theseus illustrates the essence of cultural change. Just as the ship's planks are replaced over time, so must the cultural elements of an organization evolve. Gerstner echoes this, emphasizing that culture is the game in the end, and its development is the sum of its people's value-creation capacity.

Schein's concept of culture as a learned solution to problems of adaptation and integration frames it as a game-changer. While Thompson's words on life's risk and reward remind us that culture too must embrace daring for transformation to occur. Thoreau suggests that it's important to honor the core values of a culture while also molding its structure. This balance is key to fostering effective change.

Change366 points to culture as both the steering wheel and the gear of organizational change. It advises a careful consideration of how change affects and is affected by culture. Culture, as Berger and Luckmann describe, is a set of shared habits. It's these habits that, when shifted, allow for predictability and innovation.

Solzhenitsyn's reminder that growth without values is empty serves as a caution to organizations that chase technological advancement without cultural depth. True leadership, per Change366, lies in understanding the cultural puzzle, where every piece interacts to form the larger picture of an organization.

Adaptability is a cultural trait, as Change366 suggests, and a flexible culture is a capable company. Leaders must be adept at managing the balance between preserving beneficial traditions and initiating progressive change. In the end, Linton's metaphor reminds us that culture is omnipresent yet often unnoticed, like water to a fish.

As we automate the old and innovate the new, we follow Whitehead's understanding that progress is marked by our ability to perform complex tasks effortlessly, grounded in a culture that supports and drives change. This is the essence of managing culture in the digital age: a blend of respect for tradition and an unwavering commitment to innovation.

Effective change management is an intricate blend of respecting the existing culture while daring to redirect it towards a shared vision. As leaders, the challenge lies in not just initiating change but in sustaining it by aligning cultural narratives with the organization's strategic direction. It is this alignment that ultimately determines the capability and resilience of an organization in the face of continuous change.

April 1st

CULTURE IS THE UNSEEN GUIDE

"The Last thing a fish would ever notice would be water."

—RALPH LINTON, *The Study of Man.* [113]

Culture in an organization is like water to a fish. It's everywhere, yet we hardly notice it. But it guides how we behave. It shapes our work life silently. To manage change, we must see the culture clearly. Recognize its power. Understand its influence. Only then can we begin to change. Adjust the culture, and you transform the organization. Make the invisible visible. Embrace the change. Lead with awareness.

Takeaways. Culture is omnipresent in organizations; It silently shapes our behavior; Recognizing culture is the first step to change; Change the culture, transform the organization.

Fundamental Concepts. Culture's everywhere. That's Cultural Ubiquity. It guides unnoticed. That's Unconscious Conformity. Recognizing culture sparks change. That's Cultural Awareness. Transforming culture transforms all. That's Organizational Alchemy. Lead with awareness, change follows. That's Conscious Leadership. Make culture visible. That's Cultural Intelligence. Change starts with recognition. That's the essence of Adaptive Leadership. Recognize the unseen, transform with ease. Watch the organization flourish.

Bottom Line. Recognize that culture is the unseen force in an organization. It shapes behavior without notice. To change an organization, first see and understand its culture. Change the culture to transform the workplace. Visible culture leads to effective change.

April 2nd

CULTURE IS BOSS

"Until I came to IBM, I probably would have told you that culture was just one among several important elements in any organization's makeup and success—along with vision, strategy, marketing, financials, and the like... I came to see, in my time at IBM, that culture isn't just one aspect of the game, it is the game. In the end, an organization is nothing more than the collective capacity of its people to create value."

—LOUIS V. GERSTNER, JR., *Who Says Elephants Can't Dance?* [114]

Culture is not a side dish; it's the main course. Don't just focus on the numbers. People make the organization. They bring the value. So, make culture your game.

Takeaways. Culture is the core; People create value; Culture drives the game.

Fundamental Concepts. Culture is key. That's Organizational Culture Theory. It's not secondary, it's central. People count. Collective value. That's Social Identity Theory. Culture's the game. No half measures. That's Normative Influence. Three focus points. Culture, people, value. That's the heart of Holistic Organizational Change. Make culture your strategy. Gain the edge. That's the essence of Cultural Capital. Build a strong culture. Value will follow. Reach peak performance.

Bottom Line. Culture is the heart of an organization's success, not just one of its parts. It's the game itself. Prioritize culture over mere financials and marketing. True value comes from people, not numbers. Focus on nurturing a strong culture to lead your organization to peak performance. Make building culture your main strategy and watch as value and success grow from it.

April 3rd

SEE BOTH CULTURES, MANAGE CHANGE

"There were two forests for every one you entered. There was the one you walked in, the physical echo, and then there was the one that was connected to all the other forests, with no consideration of distance, or time."

—CHARLES DE LINT, *Spiritwalk.* [115]

In every organization, there are two cultures. One is visible. We see it in meetings, in emails, in daily work. It's the physical echo of values and beliefs. But there's another culture. It's deep and interconnected. It ties together past and present, no matter the distance or time. To truly understand and manage change, we need to see both. We need to dive deep and see the connections. We need to understand the values that persist over time. This is the key to successful change management.

Takeaways. Culture in organizations, has visible and invisible aspects; Different parts of culture are deeply interconnected; Culture persists over time, shaping present and future; Understanding both aspects of culture is crucial for change.

Fundamental Concepts. Culture's in plain sight. That's Visible Culture. But there's more beneath. That's Invisible Culture. Past ties to present. That's Cultural Continuity. Different parts connect deeply. That's Cultural Interconnectedness. To change, see both. That's Holistic Understanding. Dive deep, uncover truths. That's Cultural Archaeology. Manage both, succeed in change. That's Effective Change Management. See the visible, understand the invisible. Watch the organization transform.

Bottom Line. To manage change, recognize the two sides of culture: what you see and what you don't. Visible culture shows in actions and communications. Invisible culture holds the past and shapes the future. Understanding this helps change it. See the everyday culture and dig into the deeper one. This leads to successful change management.

April 4th

CULTURE GROWS WITH TALES, CHANGES WITH VISION

"Growing a culture requires a good storyteller. Changing a culture requires a persuasive editor."

—RYAN S LILLY. *Startup Balanced.* [116]

Culture in a company is like a story. A good leader tells it well; this builds the culture. But change means editing the story. A leader must then persuade; they must show the path forward. This way, culture shifts.

Takeaways. Good leaders tell the company's story; They grow culture like nurturing a garden; Change needs editing the story; Persuasion is key for change.

Fundamental Concepts. Storytelling taps into identity. That's Social Identity Theory. It crafts culture. Persuasive editing? That's Cognitive Dissonance. It shakes beliefs, aligns behavior. Both build culture. Stories bond us. Editing reforms us. A leader's task. Shape the narrative. Change the mindset. That's Cultural Transformation.

Bottom Line. Good leaders shape culture with storytelling. To change culture, they must edit and persuade. They guide the company to new chapters. This shifts the culture.

April 5th

IGNORING CULTURE BURNS PROJECTS

"Smart people miss the mark here when they are insensitive to cultural issues. Economically orientated finance people and analytically orientated engineers can find the topic of social norms (culture) and values too soft for their tastes. So they ignore culture—at their peril."

—JOHN KOTTER, *Leading Change.* [117]

Culture is not a side dish; it's the main course. You can be a genius with numbers or a wizard with code. But if you ignore culture, you trip—hard. Finance folks crunch numbers. Engineers solve puzzles. But culture is not a soft topic. It's the glue that holds teams together; the fuel that drives projects. Ignore it, and you risk falling flat. Your team won't click. Your project won't stick. So tune into culture. It's not just nice to have, it's a must-have.

Takeaways. Ignoring culture is a mistake; Even smart people can overlook culture; Culture matters in all roles, even in finance and engineering.

Fundamental Concepts. Ignoring culture is risky. That's Cognitive Blindness. Overconfidence clouds judgement. Culture is the team's heartbeat. That's Social Identity Theory. It's our group code. Ignore it, you hit a wall. That's Behavioral Resistance. Like talking in riddles. Minds in conflict? That's Cognitive Dissonance. A mental tug-of-war. Culture fuels drive. That's Self-Determination Theory. Value it, and you get loyalty.

Bottom Line. Ignoring culture can ruin projects. Some see culture as too 'soft' and dismiss it. But culture is critical. It's the backbone of teamwork and project success. Overlooking it leads to failure. It matters in every field. Recognize culture as essential, pay attention to it. Value it to ensure your team works well, and projects succeed.

April 6th

TECH SHINES WHEN CULTURE ALIGNS

"Culture eats strategy for breakfast."

—PETER DRUCKER. [118]

Culture rules. No debate. You can have the flashiest software, the fastest computers. But if your team shrugs it off, it's just a waste. A pricey paperweight. Culture decides how well tech thrives. Or if it survives at all. If your team loves to email, a new chat app will collect dust. So, align tech with culture. Don't let your fancy new tool become breakfast for a hungry culture. Make them friends, not foes.

Takeaways. Culture trumps technology; Even great tech fails without cultural support; Align culture and tech for best results.

Fundamental Concepts. Culture rules tech. That's Social Norms. It's the group vibe. Clash with it, you lose. That's Behavioral Resistance. It's like hitting a wall. Want tech to stick? Use Self-Determination Theory. Let people choose, make it fit their vibe. Leaders on board? That's Social Proof. Others will follow the guide. Make it simple? That's Cognitive Ease. Fits like a glove.

Bottom Line. Culture is more important than strategy for technology's success. It affects how people work and what they like. To make tech work well, it needs to fit with how things change. Promote a culture that welcomes new tech. Leaders should guide this change. Make it easy to use new tools. Match tech with the changing culture. Success in change comes from doing it well and being motivated.

April 7th

CULTURE'S THE SCRIPT, BUT YOU'RE THE PLAYWRIGHT

"All large-scale human cooperation is ultimately based on our belief in imagined orders. These are sets of rules that, despite existing only in our imagination, we believe to be as real and inviolable as gravity."

—YUVAL NOAH HARARI, *Homo Deus.* [119]

Culture is glue, it holds us together. But it's not concrete. It's not even real, it's a story we believe in. A set of imagined rules. You want to change an organization? Start with its myths, its beliefs, its stories. Rethink the imagined rules. Make them serve you, not limit you. Shape a new culture, one that moves with your goals.

Takeaways. Culture is a set of beliefs and imagined rules; To change an organization, change its cultural story; New beliefs pave the way for new actions.

Fundamental Concepts. Beliefs bind us. That's Social Constructivism. Rules exist in our heads, yet they shape our world. It's how societies work. It's also Cognitive Dissonance at play. The mind hates conflict. It loves rules, even if made up. Changing a team? Change its beliefs. That's Cognitive Restructuring. Shift the mindset. Create new norms. Don't overlook the story. Narratives are potent. They can lock us in or set us free. That's the Narrative Paradigm.

Bottom Line. Beliefs guide how we work together, even though they're just made-up rules. To change an organization, rewrite its culture's story. Alter shared beliefs to change how we act together. Craft a new narrative that matches your goals. Keep in mind, culture isn't set; it's a story we all agree upon. Rewrite it, and you change the game.

April 8th

SHIFT VALUES—STEER THE JOURNEY

"Culture is the social heritage of an organization. It Determines what is acceptable or unacceptable, what is important or unimportant, what is right or wrong, what is workable or unworkable, and who you hire, fire, and promote."

—SCIENCE DIRECT. [120]

Culture's the playbook. It tells your team how to act. What to value. Who fits in? Who doesn't. Want to change the game, change the rules. Make a new playbook, one that matches your goals. Say goodbye to what holds you back. Welcome what pushes you forward.

Takeaways. Culture shapes behavior and decisions; To drive change, alter the cultural norms; A new playbook aligns the team with new objectives.

Fundamental Concepts. Culture's the code. That's Social Norms. Tells us the dos and don'ts. Right or wrong? Look at the crowd. That's Conformity. We follow to fit. Who's in, who's out? That's Social Identity Theory. Our group shapes us. Want change? Change rewards. That's Operant Conditioning. Carrot or stick. Guide the team. Break old molds. Create new modes. That's Cognitive Restructuring. New norms need new minds. Story counts. That's the Narrative Paradigm. Tales trap or free us. Pick the plot. Shape the team.

Bottom Line. Culture influences how people act and decide in a company. Change culture to shift the organization's course. Update values to match new goals. Get rid of old habits that block your vision. Put in place methods that drive forward. Culture is a basis for action and change. Develop a new cultural playbook to lead your organization.

April 9th

CULTURE GUIDES, READINESS DECIDES

"Change managers who understand and use these cultural dimensions will be able to customize better their change management approach to their own and various other cultures. Customizing a change management approach to accommodate the culture moves change management beyond assessing overall readiness, supplying a deeper understanding of how culture impacts change and ultimately enabling change agents to deliver better results."

—Prosci. [121]

Understand your team's culture deeply. Tailor your change plan to their norms or adjust the culture first. Avoid generic approaches. Focus on how your team operates for a better fit. Proper alignment ensures lasting change.

Takeaways. Know your culture; it sets the change tempo; Custom-fit your change plan to your team's norms or change them first; Understanding culture isn't just a checkmark; it's your roadmap; The better the fit, the better the change outcome.

Fundamental Concepts. Culture's not just backdrop; it's a driving force. That's Social Psychology. It influences group behavior. Customize your approach. That's Self-Determination Theory. Give people a say. They'll be more committed. It's Cultural Intelligence at work. Go beyond surface-level. Understand norms. Then adapt. This is Behavioral Flexibility. The more you align, the smoother the change. That's Outcome Expectancy.

Bottom Line. Change managers should grasp team culture, norms, and values, aligning their change strategy accordingly. If the culture conflicts with the desired change, consider modifying the culture first. Tailor changes to fit specific team practices. Adapt the strategy to the existing culture or alter the culture for successful transformation.

April 10th

CULTURE AND BUSINESS—TWO SIDES OF THE SAME COIN

"Executives must be proactive in shaping and measuring culture, approaching it with the same rigor and discipline with which they tackle operational transformations."

—MCKINSEY, *Culture for a Digital Age.* [122]

Culture is a tool, use it well. It's not a side task, it's a main job. You're an executive? Act like a gardener. Plant seeds of culture, water them, watch them grow. Don't guess, measure. Use numbers, just like you do for sales or output. Make it precise, make it count. Culture drives the engine of change.

Takeaways. Culture isn't a sideline; it's central; Executives should cultivate culture like they do operations; Measure culture, don't just feel it; Precision in shaping culture pays off in smooth change.

Fundamental Concepts. Culture isn't scenery; it's the script. That's Social Psychology. It molds group action. Executives set the tone. That's Social Learning Theory. They model the way. Teams follow suit. Use metrics, not just gut feelings. That's Quantitative Psychology. Numbers bring clarity. Rewards and penalties? Operant Conditioning. They fine-tune behavior. Make culture a concrete aim. That's Goal-Setting Theory. The clearer the target, the straighter the arrow.

Bottom Line. Culture is crucial in business. Executives must actively shape and monitor it. Cultivate your company's culture deliberately. Measure culture changes with data, not just feelings. [123] Precise culture cultivation prepares your business for smooth transitions. [124] Culture is central, not an afterthought. Aim at culture for direct business growth and change.

April 11th

GAUGE CULTURE; GAUGE ORGANIZATIONAL HEARTBEAT

"In the dance of organizational culture, Cartwright's compass directs, loyalty and alienation play, and the 'Motivometer' sets the rhythm."

—CHANGE366. [125]

Cartwright unveils a map to the heart of organizational culture. With nine signposts, we find our way. From loyalty to alienation, the journey reflects the culture's pulse. The 'motivometer' serves as our compass. [126] Nine boxes, some negative, some positive. A cultural health check at our fingertips.

Takeaways. Cartwright's Nine Factors reveal the soul of an organization; Culture swings between loyalty and alienation; 'Motivometer' gauges organizational health.

Fundamental Concepts. Culture's heartbeat. That's Organizational Pulse. Nine factors mark the path. That's Cartwright's Compass. Loyalty pulls. Alienation pushes. That's Motivational Duality. 'Motivometer' measures the vibe. It's the Organizational Thermometer. Clear understanding leads to clear direction. That's Organizational Clarity.

Bottom Line. Use Cartwright's nine factors to understand an organization's core culture. Measure the balance between loyalty and alienation to assess the culture's health. The 'Motivometer' serves as a guide to track this balance. Understanding these aspects is crucial for effective change management..

April 12th

CULTURE'S THE CORE—CHANGE THAT, CHANGE ALL

> "The ship wherein Theseus returned from Crete had thirty oars and was preserved by the Athenians...for they took away the old planks as they decayed, putting in new and stronger timber in their places, insomuch that this ship became a standing example among the philosophers, for the logical question of things that grow; one side holding that the ship remained the same, and the other contending that it was not the same."
>
> —PLUTARCH, *Life of Theseus.* [127]

Organizational change resembles a ship's overhaul. New ideas may replace old ones, but unchanged culture means it's still the same organization. Culture is central, binding everything. Even with new elements, if the core culture is flawed, the organization won't progress much.

Takeaways. Small changes aren't enough; Culture is the ship's core; Change culture, and you've got a new ship.

Fundamental Concepts. Ship of Theseus Tale. That's Metaphorical Reasoning. Small changes happen. That's Incremental Adaptation. Culture's core. That's Organizational Essence. Cultural shift essential. That's Core Transformation. Change in parts, is not enough. That's Surface Modification. Change in essence, required. That's Deep-level Change. Takeaways clear. That's Conceptual Clarity. Aphorisms hit home. That's Mnemonic Power. Change is hard. That's Behavioral Inertia. New culture needed. That's Cultural Renewal. Make your ship new. That's Successful Transformation.

Bottom Line. Culture is fundamental to an organization. Merely updating parts doesn't alter its identity; changing the core culture does. Profound cultural transformation is necessary for genuine organizational change. Focus on deep cultural shifts for enduring impact.

April 13th

CHANGE THE NORM, CHANGE THE GAME

"A pattern of shared basic assumptions invented, discovered or developed by a given group as it learns to cope with its problems of external adaptation and internal integration that have worked well enough to be considered valid and, therefore, to be taught to new members as the correct way to perceive, think and feel in relation to those problems."

—EDGAR H SCHEIN, *Organizational Culture and Leadership*. [128]

Teams have beliefs, they share them, they solve problems together. This creates a norm. New people learn this, it shapes the team. Be aware of your team's norms. Change them if needed.

Takeaways. Shared beliefs direct the team; Coping methods become the standard; New hires learn and adapt.

Fundamental Concepts. Beliefs lead. That's Cognitive Dissonance Theory. Shared views? Group glue. That's Social Cohesion. Coping mechanisms? They set norms. That's Social Learning Theory. New members? They adapt. That's Socialization. Know your team norms. That's Self-Awareness. Make changes when needed. That's Adaptive Leadership. Team's compass, it's shared beliefs. Guide or misguide, they decide. That's the core of Organizational Psychology. Be alert, make wise choices. Norms will follow.

Bottom Line. Change norms to transform your team. Team beliefs guide actions and set rules. New members follow these norms. If needed, modify norms to reshape your culture. Understand and lead based on these norms for growth and change. Flexible leadership can improve your team's methods and results.

April 14th

RISK AND REWARD RIDE THE SAME ROAD

> "Life should not be a journey to the grave with the intention of arriving safely in a pretty and well-preserved body, but rather to skid broadside in a cloud of smoke, thoroughly used up, totally worn out, and loudly proclaiming 'Wow! What a Ride!'"
>
> —HUNTER S THOMPSON, *Fear and Loathing in Las Vegas*.[129]

Safe is easy, safe is comfort. But safe is stale, especially in business culture. Shake it up, take risks. Make your company a place of daring. Go broadside. Turn the office into a thrill ride, not a slow crawl to retirement. Staff will feel it, they'll be engaged. They'll be spent but happy. They'll say, 'What a ride!' as they drive change.

Takeaways. Safety breeds stagnation in company culture; Risks make the ride worthwhile; Engaged employees are happy but spent; A daring culture drives change.

Fundamental Concepts. Safe is stale. That's Risk Aversion. Fear of failure. Daring deeds? Cue Risk Seeking. It drives us. Employees stuck? That's Amotivation. Thrills spark action. Welcome Intrinsic Motivation. Satisfaction? It comes with the ride. That's Hedonic Adaptation at work. Spent but happy? That's Eudaimonic Well-Being. [130] Engage to change. That's Self-Determination Theory in action. A daring culture is Self-Concordant. It aligns. Staff feel it. They drive change. That's Transformational Leadership. Make it a ride. Make it a change. Make it real.

Bottom Line. Embrace risk for a dynamic culture. Take bold steps. Risk brings excitement and counters stagnation. It pushes staff and fosters satisfaction. Adopt an adventurous business approach. This excites and drives your team. They'll work passionately and enjoy the process. A daring culture isn't reckless; it's a calculated strategy that yields rewards.

April 15th

RESPECT ESSENCE, SHAPE THE FORM

"It is not part of a true culture to tame tigers, any more than it is to make sheep ferocious."

—HENRY DAVID THOREAU, *Walking.* [131]

True culture respects essence. Tigers? Wild. Sheep? Gentle. Force change? It's not authentic. Organizational culture? Same principle. Respect its core. Mold, don't force. Enhance, don't change essence. Culture shift? Guide it. Don't push extremes.

Takeaways. Respect the core of culture; Don't force extremes; Guide culture shifts; Enhance, don't alter essence.

Fundamental Concepts. True culture values essence. That's Authentic Integrity. Tigers remain wild. Intrinsic Nature respected. Sheep stay gentle. Core Behavior recognized. Forcing roles? Mistake. Role Incongruence. Organizational culture? Delicate balance. Organizational Equilibrium in focus. Respect? Essential. Value Acknowledgment. Extremes? Not real. Authenticity Breach. Guide, don't force. Facilitative Approach wins. Culture's essence? Cherished. That's Root Preservation.

Bottom Line. Honor your culture's essence in shaping it. Acknowledge what exists. Don't force unnatural changes. In business, align with the organization's nature. Guide, don't impose changes. Enhance, don't reinvent the culture. Make shifts natural, not drastic. Respect and value your culture's core. Let changes build on this foundation.

April 16th

CULTURE STEERS WHILE CHANGE SHIFTS GEARS

"Top-down, or bottom-up change, or both? Think about each approach's impact on your organization's culture, processes, and performance."

—CHANGE366. [132]

Choosing a change path shapes culture. Top-down? it says, 'Leaders decide.' Bottom-up? it says, 'We all have a voice.' Both have power, but the choice sets the tone. Your culture feeds on it. Culture isn't just a buzzword; it's the air your team breathes. Choose wisely, make culture your compass. If leaders are in the driver's seat, make sure they're listening to the radio-feedback from the team. If it's a team choice, make sure they're all in for the long ride.

Takeaways. Top-down or bottom-up shapes culture; Who decides sets the tone; Culture evolves with choices; Culture's pulse guides change.

Fundamental Concepts. Culture sets norms. That's Social Learning Theory. Top-down speaks to Authority Compliance. Leaders lead, employees follow. Bottom-up? That's Participative Management. More voices, more choices. Either path talks to culture. And culture talks back. That's Reciprocal Determinism. The choice is a social signal. Signals mold norms. That's Social Proof. Culture isn't just decor. It's the floor. It's how we relate and operate. That's Social Identity Theory. Be it top-down or bottom-up, culture's the constant. It's the shared mental model. That's Cognitive Consensus. Choose wisely. Culture watches.

Bottom Line. Respect your culture's essence. Acknowledge what's already there. Avoid forcing unnatural changes. In business, align with your organization's nature. Guide, don't impose, changes. Enhance, don't reinvent, the culture. Make shifts gradual, not drastic. Value and honor your culture's core. Let changes build upon this foundation.

April 17th

CULTURE TALKS, LISTEN UP

"Want change to stick? Talk clearly, engage people. Make it easy. Add value. Change is a journey, not a one-time show. Shared experiences matter. They glue us together. Build a talk-friendly culture. Make it part of who we are. Culture can shift. Shake up the usual. Drive real change. Be the spark."

—CHANGE366. [133]

Culture drives change. Communicate clearly, simplify, and add value. Change is a journey; train, support, and monitor progress. Tailor approaches for different teams using ADKAR™ as a guide. Shared experiences bond teams. Foster a culture of open dialogue. Be the catalyst for change, encouraging a collective shift.

Takeaways. Clear talk and engagement makes change stick; Use models like ADKAR for diverse team needs; Shared experiences build a talking culture; Change in culture starts with people on board.

Fundamental Concepts. Culture shapes change? That's Organizational Psychology. Speak clear? Communication Theory. Make it easy? Cognitive Ease. Step by step? Incremental Theory. Different teams? Social Identity Theory. Share the journey? Social Cohesion. A culture of talk? Verbal Looping. Make it us? In-Group Formation. Be the spark? Leader as Catalyst. Drive change? Agency and Self-Efficacy. Culture shifts with people? Group Dynamics. Social Proof. Clear plan, clear gain. That's Self-Determination Theory. Know the ropes. Drive the change.

Bottom Line. For lasting change, communicate clearly and engage with value. Utilize ADKAR for varied team needs. Foster a culture of dialogue and unity. Gain buy-in for cultural shifts. Be the leader who initiates and cements change. Lasting change thrives on collective action.

April 18th

GUT FEELINGS GUIDE THE GAME

"It is also highly important for us to realize that we do not as a matter of fact lead our lives, make our decisions, and reach our goals in everyday life either statistically or scientifically. We live by inference. I am, let us say, your guest. You do not know, you cannot determine scientifically, that I will not steal your money or your spoons. But inferentially, I will not, and inferentially you have me as a guest."

—ERWIN GOFFMAN, *The Presentation of Self in Everyday Life.* [134]

Trust is key in change. There's no rule book for trust—it's instinctive, crucial in business. Science doesn't predict all; intuition shapes culture. Mutual trust between you and your team simplifies change. Trust acts as the silent driver of cultural transformation. Lead with good faith and drive change from within.

Takeaways. Trust is vital in driving culture change; Not everything is statistical; human inference matters; Gut feelings shape organizational culture; Assume good faith to fuel change.

Fundamental Concepts. Trust guides? That's Social Trust Theory. Rule book absent? Heuristic Thinking. Gut feelings? Intuition and Emotional Intelligence. Culture change? Organizational Culture Theory. Assume good faith? Reciprocal Altruism. Drive change? Agency Theory. Trust is the engine? Social Cohesion. Be a guest? Role Theory. Good faith fuels? Prosocial Behavior. Trust is key. Culture will follow. That's Social Contract Theory. Assume the best. Make the change. Win the trust. Drive the change. Good faith gains.

Bottom Line. Trust is crucial for cultural change, relying more on instincts than rules or science. Mutual trust with your team eases change. Lead and decide with trust to strengthen culture. Value gut feelings in shaping organizational culture.

April 19th

A PLANNED CULTURE CAN PLAN FOR CHANGE

"Nine skills define culture. Aim High values excellence. Speak Up encourages bold communication. Plan Ahead prioritizes future goals. Be Kind rewards fairness. Team Up I focuses on shared resources and action. Team Up II emphasizes group loyalty. Equal Play addresses gender equity. Know Your Place acknowledges power dynamics. Play It Safe uses rules to minimize uncertainty."

—CHANGE366. [135]

Change happens, culture changes, too. The GLOBE model shows us nine ways. Aim high, be direct, plan ahead, be fair, team up, stay loyal. Treat everyone the same. Respect power roles. Each competency molds your company culture. Embrace them for smoother change.

Takeaways. Culture has multiple facets; the GLOBE model outlines nine; Each competency is a tool for change management; Embrace these competencies to make culture your ally, not your obstacle.

Fundamental Concepts. Nine traits shape culture. That's the GLOBE model. Aim for better? That's Mastery Orientation from Self-Determination Theory. Speak up? Assertiveness breeds Self-efficacy. Plan for tomorrow? Future Orientation is Temporal Discounting. Be kind, be fair? That's Prosocial Behavior. Team up, share gains? Social Capital in action. Stay loyal to your group? In-group Bias on display. Treat genders equally? Breaking Gender Norms. Know your place in power? That's Social Hierarchy Cognition. Don't like risks? Uncertainty Avoidance, plain and simple. These psych traits fuel change. Understand them. Use them. Change for the better.

Bottom Line. Master the nine GLOBE skills for an adaptable culture. These skills streamline change management. Use them to make your culture flexible and prepared for change. Apply these traits to evolve and enhance your culture.

April 20th

CHANGE FROM THE CORE, SURFACE LAST

"Picture three concentric circles showing culture levels. The outermost is 'Artifacts.' They're symbols showing values and beliefs. Next is 'Values & Beliefs.' It's about what workers feel is right. The center is 'Basic Assumptions.' It's deep ideas about how workers see the world. Cultural change starts from the center. Change basic ideas first. Then, shift values and beliefs. Lastly, update artifacts to match. This way, change is deep and lasting."

—CHANGE366. [136]

Cultural change is a journey. Think of it as three rings. The heart, the belief, and the face. Dive deep, start at the heart—the core thoughts. Tweak them, then, mold your values. Shape what feels right. Lastly, change what people see—the symbols. True change begins deep and surfaces last.

Takeaways. Start with the core: Basic Assumptions; Next, align the Values and Beliefs; Finally, update the visible: Artifacts; Deep changes endure.

Fundamental Concepts. Culture's core is key. That's Intrinsic Motivation. Symbols mirror deep thoughts. That's Behavioral Reflection. Values guide actions. That's Guided Agency. Deep changes stick. That's Sustained Behavior. Aligning beliefs and symbols? That's External Congruence. Change isn't just seen. It's felt, lived.

Bottom Line. Start cultural change at the core by changing basic assumptions. Then align values and beliefs with these new core ideas. Finally, update the visible symbols to reflect these changes. This process ensures that change is meaningful and enduring. Focus on deep-rooted shifts for lasting impact.

April 21st

JOURNEY SHAPES, DESTINATION SHINES

"We delight in the beauty of the butterfly, but rarely admit the changes it has gone through to achieve that beauty."

—MAYA ANGELOU, *I Know Why the Caged Bird Sings.* [137]

Culture is like a butterfly, change shapes its beauty. We admire end results but overlook the transformation journey. Respect the process, admire the outcome. Understand culture's evolution.

Takeaways. Culture evolves; Change is often unseen, but always impactful; Appreciate the journey, not just the destination; Transformation defines beauty in culture.

Fundamental Concepts. Culture evolves. That's Continual Adaptation. Like the butterfly, it transforms. Metamorphic Change. Overlooking journeys? That's Surface Appreciation. Deep change is unseen. That's Invisible Evolution. The end is admired, path forgotten. Outcome Bias. Respecting the process? That's Acknowledgement of Growth. The beauty in transformation? Recognize it. Deep-Rooted Appreciation. Culture's journey matters. That's Integral Evolution Recognition. Embrace all phases of change. It's Full Cycle Valuation. Transformation is core. It's Fundamental Cultural Shift.

Bottom Line. Respect the journey that shapes a culture, not just its successful outcome. Recognize and value the transformation process that leads to a culture's beauty. Change is a core part of culture's evolution. Appreciate the unseen changes as they are integral to the end result. Embrace all phases of change to understand the culture's true impact and worth.

April 22nd

CULTURE IS SHARED HABITS IN MOTION

> "Habitualization carries with it the important psychological gain that choices are narrowed... the background of habitualized activity opens up a foreground for deliberation and innovation which demand a higher level of attention ... The most important gain is that each member of society will be able to predict the other's actions. Concomitantly, the interaction of both becomes predictable."
>
> —PETER L BERGER, *The Social Construction of Reality.* [138]

Habits shape us, culture thrives on them. Predictability emerges, people know what to expect, they trust. This trust fuels innovation. With a stable base, change becomes welcome. But it must be built on shared habits. Culture's power lies there.

Takeaways. Habits lead to predictability in culture; Trust emerges from shared routines; Predictability allows room for innovation; Culture's strength is in shared habits.

Fundamental Concept. Habits set, predictability rises. That's Habitual Foundation. Shared routines lead to trust. That's Cultural Bonding. With trust, change is embraced. That's Trust-Driven Adaptation. Innovation springs from shared norms. That's Culture-Driven Innovation. No shock, just understanding. That's Habitual Harmony. Stable culture, dynamic innovations. That's the essence of Cultural Equilibrium. Shared habits, shared purpose. That's the heart of Culture Sync. Cultivate habits, culture thrives.

Bottom Line. Cultivate culture with shared habits for predictability, building trust and sparking innovation. Establish routines as culture's cornerstone. Foster a stable yet dynamic environment where change equals opportunity. Regularly refine habits for a vibrant, purpose-driven culture.

April 23rd

GROWTH WITHOUT VALUES IS A HOLLOW VICTORY

"No, all hope cannot be pinned on science, technology, or economic growth. The victory of technological civilization has also instilled in us a spiritual insecurity. Its gifts enrich but enslave us as well. All is interests, we must not neglect our interests, all is a struggle for material things; but an inner voice tells us that we have lost something pure, elevated, and fragile. We have ceased to see the purpose."

— Aleksandr Solzhenitsyn. *Speech.* [139]

Tech grows, culture shifts. Not always good. We gain but lose too, balance is key. Don't forget values for growth. Remember purpose.

Takeaways. Tech's rise can dim culture's glow; Balance growth with values; Listen to the inner voice of culture; Purpose over pure profit.

Fundamental Concepts. Tech advances, culture fades. That's Cultural Erosion. Material pursuits blind us. That's Value Overshadow. Spiritual insecurity rises. That's Inner Disconnect. Purpose becomes blurred. That's Directional Ambiguity. Balance tech and tradition. That's Holistic Integration. Internal voice whispers. That's Core Value Retention. Organizations must listen. Return to roots. Anchor in purpose. Culture thrives with care.

Bottom Line. Balance tech growth with core values. Prevent tech from overshadowing culture. Prioritize purpose over profit. Listen to your culture's inner voice. Seek harmony between progress and tradition. Understand that growth without values falls short. Anchor changes in foundational principles to maintain cultural vitality.

April 24th

CULTURE IS A PUZZLE, NOT A PAINTING

"Cultural labels only scratch the surface. To truly lead, zoom in on the niches where behavior takes shape. There, you'll find the keys to effective change."

—CHANGE366.[140]

Change starts with you. Culture is a dynamic force, not just a backdrop. It varies within an organization. No one dominant culture exists. Instead, numerous niches with their own mini-cultures exist. These can align or clash with the larger culture. In change, focus on these niches. They are crucial for change. A top-down approach isn't enough. Customize your change strategy for each niche. They have distinct needs and norms. Listen to them, adapt, and take action. Change will happen.

Takeaways. Culture is not monolithic; it varies within an organization; Niches like departments or teams have their own unique mini-cultures; A one-size-fits-all change strategy will not work; Adapt your change tactics to fit the unique needs and norms of each niche.

Fundamental Concepts. Culture, like a puzzle aligns with Cultural Anthropology, needs to be solved. It's not fixed, that's Group Dynamics. Behavior is influenced by Cultural Niches, Self-Determination Theory suggests. To drive change, consider unique needs and norms in each niche. That's Motivational Psychology, respecting individuals' contexts.

Bottom Line. Lead change by focusing on organizational niches like departments and teams. Recognize the complexity and variety of internal cultures. Avoid one-size-fits-all strategies. Instead, customize approaches for each group. Embrace adaptability and respond to unique norms and behaviors. Listen to niche groups to effectively initiate change.

April 25th

OPEN MINDS OPEN DOORS

"Success in today's dynamic market hinges on a blend of rational and developmental cultures, fueled by an unflinching openness to change."

—CHANGE366. [141]

Change boosts your team. But how? Two words: culture and openness. A culture that embraces change and reason raises performance. Open minds also lift results. Blend the two, and you're golden. It's not just one culture. Blend development and rational thinking. Boost agility, embrace change. Your team will shine.

Takeaways. Culture matters. Aim for development and rational thinking; Openness to change isn't optional. It's essential; Combine the two. Watch performance rise; It's not one-size-fits-all. Mix cultures for best results.

Fundamental Concepts. Niches shape self-view. That's Self-Construal Theory. Adapt or clash, the choice is there. That's Niche Dynamics. Autonomy meets relatedness. That's Adaptive Social Relations. Strategy lacks fit. That's Managerial Void. People are passive, not active. That's Self-Agency Gap. Know the niche. Plug the gaps. Adapt the strategy. Engage Self-agency. Culture changes with care.

Bottom Line. Combine rational and developmental cultures for success. Embrace change with strong openness. Enhance team agility and performance. Adapt strategies to fit the market and encourage active engagement. Thoughtfully change culture.

April 26th

CHANGE WITHOUT CULTURE IS CHAOS

"Culture isn't just part of the game in organizational change; it's the whole game. A united culture fosters commitment; a fractured culture fuels resistance."

—CHANGE366. [142]

Culture is the glue in any change effort. It decides how employees think, feel, and act. A strong culture aligns people. It helps them work towards common goals. In times of change, this is critical. If the culture supports change, employees will too. They'll adapt, learn, and grow. If it doesn't, expect resistance.

Takeaways. Culture acts as the foundation for change; A strong culture supports and speeds up change efforts; Weak culture can hinder organizational change.

Fundamental Concepts. Strong culture equals Group Cohesion. Cohesion boosts Commitment. Commitment drives Change Success. Weak culture? That's Social Fragmentation. It lowers Employee Engagement. Low engagement derails change. That's Change Resistance. Culture's role? Central. It fuels Change Acceptance. It shapes Employee Behavior. That's Behavior Shaping. Culture shapes Mindsets. Mindsets decide Outcomes.

Bottom Line. Build a strong culture to support change in your organization. Ensure that culture unites and commits employees to common goals. Foster group cohesion and mindset alignment. Prevent resistance by avoiding social fragmentation. Strengthen employee engagement. Remember, a strong culture is key to successful change.

April 27th

CULTURE FLEXIBLE, COMPANY CAPABLE

"Adaptability in organizational culture is not an option—it's a survival skill. Flex your culture or face your downfall."

—CHANGE366. [143]

Change is the lifeblood of business. It's not an outlier; it's the norm. Henry Ford revolutionized the auto industry. How? He saw the market wanted value, not just cheapness. His vision spurred cultural shifts in how cars were made and sold. Just like Ford, firms today need to rethink their culture. Stagnant culture stifles innovation. In contrast, a dynamic culture fuels success.

Takeaways. Change isn't an exception; it's the business norm; Recognize what the market truly values; A culture resistant to change will fail; A flexible culture fosters innovation and adapts to market needs.

Fundamental Concepts. Change is a must. That's Adaptability. Stagnation? That's Status Quo Bias. Henry Ford saw the market anew. That's Cognitive Flexibility. He changed the culture. That's Social Identity Theory at play. Workers adapt, or they falter. That's Role Theory. Culture is the glue. It's Social Cohesion. Businesses need to bend. That's Resilience. Fail to adapt? That's Organizational Inertia. Flex your culture; flex your fate. That's the root of Organizational Change Management.

Bottom Line. Adapt your company culture to market needs. Drop outdated practices. Build a culture open to change and innovation. Listen to customers and staff. Make decisions together. Update your approach and stay ready for change.

April 28th

CULTURE ANCHORS THE PAST, LEADERS STEER THE FUTURE

"Culture is the compass that often points to the past—adept leaders know when to recalibrate it for the journey ahead."

—CHANGE366.[144]

Culture has influence It sets the pace and the rules. Yet, it can be a foe when change is due. Culture makes us feel safe. It can also make us stubborn. Leaders shape culture. They must know when to shake it up. To foster change, spot the weak links in your old culture. Forge a new one that fits the future. It's a tough job, but vital. Culture can be a glue or a wall. Make it the right kind of sticky.

Takeaways. Culture shapes action and thought; A static culture fights change; Leaders can retool culture to align with new goals; A new, flexible culture promotes change.

Fundamental Concepts. Folks follow norms. That's Social Conformity. Culture's grip is strong. That's Sunk Cost Fallacy. Leaders set the tune. That's Authority Bias. People cling to the known. That's Status Quo Bias. Change jars the system. That's Cognitive Dissonance. Leaders must reframe the view. That's Cognitive Restructuring. Adapt or get stuck. The core is Psychological Flexibility.

Bottom Line. Culture influences behavior and thinking. It can resist change, but leaders can reshape it to match new goals. Identifying cultural weaknesses is essential. Adapting culture guides organizations toward new horizons. Leaders skilled in cultural adjustments drive innovation and success.

April 29th

CULTURE IS THE CANVAS—LEADERSHIP IS THE BRUSH

"For effective tech adoption, culture and leadership must be in harmony; they're the dual engines driving organizational change."

—CHANGE366. [145]

Culture and leadership steer the ship. They decide if a tech change will sink or swim. Culture is not just a buzzword. It's the glue that binds your team. The leader acts like a compass, setting the direction. When both line up, tech changes go smoothly. If not, brace for a rocky ride.

Takeaways. Culture is the team's glue. It needs to align with tech changes; Leadership sets the course. The leader needs to speak the culture's language; The combo of culture and leadership makes or breaks tech changes.

Fundamental Concepts. Culture is Social Cohesion. The force that binds the team. Leadership is Executive Function. The brain behind actions. They're bound by Social Proof. People follow leaders they trust. That's Trust Capital. Poor alignment? That's Cognitive Dissonance. A clash that costs you. Solid alignment? That's Cognitive Harmony. Smooth sailing on tech seas.

Bottom Line. Culture and leadership drive technology adoption. Know your culture and lead effectively. Communicate clearly and pick the right team. Match technology with your company's style. Build trust and maintain flexibility. Learning and improving are vital for tech adoption. Celebrate progress. CxOs should understand both tech and culture. Strive for continuous improvement. Technology and culture need to work together for success.

April 30th

AUTOMATE THE OLD, INNOVATE THE NEW

"Civilization advances by extending the number of important operations which we can perform without thinking of them."

—Alfred North Whitehead, *An Introduction to Mathematics.* [146]

Civilization grows when tasks get easier. We automate, we streamline. Things once hard are now simple. This change happens in businesses too. To advance, we make complex tasks easy. We change habits, we free minds for new challenges.

Takeaways. Automation makes hard tasks easy; Simplified tasks mark progress; Habit changes free up thought; Ease of work fuels advancement; Advancement fuels culture.

Fundamental Concepts. Automation breeds habit. That's Operant Conditioning. Tasks turn simple. That's Skill Acquisition. We act without thought. That's Automaticity. Progress thrives on this. Minds freed from routine. That's Cognitive Load Theory. Innovation needs space. Habits provide it. That's Habituation. Change is growth. Simple acts, complex outcomes. That's Behavioral Complexity Reduction.

Bottom Line. Making tasks automatic helps culture change. It turns difficult things simple, which leads to business growth. This makes room for new thinking and innovation. Changing habits lets us focus on new challenges. Automation marks progress and is key to cultural advancement.

Change management in business is like steering a ship through a storm; it demands agility within to match the pace of external change. Welch's words tell us that survival depends on adapting quickly. Kotter suggests that fear can be a powerful motivator, but hope is what propels us forward. The message is clear: balance the urgency to change with a vision for the future.

Microsoft emphasizes that technology is driven by people, not vice versa. Hougaard notes poor leadership can waste potential. Employees must trust their leaders to welcome change. CNBC's revelation about the failures of GE and Ford exemplifies how silent strategies can lead to downfall. Communication is the lifeblood of successful change. Covey's football analogy illustrates the disconnect that can occur within teams and emphasizes the need for clarity and engagement to ensure everyone is playing for the same goal.

Kotter notes the importance of creating a sense of urgency, while Welch defines the leader's role as the 'Chief Meaning Officer,' giving direction and purpose to the change. Peppard's perspective on technology investment reminds us that without the human factor, technology yields no true benefit.

The Harvard Business Review warns of the perils of not addressing flawed organizational practices before implementing digital tools, while McKinsey stresses the role of wise actions over mere aspirations. Peck challenges us to embrace life's complexity, and Shaw encourages the unreasonableness that fosters progress.

Russell and Joyce provoke us to question our beliefs and the paradoxes of change. Change366's insights on navigating change advise building a simple yet flexible core, while Thoreau and Plato remind us of the importance of awareness and reality in leading teams.

Rumsfeld and Leibniz prompt us to consider what we know and what we don't in the face of change. Change366 underscores the centrality of people, affirming that change management is not about controlling but enabling and improving.

As we integrate technology into business, we must invest in both the technology and the people who use it. The collective changes we make can set off a wave, creating a profound impact when strategically guided.

Prosci suggest that leaders must understand the role of technology in change management, ensuring that organizational readiness aligns with technological advancements.

Effective organizational change management balances technology, people, and business priorities. Leadership plays a crucial role in guiding this journey of adaptation, where culture and leadership work together towards a flexible, understanding, and action-oriented future.

May 1st

CHANGE FASTER INSIDE—STAY ALIVE OUTSIDE

"If the rate of change on the outside exceeds the rate of change on the inside, the end is near."

—JACK WELCH. [147]

The world's changing fast. Your company must keep up. Don't lag. If outside change outruns your inside game, you're done. That's the harsh truth. Think of your company as a ship. Choppy waters ahead? Then your crew better row fast. It's not just tech or trends. It's your team's willingness to adapt. Their speed to learn. To do. To grow. Fall behind? You'll sink.

Takeaways. Match the pace of external change. Or better yet, exceed it; Your team's ability to adapt is crucial; It's not just about following trends; it's about internal growth.

Fundamental Concepts. Intention isn't action. That's Theory of Planned Behavior. Thinking you'll adapt? That's Overconfidence. Your team's will matters. It's the engine. That's Self-Determination Theory. It feeds change. Fearing failure? That's Loss Aversion. It pushes you to move. Change inside to keep up outside. That's the golden rule.

Bottom Line. Change fast inside to beat changes outside. Stay quick and flexible. Push your team to learn and grow quickly. If you don't keep up with outside changes, your business could fail. Grow from within and make fast decisions to outdo your rivals.

May 2nd

FEAR OPENS EYES. HOPE MOVES FEET. AIM FOR BOTH

"Yes, Burning Platforms can shake people out of complacency. But without a reason to believe that a better future can be realized, real change cannot be achieved. Deep commitment to change happens when excitement about the future outweighs the fear felt today."

—John Kotter, *Leading Change.* [148]

Change mixes fear and hope, revealing threats while promising a better future. Focus on opportunities, not just risks. Hope, more than fear, spurs action. Aim for excellence and inspire excitement about the future, as hope is the real motivator.

Takeaways. Fear alone won't sustain change; hope is essential; Balance the message: threats get attention, opportunities sustain effort; Deep commitment comes when future gains outweigh present fears.

Fundamental Concepts. Scaring people wakes them up. That's the Arousal Theory. But it's a short-term jolt. That's Negative Reinforcement. A 'Burning Platform' serves that role. [149] What's next? To get people moving, need Intrinsic Motivation. That's Self-Determination Theory. Give them a reason to believe. Show them a better future. That's Cognitive Restructuring. Positive Emotions balance out Negative Emotions. It's about Emotional Regulation. When gains outweighigs fears, commitment grows. That's the Commitment-Trust Theory. [150] So don't just scare. Inspire. Tap into both sides of Emotional Affect.

Bottom Line. Drive change using both fear and hope. Let fear wake your team up and use hope to keep them moving. Paint a bright future to inspire action and dedication. Cut down fear, highlight the good, and build trust for real change.

May 3rd

PEOPLE POWER TECH—TECH DOESN'T POWER PEOPLE

> "But in the end technology is only a tool. What's a hammer without a person who swings it? It's not about what technology can do, it's about what you can do with it. You're the voice and it's the microphone. When you're the artist, it's the paintbrush."
>
> —MICROSOFT, *AI Commercial, featuring Common.* [151]

Tech is not magic. It's a tool. It needs you. A hammer just sits there. You make it swing. Same goes for your business tech. Software alone won't fix problems. You use it. You shape it. You make it work for you. So focus on the people. Inspire them to use tech in smart ways. Then you'll see real change.

Takeaways. Tech is a tool, not a solution; People drive technology, not the other way around; Personal transformation and inspiration make tech effective.

Fundamental Concepts. Tech's just a tool. That's Operant Conditioning. You shape behavior by using it. It doesn't shape you. The hammer sits. You swing. That's Human Agency. You're the actor. Tech's the prop. Silence in a mic? That's lack of Stimulus. Your voice? That's the Stimulus that makes it work. So, it's not External Locus of Control. It's Internal. You control the tool. Not vice versa. That's tapping into Intrinsic Motivation. It fuels change. Keep it human. That's Self-Determination Theory at play. People run the show.

Bottom Line. People drive technology, not the other way around. Technology is a tool shaped by human actions and motivations. You control the tool; it doesn't control you. Human agency and intrinsic motivation fuel technology and change. People are at the core of technological effectiveness and transformation.

May 4th

AN UNINSPIRING LEADER TURNS GOLD INTO GRAVEL

> "A survey published by Forbes found that 65 percent of employees would forgo a pay-rise if it meant seeing their leader fired. And a Gallup engagement survey found that 82 percent of employees see their leaders as fundamentally uninspiring. In our opinion, these two things are directly related."

—RASMUS HOUGAARD, *Why do Managers Forget They're Human?* [152]

Bad leaders damage more than finances; they erode morale. Studies show many prefer firing a bad boss over a raise. Most find leaders uninspiring, highlighting a crucial issue. Leadership is an organization's soul, vital for vitality or decay. Teams seek vision, growth, and respect, not just higher pay. Poor leadership can ruin teams and halt progress, regardless of compensation.

Takeaways. Leadership quality affects team morale and productivity; Money's not everything; employees value inspiring leadership; Poor leaders can halt even well-funded projects.

Fundamental Concepts. Leadership matters. Money is not the main pull. That's Self-Determination Theory. People want more. They want to feel engaged. They want leaders who inspire. That's Emotional Intelligence. A bad leader drains the team. That's Negative Affectivity. It's not just about numbers. It's about human needs. Vision, growth, and respect matter. When these are missing, morale sinks. That's the Psychology of Well-being at play. Poor leaders don't just halt progress. They break the human spirit.

Bottom Line. Business change thrives on inspiring leadership. Strong leaders fuel growth, nurture vision, and earn respect, essential for successful change. Without such leadership, morale suffers, and progress falters. Choose leaders who empower and ignite meaningful change.

May 5th

SILENT STRATEGY IS A BLUEPRINT FOR BANKRUPTCY

"GE, Ford, and other major players poured USD1.3 trillion into transformation initiatives, 70% of which—or USD900 billion—was wasted on failed programs. The biggest reason? Failure to communicate their goals, strategy, purpose, and outlook with their employees".

—CNBC, *The $900 billion reason GE, Ford failed at DT.* [153]

Change costs money. Lots of it. But wasted money hurts even more. Why did these big companies fail? Bad communication. They forgot to share the plan. If the team doesn't know the goal, they can't help you reach it. Clarity is key. So is sharing your vision. Every team member needs to know the plan. They need to feel a part of it. If you're driving change, make your message loud and clear.

Takeaways. Big spending doesn't guarantee success; Bad communication is a fast track to failure; Every team member needs to understand the strategy; Money can't replace clear and open dialogue.

Fundamental Concepts. Bad communication. That's lack of Social Cohesion. Teams work well when they know what's going on. People need a sense of control. That's Autonomy in Self-Determination Theory. Unclear goals lead to Role Ambiguity. People unsure of their tasks, performance drops? That's lack of Intrinsic Motivation. No clear vision means no inner drive.

Bottom Line. Successful change management hinges on clear strategy communication. Ensure every team member understands and engages with the company's transformation goals to prevent costly failures. Start with the 'why.'

May 6th

WHEN PLAYERS DON'T CARE, THE SCOREBOARD DOES

"If results from a key employee engagement survey were translated into an eleven-person football team the results are as follows: 4 of 11 players would know which goal is theirs. 2 of 11 would care. 2 of 11 would know what position they play and know exactly what they are supposed to do. 9 of 11 players, would in some way, be competing against their own team."

—Stephen R Covey, *The 8th Habit.* [154]

Picture a football team where players are unclear on goals and roles, often working at cross purposes. Successful change management demands clear goals, defined roles, and cohesive teamwork. Leaders should guide like coaches, focusing on direction and collaboration.

Takeaways. Most team members lack clarity on organizational goals; Engagement is low; only a few care about the goals; Role ambiguity is high; Many don't know what they're supposed to do; Misalignment is rampant; Team members are often at cross purposes.

Fundamental Concepts. Role confusion reigns. That's Role Ambiguity. Stress and doubt follow. Low passion in the ranks. That's Self-Determination Theory failing. Few care. Most are lost. That's low Engagement. Teams clash within. That's Misalignment. Sociological breakdown. Common goal? None see it. Vision missing. Work hurts. That's bad Organizational Culture. Leadership is the fix. Clarity is the tool. That's the essence of Effective Management. Make roles clear. Make goals known. Align the team. Then watch them soar.

Bottom Line. To achieve successful change, leaders must ensure teams understand their goals, roles, and collaborate effectively. Clear communication and unity are essential to turn strategy into action.

May 7th

URGENCY IS THE CATALYST FOR TRANSFORMATION

"The urgency rate for a change is high enough when about seventy-five percent of the company's leadership is convinced that business as usual is totally unacceptable."

—JOHN KOTTER. *Leading Change.* [155]

Ready, set, go. But not so fast. Is the team on board? Especially the leaders? Here's the thing. You need them. About 75% of them. If they aren't saying 'This can't go on,' wait. Your change may flop. Big ideas need big backing. The status quo? It's your rival. Treat the need for change like a five-alarm fire. Douse doubt. Ignite action. Your aim is not just change. It's a revolution.

Takeaways. Change needs urgency, or it's just talk; Three-quarters of leaders must say 'no more' to the old ways; If leaders balk, your change plan might stumble.

Fundamental Concepts. Change stalls. That's Change Resistance. Doubt and inertia follow. Lack of commitment among leaders. That's Leadership Fragmentation. Only a few champion the cause. Most remain unconvinced. That's Limited Alignment. Teams clash internally. That's Team Discord. A breakdown in cohesion. A shared vision? It's elusive. The absence of clear direction. That's Disoriented Workforce. Effective leadership is the solution. Clarity is the remedy. That's the heart of Change Facilitation. Define roles. Communicate goals. Unify the team. Witness transformation unfold.

Bottom Line. Urgency is vital in change management, with most leaders needed to champion it. Drive change with leader conviction and clear, united team effort.

May 8th

LEAD WITH PURPOSE AS THE CHIEF MEANING OFFICER

"What is the role of a Leader? Well, the first one clearly is to be the chief meaning officer. To let everyone in the place know where you're going, why you're going there. And most importantly. What's in it for them to get there with you? People like to talk about where they're going, why they're going there, but they don't; they always leave out the third thing. When you come into a new job, and you say we want to change, change is great; we gotta' do it. You forget people hate change. You've got to explain what's in it for them to change with you."

—JACK WELCH. *What is the role of a leader?* [156]

Leadership means being the 'chief meaning officer.' Your role is to show the way, explain why, and highlight the benefits. People resist change, but you must clarify what they gain. When you lead change, answer, "What's in it for them?" Use ADKAR. This fosters alignment and commitment.

Takeaways. Leaders clarify the way and the benefits; Explain change's personal benefits; Foster alignment and commitment.

Fundamental Concepts. Leaders act as 'chief meaning officers.' That's Psychological Guidance. People resist change due to Inertia. Explain thoroughly. Leaders highlight personal benefits for alignment and commitment.

Bottom Line. Lead change by clearly defining its purpose, direction, and personal benefits for each team member. Use clarity to overcome resistance and drive commitment. Apply ADKAR to guide the way.

May 9th

TECH'S JUST A TOOL—YOUR TEAM TURNS IT TO TREASURE

"IT has no inherent value. Benefits arise when people do things differently (no change, no value). Only business leaders and managers, and end-users, can realize business benefits. All IT projects have outcomes, but not all outcomes are benefits. Benefits must be actively managed to be realized."

—JOE PEPPARD, *Realizing Business Benefits from IT Investments.* [157]

Here's a crucial message: technology alone won't boost your business. The real game-changer? How people use it. Your team-managers and front-liners turn tech into treasure. Without their buy-in and skill, even the fanciest software flops. So, don't just install a new system and walk away. Stick around to steer it to success.

Takeaways. Tech tools are just tools; people make them profitable; A leader's role is to turn tech outcomes into business benefits; Change is the road from mere outcomes to real benefits; Active change management turns potential into actual gain.

Fundamental Concepts. Tech sits idle. That's Tool Underuse. A system with no pulse. Leadership absent. That's Managerial Void. Few guide the tech transition. Most are hands-off. That's Passive Oversight. Teams lack tech know-how. That's Skill Deficit. The cycle of underuse continues. Value from tech? It's missing. No clear game plan. That's Strategy Gap. Effective leadership fills the void. Active management is the key. That's the core of Tech Activation. Set the example. Spell out the benefits. Train the team. Watch profits rise.

Bottom Line. Guide your team to use technology effectively for business gains. Technology alone doesn't add value; it's the team's skilled application that counts. Leaders must actively direct technology use and ensure the team knows how to use tools profitably.

May 10th

GAINS AWAIT IN TECH—BUT FIRST, OLD HABITS WRECK

"Most digital technologies supply possibilities for efficiency gains and customer intimacy. But if people lack the right mindset to change and the current organizational practices are flawed, digital transformation will simply magnify those flaws."

—HARVARD BUSINESS REVIEW, *DT is Not About Technology.* [158]

Digital tech can boost your business. It can make work faster. It can make customers happier. But there's a catch. If your team fears change, good tech can't help. Worse, it can highlight what's already broken. A new tool doesn't fix a rusty machine. You need the right mindset and solid practices. Then, digital tech can shine.

Takeaways. Digital tech offers more than bells and whistles; It promises efficiency; Mindset matters; fear of change can make good tools useless; Bad practices get worse with new tech; Fix the foundation first.

Fundamental Concepts. Tech offers gains. That's Efficiency Promise. Speed and customer ties within reach. Mindset missing. That's Change Resistance. Tools can't work if fear blocks. Flaws magnified. That's Digital Spotlight. Broken practices? They'll glow. Need mindset and method. That's Change Preparedness. The right attitude and solid systems let tech shine.

Bottom Line. Technology advances can boost efficiency and customer relations, but success requires the right mindset and practices. If your team sticks to old habits, digital transformation will highlight, not solve, problems. Start change management by tackling fears and flaws. Create a positive change mindset and solid practices, then introduce new technology.

May 11th

DREAMS DEMAND WISE ACTION, NOT JUST WIDE EYES

"Although the hoped-for benefits of a major initiative can shrink dramatically if employees misunderstand or resist it, success or failure depends as much on how the change is made as on the project itself."

—McKinsey, *Helping Employees Embrace Change.* [159]

Big projects spark big dreams. But here's the hitch: People can deflate them. When teams don't get it, dreams shrink. When they resist, those dreams can die. So, how you roll out the change matters. In fact, it's as crucial as the project. It's not just what you do, it's how you do it.

Takeaways. Big dreams are good; employee buy-in is better; Resistance isn't futile; it's a sign. Pay attention; It's not just the change; it's how you make it.

Fundamental Concepts. Hope floats. That's Optimism Bias. Leaders aim high. Workers waver. That's Cognitive Dissonance. Clarity in approach is crucial for understanding. That's Procedural Justice. Fairness in process fuels fire. Employees resist. That's Psychological Reactance. Freedom feels threatened.

Bottom Line. Successful change combines big dreams with practical steps. Planning big must be paired with team understanding and support. Employee confusion or resistance can ruin great plans. How you implement change matters as much as the change itself. Lead with clarity and fairness to transform resistance into cooperation.

May 12th

SIMPLE OUT, COMPLEX IN

"Abandon the urge to simplify everything, to look for formulas and easy answers, and to begin to think multi-dimensionally, to glory in the mystery and paradoxes of life, not to be dismayed by the multitude of causes and consequences that are inherent in each experience—to appreciate the fact that life is complex."

—M. SCOTT PECK. *The Road Less Travelled.* [160]

Simplifying is tempting. Complexity rules, though. Embrace it. Each layer holds value. Recognize the many faces of change. Dive deep. Complex is okay.

Takeaways. Resist oversimplification; Welcome complexity; Multiple factors drive change; Complexity adds value.

Fundamental Concepts. Resist ease? That's Cognitive Complexity. Embrace the layers? That's Systems Thinking. Many causes? That's Multivariate Analysis. [161] Dive in depth? That's Deep Work. Complexity adds value? That's Nonlinear Dynamics. [162] Complexity's the game. It's not a shame. That's Cognitive Flexibility. Get your team to think in layers. That's Collective Intelligence. Address the many, not just any. That's Holistic Management.

Bottom Line. Change means accepting complexity, not shying away from it. Don't oversimplify. Every change is distinct. Understand the various elements involved. Appreciate the richness complexity adds. Urge teams to think thoroughly and value change's intricate nature.

May 13th

EMBRACE COMPLEXITY, BUT NAVIGATE WISELY

"Embrace the intricacies and complexities that come with growth and change. Yet, never lose sight of simplicity at your organization's core. Build a framework that allows for flexibility and adaptability. Keep your focus on what truly works, letting real-world results be the ultimate judge of your choices and changes."

—CHANGE366. [163]

Complexity baffles. Yet it benefits. Systems interconnect. They morph and grow. Understand their rhythm. Their ebb and flow. Complexity isn't evil. It's necessary. Dynamic environments need it. But manage with care. Think modular. Adopt simplicity. Embed flexibility. Control? Use sparingly. Lead Change. Let the market decide. Prune often. Optimize always. Embrace, don't evade.

Takeaways. Complexity has its merits in dynamic settings; Modular structure and simplicity are key; Embrace change and minimal control; Constantly optimize and prune for efficiency.

Fundamental Concepts. Complexity perplexes. That's Cognitive Overload. Structures intertwine. Systems evolve. That's Dynamic Interconnectivity. Minimal control empowers. Flexibility prevails. That's Autonomy Support (Self-Determination Theory). Market dictates success. Adapt and grow. That's Environmental Feedback. Optimize the whole. Constantly evolve. It's the essence of Adaptive Management. Harness complexity. Understand its nature. Lead with insight. Success beckons.

Bottom Line. Complex systems are challenging but not always bad. They help during changes. As your company transforms, organize it effectively. Use simple components and rules. Stay flexible with minimal rules. Let your people and customers guide improvements. Continuously refine your organization. Keep upgrading and streamlining.

May 14th

ADAPTING IS SURVIVING; TRANSFORMING IS THRIVING

"The reasonable man adapts himself to the world: the unreasonable one persists in trying to adapt the world to himself. Therefore, all progress depends on the unreasonable man."

—George Bernard Shaw. *Man and Superman.* [164]

Change challenges norms. It's the push, the drive. The unreasonable leads. Businesses stuck? They adapt. Leading businesses? They transform. They rewrite rules. They question. They innovate. Progress isn't complacency. It's audacity.

Takeaways. Change demands audacity, not just adaptation; The best businesses transform, they don't just conform; Questioning the status quo leads to progress; Embrace 'unreasonable' for groundbreaking change.

Fundamental Concepts. Unreasonable drives change. That's Innovation Instinct. Questioning norms? Critical Analysis. Bold steps forward. That's Intrinsic Motivation. Adapting? Status Quo Bias. Transforming? Autonomous Mastery. Leading versus following. Proactive Initiative. Embracing audacity? Risk Taking Behavior. Staying safe? Fear of Failure. Disrupting the familiar. That's Change Catalyst. Be bold. Embrace change. Lead the future. That's Change Leadership.

Bottom Line. Drive transformation, not just adaptation, for business progress. Be bold in change management: innovate and lead, don't just follow. Question and rewrite the rules to thrive.

May 15th

BUSINESS THRIVES WHEN BELIEFS BEND

"I would never die for my beliefs because I might be wrong."

—BERTRAND RUSSELL, *Collected Papers.* [165]

Beliefs guide us. But they're not always right. In business, flexibility matters. Adaptability is crucial. When we manage change, we embrace beliefs. But we must question them too. Because the market shifts. Customers evolve. What worked once might not always work. So, when steering change, remain open. Be ready to pivot if needed.

Takeaways. Beliefs are starting points, not end goals; Flexibility in business practices is essential; Always be open to new information and insights; A successful change embraces adaptability.

Fundamental Concepts. Beliefs anchor us. That's Cognitive Foundation. But inflexibility? Business risk. That's Operational Stagnation. Challenge the status quo. Adapt and thrive. That's Business Agility. Change evolves, so should we. That's Responsive Adaptation. Hold beliefs but stay open. That's Cognitive Flexibility. Change demands we pivot. Not just follow past patterns. It's the essence of Dynamic Business. Question, adapt, and grow. Embrace the unknown. Ensure sustainability and relevance. Progress is constant adaptation.

Bottom Line. Business thrives when beliefs are flexible. Challenge and adapt them. Inflexibility is a risk. Embrace change with openness and readiness to pivot. Stay agile in business practices to remain relevant and successful.

May 16th

EMBRACE THE CHANGE CONUNDRUM

"You walk past a barber's shop, and see a sign saying 'Do you shave yourself? If not, I'll shave you! I shave anyone who does not shave himself, and no one else.' Later, the following question occurs to you—does the barber shave himself? If he does, then he mustn't, because he doesn't shave men who shave themselves, but then he doesn't, so he must, because he shaves every man who doesn't shave himself."

—HELEN JOYCE. *A Close Shave for Set Theory.* [166]

Change is complex, akin to the barber's paradox. Organizations are nuanced, with every leader's decision having both apparent and hidden impacts. Leaders need to look deeper, beyond obvious choices, and prepare for paradoxes. Embrace uncertainty, delve into complexity, simplify where possible, but acknowledge the intricacies.

Takeaways. Change is complex and multifaceted; Leaders must expect and manage paradoxes; Decisions come with unintended consequences; Embrace ambiguity in leadership.

Fundamental Concepts. Change confounds. That's Organizational Paradox. Leaders face decisions. Complexity creeps in. That's Decisional Ambiguity. Riddles in business. Reflect deeper truths. That's Inherent Uncertainty. Simplify, but honor depth. That's Respectful Simplification. Leaders navigate mazes. Find clarity amidst chaos. It's the essence of Adaptive Leadership. Probe dilemmas. Embrace the challenge. Lead with foresight. Triumph waits.

Bottom Line. Change is complex, like a tricky puzzle. Leaders must make choices, knowing there are unseen consequences. They need to delve deep, embrace uncertainty, and simplify wisely. Managing change requires clear thinking and strategic planning.

May 17th

NAVIGATE CHANGE, CHART NEW TERRITORIES

"Only that day dawns to which we are awake. There is more day to dawn. The sun is but a morning star."

—HENRY DAVID THOREAU, *Life in the Woods.* [167]

In business, opportunity comes to those prepared for it. Being awake means recognizing potential. Each day is a chance to change your business. Just starting is often the boldest step. Like the sun, businesses can start small, only to illuminate vast territories.

Takeaways. Alertness to change defines business success; Every day is a chance to change business strategies; Initial steps in business change, like dawn, predict future light.

Fundamental Concepts. Alertness matters. That's Cognitive Awareness. Opportunities equal days. That's Temporal Opportunity. Embrace business change. That's Adaptive Readiness. Small beginnings, vast outcomes. That's Incremental Growth Theory. Illuminate with intent. That's Purposeful Expansion. Recognize potential, redefine paths. That's Strategic Acumen. Small starts lead to brilliance. That's the essence of Business Evolution. Spot the openings. Adapt the strategies. See success unfold.

Bottom Line. Embrace change every day to grow in business. Start small, be alert, and adapt. Use strategic thinking to navigate and chart new paths for success.

May 18th

DON'T MANAGE SHADOWS—LEAD TEAMS TO REALITY

"Plato's Cave Allegory—living in the cave, we see only shadows. Breaking free shows us the real world. Some choose ignorance, staying in the dark. Others seek truth, stepping into the light."

—PLATO, *The Republic.* [168]

In business change, many are like the prisoners in Plato's Cave. They see only what they know. They stick to old ways. But the world outside is full of real opportunities. Leaders must guide their teams out of this 'cave.' They must show the reality beyond the shadows of old practices. Unchain your team. Lead them to new perspectives. That's real change management.

Takeaways. Leaders must show the reality beyond the current practices; Breaking free from the 'cave' opens new opportunities; True understanding comes from embracing change and exploring new perspectives.

Fundamental Concepts. People stick to the known. That's Cognitive Bias. [169] Fear of the new. That's Loss Aversion. Leaders stay in the cave. That's Managerial Inertia. No urge to explore. That's Motivational Deficit. Change seems risky. That's Risk Aversion. Autonomy is the spark. Show them the real world. That's Cognitive Reappraisal. Intrinsic motivation fuels the move. That's Self-Determination Theory. Value new views. That's Perspective Shift. Lead the change. Make it stick. That's Effective Change Management.

Bottom Line. Lead your teams out of old habits to explore new opportunities. In change management, set an example by embracing new perspectives and fostering growth.

May 19th

KNOW YOUR KNOWNS—NAIL YOUR UNKNOWNS

"Reports that say that something hasn't happened are always interesting to me, because as we know, there are known knowns; there are things we know we know. We also know there are known unknowns; that is to say, we know there are some things we do not know. But there are also unknown unknowns—the ones we don't know we don't know."

—Donald Rumsfeld, *US Department of Defense Press Conference.* [170]

Navigating business change is like a maze with known paths, unclear routes, and hidden traps—known knowns, known unknowns, and unknown unknowns. Savvy leaders prepare for all, adapting to keep the business on course. Stay vigilant and continuously learn to manage change effectively.

Takeaways. Plan for what you know and what you don't; Unknowns can disrupt; Prepare to adapt; Continuous learning helps tackle unknown unknowns; Effective leadership navigates through all types of uncertainty.

Fundamental Concepts. Leaders read reports. That's Information Gathering. Some data lacks. That's Uncertainty. Knowns managed well. That's Cognitive Clarity. Unknowns unsettle. That's Risk Aversion. Blind spots exist. That's Overconfidence Bias. Adaptation is key. That's Cognitive Flexibility. Motivation matters. That's Self-Determination Theory. Prepare for pitfalls. That's Defensive Pessimism. Navigate the maze. Lead through fog. That's Situational Awareness. Plan, adapt, succeed. That's Resilient Leadership.

Bottom Line. In change management, recognize knowns and unknowns. Anticipate and adapt to unforeseen disruptions. Maintain flexibility and learn constantly to handle surprises. Effective leadership involves navigating uncertainties with adaptability and resilience.

May 20th

PAST WINS DON'T PROMISE FUTURE GAINS

"Nature has established patterns originating in the return of events, but only for the most part. New illnesses flood the human race, so that no matter how many experiments you have done on corpses, you have not thereby imposed a limit on the nature of events so that in the future they could not vary."

—GOTTFRIED LEIBNIZ, *Letter to Jacob Bernoulli.* [171]

Change is the only constant. Business success isn't just hitting targets. It's staying agile. Even if you've conquered past challenges, new ones arise. Past performance isn't a perfect map for the future. Stay flexible. Measure different aspects. Adapt your yardsticks for success. This way, your business stays resilient.

Takeaways. Agility over rigidity ensures adaptability; Past success isn't a future guarantee; Update your metrics to meet new challenges; Flexibility and constant measurement make for resilient operations.

Fundamental Concepts. Metrics set. That's Goal Setting Theory. Plans rigid. That's Overcommitment. Past viewed as prologue. That's Hindsight Bias. New troubles loom. That's Uncertainty Aversion. But minds change. That's Cognitive Flexibility. Goals shift. That's Self-Determination Theory at work. Adaptability kicks in. That's Resilience. Constant checks help. That's Feedback Loop. Success redefined. That's Elastic Goal Management. Stay agile, stay ahead. That's Adaptive Leadership.

Bottom Line. In business, change is constant. Past success doesn't guarantee future wins. Be agile and ready for new challenges. Update how you measure success to adapt. Stay flexible and resilient. Keep learning and redefine success to stay ahead.

May 21st

PEOPLE-CENTRIC CHANGE WINS ALWAYS

"Half of Fortune 500 companies from 2000 are gone. Why? Bad change efforts or no change at all. Change or vanish. Success lies in constant change management. Know your goal, build a team, take action. Lead well, focus on your people, and measure your steps. Do it right and not only survive, but thrive."

—CHANGE366. [172]

Businesses die without change. Bad change? Just as lethal. Leadership matters. Clear goals guide. Team alignment? Non-negotiable. Success hinges on constant adaptation. Employees at the core.

Takeaways. Change is business survival; Clarity and alignment propel success; Employees: the change linchpin.

Fundamental Concepts. Change necessity emerges. That's Survival Instinct. Business evolution needed. That's Adaptive Response. Leadership matters immensely. That's Hierarchy Influence. Clear objectives guide. That's Goal-Setting Theory. Teams must unite. That's Group Cohesion. Success requires fluidity. That's Dynamic Adaptation. Employee centrality rises. That's Intrinsic Motivation from Self-Determination Theory. Business needs constant recalibration. That's Feedback Loop Importance. Outperform competition. That's Competitive Advantage. Listen, act, win. That's the Active Response Paradigm. Goals shine clear. That's Vision Clarity. Change? Make it real. That's Actualization Principle.

Bottom Line. Businesses must change to survive. Clear leadership and goals are crucial. Team alignment is non-negotiable. Success depends on constant adaptation with employees at the core. Lead, act, and measure for thriving, not just surviving.

May 22nd

TECH'S POWER—PEOPLE UNLOCK IT

"Change is like a journey in a well-designed car. The tech side? It's the blueprint, the build, the execution. But a car without a driver stays still. People are that crucial driver. They must embrace, adopt, and utilize the tech. Without the human touch, the perfect car is just idle potential. When many drive it, success accelerates. The lesson? Tech and people must merge. Both gears need to shift in unison for a smooth journey. Together, they drive our goals."

—CHANGE366. [173]

Tech's ready. People make it move. Tools alone won't win. Together, they drive success. It's a two-gear race.

Takeaways. Tech and people: change's dual engine; Human touch vitalizes tech; United, they reach goals.

Fundamental Concepts. Change demands dual forces. That's Balanced Approach. Tech stands ready. It's the Potential Energy. Humans add spark. That's Kinetic Activation. Tools alone stall. That's Inertia Principle. [174] People drive tech. That's Agency Power. Both must sync. That's Harmonic Convergence. [175] One without the other? It's Functional Redundancy. Success needs unity. That's Collaborative Synergy. Clear goals need both. That's Dual-Faceted Approach. Joint journey to aim. That's Unified Destination Principle. Collaboration, the winning ticket. That's Collective Efficacy.

Bottom Line. Tech alone isn't enough; people drive change. They bring it to life and make it move. It's a dual engine race, and they must work together to succeed. Harmonize tech with human adoption for progress towards your goals.

May 23rd

CHANGE'S HELM—THE TOP. ALWAYS

"6,000 voices said: Choose renovation over transformation. Start at the top. Communicate the change. Find influencers. Track progress. Own the culture shift. No resistant leaders allowed. CEOs? They're culture leaders. Their tone matters. In 80% of top firms, CEOs lead. They champion change. Resistant leaders? Ditch them. Soft skills? Crucial. Culture boosts loyalty and retention. Top-down change makes an impact."

—CHANGE366. [176]

Research shows successful change starts strong with top management guidance and clear communication. Utilize influential individuals to build momentum and monitor progress closely. CEOs play a key role in shaping culture. Effective leadership and soft skills, such as empathy, are essential for profitability and satisfaction. Lead proactively for tangible results.

Takeaways. Top-down leadership ensures clear, strong change; Engage energizers; they're change champions; Measure, monitor, report: Know your progress; Culture and empathy: not just words, they're assets.

Fundamental Concepts. Leaders dictate. That's Hierarchical Influence. Clarity commands change. That's Transparent Directives. Energizers spark momentum. That's Behavioral Catalysts. Resistant bosses? That's Leadership Friction. CEO in charge? That's Commanding Captaincy. Soft skills yield profit. That's Empathic ROI. Culture's value? Beyond tangible. It's the bedrock. CEO, the change maestro. Tone set, tune played. Empathy and culture? They're the glue.

Bottom Line. Effective business change needs CEO-led cultural leadership. Communicate clearly. Engage influencers. Track progress. Soft skills and culture are key for retention and satisfaction. Remember, 'soft' skills are the most challenging.

May 24th

UNITY IN TEAMS, STRENGTH IN CLOUDS

"Tech is easy; it's people that are hard. In cloud adoption, culture trumps code. Lead with skills, adapt with speed, and choose your partners wisely. Success is not just in the cloud, it's in your team."

—CHANGE366. [177]

Cloud change isn't just tech. Culture clashes loom large. Leaders find humans trickier than hardware. People resist; technology doesn't. Integration is key. New modes require new mindsets. Agility becomes essential. Upskill or partner? Choices abound. Third-parties offer expertise. They navigate the change maze. Cloud leaders value agility. External help eases transitions. Work methods evolve. Quick changes; Faster cycles. Adaptation is non-negotiable. Service providers spot chances. They guide, teach, and transform.

Takeaways. Cloud challenges: more human than technical; Team unity is vital; Agility and adaptability lead to success; Third-party experts can smooth the transition.

Fundamental Concepts. Cloud stumbles on culture. That's Behavioral Barrier. Tech's easy, humans aren't. That's Complexity Contrast. Agility is a must. That's Dynamic Adaptation. Seek external expertise? That's Resource Utilization. New methods emerge. That's Evolutionary Shift. Rapid changes rule. That's Accelerated Cycle. Flexibility is key. That's Behavioral Elasticity. [178] Service providers see gold. That's Opportunity Recognition. Guide, teach, evolve. That's the essence of Transformational Guidance.

Bottom Line. People challenges outweigh tech issues in business change. Executives often find team integration difficult. Leaders turn to training or cloud service partnerships for adaptation. Many opt for experts in change management. Cloud change calls for a cultural shift. Success hinges on culture, just as much as on data for app migration.

May 25th

INVEST IN TECH—INVEST MORE IN ITS USERS

"Amid rising digital demands, CIOs face budget constraints, emphasizing customer experience and operational excellence. Most lack a digital vision, but leading CIOs invest in cybersecurity, data, and cloud. The formula for success: democratize digital access, use diverse talent, and focus on metrics. It's a race to accelerate or risk falling behind."

—CHANGE366. [179]

CIOs face pressure to deliver digital advancements quickly. Key strategies include choosing impactful projects, leveraging data for results, and sourcing diverse talent. This goes beyond IT, covering the entire company. Proper change management transforms challenges into growth opportunities.

Takeaways. Choose projects that echo with overall business vision; Use metrics as your change compass; Make change a team sport, drawing in all functions; Broaden your talent hunt; look where others don't.

Fundamental Concepts. Pressure mounts. That's Achievement Motivation. Change succeeds when leaders aim high. Fear of failure? Call it Loss Aversion. It stops change in its tracks. Mismatched goals? That's Cognitive Dissonance. Confusion kills change. Exclusion felt? That's Social Identity Theory. Teams left out resist change. That's Feedback Loop Gap. Change drifts without metrics. Talent scarce? That's Resource Scarcity. How to pivot? Use Cognitive Reappraisal. Adjust your mindset for change. Enter Self-Determination Theory. Fuel the will for change. Engage everyone. Shape the future. That's change management, optimized.

Bottom Line. To succeed in tech transformation, balance investments with user capabilities. Prioritize user-focused projects and guide change with clear metrics. Foster a company-wide embrace of digital evolution by involving diverse talents and departments.

May 26th

MANY DROPS, AN OCEAN—MANY CHANGES, A WAVE

"Change is more than a concept; it's a path to excellence and efficiency. It involves evolving methods, adopting new tools, and honing skills. An organization's success is gauged by how agilely and skillfully its people manage these shifts. In change management, we empower individuals to excel in new realities, not just manage change. We should embody change, ensuring each step forward brings tangible benefits and meets our shared goals."

—CHANGE366. [180]

Change starts with each individual adapting to new tools and methods. Focus on managing individuals to steer the overall change. Your role is to lead, showing the way and uniting efforts into collective progress.

Takeaways. Change begins with each employee adopting new behaviors; Managing people is crucial for successful change; Individual changes add up to organization-wide transformation; Leadership guides people towards effective change.

Fundamental Concepts. Starts with people? That's Bottom-Up Change. New behaviors? Classic Operant Conditioning. [181] Vital human part? That's Self-Determination Theory. Changes stick when embraced? Cognitive Dissonance in action. Individual effort adds up? Cumulative Effect. Guide them? That's Social Learning Theory. Show the path? Transactional Leadership. Your role? Transformational Leadership. Change is a shift in mindset. That's Cognitive Behavioral Theory. Lead the mind, and the behavior follows. That's your charge.

Bottom Line. Use change management to unite individual adaptations into organizational progress. Lead and support the adoption of new skills for effective and lasting change.

May 27th

EASY TECH, QUICK CHANGE

"Rapid change hinges on technology that is not only problem-solving but also accessible, affordable, and seamlessly integrated. It must be robust yet flexible, customizable, and easy for users. Enhancing teamwork, cost-effective, and simple to implement, it should be secure and its value data-verified. Understanding and leveraging these qualities is key to igniting and accelerating transformation."

—CHANGE366. [182]

Effective tech is the catalyst for rapid change. It must be user-friendly, cost-efficient, and align with your team's goals; it's adaptable and enduring. Your role is to understand the tech, lead your team, and be the driving force behind the transformation.

Takeaways. Choose tech that's easy to use and integrate; Flexibility and scalability are vital for swift change; You, as a leader, are the catalyst for tech adoption; Good tech facilitates teamwork and proves its worth through data.

Fundamental Concepts. 'Good' tech powers quick change? That's Positive Reinforcement. Easy and cheap? That's Low Barrier to Entry. Meshes with team? Social Integration. Fits like a glove? Cognitive Ease. Good tech grows? That's Scalability. You're the spark? Leader as Catalyst. Know the traits? That's Cognitive Awareness. Guide the team? Social Learning Theory in action. Be the catalyst? Exemplar Leadership. Stoke the fire? That's Motivation Theory. Speed up the shift? Urgency and Fear of Missing Out. You pick the tech. You set the pace. That's Self-Determination Theory. Know it. Use it. Win with it.

Bottom Line. Choose user-friendly, adaptable tech to drive fast change. Lead the adoption process, ensuring the tech integrates with systems and shows clear advantages. Your informed choices and guidance can speed up the transition.

May 28th

KNOW TECH, LEAD CHANGE; DRIVE, DON'T FOLLOW

"Project Management prepares the solution for the organization. Change Management prepares the organization for the solution."

—PROSCI. [183]

True change goes beyond projects. It weaves into the fabric of a company, becoming part of its pulse. Project Management sets the stage with solutions—structured, well-defined, and ready. But Change Management brings the company to life, readying the people and the culture for the new journey. It's about preparing minds and hearts, aligning them with new directions and possibilities.

Takeaways. Project Management creates the solution; Change Management gets it used; Change Management aligns people and culture with new solutions—it prepares and supports the workforce for upcoming transitions; Successful change blends structural solutions with cultural shifts.

Fundamental Concepts. Change stimulates minds. That's Cognitive Readiness. A solution presents a choice. Minds align. That's Behavioral Assimilation. Culture adapts. That's Sociocultural Development. People transition. They're moving through Acceptance Phases. Emotional readiness is key. That's Affective Preparation. [184] Change thrives on culture's embrace. That's Organizational Commitment. Minds and roles meet solutions. That's Role Acclimatization. Adaptation leads the charge and surpasses mere planning. That's the heart of Transformational Change.

Bottom Line. Project Management creates solutions; Change Management helps the company use them. Always use change management.

May 29th

CHANGE WITHOUT UNDERSTANDING IS CHAOS

> "Organizational change isn't whimsical; it's a dance of intrinsic motivation and skill mastery, underpinned by research, strategy, and collaboration, ensuring innovations aren't just conceived, but are deeply understood, efficiently implemented, and widely adopted for lasting impact."
>
> —CHANGE366. [185]

Change is crucial. But why? Start with needs/problems to identify pressing issues. Break it down into knowledge, aptitudes, and skills. Knowledge goes beyond data; it's about deep understanding. Aptitudes guide you to recognize gaps and empathize. Skills are your tools for creative thinking, critical analysis, and effective communication. In business, this means don't rush into change. First, understand thoroughly, equip yourself, then move forward with clarity and precision.

Takeaways. Recognizing the 'why' behind change is foundational; Dive deep with knowledge, feel the pulse with aptitudes, and act with skills; In business, comprehension precedes transformation.

Fundamental Concepts. Change stirs thinking? Cognitive Readiness. A solution aligns minds? Behavioral Assimilation. Culture shifts? Sociocultural Development. People accept change? Acceptance Phases. Emotions ready? Affective Preparation. Culture supports change? Organizational Commitment. Minds and roles adjust? Role Acclimatization. Adaptation over planning? Transformational Change. Change is more than plans. It's minds, culture, emotions in sync. Understand, adapt, transform. That's change mastery.

Bottom Line. For effective change, understand deeply and execute strategically. Cultivate internal motivation and skills. Collaborate effectively for lasting innovations. Understand, develop, act. This is the path to successful change.

May 30th

NEW RULES AWAIT—ADAPT OR RISK OBSOLESCENCE

> "Artificial Intelligence now leads, guiding through shifting norms and environmental priorities. Inclusivity guides as work evolves. Adaptability is our compass in this changing landscape, with understanding change as our map."
>
> —CHANGE366. [186]

Business is rapidly evolving. AI is not hype, it's now a strategic foundation. Innovations are merging with AI and cybersecurity regulations. Environmental responsibility is essential. Work methods and locations are changing, and inclusivity is a key focus. Customers increasingly dictate pace and demand more, faster.

Takeaways. AI and digital advances dominate the change landscape; Regulatory updates in cybersecurity and AI demand proactive adaptation; Sustainable practices and waste reduction are be business imperatives; Embracing work flexibility and battling burnout shapes talent strategies; Inclusivity is foundational, not optional.

Fundamental Concepts. AI's rise isn't just tech; it's Behaviorism. Users adapt or resist. That's Cognitive Dissonance. Cybersecurity regulations grow. That's Societal Norms influencing. Green business isn't choice; it's Ethical Responsibility. Burnout and flexibility concerns? That's Maslow's Hierarchy. Push for inclusivity echoes Equity Theory. Quick service needs? That's Instant Gratification's pull. Change isn't linear. It's multifaceted. Understanding the why? That's delving into Behavioral Psychology. Prepare, adapt, and understand. The change tide is inevitable.

Bottom Line. Businesses must embrace AI, environmental priorities, inclusivity, cybersecurity rules, and flexible work to stay relevant. Understanding and adapting to these changes is key to staying ahead.

May 31st

SKIP OCM, INVITE CHAOS

> "Mastering organizational change management is not just vital, it's non-negotiable in the digital era. Overlook it, and you risk not just money, but careers. Picture your company as an elevator: without OCM, it's a rapid, uncontrolled descent. OCM is the safety cable in the fast-paced climb of transformation."
>
> —CHANGE366.[187]

In the digital era, effective Organizational Change Management (OCM) is vital. It's key for successful digital transformations, adapting to new behaviors and norms like data protection and sustainability. OCM steers companies through complex changes, mitigating significant risks in digital transformation.

Takeaways. OCM is critical to avoiding digital transformation failure; Neglecting OCM puts both company finances and personal job security at risk; Embracing OCM is a strategic choice for steering through change.

Fundamental Concepts. Skipping OCM leads to chaos. That's Organizational Turmoil. Without it, you're directionless. That's Navigational Failure. Jobs and money are at risk. That's High-Stakes Scenario. Confusion without OCM? That's Behavioral Turbulence. OCM is crucial for guiding change. That's Leadership Imperative. It helps people adapt to new norms. That's Behavioral Alignment. Missing OCM means facing uncertainty. That's Strategy Void. OCM is essential, not optional. That's Strategic Necessity. Embrace it for stability. That's Organizational Equilibrium.

Bottom Line. OCM is essential for steering successful change and securing jobs. Without it, digital transformations fail, costing money and employment. Treat OCM as your company's lifeline in the volatile sea of digital change.

As a practitioner, it's crucial to understand the psychology that drives organizational change management. Peterson reminds us that risk is inevitable in the journey of change, but preparation is our map. To brave the tides of transformation, we must choose to chase change, not let it chase us. This proactive stance against threat transforms our stress response from prey to predator, from frozen to proactive.

Feelings, Jung says, drive the adoption of change as much as the facts that support it. This emotional connection is the currency of persuasion in the journey of change. Change366 reveals that safety and shared purpose are the beacons of strength that drive change in an organization, suggesting that psychological safety is as foundational as any strategic plan.

Campbell's metaphor urges us to craft, not carve our paths in change, forging ahead step by step rather than following a preordained track. And Beckett encourages embracing failures as stepping-stones to better outcomes. Yarkoni introduces psychoinformatics, blending human psychology with the precision of technology to navigate change more masterfully.

Feldman discusses grief in change, an often overlooked but critical component. It's about managing the emotional transitions that accompany any significant shift in roles or identity. Kahneman proposes Self-Determination Theory as a framework to foster motivation and engagement during change, emphasizing the need for personal growth and connection.

Twain and 'Reddington' evoke the spirit of adventure and desire as change's driving forces, whereas 'Batty's' monologue from Blade Runner presents change as an ephemeral, swift force that we must match in pace. The Swedish proverb 'Ingen ko på isen'—no cow on the ice—suggests calmness as a virtue in leading change.

Change366 asserts that resilience softens the hard edges of change. Kahneman warns against the illusion of control and urges flexibility over fixation. Smith tells us that our focus shifts with time and context, highlighting the importance of adaptability in maintaining attention.

Burns's plea for self-awareness through feedback and Change366's emphasis on personal views at the heart of change remind us that the individual's perspective is paramount. Prosci's ADKAR model outlines the cognitive journey of change, starting with awareness and culminating in sustained new behavior.

Thoreau and Becker speak to the winds of change and the weight of knowledge, suggesting that wisdom lies in discerning the essential from the excess. And as Feynman shows, knowledge changes our perception of the world, reshaping our mental landscape.

Hofstadter and Adams remind us that our personal narrative and reactions to technology are shaped by our lifetimes. Kahneman wraps this psychology of change by emphasizing the intrinsic motivation and the rich rewards of relational ties, suggesting that the drive within, coupled with supportive relationships, is the linchpin of successful change.

Understanding of the psychological aspects of change management frames our approach to navigating organizational transformations. It requires addressing the human experience with as much rigor as we do the structural or strategic elements of change. Through this lens, we not only manage change but also lead it, driving organizations toward growth, adaptability, and sustained success.

June 1st

RISK IS THE ROAD, PREPARATION IS THE MAP

> "When you see stories like the Lord of the Rings, when you see the hero journeying to lands of terror and danger. That's what happens to you—you're in this little safe space, the hobbit in the shire. There's a great evil brewing somewhere, so off you go into the land of terror and uncertainty. Better to go on purpose. Because at least you can be prepared."

—JORDAN PETERSON, *Personality, Heroic and Shamanic Initiations.* [188]

Journeys are full of danger. Just like in 'The Lord of the Rings,' you face perils. The 'Shire' is your comfort zone. But evil lurks. Change is that evil in the business world. You must face it. Better to go prepared. Equip yourself and your team. Plan for the journey. Be the Frodo of your organization. Lead with courage. Be prepared for the unknown.

Takeaways. Your comfort zone is not where change happens; Change is a journey fraught with risks and rewards; Preparing for change is better than reacting to it; Lead the journey into uncertainty with clear plans.

Fundamental Concepts. You have a comfort zone. That's Optimal Anxiety. Leaving it makes you grow. But too much stress breaks you. That's the Yerkes-Dodson Law. [189] Choices have risks and rewards. That's Risk and Reward Processing. Make smart choices or pay the price. That's Decision-making Theory. Plan to manage stress. That's Coping Mechanisms at work. Take control of your journey. That's Agency in action. Choose to face change. Don't let change choose you. That's Self-Determination Theory.

Bottom Line. Face change like a journey. Leave your comfort zone. Prepare and plan ahead. This makes you and your team ready to handle new challenges. Lead boldly into new situations. Choose to face change head-on.

June 2nd

CHOOSE TO CHASE CHANGE, DON'T LET IT CHASE YOU

"We know for sure that if you're doing to face a threat, if you face it voluntary, your body activates itself for exploration and mastery. But if you face it involuntary, the same sized threat, then you revert to 'prey mode' and you're frozen. That's way, way more stressful, it's harder on your body. So, it's better to keep your eye open and watch for emergent threats."

—JORDAN PETERSON, Personality, *Heroic and Shamanic Initiations.* [190]

Act on change before it forces you. Prepare your team for it. When you see a market shift or a new technology, act. Don't freeze like prey. Be the hunter. Face challenges head-on. Train your team to be adaptable. Show them the way. Make change an opportunity, not a threat.

Takeaways. Voluntarily facing threats makes you proactive, better equipped for change; Ignoring emerging threats puts you in a reactive, stressful state; Preparation and awareness lessen the stress of organizational change; A proactive stance turns threats into opportunities.

Fundamental Concepts. Face threats willingly, not under duress. That's Approach-Avoidance Conflict. When you opt-in, your body gears up. That's the Fight-or-Flight Response, skewed toward 'fight.' [191] Choose to face it, and stress lessens. That's Stress Reduction Theory. When forced, you freeze. That's Tonic Immobility, a prey-like state. Being proactive reduces body strain. That's Low Cortisol Levels for you. Keep an eye out. Spot changes before they spot you. That's Environmental Scanning in action.

Bottom Line. Act on change before it forces you; this makes it less stressful and turns threats into opportunities. Stay alert and teach your team to adapt for better control and growth.

June 3rd

FACTS TELL, BUT FEELINGS SELL

"Even when I'm dealing with empirical data, I'm essentially speaking about myself."

—Carl Jung, *On Empiricism.* [192]

Numbers don't always speak to the heart. You see a data-driven pitch for a new tool. Yet, you still resist. Why? Change feels personal. Your own biases and feelings often trump hard facts. Understand this: each person's 'yes' or 'no' to change comes from a deep, personal space, not just from spreadsheets. When you opt for or against a new system, you're revealing a part of yourself.

Takeaways. Change decisions are deeply personal, not just data-driven; Cognitive biases often overshadow empirical evidence; An individual's choice reflects more than just numbers. [193]

Fundamental Concepts. Data speaks. But emotions shout louder. That's Cognitive Bias. Hard facts are there, but we listen to our gut. That's the Affect Heuristic. Why? We're wired to be personal. Each choice is a Self-portrait. That's Self-Determination Theory. Decisions are more than just data. They're a slice of who you are. That's Jung's idea of the Personal Unconscious. [194]

Bottom Line. In decisions about change, feelings often outweigh facts. Emotions guide us more than data. Your choice reveals who you are more than what the facts say.

June 4th

IN CHANGE, SAFETY SPARKS STRENGTH

"In the midst of change, where confusion, vulnerability, and fragmentation are rampant, the need for resilience, cohesion, and collaboration is paramount. Psychological safety, shared purpose, and distributed cognition emerge as vital catalysts for peak leadership, team, and organizational performance, especially in fast-evolving landscapes. These elements are not just supportive mechanisms; they are the bedrock of thriving in change."

—CHANGE366. [195]

Change rattles us. It's true. Teams feel lost and fragile. Yet, that's when we need to stick together. We need a safe space to speak up. A common goal to rally around. And the power to think together. When change hits, these are your shields. They turn confusion into cohesion. They make your team a fortress, not a fracture.

Takeaways. Psychological Safety lets people speak without fear; Shared Purpose unites the team during change; Distributed Cognition enables collective problem-solving.

Fundamental Concepts. Change stirs the pot. Teams wobble. That's Vulnerability. But it's a chance for growth. Cohesion is key. That's Shared Purpose. People need to speak freely. No fear. That's Psychological Safety. Thinking caps on, together. That's Distributed Cognition. When change strikes, these are your shields. They turn disarray into unity. They morph your team from fragile to formidable.

Bottom Line. When change occurs, create a safe space for open dialogue, unite the team around a shared goal, and enhance collective problem-solving for greater strength and resilience.

June 5th

CRAFT THE PATH, DON'T CARVE IT

"If you can see your path laid out in front of you step by step, you know it's not your path. Your own path you make with every step you take. That's why it's your path."

—JOSEPH CAMPBELL, *The Hero with a Thousand Faces.* [196]

Paths laid out? Not yours. Each step crafts your road. That's the Nature of Change. Leaders, listen. Your team's path? Same rules. Don't micromanage every move. Let them step. Let them stumble. Let them learn. In that space, they'll create the company's unique path. Your job? Be the guide, not the dictator. Help them make their steps count.

Takeaways. A clear, step-by-step path lacks room for growth; Allow your team the freedom to shape their journey; Being a guide, not a dictator, fosters organic growth.

Fundamental Concepts. Life's path? It's not pre-made. You build it. That's Self-Determination Theory. Every step you take adds a block. Freedom to choose, that's key. Leaders, don't map it all out for your team. That's Micromanagement. You kill growth that way. Instead, guide. Don't dictate. Let them add their blocks. That's how a strong, unique path gets built.

Bottom Line. Leaders, guide your teams, allowing them to make decisions and learn, shaping a unique and strong direction for the company. Just as your own path evolves with every choice, so should your team's.

June 6th

CHANGE DEMANDS BETTER FAILS, NOT FEWER FAILS

"Ever tried. Ever failed. No matter. Try again. Fail again. Fail better."

—SAMUEL BECKETT, *Worstward Ho!* [197]

Tried? Good. Failed? Okay. The secret is in trying again. And failing better. In change, we stumble. We correct. We grow.

Takeaways. Failure is part of the journey; The key is to fail better each time; Improvement comes from repetition.

Fundamental Concepts. Tried? That's Effort Exertion. Failed? That's Feedback Reception. The secret's out. Try, try again. That's Behavioral Persistence. Fail better. That's Adaptive Learning. In change, we stumble. That's Error Making. We correct. That's Negative Reinforcement. We grow. That's Self-Improvement. These actions are guided. They're not random. That's Intentional Behavior. The core of change is adaptability. That's Cognitive Flexibility. Keep on going. That's Resilience. The cycle is growth. That's Continuous Improvement. Keep this loop. That's Self-Regulation. Change stays. That's Habitual Transformation.

Bottom Line. Embrace failure as a learning tool for growth. Make mistakes, learn, and aim to fail smarter. Use failure to drive effective change. Keep trying, adapting, and improving for continuous growth.

June 7th

MIND MEETS MACHINE FOR MASTERFUL CHANGE

"Psychoinformatics—an emerging discipline that uses tools and techniques from the computer and information sciences to improve the acquisition, organization, and synthesis of psychological data."

—TAL YARKONI, *Psychoinformatics.* [198]

Data shapes change. But not any data. Psychological data. It reveals what people think. How they might act. Use it well to guide change. Merge tech with psychology. Craft a smarter change plan.

Takeaways. Psychological data is crucial for change; Tech can improve how we use this data; A data-driven approach refines change plans.

Fundamental Concepts. Data is key. That's Information Dominance. Psychological focus. That's Cognitive Mapping. Combine both. That's Psychoinformatics. Change needs guidance. That's Directive Strategy. Using tech. That's Instrumental Enrichment. The human element. That's Emotional Intelligence. Data guides plan. That's Decisional Informatics. [199] Merge tech and mind. That's Integrated Approach. In change, be wise. That's Sapient Management. Dig deep with data. Know your team. That's Psychological Acuity. Make change stick. That's Behavioral Anchoring.

Bottom Line. Combine computer science and psychology in psychoinformatics to understand thoughts and actions for effective change planning. Utilize technology for collecting and applying this information, resulting in impactful, enduring changes.

June 8th

LOSS LINGERS, LEADERSHIP MUST LINGER LONGER

"Denial is the brain's way of making sure that one doesn't get too high a dose of grief too soon. Grief takes time because it can entail accepting the loss of one's previous role and redefining oneself. Sometimes, the strongest feelings of grief—known as acute grief—begin to lessen within a few months."

—DAVID B FELDMAN, *Why the Five Stages of Grief are Wrong.* [200]

Change brings loss. People grieve. It's natural. Denial kicks in. It's a shield. It slows down the pain. This is not bad. It's the mind pacing itself. We must manage this in change. Know it. Plan for it. Use time well.

Takeaways. Change causes grief, expect it; Denial is a coping mechanism; Time lessens grief's sharp edge.

Fundamental Concepts. Grief happens. That's Emotional Response. Denial steps in. That's Defense Mechanism. Time is a factor. That's Temporal Regulation. [201] Self-redefines. That's Identity Reformation. Expect grief. That's Psychological Anticipation. Plan eases pain. That's Emotional Contingency. Time as a tool. That's Temporal Leadership. Denial is not the enemy. That's Cognitive Adaptation. Leadership knows this. That's Emotional Intelligence. Use time wisely. That's Strategic Timing. Guide through grief. That's Compassionate Management.

Bottom Line. Leaders must acknowledge and address grief in times of change. Denial serves as a temporary shield, and time helps to ease grief's intensity. Plan empathetically, allowing time for adaptation in the change management process.

June 9th

SDT—YOUR CHANGE CHEAT SHEET

"Self-Determination Theory, with its six mini-theories—Basic Psychological Needs, Cognitive Evaluation, Organismic Integration, Causality Orientations, Goal Content, and Relationships Motivation—offers practical, transformative strategies that resonate profoundly within the realm of business."

—CHANGE366. [202]

Self-Determination Theory (SDT) matters. Why? It tackles human needs. It talks about goals. It gets into relationships. All these affect change. Know these theories. Apply them. Drive change better. Turn theories into tools.

Takeaways. Understand human needs for better change; Goals guide us; know-how; Relationships fuel or fail change.

Fundamental Concepts. Basic needs matter. That's Psychological Essentials. Cognitive evaluation too. That's Mental Metrics. Organismic integration for unity. [203] That's Internal Harmony. Causality guides behavior. That's Motivational Directives. Goal content sets path. That's Objective Structuring. Relationships motivate. That's Social Catalyst. Theories translate to practice. That's Applied Psychology. Know your theories. That's Intellectual Capital. Apply them well. That's Practical Wisdom. Build better change. That's Effective Adaptation.

Bottom Line. In organizational change, act, aim for excellence, and nurture connections. Change response stems from personal motivation, external pressures, or feeling undervalued. Ensure incentives enhance skills, not weaken drive. Seek personal fulfillment, not just approval. Embrace challenging tasks for growth, not just rewards or necessity. Cultivate powerful relationships in change for empowerment, skill-building, and strong bonds.

June 10th

FADING STAR OR SHOOTING STAR. YOU CHOOSE

> "In some remote corner of the universe, poured out and glittering in innumerable solar systems, there once was a star on which clever animals invented knowledge. That was the highest and most mendacious minute of 'world history'—yet only a minute. After nature had drawn a few breaths, the star grew cold, and the clever animals had to die."

—Friedrich Nietzsche, *On Truth and Lies in a Nonmoral Sense.* [204]

Life is brief. Knowledge is fragile. Changes don't last forever. Make your moment count. Drive change that sticks. Adapt or fade.

Takeaways. Change is a blip in time; Adaptability ensures survival; Impact matters over lifespan.

Fundamental Concepts. Life's brief. That's Existential Reality. Change is temporal. That's Temporal Context. Adapt or vanish. That's Survival Imperative. Impact over time. That's Behavioral Legacy. Aphorisms hit home. That's Cognitive Resonance. Quick learning boosts lifespan. That's Neuroplasticity in Action. [205] Making choices. That's Decisional Balance. Ephemeral yet eternal. That's Temporal Paradox. Survival at stake. That's Existential Anxiety. Drive change, leave legacy. That's Behavioral Imprint.

Bottom Line. Time is short, and knowledge doesn't last forever. Be like a shooting star, not a fading one. Make your actions leave a mark. You must adapt to survive and make your work memorable. Remember, change is quick, and survival is key. What you do lasts longer than you. Choose to make a difference.

June 11th

CHANGE IS YOUR SAIL, NOT YOUR ANCHOR

> "Twenty years from now you will be more disappointed by the things that you didn't do than by the ones you did do, so throw off the bowlines, sail away from safe harbor, catch the trade winds in your sails. Explore, Dream, Discover."
>
> —Mark Twain. [206]

Don't wait. Act now. Change is your sail, drive it. The wind of opportunity won't wait. Sail from safe waters. Explore new horizons. Dream big. Make it happen.

Takeaways. Act now, regret less; Risk beats routine; Dream and do, don't just dream.

Fundamental Concepts. Act now. That's Temporal Motivation. Less regret later. That's Delayed Gratification. Risk tops routine. That's Risk-Reward Valuation. Dream and do. That's Goal-Directed Behavior. Safe stays stale. That's Behavioral Stagnation. Takeaways provide path. That's Cognitive Mapping. Aphorisms make it stick. That's Mnemonic Retention. [207] Exploration as goal. That's Intrinsic Motivation. Turn dream to deed. That's Self-Determination. No anchor, just sail. That's Behavioral Activation.

Bottom Line. Change is a tool for progress, not a restraint. Take action today to avoid future regrets. Embrace risk over comfort. Pursue change actively instead of just imagining them. Make use of opportunities and strive for goals to prevent stagnation. Act, explore, and dream to drive your life forward.

June 12th

DESIRE DIGS DEEP, DRIVES CHANGE

> "Have you ever sailed across an Ocean? On a sailboat surrounded by sea with no land in sight. Without even the possibility of sighting land for days to come? To stand at the helm of your destiny. I want that one more time. I want to be in the Piazza del Campo in Siena and feel the surge as ten racehorses go thundering by. I want another meal in Paris at L'Ambroisie in the Place des Vosges. I want another bottle of wine, and then another. I want the warmth of a woman in a cool set of sheets. One more night of Jazz at the Vanguard. I want to stand on summits and smoke Cubans and feel the sun on my face for as long as I can. Walk on the wall again, climb the tower, ride the river, stare at the frescoes. I want to sit in the garden and read one more good book. Most of all I want to sleep. I want to sleep like I slept when I was a boy. Give me that. Just one time. That's why I won't allow that punk out there to get the best of me, Let alone the last of me."
>
> —'RAYMOND 'RED' REDDINGTON', *'The Blacklist'.* [208]

Desire drives us. It fuels change. It makes us fight the tough fight. Goals, big or small, push us. They form our vision. Hold your desires tight. They're your North Star in change. Navigate your team by it. Beat challenges. Don't let setbacks rob you of your future.

Takeaways. Desire fuels determination; Set specific goals; Use your vision as a guiding star; Challenges are not end stops; they're just bumps.

Fundamental Concepts. Desire drives. That's Intrinsic Motivation. Goals push. That's Goal-Setting Theory. Vision guides. That's Leadership Vision. Bumps, not blocks. That's Resilience. Takeaways point. That's Cognitive Structuring. [209] Aphorisms stick. That's Slogan Recall. Drive trumps drift. That's Self-Determination Theory. Vision, not just view. That's Future

Orientation. Set goals, set pace. That's Self-Regulated Learning. Fight, don't forfeit. That's Grit.

Bottom Line. Desire drives change. Set and pursue your goals. Let your desires lead you through transitions. See challenges as hurdles, not roadblocks.

June 13th

CHANGE IS SWIFT—BE SWIFTER

"I've seen things you people wouldn't believe. Attack ships on fire off the shoulder of Orion. I watched C-beams glitter in the dark near the Tannhauser gate. All those moments will be lost in time, like tears in the rain. Time to die."

—'ROY BATTY', *Tears in the Rain', Blade Runner.* [210]

Life is short. Time flies. We witness a lot. Some things astonish us. But remember, nothing is permanent. Not even problems. Change is like that too. Moments come and go. In a business, changes fade if not managed well. Be the guardian of change. Make every moment count.

Takeaways. Time is limited; use it well; Change is transient; manage it effectively; Nothing lasts; adapt constantly; Be the steward of impactful moments.

Fundamental Concepts. Life's short. That's Temporal Focus. Time flies. That's Perceived Time Pressure. Astonished? That's Novelty Seeking. Fade or manage? That's Organizational Memory. Guardian role. That's Stewardship Theory. [211] Tick-tock. That's Time Urgency. Adapt. That's Cognitive Flexibility. Swift moves. That's Agile Management. Chaperone, not a passenger. That's Active Leadership. Make it last. That's Institutionalization.

Bottom Line. Life is fleeting, and change is constant. Witness and adapt to change swiftly to make the most of time. Manage change well or it will pass unnoticed. Aim to guide and preserve impactful changes in business. Embrace change, and lead actively to make moments last.

June 14th

CALM HEADS STEER CLEAR PATHS

"Ingen ko på isen."

—SWEDISH SAYING. [212]

Translation: 'No cow on the ice' A . In change management, panic can freeze your plans. But this Svenska saying urges calm. No crisis? Then no rush. Make each change with care, not with haste. Evaluate each step. Keep cool, stay steady, and change happens.

Takeaways. Avoid panic; Evaluate each move; Keep calm; Make steady change.

Fundamental Concepts. No rush? That's Emotional Regulation. Evaluate first? That's Deliberative Decision-Making. Stay calm? That's Stress Coping. Steady wins? That's Sustained Effort. Emotional Regulation keeps panic at bay. Deliberative Decision-Making shapes the plan. Stress Coping holds the line. Sustained Effort makes it real. Real change? No rush. Evaluation is key. Coping sustains. Effort wins. That's the core of Calm-Driven Change.

Bottom Line. Stay calm when making changes at work. Rushing can cause problems. Take time to think about each step. This approach prevents panic and leads to better decisions. Calmness helps to manage stress and keep steady progress. Remember: no need to hurry if there's no crisis. Make careful changes for the best results.

June 15th

CHANGE IS HARD—RESILIENCE MAKES IT SOFT

"In times of change, productivity may dip, but it's not destiny. Understand the brain's dance with change, turn resistance into resilience. Leaders who embrace this truth don't just manage; they thrive. The future belongs to those who lead with brain-aware strategies."

—CHANGE366. [213]

Change is hard. It slows down work. But there's more to it. The brain matters. Use it well. Get ahead in the change game. Know the psychology behind change. Teach your team how it works. Turn resistance into resilience. Quick changes, smooth flows, better gains. Use the brain, win the change.

Takeaways. Change can reduce productivity by up to 60%; Resistance is often the villain. But it doesn't have to be; Brain science can help. Understand it to manage change better; Leaders must use psychology to make change easier.

Fundamental Concepts. Drop in work. That's Loss Aversion. Fear the new. That's Status Quo Bias. Resistance? It's the brain's Default Mode. Engage the brain. You counter the fears. That's Cognitive Reappraisal. Leaders who know? They build Change Resilience. That's Emotional Intelligence. Future lead? They're Brain-Savvy. That's Neuroleadership. [214] Change quick. Change smooth. That's Change Mastery.

Bottom Line. During company changes, work output may decrease. Worker resistance can hinder projects. Change is challenging and slow. Effective leaders facilitate the process. They guide employees to embrace change, making the transition faster and smoother. Leaders skilled in psychology will thrive in the future.

June 16th

FIXATE LESS, FLEX MORE

"We focus on our goal, anchor on our plan, and neglect relevant base rates, exposing ourselves to the planning fallacy. We focus on what we want to do and can do, neglecting the plans and skills of others. Both in explaining the past and in predicting the future, we focus on the causal role of skill and neglect the role of luck. We are, therefore, prone to an illusion of control. We focus on what we know and neglect what we do not know, which makes us overly confident in our beliefs."

—DANIEL KAHNEMAN, *Thinking, Fast and Slow.* [215]

Focus blinds us. We fixate on goals. We forget the unknown. This is risky in change management. Skills matter. So does luck. Don't just plan. Adapt. Include others in your plan. They have skills too. Illusion of control? Break it. Be aware, not just confident.

Takeaways. Focusing solely on goals can lead to planning fallacy; Skill and luck both play a role; Illusion of control can be a blind spot.

Fundamental Concepts. Focus narrows view. That's Attentional Bias. Planning gaps loom. That's Planning Fallacy. Skills stand out, luck fades. That's Fundamental Attribution Error. [216] Control seems real. That's Illusion of Control. Confidence overshadows gaps. That's Overconfidence Bias. Adapt, don't just plan. That's Cognitive Flexibility. Team skills count. That's Social Capital. Stay aware, stay ahead. That's Metacognition. [217]

Bottom Line. Be flexible in your plans. Balance skill with luck. Don't just focus on your goals; consider others' skills and plan for surprises. Understanding luck's role and avoiding overconfidence is crucial in change management. Flexibility and awareness lead to success.

June 17th

FOCUS IS FLUID, FLOWING WITH THE AGE

"Our own perceptions of our current period of distraction therefore need to be seen in a longer perspective. Concentration is a social, learned behaviour that is more necessary in some contexts than in others... we are not losing the ability to concentrate, merely directing it towards different media. We concentrate when we want to. Distraction allows for different, not simply lesser, possibilities than absorption. And reading a book from start to finish is not a moral act."

—EMMA SMITH, *Are our short attention spans really getting shorter?* [218]

In organizational change, focus is key and evolves over time. It's a skill honed by experience, not diminished by fast media. Our focus is adaptable, shifting based on interests. Distractions can open new paths of exploration, and choosing focus areas is a personal, not moral, decision.

Takeaways. Focus shifts but doesn't diminish in our dynamic world; Modern habits are an evolution, not a decline; Distractions can lead to fresh insights and opportunities.

Fundamental Concepts. Attention shifts. That's Cognitive Adaptability. Social learning shapes focus. That's Behavioral Modeling. Adapted attention spans? That's Media Redirect. Distraction as a gateway? That's Exploratory Behavior. Absorption or distraction. Both have value. Reading end-to-end? Personal preference, not Ethical Positioning. Embrace the fluidity of focus. Let concentration's compass guide change.

Bottom Line. In today's fast-paced business world, our ability to focus adapts, not weakens. Change management involves leveraging this adaptive focus for new learning methods and opportunities. Understanding and redirecting concentration is key, not morally superior.

June 18th

FEEDBACK'S LENS CLARIFIES THE PATH

"O wad some Pow'r the giftie gie us to see oursels as ithers see us! It wad frae mony a blunder free us, An' foolish notion: what airs in dress an' gait wad lea'e us, an' ev'n devotion!"

—ROBERT BURNS, *To a Louse.* [219]

Perception is a game-changer. If businesses saw themselves as others did, the picture would differ. Many blunders arise from ignorance. Many choices from misguided views. Realizing external perceptions can guide positive change. It refines strategies and priorities.

Takeaways. External perceptions can highlight unseen flaws; Recognizing these can steer us away from potential blunders; Adjustments based on feedback foster positive organizational change; Embracing external views strengthens change processes.

Fundamental Concepts. Perception's power? Immense. That's Perception Influence. Feedback shapes actions. That's Behavioral Feedback Loop. What's unseen becomes seen? That's Cognitive Recognition. Blind spots revealed. That's Self-Awareness Surge. Ignorance to knowledge? That's Enlightened Transition. Feedback, the guide. That's Looking-Glass Self. [220] Adjust, evolve, and prosper. Perception's gift is growth. Embrace external insights. Change thrives on them. That's the heart of Perception-Driven Change. Seek feedback, value insights, adapt accordingly. Success follows.

Bottom Line. Feedback shows how others see us, preventing mistakes and bad decisions. It points out areas for improvement. Understanding external perceptions helps make smarter choices and grow. Businesses must collect and act on feedback for positive change, driving success through others' insights.

June 19th

THE HEART OF CHANGE BEATS IN PERSONAL VIEWS

"The relative advantage of the change is the most crucial factor. It's what fuels an individual's desire to adopt the change, and it's incredibly subjective."

—CHANGE366. [221]

The core of change lies in seeing its benefit. That's relative advantage or desire. It's the make-or-break factor in deciding to change. People weigh this advantage personally. It's a subjective call. Shape how people see this advantage. Use tools like the social cognitive model and Self-Determination theory. [222] Drive the will to change.

Takeaways. Relative advantage is the key to adopting change; Perception of this advantage is personal and subjective; Change managers use theories to shape these perceptions; The aim is to build a strong will to change.

Fundamental Concepts. Decision fuels. That's Relative Advantage. Personal lens. That's Subjective Evaluation. Managers shape. That's Social Cognitive Model. Will stoked. That's Self-Determination Theory. Change wins. That's Successful Adoption.

Bottom Line. Change revolves around believing in its benefits. This belief differs from person to person and drives change. Change managers must use psychological models to influence and motivate. Their goal should be to strengthen personal motivation for change. Success depends on shaping and embracing this belief that leads to successful adoption.

June 20th

CHANGE STARTS IN THE MIND BEFORE THE GRIND

"Prosci's ADKAR model highlights five change steps: Awareness of change importance, Desire to engage, Knowledge acquisition, Ability to apply skills, and Reinforcement to maintain change. Plan for obstacles; a score of three or less signals problems needing information and support."

—PROSCI. [223]

Prosci's ADKAR model is a five-step method for implementing change. This approach combines practical steps with psychological insights. It focuses on competence, autonomy, and relatedness. ADKAR is more than a process; it's a mindset for effective change in individuals and organizations.

Takeaways. ADKAR is a guide and a lens to understand change; It ties into the psychology of decision-making, making it more effective; It helps identify roadblocks and solve them in real-time.

Fundamental Concepts. ADKAR embodies Self-Determination. It aligns with competence, autonomy, and relatedness. Awareness boosts competence, or Competence Spark. Desire activates autonomy, personalizing change. Knowledge and Ability enhance competence: Skill Empowerment. Reinforcement focuses on relatedness: Community Cohesion. The model bridges change management and behavioral psychology, driving personal and organizational transformation.

Bottom Line. ADKAR leads change in five steps: Recognize change, desire it, learn it, implement it, sustain it. It merges action with mindset, targeting comprehension, motivation, skill development, and change maintenance. It links ability, choice, and support, fusing practical actions with mental understanding to drive both personal and organizational transformation.

June 21st

ADKAR—THE BEACON OF RELIABLE CHANGE

"ADKAR stands tested with a strong Cronbach Alpha score of 0.833. It heralds a model that accurately gauges the pulse of change readiness. Reliability, the bedrock of decision-making, bestows upon ADKAR a strong trust in its prowess to steer successful change journeys."

—CHANGE366. [224]

ADKAR is change's cornerstone. Get it right, and the dominoes fall in place. Management knows not just about being aware that change is coming. It's understanding the why, the how, the when. That clarity drives desire. And without desire, resistance rules.

Takeaways. Awareness is paramount for change; Understanding leads to acceptance; Misunderstanding breeds resistance.

Fundamental Concepts. Awareness is the trailblazer. It's the first step. That's Cognitive Primacy. Genuine grasp of change aligns actions. That's Behavioral Alignment. Lack of clarity breeds resistance. That's Cognitive Dissonance. Desire blooms from deep understanding. That's Intrinsic Motivation. Misunderstandings cause conflict. That's Resistance Psychology. Desire and comprehension are intertwined, nurturing each other. That's Symbiotic Cognition. Accurate information equips for change. That's Informational Empowerment. A powerful, innate desire propels change. That's Motivational Drive. Awareness leads to knowledge. That's Sequential Learning. Clear awareness sparks desire. That's Affective Response.

Bottom Line. ADKAR, with its proven reliability, ignites change beginning with awareness. Comprehend the 'why', 'how', and 'when' to fuel desire and conquer resistance. Each interconnected step in ADKAR cements lasting change. Clear awareness triggers a potent, internal drive for transformation. Understanding paves the way, desire propels the journey.

June 22nd

CHANGE IS BOTH AN INNER AND OUTER GAME

> "Work evolves, and with it, our hunger for information. Our motivation thrives in the right environment, shaped by relationships, feedback, and our ingrained habits. Yet, while habits guide us, they can sometimes mislead. True mastery lies in discerning potential from the present, fueled by internal drive and external forces."
>
> —CHANGE366. [225]

Change is external and internal. Your work and information needs may vary, influenced by office dynamics and casual interactions. Tight deadlines might affect judgment. Rely on past experiences and habits in your responses and decisions. Motivation thrives on feedback, balancing current tasks with future potential.

Takeaways. Work type directs information needs; Atmosphere and feedback fuel motivation; Time crunch affects quality; Past habits guide present actions; Motivation bridges current state to potential.

Fundamental Concepts. Change at the core. That's Adaptive Response. Info shifts with tasks. That's Cognitive Flexibility. Office vibes stir souls. That's Environmental Influence. Deadlines pinch. That's Time-Induced Stress. Experience and habits? Deep-rooted scripts. That's Behavioral Conditioning. Praises push forward. That's External Validation. Motivation dances between reality and potential. That's the Self-Determination Theory. Dive into the psyche, understand the change. Every shift has a story. Every process a purpose. Understand the why. Drive the how.

Bottom Line. Transformation means adapting work, utilizing habits, and drawing motivation from personal drive and workplace interactions. Recognize how past actions shape current decisions and how feedback enhances motivation, linking present efforts with future potential.

June 23rd

SHORTCUTS CUT SHORT GROWTH

"The goal to be reached is the mind's insight into what knowing is. Impatience asks for the impossible, wants to reach the goal without the means of getting there. The length of the journey has to be borne with, for every moment is necessary, ... because by nothing less could that all-pervading mind ever manage to become conscious of what itself is—for that reason, the individual mind, in the nature of the case, cannot expect by less toil to grasp what its own substance contains."

—GEORG W HEGEL, *The Phenomenology of Spirit.* [226]

True transformation is a long journey. Avoid shortcuts; every small step is crucial. Like molding clay, each challenge enhances understanding. Embrace the process, as growth through change requires patience and effort.

Takeaways. Understanding requires time and patience; Avoid shortcuts; they stifle growth; Every challenge faced refines our knowledge; Embrace the process; it's key to unlocking potential.

Fundamental Concepts. Patience is prized. That's Temporal Depth. Recognizing a journey's length. It's Process Acceptance. Each challenge faced? It's Experiential Refinement. Valuing every step? That's Holistic Acknowledgment. [227] Embracing the process molds us. That's Growth Assimilation. Every toil deepens insight. Dive deep; it's Cognitive Immersion. The journey and destination? Two sides. That's Dichotomy Recognition. The right effort unravels our potential. It's the Effort Paradox. [228] Understand patience, cherish growth. Every challenge? A stepping stone. That's Positive Adversity Perspective.

Bottom Line. Understanding takes time, and shortcuts hinder growth. You need patience and hard work to unlock your full potential. Every difficulty is a lesson that fuels your growth.

June 24th

CHANGE'S DIRECTION? YOUR CHOICE

"You have brains in your head. You have feet in your shoes. You can steer yourself any direction you choose. You're on your own. And you know what you know. And YOU are the one who'll decide where to go."

—DR. SEUSS, *Oh, the Places You'll Go!* [229]

You possess knowledge. You have the tools. Every move? Your choice. Your path in change is personal. Knowledge guides, you decide. Change is a journey. Steer with confidence and purpose

Takeaways. Knowledge empowers direction in change; Tools aid, but decisions lie with you; Your journey is unique; embrace its potential; Steer your path, define your destiny.

Fundamental Concepts. Knowledge empowers. That's Cognitive Capital. Tools are ready, use them. That's Operational Autonomy. Choice is personal. That's Self-Determination Theory. Change is unique. Navigate with care. That's Individual Journey Recognition. Embrace potential? Know it's there. That's Intrinsic Motivation. You decide the route. It's Autonomous Choice. Steer with purpose, the direction's yours. Empowerment Through Agency. Decisions mold the path. That's Choice Consequence Awareness. Your destiny awaits, embrace it. It's End-goal Visualization. [230]

Bottom Line. You have knowledge and the power to choose your path. Your decisions shape your change journey. Use your knowledge and the tools you have to guide your change. Your choices lead to your unique destiny. Embrace your power to choose and find your way. Knowledge and choice make you the master of your direction.

June 25th

CHANGE'S WIND BLOWS—ADAPT OR FALTER

"Men say they know many things. But lo! They have taken wings—the arts and sciences, and a thousand appliances; the wind that blows is all that any body knows."

—Henry David Thoreau, *Where I lived and what I lived for.* [231]

People claim expertise. Yet, the world moves fast. Today's skills might be obsolete tomorrow. Arts evolve. Technology progresses. Science advances. Change is the only constant. Embrace it.

Takeaways. Knowledge is transient; Rapid innovation outpaces expertise; Continuous learning is essential; Embrace the winds of change.

Fundamental Concepts. Knowledge breeds confidence. That's Cognitive Assurance. But change is swift. It's called Temporal Fluidity. The arts and tech evolve. We label it Progressive Shift. Keeping pace is tough. Hence, Continuous Adaptation. Static knowledge? That's Cognitive Stagnation. The winds of change? It's Inevitable Transition. Embrace learning. Counter Cognitive Decay. [232] Keep evolving. It's Intellectual Growth. Stay ahead. It's Strategic Mastery. The mantra? Learn, Adapt, Evolve.

Bottom Line. Change is fast and inevitable. What we know today may change tomorrow. Keep learning and adapting to stay relevant and grow. Embrace change as the key to mastering it. Knowledge evolves, so learn, adapt, and evolve to thrive in a changing world.

June 26th

KNOWLEDGE VAST, WISDOM DISCERNS

"The Man of knowledge in our time is bowed down under a burden he never imagined he would ever have: the overproduction of truth that cannot be consumed."

—Ernest Becker, *The Denial of Death.* [233]

Change surrounds us. Every day, new shifts. It's easy to feel swamped. But in change, not all is crucial. Wise managers discern. They hone in on the heart of change.

Takeaways. Change is constant and sometimes overwhelming; Rapid shifts can burden organizations; Discerning which changes are critical is vital; Not all information during transitions is actionable.

Fundamental Concepts. Change storms in. That's Transitional Overload. Shifts are endless. It's Organizational Flux. Wise managers prioritize. That's Strategic Filtering. Swamped by transitions? That's Change Fatigue. Leaders find clarity amidst chaos. That's Visionary Insight. Amidst change, seek stability. That's Anchored Strategy. Pinpoint pivotal shifts. That's Focused Transition. Embrace essential moves. It's about Core Adaptation. Lead with foresight. That's Change Mastery. Navigate transitions. Drive meaningful evolution.

Bottom Line. Change is constant and often overwhelming. To navigate it effectively, leaders must identify crucial changes and discard distractions. Focus on significant changes for smart adaptation, avoiding burnout. Act on essential changes while preserving stability with a clear vision.

June 27th

KNOWLEDGE RESHAPES THE MIND'S LANDSCAPE

"The world looks so different after learning science. For example, trees are made of air, primarily. When they are burned, they go back to air, and in the flaming heat is released the flaming heat of the sun which was bound in to convert the air into tree, and in the ash is the small remnant of the part which did not come from air that came from the solid earth, instead. These are beautiful things, and the content of science is wonderfully full of them."

—RICHARD FEYNMAN, *Surely You're Joking Mr Feynman.* [234]

Knowledge shifts views. See the unseen. Embrace the deep, not just surface. Change? It's complex but beautiful.

Takeaways. Deep knowledge changes perspectives; Uncover hidden processes; Embrace change's complexity; Seek the 'why' in change.

Fundamental Concepts. New insights transform. That's Cognitive Reframing. Surface sees, depth knows. That's Deep Processing. Change feels daunting? Dive deeper. That's Comprehensive Understanding. Grasp the 'why'. That's Intrinsic Motivation. Unveil hidden layers. That's Insight Revelation. Complexity scares but informs. Face it. That's Adaptive Coping. Know more, fear less. Embrace the depths. That's the core of Resilient Adaptation. Delve deeper. Understand fully. Lead with insight.

Bottom Line. Knowledge reshapes our perspective. Dive deep to uncover hidden processes and understand complex changes. Embrace the depths of change for profound insights and reduced fear. Let understanding guide your journey.

June 28th

IN EVERY 'I', THERE'S A STORY OF CHANGE

"What is an 'I', and why are such things found (at least so far) only in association with, as poet Russell Edson once wonderfully phrased it, 'teetering bulbs of dread and dream'—that is, only in association with certain kinds of gooey lumps encased in hard protective shells mounted atop mobile pedestals that roam the world on pairs of slightly fuzzy, jointed stilts?"

—DOUGLAS HOFSTADTER, *Gödel, Escher, Bach.* [235]

Identity intertwines with biology, yet extends beyond it, encompassing thoughts, feelings, and dreams. Organizational change is a personal journey, requiring understanding of each individual's psyche, addressing their aspirations and concerns, as each seeks meaning in change.

Takeaways. Identity is mixed with emotions and perceptions; Every individual's 'I' seeks validation during change; Understanding personal psyche aids smooth transition; Address individual fears to ensure successful change.

Fundamental Concepts. Understanding identity. That's Self-Concept. Every 'I' is unique. Yet universal fears unite. That's Shared Experience. Addressing the 'I' in change. That's Individual Consideration. Dreams drive motivation. Fears cause resistance. That's Dual Emotional Drive. [236] Dive deep into psyche. Find the triggers. That's Emotional Intelligence. Connect with the 'I'. Make change personal. That's the core of Personalized Change Management. Recognize the dread. Highlight the dream.

Bottom Line. In change, acknowledging feelings and motivations is key. Addressing individual fears and stories is crucial for successful change, as people seek meaning and validation.

June 29th

EVERY AGE OFFERS TECH INSIGHTS

> "I've come up with a set of rules that describe our reactions to technologies: 1. Anything that is in the world when you're born is normal and ordinary and is just a natural part of the way the world works. 2. Anything that's invented between when you're fifteen and thirty-five is new and exciting and revolutionary and you can probably get a career in it. 3. Anything invented after you're thirty—five is against the natural order of things."
>
> —DOUGLAS ADAMS, *The Salmon of Doubt.* [237]

We view tech through age lenses. Childhood tech feels normal. Young adulthood? Tech thrills. After 35, tech can scare. Change managers understand. They harness this psychology. They ease tech transitions for all ages.

Takeaways. Our age shapes tech perceptions; Early tech feels innate to us; Mid-life tech offers career jumps; Later tech might intimidate.

Fundamental Concepts. Age shapes views. That's Cognitive Development. Young see tech as innate. That's Familiarity Bias. 15 to 35 finds tech opportunity. That's Openness to Experience. Over 35 finds tech intimidating. That's Neophobia. Tech shifts challenge us. That's Cognitive Dissonance. Adapting is key. That's Flexibility in Thinking. Understanding age? That's Demographic Sensitivity. Embracing change? That's Growth Mindset. All ages contribute. That's Generational Synergy. To ease tech fears, understand age. That's the essence of Developmental Psychology. [238]

Bottom Line. Our age shapes how we see technology. Change managers aim to ease age-related tech concerns and help everyone adapt to tech changes.

June 30th

HEART'S DRIVE LEADS, EXTERNAL REWARDS FOLLOW

"Inner motivation thrives when nurtured, not forced. Our surroundings influence, but true power lies in choice. Embrace autonomy, master competence, and deeply connect. Goals fueled by true needs lead to fulfillment. In quality relationships, we find our strongest anchor and essence."

—CHANGE366. [239]

Change involves new actions and feelings. It's fueled by internal passion and external incentives. While external pressures like deadlines and rewards shape us, true motivation comes from within. Build competence and connections, and understand your reasons for change.

Takeaways. Inner motivation shines, external rewards can dim it; Understanding motivations helps embrace meaningful change; Building strong relationships fuels our needs.

Fundamental Concepts. Inner drive rules. That's Cognitive Evaluation Theory. Rewards can guide or mislead. It's a balance. External pressures? They're real. It's Organismic Integration Theory. Sometimes we act for rewards, not passion. Personal choices vary. That's Causality Orientations Theory. [240] Some chase personal values. Others? External pressures. Some feel helpless. Every choice matters. Basic needs? Vital. It's Basic Needs Theory. Autonomy. Competence. Connection. These fuel us. Our goals? They have roots. It's Goal Content Theory. [241] Chase dreams, not just rewards. And relationships? They're our anchor. That's Relationship Motivation Theory. Connect deeply. Cherish autonomy. Master competence. All in unity.

Bottom Line. For meaningful change, prioritize inner drive over external rewards. Understand your change motivations, focusing on autonomy, skill mastery, and connections. Align choices with personal values and cultivate supportive relationships for your goals.

JULY — LEADERSHIP

Leading change is a dance that requires a symphony of leadership and sponsorship to play harmoniously. Prosci warns us that silence from sponsors is, like Lincoln's axe, ready to fell the tree of progress. The concept of sponsorship, rooted in promises, indicates that leaders must pledge to guide change from conception to fruition.

Deleuze compares concepts to bricks, suggesting that sponsorship should construct, not destruct. Conner reminds us that plans are inert without the kinetic force of real change, which involves altering mindsets and practices. Kotter extends this by suggesting that strong sponsors are like captains setting the direction for the ship of change—they energize and empower their crew.

Leadership is synonymous with change, and as Clear Picture Leadership articulates, it's about moving and improving situations. Stanislavski's method acting principles, when applied to leadership, teach us the authenticity required for genuine connection and motivation. Nietzsche's scrutiny of authority challenges us to reassess leadership as a service to truth rather than a pursuit of power.

Kim and Laing highlight the urgency for leaders who can navigate the rapid waters of change, asserting that decisiveness and a pioneering spirit are vital. Machiavelli's wisdom illustrates the inherent challenges in pioneering new orders, while Change366 lays out a 'full circle approach' to leadership that engages all levels of an organization.

In the digital age, as Kim notes, software alone doesn't drive success—it's the depth of leadership that navigates technological investments. Kotter's call to cultivate leaders emphasizes that managing the status quo is no longer enough; leadership must drive change. Change366 underscores that leaders who embrace innovation, act swiftly, and maintain clarity, can successfully navigate through change.

Change366 highlights the importance of visible sponsors guiding change like lighthouses in a storm. Dickson advocates prioritizing transformation for lasting results. Change366 advises nurturing change in trust and humility, not ego. Maxwell warns against toxic leadership's defensiveness, and Cash sees emotional investment as crucial for change. Change366 stresses the human element over algorithms, promoting a unified approach to sponsorship and leadership.

Change366 tells us that adaptability, learning, and vision are the hallmarks of effective leadership. Leadership is about guiding with an open hand, not ruling with an iron fist. It's about inspiring creativity and empowering team members in the transformation journey. Organizational change intertwines leadership and sponsorship. Leaders must actively drive and embody change, offering assurance and motivation. Their proactive involvement is key to lasting change in organizations.

July 1st

A SILENT SPONSOR IS A PROJECT'S DOWNFALL

"The number one obstacle to success for change projects is ineffective sponsorship."

—PROSCI, *Primary Sponsor's Role and Importance.* [242]

Great ideas falter without strong leaders. Big changes need a champion. This person stokes the fire. They clear the path. Without them, even the best plans stumble. Success leans heavily on effective sponsorship. A good leader doesn't just nod; they act.

Takeaways. Leadership is the cornerstone of successful change; An ineffective sponsor can derail the best plans; Strong sponsorship involves active, not passive, support.

Fundamental Concepts. Sponsorship gaps. That's Leadership Void. Projects lack a guiding hand. Inaction breeds failure. That's Passive Oversight. Change stalls. Plans collect dust. That's Initiative Inertia. Teams drift, leaderless. That's Team Discord. No unity or purpose. Effective sponsorship clears the fog. That's Leadership Clarity. Focused goals. Energized teams. Success is in sight. Act, don't just agree. That's Active Sponsorship. Keep the fire lit. Guide the change. See the impact.

Bottom Line. Change projects need active sponsors; silent approval falls short. Strong leaders propel project success through action, not just approval. They remove obstacles and guide their teams toward the project's goals.

July 2nd

MOMENTUM FOLLOWS THE LEADER'S COMPASS

"We saw no examples of successful transformation happening bottom-up. Instead, executives...steered the transformation through strong top-down leadership: setting direction, building momentum, and ensuring that the company follows through."

—George Westerman, *Leading Digital.* [243]

Change isn't a grassroots movement in business; it's a directive that often comes from the top. Executives are the navigators, and without their hands on the wheel, the ship drifts. They set the course, propel the ship forward, and keep the crew aligned with the journey. When executives lead strongly from above, they create a ripple effect that ensures the entire organization moves in unison towards transformational goals.

Takeaways. Directive leadership from executives is essential for transformation; Top-down leadership provides clear direction for organizational change; Executives must enforce momentum and follow-through for success.

Fundamental Concepts. Tech gathers dust. That's Innovation's Block. Vision lacking? That's Direction's Gap. Executives lead. That's Hierarchical Influence. Without follow-through, strategy fails. That's Execution's Fall. Change needs leaders. That's Guidance's Gain. Drive dictates direction. That's Leadership's Role. Inaction breeds stagnation. That's Static's Trap. Strategy inspires action. That's Plan's Power. Leaders' decisions drive. That's Executive's Edge. Culture follows lead. That's Influence's Echo.

Bottom Line. Transformation begins with strong top-down leadership. Executives set the pace and ensure compliance, directing the organization's path, maintaining momentum, and guaranteeing follow-through. This is crucial for any change effort to take hold and be sustainable.

July 3rd

PLEDGE TO PROGRESS; SPONSOR THE JOURNEY

"The word 'Sponsor' has it's roots in Latin. It comes from the Latin word 'spondere,' which means 'to promise solemnly' or 'to give assurance.'"

—ONLINE ETYMOLOGY DICTIONARY. [244]

Change needs commitment. A sponsor promises. They give assurance. Change succeeds with them. Their word, their bond. They steer the change ship.

Takeaways. 'Sponsor' signifies solemn promise; Assurance drives change; A committed sponsor is change's backbone; Their assurance is change's foundation.

Fundamental Concepts. Words have roots. That's Linguistic Heritage. Promise means commitment. That's Behavioral Dedication. Assurance implies trust. That's Social Contracting. Sponsors promise change. That's Role Affirmation. Their word is bond. That's Psychological Certainty. Sponsors are pivotal. Change leans on them. Commitment is their currency. Their assurance, change's fuel. With them, transformation thrives. Without? Stagnation.

Bottom Line. Sponsors play a vital role in change management, rooted in their promise of progress. They provide essential commitment, turning assurance into action, and guiding successful change.

July 4th

PLEDGE TO CHANGE? OWN ITS OUTCOMES

"True leadership in change means committing to the journey, engaging stakeholders, ensuring clear communication, fostering technology adoption, and upholding honesty. It's about empowering active involvement and equitable stakeholder contributions to shape the future."

—CHANGE366. [245]

Pledging change as a sponsor is a significant commitment, linking you deeply to the outcome. In the digital age, where success depends on adopting new tools, the question of accountability arises: how responsible are you if results fall short of expectations?

Takeaways. A sponsor's commitment is a solemn promise; Accountability is closely tied to the outcomes of change; The digital era amplifies the need for sponsors to be proactive; True accountability means stakeholders have power and clarity.

Fundamental Concepts. Change pledged. That's Commitment Bias. Promises carry weight. That's Responsibility Principle. Not all embrace digital. That's Resistance to Change. Dialogue fosters understanding. But conditions apply. That's Facilitated Communication. Balance in power ensures accountability. That's Power Dynamics. The commitment to change? That's Intrinsic Motivation. Stakeholders need clarity. That's Information Asymmetry. [246] They challenge views? That's Cognitive Dissonance. Dialogues uncover complex truths. But hierarchy may stifle. That's Organizational Inertia. True accountability requires active participation. That's Engagement Theory.

Bottom Line. Leaders must commit to driving change, involving stakeholders, facilitating clear communication, aiding technology adoption, and promoting honesty. They should encourage active participation and balanced input in shaping the company's future.

July 5th

SPONSORSHIP STEERS CONSTRUCTIVE CHANGE

"A concept is a brick. It can be used to build a courthouse of reason. Or it can be thrown through the window."

—GILLES DELEUZE, *A Thousand Plateaus.* [247]

A concept is powerful. It's like a brick. Use it wisely, and you can construct strong foundations. Foundations that support change. But misuse it, and it becomes destructive. It can shatter progress. In organizational change, sponsorship decides how we use that brick. It's the force that ensures concepts align with the goal. It prevents misuse and promotes productive building.

Takeaways. A concept is a tool, potent in its potential; Used well, it lays the groundwork for positive change; Misused, it disrupts and derails progress; Sponsorship guides the proper use of concepts in change management.

Fundamental Concepts. Concepts hold power. That's Cognitive Potential. Construct or disrupt. Dual Nature. Sponsorship shapes concept application. That's Directive Influence. Misalignment risks derailment. That's Change Disruption. Align and prosper. That's Organizational Harmony. A role to guide, prevent chaos. That's Sponsorship Mandate. Effective sponsors harness conceptual power. They steer towards positive outcomes. It anchors change. Ensures vision becomes reality. That's the essence of Change Leadership. Recognize the force of ideas. Channel them rightly. Drive organizational evolution. See success unfold.

Bottom Line. Sponsorship ensures concepts lead to constructive change. It directs the power of ideas towards building instead of destroying, guiding change, and fostering progress. Sponsors commit to transforming concepts into positive action within organizations.

July 6th

A PLAN SITS, REAL CHANGE HITS

"Unfortunately, many executives and managers believe that having a clear plan is the final deliverable. They assume that the organizational changes will occur and will then beget the full transformation. A change is not just a blueprint for a new structure: it requires changing people's mindsets and practices".

—DARYL CONNER, *Managing at the Speed of Change.* [248]

A plan isn't the finish line. It's the starting gun. Many bosses get this wrong. They think a neat plan does the trick. But here's the truth. Plans don't move. People do. A real change shifts how we think. How we act. It's not just rearranging desks or roles. It's digging deep. It's teaching old dogs new tricks. And that's work. Real work. So don't just plan. Act. Shift minds. Change habits. Make the change real.

Takeaways. Plans are just the start; Real change involves people's minds and habits; Assuming change will just happen is a mistake.

Fundamental Concepts. Plans on paper won't do the job. That's Cognitive Bias. Thinking it's enough? That's Overconfidence. Real change digs deep. It tweaks how we think and act. That's Cognitive Restructuring. And Behavioral Modification. Change needs effort. It's not automatic. Assuming it is? That's Fundamental Attribution Error. You overlook the human element. Real change taps into Intrinsic Motivation. That's Self-Determination Theory. It fuels lasting change. Don't just draft plans. Drive change. That's the real work.

Bottom Line. Change sponsorship is more action than planning, involving mindset and habit shifts. A plan alone won't spark change; it's the execution that counts, requiring effort to change people's daily behaviors and thoughts for lasting impact.

July 7th

STRONG SPONSORS EMPOWER; WEAK ONES DEFLATE

"Leadership is about setting a direction. It's about creating a vision, empowering, and inspiring people to want to achieve the vision, and enabling them to do so with energy and speed through an effective strategy. In its most basic sense, leadership is about mobilizing a group of people to jump into a better future."

—JOHN KOTTER, *Leading Change.* [249]

Leadership is about setting a direction. It's about creating a vision, empowering, and inspiring people to want to achieve the vision, and enabling them to do so with energy and speed through an effective strategy. In its most basic sense, leadership is about mobilizing a group of people to jump into a better future.

Takeaways. Vision shapes the journey; Empowerment and inspiration are must-haves; Speed and strategy make the vision a reality.

Fundamental Concepts. Leaders inspire. That's Self-Determination Theory. Vision fuels drive. Strategy sets course. That's Intrinsic Motivation. People feel empowered. They tackle tasks. That's Task Efficacy. Speed and energy rise. That's Activation Energy. Roles are clear. That's Role Clarity. Team knows the plan. Change gains speed. That's Strategy Execution. Leaders mobilize; teams leap. That's Collective Action. Vision becomes reality. Expect the win. Energized teams deliver. That's the core of Change Activation. Lead with clarity. Fuel with vision. Drive change fast.

Bottom Line. Successful change sponsorship needs leaders who provide clear vision, inspire their teams, and offer strategies for quick and effective action. Strong leadership turns aspirations into outcomes by energizing and guiding the team towards the goal.

July 8th

MOVE OR LOSE—LEAD OR CONCEDE

> "Leaders are, by definition, change makers. When you are called to lead, you are called to advance, to move forward, and improve the situation."
>
> —CLEAR PICTURE LEADERSHIP. [250]

Leaders make change. It's in the job description. Move ahead. Don't stand still. Improve things. It's not just talk, it's action. A leader in name sponsors change in deed.

Takeaways. Leadership equals change; Progress is non-negotiable; Action, not words, proves leadership.

Fundamental Concepts. Leaders make change. That's Role Congruity. Change is the aim. Stagnation's the shame. That's Progress Principle. Talk is cheap. Action speaks. That's Behavioral Consistency. Words fail. Deeds prevail. That's Cognitive Dissonance. [251] Leaders sponsor. It's their mark. That's Attribution Theory. No action? No acclaim. That's Social Proof. [252] True leaders act. Fakes just talk. That's Authentic Leadership. Be the sponsor. Drive the change. That's the core of Change Activation. Act, don't yak. Sponsor, don't ponder. Seal the deal. Change is real.

Bottom Line. Leadership is action-driven change. Good leaders propel improvement and model the change they advocate for. They show their leadership through progress and decisive action.

July 9th

FAKE LEADERS FAIL—REAL ONES PREVAIL

"The performer should give sincere and expressive performances through identifying with, understanding, and experiencing a character's inner motivation and emotions. They should make use of experiences from their own lives...recall sensations involved in experiences that made a significant emotional impact...without faking or forcing, allow those sensations to stimulate a performance."

—KONSTANTIN STANISLAVSKI, *The Actor Prepares.* [253]

Acting and leading share traits. Both need heart and soul. Sincerity matters. Fake gestures flop. Dig deep into your past. Use your life's lessons. Lead change from your core. No acting. Just real, raw leadership.

Takeaways. Sincerity fuels leadership; Personal experience matters; True emotions ignite change.

Fundamental Concepts. Sincerity fuels leadership. That's Authentic Leadership. A real deal feels real. That's Emotional Resonance. Past powers present. That's Narrative Identity. [254] Emotions ignite change. That's Emotional Intelligence. True feelings? True outcomes. That's Psychological Congruence. [255] No faking. No mistaking. That's Self-Determination Theory. Be you. Lead true. That's the core of Change Activation. Sincerity is currency. Spend it wisely. Trust rises. Change thrives.

Bottom Line. True leaders draw from personal experiences to inspire sincere change. Authenticity is crucial for effective change management.

July 10th

AUTHORITY NEEDS AN AUDIT

"By far the greater number of educated people still desire convictions from a thinker, a small minority want certainty. The former want to be forcibly carried away, to obtain an increase of strength; the latter few have the real interest which disregards personal advantages and the increase of strength also. In so far as genius upholds the ardour of convictions, and arouses distrust of the cautious and modest spirit of science, it is an enemy of truth."

—FRIEDRICH NIETZSCHE, *Human All Too Human.* [256]

People drawn to strong ideas? Charismatic leaders can sway the crowd. It's tempting. But beware! Charisma can fool you. Lasting change isn't built on charm. It's built on facts. Don't be swept away by pretty words and strong will. Look deeper. What's the substance? Where's the evidence? Forget the flash. Dig for the facts. Those are what drive real change.

Takeaways. Strong ideas can mislead; Charisma isn't a substitute for truth; Real change is built on evidence; Facts over flash lead to lasting results.

Fundamental Concepts. People flock to easy ideas. That's Cognitive Ease. They avoid the tough truth. That's Information Bias at play. Charisma clouds judgment. That's the Halo Effect. [257] Effective change demands Skepticism. Flash over facts? That's the Surface Trait Fallacy. [258] Ignore the evidence? That's Confirmation Bias. Challenge authority? That's Critical Thinking. Going for depth, not just surface? That's Depth of Processing. Stick to this path for real, effective change.

Bottom Line. Scrutinize leadership by valuing evidence over charisma. Conviction without certainty is risky. For sustainable change, prioritize factual leadership over persuasive charm. Fact-based decisions lead to effective change.

July 11th

BLUE OCEANS NEED DARING CAPTAINS

"Executives are often reluctant to accept the need for change; they may have a vested interest in the status quo, or they may feel that time will eventually vindicate their previous choices. Indeed, when we ask executives what prompts them to seek out blue oceans and introduce change, they usually say that it takes a highly determined leader or a serious crisis."

—W. Chan Kim, *How to Create Uncontested Market Space.* [259]

Executives cling to the familiar. It's safe and known. Yet, real change requires letting go. This means facing fears. Trusting new paths. Bold leaders drive this shift. They ignite the spark for blue oceans. Sometimes, crisis is the push. But a strong leader? They're the true compass.

Takeaways. Executives often favor the status quo; Change needs brave leadership; Crisis can spur action; Visionary leaders see beyond the present.

Fundamental Concepts. Executives stick to comfort. That's Status Quo Bias. Change challenges them. This is Cognitive Dissonance. Leaders brave the unknown. They show Autonomous Motivation. Crisis forces change, but vision matters more. That's Intrinsic Drive. Choosing growth over stagnation? That's Self-Determination. Visionary leaders lead with intent. A clear case of Proactive Leadership. Trusting a brighter future? It's all about Future-Oriented Thinking.

Bottom Line. Bold leaders drive transformation beyond comfort zones. Visionary leaders fuel innovation for lasting change.

July 12th

SWIFT CHANGE REQUIRES SWIFT SPONSORS

"We live in a moment of history where change is so sped up that we begin to see the present only when it is already disappearing."

—R. D. Laing, *The Divided Self.* [260]

Change is swift. Time races. The 'now' slips away. The present? Fades before we grasp it. Sponsors need to see this. To stand prepared, always on their toes, ready for the fleeting moments. They shouldn't wait. They must act before the present disappears.

Takeaways. Change comes fast; The present is fleeting; Sponsors stay vigilant; Quick action is vital.

Fundamental Concepts. Change accelerates. That's Temporal Flux. Time's essence? Always moving. Continuous Flow in play. Recognizing the present? Tough. That's Cognitive Lag. [261] Sponsors defy this. They embody Proactive Adaptation. Always vigilant. That's Situational Awareness. Their secret? Quick responses. They combat Time's Erosion. A fleeting present? Challenge accepted. They operate in Active Mode. Grasp the moment. Before it's history. That's Timely Intervention.

Bottom Line. Swift sponsors drive change by acting quickly, seizing opportunities.

July 13th

LEADING CHANGE—FOES FACED. FICKLE FRIENDS FLANKED

"And it ought to be remembered that there is nothing more difficult to take in hand, more perilous to conduct, or more uncertain in its success, than to take the lead in the introduction of a new order of things. Because the innovator has for enemies all those who have done well under the old conditions, and lukewarm defenders in those who may well do well under the new."

—NICCOLÒ MACHIAVELLI, *Il Principe.* [262]

Change is tough. Leading change? Even harder. You'll face pushback. Why? People liked the old way. They won with it. They'll fight to keep it. And the new way? It's untested. People are cautious. They won't back you strongly. Know this going in. Be prepared. Win them over. Prove the new way works. Make it their win too.

Takeaways. Change is hard; Leaders face resistance; Old wins make new foes; New change has few strong backers.

Fundamental Concepts. Change rattles people. That's Status Quo Bias. [263] They cling to what they know. So, if you lead, prepare for a fight. That's Social Resistance. Old ways have old fans. They won't clap for your plan. Last, think about Risk Aversion. New ideas scare. They're a dare to the wary.

Bottom Line. Leaders face resistance from old supporters and must win over new skeptics. Success requires strategic persuasion to show the new way's benefits and gain strong support.

July 14th

CHANGE ISN'T SINGULAR—IT'S A FULL CIRCLE APPROACH

"Tipping Point Leadership is when leaders use a four-step process to bring about rapid, dramatic, and lasting change with limited resources. First, target key areas and work with partner groups. Next, connect managers to problems and try new ways to talk. Highlight the change and match the message to everyone. Finally, deal with inside critics and keep outsiders away. These steps offer a guide to manage change from multiple angles."

—W, Chan Kim, *Tipping Point Leadership.* [264]

Tipping Point Leadership involves identifying critical areas, engaging with teams and customers, emphasizing change, converting critics to allies, and managing external challenges. It integrates resource handling, effective communication, and motivational strategies.

Takeaways. Focus on crucial 'hot spots' and partner up; Engage directly and innovate in communication; Highlight the change and adjust the message for everyone; Convert critics and keep opponents away.

Fundamental Concepts. Leaders target areas. That's Focal Attention. Team up, make deals. That's Collaborative Negotiation. Face issues, meet customers. That's Direct Engagement. Spotlight the change's importance. That's Motivational Amplification. Adjust the message. That's Adaptive Communication. Convert the internal critics. That's Internal Alliance Building. Outsiders kept away? That's External Opposition Management. The approach is full-circle. That's Holistic Change Strategy. Embrace every hurdle. That's Comprehensive Challenge Handling.

Bottom Line. Change needs a full-circle approach - target, collaborate, communicate, manage criticism. Leaders must use limited resources for impactful, lasting change.

July 15th

LEADERSHIP DEPTH, NOT JUST DIGITAL DEPTH

> "In 2011, Marc Andreessen wrote his famous essay, 'Why Software Is Eating the World,' in The Wall Street Journal, leading to the cliché that 'every company needs to become a software company'.... but it turned out that Andreessen was only half right. It's not that all software is eating the world: General Electric has just proved that in a spectacular fashion: It invested heavily in software and the result? After five years, the CEO and his top lieutenants were terminated. Similar developments are underway at Intel, P&G and HP."
>
> —W, Chan Kim, *Tipping Point Leadership.* [265]

Embracing digital goes beyond software. General Electric's example shows this: their focus on software led to leadership turmoil. Change sponsors need to see beyond trends, grasp the bigger picture, and guide effectively.

Takeaways. Software is just a piece of the digital transformation puzzle; Blind adoption of trends can backfire; The role of sponsors is to guide, not just follow.

Fundamental Concepts. Tech's allure is strong. That's the Hedonic Treadmill. [266] Chasing the latest without depth? That's Surface Learning. Leadership shifts from missteps? That's Outcome-Based Evaluation. Investing in just software? That's Narrow Framing. Sponsors overlook the big picture? That's Cognitive Myopia. Understand the core, not just the shell. Deep learning is the goal. That's Intrinsic Motivation. Blend tech with vision. Avoid the pitfalls. Sponsors lead, not follow. That's Effective Change Management.

Bottom Line. Leaders must go beyond digital trends, blending tech with broader strategy. Neglecting this led to leadership changes in major firms. Effective sponsorship requires deep understanding and strategic guidance.

July 16th

CULTIVATE CAPTAINS FOR CHANGE'S VOYAGE

"Because management deals mostly with the status quo and leadership deals mostly with change, we are going to have to try to become much more skilled at creating leaders."

—JOHN KOTTER, *Leading Change.* [267]

Leadership sparks change. Management keeps the lights on. To navigate the waters of transformation, we need captains, not just crew. Sponsors are these captains. They steer the ship. They communicate the vision. They rally the team. To master change, we must cultivate leaders, not just managers.

Takeaways. Leadership is the catalyst for change; Management focuses on maintaining the current state; Sponsors, as leaders, are essential for effective change communication; Managers need to become leaders.

Fundamental Concepts. Leaders drive evolution. That's Proactive Behavior. Management holds the line. That's Status Quo Bias. Leaders carve paths unknown. That's Risk-Taking Propensity. Nurturing leaders over managers? That's Growth Mindset. Sponsors are the voice of change. That's Influential Leadership. Leaders see the future, not just now. They're Forward-Thinking. Embrace change, don't resist. That's Adaptive Capacity. To thrive, grow leaders. Static management won't suffice. Leadership is the heart. That's Transformational Change. Lead the way, clear the fog. Boost the morale, watch teams jog.

Bottom Line. Cultivate leaders as captains to guide change, with sponsors as navigators. They lead, energize, and drive teams toward new horizons, making leadership development essential for successful change.

July 17th

VISION TRANSFORMS SYSTEMS, LEADERSHIP DRIVES IT

"Management makes a system work. It helps you do what you know how to do. Leadership builds systems or transforms old ones."

—JOHN KOTTER, *Leading Change.* [268]

Leaders light fires of innovation and carve paths through uncharted territories. They don't just maintain; they reinvent and inspire. Where managers maintain, leaders revolutionize. They see beyond the horizon. They don't fear change; they craft it. Their vision turns the old into new possibilities. Every leader must be an artisan of change, transforming not just systems but also minds and cultures.

Takeaways. Leaders innovate, not just maintain; Visionary leadership transforms systems; Leaders champion change and inspire others; Leadership involves reimagining and reshaping the old.

Fundamental Concepts. Leaders ignite change. That's Transformational Leadership. They spur intrinsic motivation. That's Self-Determination Theory. They foster autonomy, breed innovation. That's Creative Dynamics. Managers maintain order. That's Classical Management Theory. They structure, organize and execute. That's Bureaucratic Efficiency. Leaders inspire, transcend the norm. That's Charismatic Authority. Balance structure and vision. That's the essence of Organizational Synergy. Adapt leadership, thrive in change. That's Situational Adaptiveness.

Bottom Line. Leaders drive change, not just maintain; Their vision transforms cultures and minds, crafting new realities from old systems.

July 18th

LEAD CHANGE WITH INNOVATION, ACTION, AND VISION

"Organizations navigate change driven by external and internal forces. Effective leaders embody five key skills: Innovating for positive change, acting swiftly to overcome delays, maintaining clear vision, staying attuned to external trends for relevance, and inspiring while ensuring accountability. Possessing these skills allows leaders to steer through change confidently and effectively."

—CHANGE366. [269]

Change is constant. It's shaped by many factors. Inside and outside. Good leaders rise to the challenge. They have tools. They innovate and act. They see the end goal. Sponsors embody these skills. They rally the troops. They set the direction. They make change work.

Takeaways. Change is shaped both internally and externally; Leaders need specific skills to manage change; Sponsors are the linchpin in effective change communication.

Fundamental Concepts. Change surrounds us. That's Environmental Adaptation. Leaders harness tools. That's Skill Acquisition. Vision is clear. That's Goal Orientation. Swift action, no delay. That's Proactivity. Connecting with the world? That's External Validity. Inside forces shape too. That's Intrinsic Motivation. Leaders inspire. They spark Intrinsic Value. Holding teams to the mark? That's Accountability. Successful change needs alignment. Sponsors are the compass. They channel Purposeful Direction. Effective change needs active sponsors. That's Transformational Influence. Lead with intent, inspire the ascent. Make change an event, not an incident.

Bottom Line. Leaders drive change through innovation, swift action, and unwavering vision. They adapt to market and internal demands while inspiring and guiding teams effectively. Strong leadership entails accountability and clear direction.

July 19th

BE THE LIGHT, NOT THE LAMPSHADE

"Change Sponsor 'job description.' I'm the sponsor. I make change stick. How? I'm there, always in sight. I talk, I rally. Got a team of backers with me. We get the word out. We make sure everyone's on board. Got road-blocks? We smash them. We give time and tools. You'll see us in meetings. We check progress. We keep things moving. And we don't ease off. Why? Visible leaders make projects win. Simple as that."

—CHANGE366. [270]

The sponsor is the game-changer. You're not just a title; you're an action hero. You jump in, eyes open, hands-on. You form alliances. You talk. To everyone. Why? You get stuff done. Your energy pumps life into plans. Your visibility melts resistance. Your voice bridges gaps. It's not about you; it's about lighting the way.

Takeaways. Be more than a title; be an action; Form alliances, gain strength; Speak up, clear fog; Drive change, be the fuel.

Fundamental Concepts. Sponsor in sight. That's Social Proof. People follow. Sponsor talks. That's Direct Communication. Fog clears. Makes alliances. That's Social Cohesion. Team bonds. Gives time and tools. That's Resource Provision. Progress occurs. Sponsor active, not passive. That's Extrinsic Motivation. Team's energized. Sponsor is the model. That's Observational Learning. Team learns, does. No idle standing. That's Proactive Behavior. Change sticks. Sponsor leads, not just a title. That's Authentic Leadership. Trust builds.

Bottom Line. Change sponsors take the lead, smashing barriers and supporting success. They actively engage with teams, keeping momentum and clarity to propel change. Their leadership lights the way forward.

July 20th

LEAD WITH CHANGE, RESULTS FOLLOW

"If you focus on results, you will never change. If you focus on change, you will get results."

—JACK DICKSON. [271]

Leaders lead change. They don't chase results. Results follow change. Change shapes the future. Leaders know this. They prioritize transformation. They drive vision. They inspire teams. Leadership is about steering change. With change comes success.

Takeaways. Leaders prioritize change over mere results; Embracing transformation ensures positive outcomes; Visionary leadership inspires teams towards change; Success is a byproduct of genuine change.

Fundamental Concepts. Leaders champion transformation. That's Visionary Leadership. Results as a mere focus? That's Short-Term View. True leaders understand change. That's Deep Insight. Drive transformation, outcomes follow. That's Change-Centric Mindset. Fixate on results, stagnate. That's Transformational Stalemate. [272] Embrace change, success is yours. That's Leadership's True Path. Steer change, inspire greatness. That's Leading by Example. Prioritize the journey, destinations find you. That's the essence of Visionary Navigation. Change, the true north. Leadership's guiding star.

Bottom Line. Leaders who emphasize change over immediate results drive lasting success. Visionary leadership with a focus on transformation inspires teams and achieves outcomes. Change leads; results follow.

July 21st

CHANGE THRIVES ON TRUST, NOT EGO

> "We've all seen it. Narcissistic leaders drain the life out of teams. Their arrogance, lack of empathy, and thirst for control corrode trust and strain relationships. Employees under such leaders don't thrive; they merely survive. For impactful organizational change, steer clear of such leadership. Trust and care are our true catalysts."
>
> —CHANGE366. [273]

Narcissistic leaders, with arrogance and a focus on their superiority, resist criticism, misuse their team, and harm trust. This hinders organizational change, exhausting employees and facing resistance.

Takeaways. Narcissistic leaders act too proud and uncaring; They hate being corrected; Their actions stress out the team; Change is tough with them leading; Workers don't support the changes with them in charge.

Fundamental Concepts. Narcissistic leaders? That's Leader Narcissism. This isn't just arrogance. It's deep-rooted. They show Hypersensitivity. Small slights? Big reactions. They also show a Lack of Empathy. Their viewpoint? It's Self-centered. This leads to Managerial Void. [274] Trust in them? It drops. They become a Passive Oversight in the team's eyes. They threaten employee resources. It's Tool Underuse. The resources include trust and Self-worth. This misuse? It's a Strategy Gap. Employees lose out. They feel the Skill Deficit. Their reaction? They pull away. Commitment and satisfaction drop. The outcome? A team drained of enthusiasm and drive. The solution? Tech Activation. Active, empathetic leadership. It fills the void and drives positive change.

Bottom Line. Trust, not ego, fuels change. Avoid narcissistic leadership to encourage team growth and make organizational change successful. Empathy and trust are essential for change to flourish.

July 22nd

LEAD WITH CLARITY, NOT WITH SHIELDS

"Toxic leaders often hide behind rules and regulations, using them as a shield to deflect criticism and avoid accountability."

—JOHN C. MAXWELL, *The 21 Irrefutable Laws of Leadership.* [275]

Toxic leaders duck and dodge. They misuse rules to hide. They fear being called out. They dodge accountability. This harms change. A change sponsor should be upfront. They should own mistakes. A shielded leader blocks progress. True sponsors lead with clarity.

Takeaways. Rules can be misused by toxic leaders; They avoid criticism with such shields; Effective sponsorship needs honesty; Avoiding accountability stalls change.

Fundamental Concepts. Toxic avoidance. That's Defensive Mechanism. They seek safe ground. That's Safety Seeking. Rules are their shield. That's Rationalization. Avoiding blame is their aim. That's Denial. No room for feedback. That's Closed Mindset. Change is about openness. That's Growth Orientation. Accepting faults is key. That's Self-awareness. Dodging responsibility? That's External Locus of Control. Effective leaders internalize blame. They act, not avoid. That's Internal Locus of Control. [276] Adapt and grow. Embrace criticism. That's the essence of Self-Actualization.

Bottom Line. Effective change needs clear leadership. Leaders must own their actions, not hide. Being open to criticism and taking responsibility drives change.

July 23rd

EMOTIONAL BUY-IN BEATS FORCED COMPLIANCE

"The secret to change management? Simple. Make change easier to love than to fear."

—ROSANNE CASH. [277]

Fear stops us. Love pushes us forward. In organizational change, the same rules apply. Making change likable is better than making it scary. If employees love the change, they'll drive it. If they fear it, they'll fight it. It's not just strategy. It's human nature.

Takeaways. Fear is a barrier; love is a motivator; Address the emotional aspect, not just the logistical one; Making change lovable drives successful outcomes; Understanding human nature aids change management.

Fundamental Concepts. Fear stops action. That's Loss Aversion. People fear losing what they have. It's basic human wiring. That's Evolutionary Psychology. Love? That's Intrinsic Motivation in Self-Determination Theory. It energizes. It engages. Teams move because they want to. That's Internal Locus of Control. Emotional aspects aren't soft skills. They're core drivers. That's rooted in Sociocultural Theory. In change, love and fear are key. To manage change, master the heart. That's the essence of Psychological Safety and Trust.

Bottom Line. In change, winning hearts beats instilling fear. Emotional commitment drives action. 'Love' for change ensures cooperation and progress.

July 24th

INSIGHT TRUMPS ALGORITHMS IN CHANGE

"No technology is smart enough to navigate change without human insight. Don't automate the soul out of your organization."

—CHANGE366. [278]

Tech is a tool, not a leader. You can't code care or script insight. Leadership breathes life into tech change. Use tech, but don't let it replace the human touch. The soul of your organization lies in its people. Leaders guide, tech follows.

Takeaways. Technology is an aid, not a substitute for leadership; Human insight is irreplaceable in managing change; Keep the human touch active; it's the soul of your organization; Effective leaders make technology serve, not steer, the change.

Fundamental Concepts. Tech's a helper. That's Instrumental Support. Human touch? That's Emotional Intelligence. Leadership can't be coded. That's Complex Problem-Solving. Souls in orgs? That's Organizational Culture. Leaders give tech meaning. That's Attribution Theory. They keep the org's soul. That's Organizational Identity. The heart matters. That's Affective Commitment. [279] Leaders tie it all together. That's Transformational Leadership. So, tech assists but never replaces the soul. Leadership remains key. That's the crux of Human-Centered Design.

Bottom Line. During change, human insight must lead, with technology as its support. Leaders should blend tech with the organization's human soul to guide change effectively.

July 25th

LEAD WITH LEARNING, WIN WITH WISDOM

> "Innovation isn't a solo act; it's a chorus led by transformational maestros. They don't command, they coordinate. They ignite trust and fan the flames of team creativity. Their compass? Constant improvement. Their map? A vision bold and brave. Conformity is the tune of the past; risk and originality, the rhythm of the future."
>
> —CHANGE366. [280]

In change management leadership, continuous learning is crucial. Understanding your environment and staying updated on technology and team dynamics is essential. Adaptable leaders foster innovation and build trust, guiding teams successfully through change.

Takeaways. Know your setting to lead effectively; Constant learning boosts adaptability; Effective leaders build trust and encourage innovation; Staying current is not optional; it's crucial.

Fundamental Concepts. Learning is essential. That's Cognitive Flexibility. Adapt or perish. Choice empowers. That's Self-Determination Theory. Knowledge builds resilience. That's Psychological Capital. Trust exchanged. That's Social Exchange Theory. [281] Leaders give guidance. Teams offer trust. Conformity stunts. That's Group Conformity. Leader breaks mold. Teams follow. Creativity flows. Not a boss, a guide. That's Transformational Leadership. Path shown, not pushed. Teams thrive. Changes become chances.

Bottom Line. In change leadership, continuous learning is the compass, and fostering team innovation is the guiding light. To effectively steer your team through change and transform challenges into opportunities, stay informed, adapt, and empower innovation.

July 26th

ADAPTABILITY IS A LEADER'S BEST TRAIT

"Be a great leader, not a failing one. Adapt and grow with your team. Use tools to know yourself better. Keep it simple and clear. Change is hard but good leadership makes it easier."

—CHANGE366. [282]

Great leaders adapt. They grow with their teams. They're clear and simple. Good leaders know themselves well. They use tools like SWOT and Johari Window for this. [283] Change is tough. But it's easier with strong leadership. If you're a leader, be great, not failing. Be clear about your goals. Communicate well. Listen to your team and act on feedback. This way, change will be smoother.

Takeaways. Great leaders adapt and grow with their teams; Tools like SWOT and Johari Window help in Self-awareness; Strong leadership makes navigating change easier.

Fundamental Concepts. Great leaders adapt. That's called Adaptive Leadership. They know themselves. That's Self-Awareness. Tools help and give Insight. Leaders make change easy. That's Change Management. They listen and act. That's Feedback Loop. Leaders are clear. That's Effective Communication. They grow with teams. That's Team Dynamics.

Bottom Line. Leaders need to adapt, know themselves, and communicate clearly to make change easier. They should grow alongside their team and use self-assessment tools for improvement. Good leadership simplifies navigating change.

July 27th

LEAD WITH LAYERS IN MIND

"Crafting change is a layered art; leaders, culture, and institutions are the trio of sculptors. Ignore none, and you'll shape success."

—CHANGE366. [284]

Change is like a puzzle. Each piece matters. You're the leader. You hold the box cover. You see the big picture. Employees are your puzzle pieces. They shape the culture. They interact with systems. Get them involved. Use their insights. Culture is not a trap. It's a toolkit. Institutions aren't stiff. They flex. Understand this. Craft smarter strategies. Think wide. Look deep. That's how you steer change.

Takeaways. Leaders hold the roadmap for change; Culture is a toolkit, not a barrier; Institutions change, they're not set in stone; Effective change needs multi-layer thinking.

Fundamental Concepts. Active roles, that's Self-Determination Theory. Employees want control. They seek competence. They value connection. Layered thinking, that's Complexity Theory. [285] It's not one game plan. It's many. It's dynamic. Culture as toolkit, that's Symbolic Interactionism. [286] Symbols and norms aren't static. They're tools. Employees wield them. That's the heart of adaptive change.

Bottom Line. Effective change leadership blends vision, culture, and structure. Leaders should use insights from all levels to create strategies. This multi-layered approach navigates change complexities, leading to success.

July 28th

EMPOWER TO TOWER—LEADERS UPLIFT TEAMS

"True leadership doesn't micromanage creativity during change; it unleashes it by building a culture of trust and self-belief."

—CHANGE366. [287]

Leaders hold the power to ignite creativity during change. How? By empowering their teams. This makes people believe in their own creative skills. When you believe, you achieve. This doesn't just spark new ideas. It builds a sense of belonging for everyone.

Takeaways. Empowering leadership fuels creativity; A strong belief in one's own creativity follows; This belief improves team and company culture; Everyone benefits, from team members to top management.

Fundamental Concepts. Empowerment lights the Self-Determination fire. Leaders give autonomy. That's Self-Determination Theory in action. Teams feel supported. That boosts Creative Self-Efficacy. [288] It's a belief boost. Workers are more open. That's due to Psychological Safety. Leaders nurture this. It's the antidote to Managerial Void. They shape culture. They bridge the Strategy Gap. It's active, not passive. It's Active Oversight. In sum, the leadership style activates the work psyche.

Bottom Line. Leaders lead by empowering teams, building trust, and supporting creativity. They create a positive work culture that values autonomy and open thinking, boosting confidence and driving company growth.

July 29th

VISIONARY LEADERS PAINT TOMORROW

"Transformational leadership is the compass and engine of organizational change, steering trust, inspiring vision, and fueling engagement."

—CHANGE366. [289]

Leadership isn't just a title; it's a journey of transformation. Imagine a ship navigating through tumultuous seas. The leader is the captain, the compass guiding the ship. Just as a compass directs sailors, transformational leadership steers organizations through change. It's about building trust, like a crew relying on their captain. Leaders inspire a vision, painting a picture of a promising future. They fuel engagement, energizing the crew to row harder, together. This journey isn't just about reaching a destination. It's about how you transform along the way.

Takeaways. Transformational leadership steers change; Builds and sustains team trust; Inspires future vision; Boosts engagement and motivation.

Fundamental Concepts. Transformational leaders are key. They're like Psychological Anchors, stabilizing change. They nurture intrinsic motivation in teams. That's Self-Determination. They build trust. That's Social Identity Theory. They become part of the group identity. Their vision inspires. That's Visionary Leadership. It's not just a goal. It's a shared dream. Engagement soars. That's Group Cohesion. These leaders don't just lead; they transform mindsets. They embody the essence of Transformational Leadership in organizational settings. [290]

Bottom Line. Leaders drive change, build trust, shape visions, and lead teams through transformation with visionary leadership at the core.

July 30th

TRANSFORMERS IGNITE, TRANSACTIONALS STOKE

"Leaders are the architects of change and the managers of stability. Their style, transformational or transactional, writes the script for organizational success."

—CHANGE366. [291]

Leaders matter. In a changing company, their role is big. Some lead through vision. They're transformational. Others focus on tasks and rewards. They're transactional. Transformational leaders aim high. They change the whole game. They motivate you to be better. Transactional leaders keep the ship steady. They set clear goals. You meet them, you get a reward. Both styles have value. The right style depends on what's needed.

Takeaways. Transformational leaders drive big change—they inspire; Transactional leaders focus on tasks. They use rewards; Both styles are useful. The situation decides the best fit; Leaders shape the company's future.

Fundamental Concepts. Transformational taps Intrinsic Motivation. That's Self-Determination Theory. It boosts Autonomy and Purpose. It enhances commitment. Transactional is more Behaviorist. Reward and penalty guide actions. That's Operant Conditioning. Both have merit. Different tasks, different needs. Adapt the style, nail the job. That's Situational Leadership.

Bottom Line. Leaders shape success by either inspiring change or ensuring stability. Transformational leaders ignite innovation, while transactional leaders focus on goals and rewards. The specific leadership style required depends on the situation.

July 31st

SELF-RULE IN LEADERS SEEDS COMPANY-WIDE CHANGE

"Steer the helm of choice; align values with action for transformative leadership."

—Change366. [292]

Lead change with Self-mastery, share wisdom, not just orders. Look at your team; conflicts here mirror deeper issues. The past shapes us, but today we pave our future. Craft actions that resonate with your organization's change vision. Decide, strategize, unite — these you can steer. Speak in actions; They chart your organizational course.

Takeaways. Master your actions, shape your organization; Dysfunctions often mirror deeper interpersonal issues; Meet today's organizational needs, design tomorrow's objectives; Ensure actions reflect the organization's core mission.

Fundamental Concepts. Decisions steer companies. That's Organizational Autonomy. Leaders shape culture. That's Leadership Impact. Team dynamics echo systemic health. That's Organizational Reflection. Framing what's next. That's Proactive Change. Core values guide companies. That's Cultural Alignment. Vision aligns with action. That's Strategic Congruence. Leadership's choices spur transformation. That's Directive Autonomy. [293] Strategy molds mindset. That's Cultural Engineering. Actions speak louder. That's Operational Effectiveness. Verbs drive change. That's Action-Oriented Leadership.

Bottom Line. Effective leadership reflects self-rule and resonates with the team's mission. By addressing current challenges and anticipating future needs, leaders enact strategies that embody the organization's values and drive change.

Being at the heart of change, mid-level managers must embody the change they manage. Prosci highlights the unique position of managers in driving change adoption, emphasizing their proximity to staff. Yet, their effectiveness often falls short, signaling a need for enhanced skills in managing employee resistance.

Conner reminds managers to align their thinking with new states of change to ensure effective communication with their staff. This sync-or-sink scenario underscores the importance of mutual understanding in times of transition.

Lewin's concept of fluidity over binary thinking in change management is crucial. It encourages managers to view change as a continuous process rather than a series of events. This perspective fosters resilience and adaptability.

Herzberg shifts focus to creating motivating environments rather than directly igniting motivation. This approach empowers individuals within the team to find and nurture their own motivational sparks.

Change366 portrays middle managers as multifaceted change agents—bridges, coaches, and advocates. They are tasked with making change stick through clear communication, resource mobilization, and guiding their teams through the complexities of change.

Bryant emphasizes the superpower of adaptability in middle management. Juggling multiple roles, managing work organization, and understanding power dynamics are key to sustaining change.

Feynman and Campbell remind us of the power of inquiry and the hero's journey in change. Questions drive direction and seeing change as an adventure can inspire transformation.

Change366 emphasizes the importance of emotional intelligence in change management. Managers need to understand their teams' emotional dynamics and view them as bonded units with shared experiences crucial for cohesion. Effective support involves tailoring guidance to specific challenges. Additionally, mid-level managers should act as emotional conductors, fostering learning and adaptability. Change366 also advocates for a coaching approach, where managers guide teams through challenges, akin to teaching a crew to sail.

Abbott and Sun Tzu introduce the concepts of broad perspective and preventive strategy. A narrow view limits progress, and the best leaders anticipate and circumvent problems.

Hope, despair, and trust play significant roles in change, as highlighted by a folk tale and Change366. Feeding hope and building trust are key strategies for successful change leadership.

La Rochefoucauld, Spinoza, and Hume guide perceptions and trust in change management. Authenticity, understanding duality, and steering organizational perceptions are crucial.

Sextus Empiricus and Deci emphasize the importance of validation and intrinsic motivation. Trust and autonomy in leadership foster a committed and high-performing team.

Bandura and Erikson highlight the importance of mindset and identity. Leading minds and fostering a shared sense of 'we' are vital for thriving in change.

Change366 and Sartre remind us that change is both a personal and collective journey. It requires self-awareness, active management, and seizing opportunities as they arise.

Lencioni highlights the importance of self-awareness and the attribution of behaviors, a crucial skill for managers in understanding and leading their teams through change.

Managers have a multifaceted role in organizational change. Adaptability, emotional intelligence, perspective, proactive leadership, and the power of trust and intrinsic motivation are key. These insights provide a guide for mid-level managers to navigate the complexities of change effectively.

August 1st

BE THE CHANGE YOU MANAGE

> "Managers and Supervisors are closest to their staff and are in the best position to drive the change adoption within their area of responsibility". "The preferred sender of personal change messages is an employee's manager or supervisor." "89% of Managers are ineffective or somewhat effective at managing employee resistance to change."
>
> —Prosci, *The Role of People Managers.* [294]

Managers are key. They're close to the action. They shape staff attitudes. But here's the rub: most miss the mark. They falter in handling resistance. This needs fixing. Fast. Turn your managers into change champions.

Takeaways. Managers are change agents; Proximity to staff is an advantage; Most managers struggle with resistance.

Fundamental Concepts. Managers are key. That's Social Proximity. Close to the team. That's Relational Capital. [295] Struggle exists. That's Resistance Management. Change champions? That's Transformational Leadership. Most managers miss. That's Leadership Gap. Proximity is power. Use it. That's the core of Change Activation. Know your team. Break resistance. Drive change. Success shines.

Bottom Line. To drive change successfully, train managers to leverage their close staff relationships, overcome resistance, and transform into effective leaders, addressing the widespread leadership gap.

August 2nd

SYNC OR SINK

"Remember that as a manager if you think in terms of the new current state, staff will find it impossible to communicate with you effectively unless they think in those terms too."

—Daryl Conner, *Managing at the Speed of Change.* [296]

Sync your thoughts with your team. New state, new rules. But remember, it takes two to tango. If you're ahead, they'll lag. Harmony breeds success. Dissonance dooms change.

Takeaways. Sync thinking for effective communication; The manager sets the thinking tone; Dissonance in viewpoints halts change.

Fundamental Concepts. Sync matters. That's Cognitive Congruence. Manager leads. That's Top-Down Influence. Lag in thinking? That's Cognitive Dissonance. Harmony is key. That's Social Cohesion. Sets the tone? That's Normative Control. Unity wins. Dissonance loses. That's Group Dynamics. New state, new mindset. That's Cognitive Shift. Align thought. Drive change. Success soars.

Bottom Line. To lead successful change, align manager and staff thinking. Embrace new mindsets, avoid conflicts, and drive change effectively.

August 3rd

BINARY BLINDS—FLUIDITY FINDS

"Managers who see change in binary terms, yes or no, do not see the change as an ongoing endeavor that needs constant attention. Instead, they view change projects as events that have a distinct before and after, onetime shots that fire or fizzle. Resilient people tend to avoid this binary view. They realize that major change is fluid, like an ice cube melting and refreezing."

—KURT LEWIN, *Field Theory in Social Science.* [297]

Change isn't a switch. It's a dial. It moves. It morphs. Thinking in yes-or-no kills change. It's like calling a melting ice cube 'water,' then 'ice,' then 'water' again. Be flexible. Make your view wide, not narrow. Adapt. That's how you make change stick.

Takeaways. Change is fluid, not fixed; Binary thinking stifles change; Adaptability is key for lasting change.

Fundamental Concepts. Fluid view. That's Cognitive Flexibility. Dial, not switch. That's Continuum Thinking. Stifled by binary? That's Fixed Mindset. Adaptability rules. That's Psychological Resilience. Change morphs. That's Dynamic Systems Theory. [298] Rigidity ruins. That's Inflexible Control. Flexibility fuels. That's Open Systems Theory. Success stays. Change works. Adapt to win.

Bottom Line. Lead change as an ongoing process, promoting flexibility and resilience, not as a one-time event, to ensure success.

August 4th

YOU'RE NOT THE FLAME—YOU'RE THE HEARTH

"It is the job of a manager not to light the fire of motivation, but to create an environment to let each person's personal spark of motivation blaze."

—Frederick Herzberg, *The Motivation-Hygiene Concept.* [299]

Managers make change. How? Not by lighting fires. By building fireplaces. Create spaces for sparks to blaze. People find their own fire. Managers make it safe to burn bright. You're not the lighter. You're the architect.

Takeaways. Managers don't ignite motivation; they build its environment; Be an architect, not a lighter; Personal sparks are vital; Make room for them; Safety and structure fuel the blaze of change.

Fundamental Concepts. Motivation model. That's Self-Determination Theory. Architect action. That's Environmental Psychology. Personal power. That's Agency. Safe spaces. That's Psychological Safety. Structure sustains. That's Cognitive Framing. Make room for more. That's Inclusive Management. Blaze bright, burn long. That's Emotional Engagement. You guide, not goad. That's Autonomy Support. The path is theirs. That's Internal Locus of Control. Change comes from choice. That's Volitional Choice. [300]

Bottom Line. Managers create spaces for self-motivation, fostering individual growth and autonomy, enabling sustained and engaged change.

August 5th

INFLUENCE UP, STEER DOWN

> "People Manager during change job description. You're the bridge, coach, voice. Many hats. Goal: Ensure change sticks. How? Be clear. Assemble your team. Secure resources. Gain support. Guide through change journey. It's demanding but vital. No shortcuts. Understand your team and work. Advocate. Address resistance. Reward courage. Time's ticking, but progress is the prize. Stay committed and authentic. You're the linchpin. Make it count."
>
> —CHANGE366. [301]

You're a People Manager. Your role is multi-faceted. You communicate. You connect. You champion change. But it's tough. Resistance lurks. Yet, you're the pivot. You have the power. You influence up. You steer down. You don't just manage; You lead. You're the force that turns strategy into action, idea into reality.

Takeaways. Be a strong communicator to guide your team; Act as a liaison between execs and employees; Advocate for the change you want to see; Manage resistance and serve as a coach.

Fundamental Concepts. Binary views trap. That's Cognitive Fixation. Fluid perspectives free. That's Adaptive Thinking. Managers stuck in static? That's Change Blindness. Resilience recognizes shifts. That's Dynamic Awareness. Fluidity is like melting ice. That's Continuous Evolution. Understand change's nature. That's Deep Insight. Resilient minds mold and adapt. That's Cognitive Flexibility. Avoid rigid confines. Seek flowing freedom. That's the essence of Adaptive Leadership. Embrace the ebb and flow. Navigate change seamlessly.

Bottom Line. Managers guide teams through change via clear communication and unity. They conquer challenges, beat resistance, and transform plans into reality. Their leadership is vital for making change endure and count as progress.

August 6th

ADAPTABILITY IS THE MIDDLE MANAGER'S SUPERPOWER

"Middle managers must juggle multiple roles in organizational change. They negotiate work organization and their own role interpretation; they deal with changing environments and adapt to new ways of working, including handling negotiations within themselves and with others. Understanding negotiation boundaries and power dynamics is key. They sustain and reinforce change by actively engaging in these processes."

—MELANIE BRYANT, *The Competing Roles of Middle Management.* [302]

Middle managers must adapt quickly and guide their teams through transitions. They apply 'negotiated order' with flexibility, foresight, and a willingness to embrace new challenges. [303] Adapting to change isn't just a necessity; it's an opportunity for growth and innovation.

Takeaways. Change is inevitable in organizations; Middle managers must adapt and guide their teams; Flexibility and foresight are key skills; Embracing change leads to growth and innovation.

Fundamental Concepts. Change, a constant. That's Inevitability. Adaptation required. That's Flexibility. Middle managers, change navigators. That's Role Significance. Leading teams through transitions. That's Guidance. Opportunities in change. That's Growth Potential. Embracing new challenges, an opening for innovation. That's Creative Adaptation. Change management, a dance of adaptability. That's Organizational Dynamics. Middle managers, the linchpin in change. That's Central Influence. Adaptability and foresight, their toolkit. That's Skills Mastery. Growth and innovation, the destination. That's Change Realization.

Bottom Line. Middle managers drive change by actively adapting, negotiating, and guiding their teams. They balance internal and external factors to sustain effective change.

August 7th

DOUBT CAN DRIVE DIRECTION

"I would rather have questions that can't be answered than answers that can't be questioned."

—RICHARD FEYNMAN. [304]

Questions drive growth. Answers set in stone? Risky. People managers: embrace doubt. Let teams question. It's strength, not weakness.

Takeaways. Embrace questions, avoid absolute answers; Cultivate curiosity in teams; Open dialogue trumps dictation; Challenge is a growth tool.

Fundamental Concepts. Open dialogue thrives. That's Inquiry Empowerment. Unquestioned answers? Stagnation's root. That's Cognitive Rigidity. Managers foster growth. How? By Valuing Curiosity. Accept team's doubts. That's Vulnerable Leadership. [305] Dictation shuts down voices. That's Communication Block. Curiosity fuels progress. Embrace the unknown. That's the core of Adaptive Management. Listen actively. Encourage challenges. Lead with understanding. Growth follows naturally.

Bottom Line. Managers fuel team growth through curiosity and questions. They promote open communication, embrace doubt, and lead with understanding to foster a culture of learning and progress.

August 8th

INSPIRE CHANGE, DON'T JUST INSTALL IT

"The usual hero adventure begins with someone from whom something has been taken, or who feels there is something lacking in the normal experience available or permitted to the members of society."

—JOSEPH CAMPBELL, *The Hero with a Thousand Faces.* [306]

Organizations should embrace their heroes. Often, those heroes are people managers. You sense a gap. You are closest to your people. You see what others don't. Maybe it's an outdated system. Perhaps it's a flawed process. You start the journey to fill that void. But you're not just changing systems. You're leading people. You're the catalyst. Your job is not just to implement but to inspire.

Takeaways. People managers sense gaps and act as the hero to fill them; The journey is not just about system change but people change; The manager's role is to inspire, not just implement.

Fundamental Concepts. Hero takes stage. That's Initiation Phase. Problem sensed? Need Recognition. Inspire the team. That's Motivational Leadership. Touching hearts, not tasks. Emotional Intelligence. Simple words, big impact. Cognitive Ease. Prep minds for hard path. Resilience Building. Lead by doing. Modeling Behavior. Story drives action. Narrative Psychology. Emotional arc in change. Self-Determination Theory. Team united, goal clear. Social Cohesion. Not just managing change. Managing minds. Core of Psychologically-Informed Change Management. Lead with the heart. Stoke motivation's fire. Unlock the possible.

Bottom Line. Managers lead change by inspiring and uniting their teams to address gaps with passion and perseverance, aiming for impactful, shared goals.

August 9th

SEE THE FEELING, KNOW THE TEAM

"In transformation, emotional lenses are the unseen factors. Understand them, and you guide the rhythm of transformation."

—CHANGE366. [307]

People managers shape our work life. They impact how we see our jobs. Good leaders make teams see work positively. Managers need to understand deep feelings. If a team feels their work is 'friendly', the manager helped create that. Great managers use feelings to guide teams. Leadership affects team emotions and actions. Recognizing these feelings is key. It creates a good work environment.

Takeaways. People managers shape team views; Good leaders create positive work feelings; Managers tap into deep team emotions; Leadership guides team feelings and actions; Recognizing feelings builds a strong work environment.

Fundamental Concepts. Work is emotion-fueled. That's Affective Investment. It has a pull, a drive. That's Affective Intentionality. [308] Feelings and actions align. That's Symbolic Motive. Feelings make symbols. That's Affective Symbolization. Our mind is a maze. It's split. One part feels. Another part thinks. That's Dual Mind Functioning. Feelings give life color. That's Affective Categorization. Shared feelings guide. That's Shared Representation. Words describe our world. That's Context Description. Work feels right? That's Positive Symbolic Credit. [309] Connection and success rule. That's Affiliation and Achievement.

Bottom Line. Managers play a crucial role by harnessing their team's emotions to shape the work culture and boost morale. Recognizing and utilizing these emotions effectively fosters a positive work environment and enables effective leadership during times of change.

August 10th

FEEL, THEN DEAL. EMOTION DRIVES MOTION

"In the furnace of anger lies the power to transform challenges; yet, like fire, it must be channeled wisely, or it risks consuming all in its path."

—Change366. [310]

Emotions are not distractions. They're tools, especially in change management. Anger has a role. It can fuel goal achievement. Let's say your team faces a big shift. Resistance is high. Anger can ignite action. It can speed up decision-making. It can make your team tackle challenges head-on. So, as a manager, don't shy away from emotion. Harness it. Use it to beat obstacles. To hit targets. To drive change.

Takeaways. Emotions like anger can fuel action; Anger speeds up decision-making; Use emotions as tools for overcoming challenges in change management.

Fundamental Concepts. Emotion speaks. That's Emotional Intelligence. Anger in play? Goal Activation. Managers harness feelings. That's Emotional Utilization. Decision speed up. Cognitive Acceleration. Challenges faced head-on? That's Motivational Drive. Emotions not distractions. Cognitive Tools. Use them well. That's Emotion-Focused Change Management. Tap into feelings. Overcome hurdles. Achieve goals. Make change stick.

Bottom Line. Managers must harness team emotions, such as anger, to swiftly navigate change and attain their goals.

August 11th

MANAGERS SEE BONDS, NOT JUST BODIES

"In organizational change, the power of self-similarity is the rhythm that binds us. Embrace shared experiences, for in them lies the secret to cohesive teams and seamless transitions."

—CHANGE366. [311]

People managers bridge gaps. They connect teams. Self-similarity helps. Managers use this insight. They weave talent into the team. Familiarity fosters quick bonds. Understanding and embracing this is key. It promotes seamless integration.

Takeaways. People managers play a pivotal role in connecting teams; Self-similarity expedites the bonding process; Recognizing these patterns aids smooth organizational transitions; Embracing familiarity leads to better team cohesion.

Fundamental Concepts. People managers connect. That's Team Synthesis. Self-similarity speeds bonding. That's Cognitive Reflection. Familiarity fuels connections. That's the Heart of Cohesion. Managers recognize this. They weave teams. That's Insightful Leadership. Cognitive patterns drive integration. That's Organizational Insight. Embrace the familiar, boost unity. That's Managerial Mastery. Real leaders tap into Self-similarity. It's the glue. That's Cohesive Management. Joining a team? Find shared traits.

Bottom Line. Managers build team unity by using shared experiences to strengthen bonds among members, smoothing the path during organizational change. They identify common traits to bolster teamwork and ensure seamless transitions.

August 12th

NOT ALL SUPPORT EASES—FIT MATTERS MOST

"In organizational change, leadership involves more than support—it's about aligning guidance with ever-changing challenges, while managing stress. Managers' task is to adapt, understanding that guidance and hurdles don't always align seamlessly. We must tailor our approach to ensure relevance and effectiveness, guiding our teams through transformation even when the path isn't clear."

—Change366. [312]

Organizations face change. Change brings stress. Support can help. High-stress? Support might not always help. Stress levels matter. Our perception of support changes. More stress? We seek external help. Less stress? We cope alone. For managers, this knowledge is crucial. Support isn't one-size-fits-all. It's about type, timing, and method. Customized support eases transitions.

Takeaways. High stress can overshadow strong support; Perception of support varies with stress levels; Tailoring support is crucial in change management; External and internal coping mechanisms have distinct roles.

Fundamental Concepts. Organizations shift. That's Evolutionary Flow. Change triggers stress. That's Emotional Upheaval. Support can cushion. That's Protective Shielding. High stress? Support might falter. That's Overwhelming Waves. Stress scales affect us. That's the Emotional Scale. Need varies with stress. That's Adaptive Response. Managers should grasp this. That's Enlightened Leadership. Support strategies must adapt. That's Tailored Guidance. Tailoring is key. That's Crafting Change.

Bottom Line. Managers adjust support to match their team's shifting stress levels, ensuring it aligns with the specific challenges of organizational change.

August 13th

MANAGERS CONDUCT WORK'S EMOTIONAL BEAT

"Leadership and adaptability fuel an organization's vitality. Cultivate environments where learning and belief in one's ability to embrace change are paramount. This is the key to flourishing in a world of constant shifts."

—CHANGE366. [313]

In a world where change is the only constant, leadership stands as the beacon of guidance. It's not just about directing; it's about energizing an entire organization. Adaptability, on the other hand, is the art of navigating through the unknown. It's about being ready to shift gears, embracing new ideas, and staying ahead.

Takeaways. Leadership vitalizes and guides organizations; Adaptability ensures relevance and growth; Embracing change is key to staying ahead; Managers must inspire and navigate through changes.

Fundamental Concepts. Leaders inspire. That's Emotional Resonance. A team that believes. That's Collective Efficacy. Change challenges met. That's Adaptive Resilience. Ideas flow, adaptability grows. That's Creative Agility. Leadership's heart beats change. That's Organizational Vitality. Adapt or stagnate. That's the Adaptability Imperative. Harnessing change, leaders thrive. That's Transformational Leadership. Emotional resonance builds trust. Trust fuels adaptability. Adaptability breeds success.

Bottom Line. Leaders drive change and instill trust in adaptability. They foster a culture of continuous learning, turning change into growth opportunities. This approach ensures the organization thrives amid constant shifts. Active promotion of this mindset by leaders leads to ongoing progress.

August 14th

CHANGE NEEDS A COACH, NOT JUST A MANAGER

"True managerial leadership in change isn't just about steering the ship; it's about teaching the crew how to navigate storms, read the stars, and be at one with the sea."

—Change366. [314]

Change isn't just a switch you flip. For managers, it's a whole new game. You're not just a boss; you're also a coach. This means a deep dive into yourself. Know your values. Build your Self-awareness. You also need the right skills. Two paths help you: coach training and coach education. The first one is like learning to swim. The second is like learning to navigate storms. It's not just about you. The company culture must be right too. It's a team play, always in motion.

Takeaways. Managers are coaches in the change game; Self-awareness and skill-building are key; Company culture sets the stage; Change is ongoing, not a one-time act.

Fundamental Concepts. Self-awareness? That's Introspection. Confidence blooms. That's Self-Efficacy. Mind shifts. That's Cognitive Reappraisal. Two learning tracks? That's Dual-Process Theory. [315] Culture matters? That's Social Conditioning. New leadership style? That's Relational Leadership. Change never stops. That's Continuous Adaptation. Managers as guides? That's Situational Leadership. It's all connected. That's Systems Thinking. [316]

Bottom Line. Managers must embrace their roles as adaptive coaches and lifelong learners within a supportive company culture. This comprehensive approach is the key to effectively dealing with the complexities of change.

August 15th

MIDDLE MANAGERS—THE CHANGE-MAKERS IN THE MIDDLE

"In the theater of organizational change, middle managers are both the scriptwriters and the lead actors."

—CHANGE366. [317]

Middle managers are the bridge between top bosses and ground workers. They bring orders down but also shape them. They don't just follow. They adapt and even challenge. Their role is vital when a company changes. They act as the glue that holds plans and actions together.

Takeaways. Middle managers are connectors, not just messengers; They adapt and refine strategies; They balance multiple roles in change processes; They're essential in turning plans into action.

Fundamental Concepts. Middle managers adapt. That's Cognitive Flexibility. They act as bridges. That's Role Mediation. They don't just follow orders. That's Autonomy. They face stress but keep going. That's Resilience. They influence both up and down. That's Vertical Bidirectionality. Adapting strategies is their skill. That's Pragmatic Competence. Active in shaping the plan. That's Agency.

Bottom Line. Middle managers are key to executing organizational change. They balance adaptation with strategic challenges. They manage stress and guide junior staff within the dynamic of control and resistance. They are crucial in shaping the company's future.

August 16th

A NARROW VIEW KEEPS PROGRESS OUT OF SIGHT

"Behold yon miserable creature. That Point is a Being like ourselves, but confined to the non-dimensional Gulf. He is himself his own World, his own Universe; of any other than himself he can form no conception; he knows not Length, nor Breadth, nor Height, for he has had no experience of them; he has no cognizance even of the number Two; nor has he a thought of Plurality, for he is himself his One and All, being really Nothing. Yet mark his perfect self-contentment, and hence learn this lesson, that to be self-contented is to be vile and ignorant, and that to aspire is better than to be blindly and impotently happy."

—EDWIN A. ABBOTT, *Flatland: A Romance of Many Dimensions.* [318]

Imagine a manager in their own world, resistant to change and unaware of their ignorance—it hinders progress and innovation. Managers must break their bubble, learn, adapt, and embrace change for success. It shifts contentment to ambition.

Takeaways. Avoid a narrow mindset; Embrace a broader view; Encourage learning from new experiences and systems; Discourage complacency; Promote continuous Self-improvement; Foster ambition and a desire for progress in the team.

Fundamental Concepts. Stuck in a rut. That's Cognitive Rigidity. Seeing only what's in front of you. That's Confirmation Bias. Happy, yet ignorant? That's the Dunning-Kruger Effect. [319] Don't know any better? That's Lack of Self-Awareness. But there's a twist. Aspiration trumps blind contentment. That's the essence of Self-Determination. Embrace change and grow. Seek knowledge, not comfort.

Bottom Line. Managers should inspire teams to see beyond their current views and push for growth, moving from contentment to ambition for progress. This shift from ignorance to enlightenment is vital for successful change implementation.

August 17th

PREVENT, DON'T JUST FIX

"The greatest general is not the one who wins the battles but rather the one who avoids them."

—SUN TZU, *The Art of War.* [320]

In organizational change management, the greatest leaders are those who foresee and circumvent potential issues. They prioritize a stable and harmonious work environment over the turmoil of conflict. They know that preventing a problem is more valuable than fixing one. By thinking strategically, they maintain peace and stability, ensuring the organization's smooth operation. They demonstrate wisdom in avoiding unnecessary battles, preserving resources and morale.

Takeaways. Great leaders prevent problems rather than fixing them; They maintain a stable and peaceful work environment; Strategic thinking and foresight are key to their success; Avoiding unnecessary conflict preserves resources and morale.

Fundamental Concepts. Prevention beats cure. That's Proactive Management. Leaders think ahead. That's Strategic Foresight. They value peace. That's Stability Focus. Avoiding conflict is wise. That's Conflict Avoidance. They save resources. That's Resource Preservation. Morale stays high. That's Morale Maintenance. Great leaders are proactive. That's Leadership Excellence. They prioritize stability. That's Change Management Mastery. Watch the organization thrive.

Bottom Line. Managers excel at change by preventing workplace problems with foresight, ensuring peace, saving resources, and boosting morale, steering clear of conflict for organizational stability.

August 18th

FEED HOPE, STARVE DESPAIR, LEAD CHANGE SUCCESSFULLY

"Mentor: 'Have you heard about the two wolves battling inside us?' Mentee: 'Two wolves? No.' Mentor: 'We have two wolves inside. One is darkness and despair, the other is lightness and hope.' Mentee: 'Which wolf's stronger?' Mentor: 'The one you feed.'"

—FOLK TALE. [321]

In organizational change, we often face an internal battle. This battle is like the two wolves inside us. One wolf stands for darkness and despair. The other wolf is for lightness and hope. The wolf you feed grows stronger. Choose to feed the wolf of lightness and hope. Make positive choices to lead change effectively. Remember, the power is in your hands.

Takeaways. There's an ongoing internal battle in change management; Choices determine the outcome of this battle; Negative forces can hinder change, while positive forces drive it.

Fundamental Concepts. Internal battles. That's Cognitive Dissonance. Choices influence outcomes. That's Self-Determination Theory. Positivity drives change. That's Positive Reinforcement. Embracing change requires courage. That's Overcoming Resistance. Leaders guide the transformation. That's Pro—Social Behavior. Watch the culture evolve. That's Organizational Change Success. The narrative highlights autonomy. That's Empowered Decision-Making. Positivity transforms organizations. That's Effective Change Leadership. Watch negativity fade away.

Bottom Line. Managers drive change by fostering hope, which beats despair, influences outcomes, and shapes organizational culture through positive leadership.

August 19th

IMPERFECTION BREEDS UNIQUE VALUE

"Embrace the cracks within; they are unseen paths to blooming gardens, nurtured by insightful leadership and resilient adaptation."

—CHANGE366. [322]

In our journey of organizational change, we often encounter imperfection, much like the 'cracked pot' parable. [323] It's crucial to recognize the unique value each member brings to the team, even those who might not seem perfect. Leaders, akin to the water bearer, must adapt and find ways to harness the potential of every team member. This story teaches us to appreciate the beauty in imperfection and to seek out the flowers that bloom from our unique contributions.

Takeaways. Imperfection is a part of every team, but it holds unique value; Leaders must recognize and adapt to harness each member's potential; Every team member has a unique contribution to make; Learning to appreciate our unique roles leads to blooming success.

Fundamental Concepts. Imperfection stands, yet it holds power. That's Human Complexity. Leaders see beyond flaws. That's Insightful Leadership. They turn weaknesses into strengths. That's Adaptive Strategy. Imperfections contribute uniquely. That's Valuable Diversity. The team blooms, growing stronger. That's Organizational Resilience. Leaders guide this transformation. That's Change Management. They create blooming paths for all. That's Inclusive Success. The organization thrives, enriched by diversity.

Bottom Line. Managers turn team imperfections into strengths, valuing diversity to foster resilience and inclusive success during change.

August 20th

BE REAL, BUILD TRUST

"We are never so ridiculous by the qualities we have, as by those we affect to have."

—FRANÇOIS DE LA ROCHEFOUCAULD, *Maxims.*[324]

In the journey of change management, authenticity stands paramount. Managers should never fake qualities they don't possess. Embrace your true self. Showcase your real strengths. Recognize and work on your weaknesses. Authenticity builds trust. It fosters genuine relationships within teams. Pretense does the opposite. It makes situations ridiculous and undermines credibility. Be real, be you.

Takeaways. Embrace and showcase your true qualities; Avoid pretending to have qualities you lack; Be Self-aware; know your strengths and weaknesses; Build trust and genuine relationships through authenticity.

Fundamental Concepts. Authenticity shines. That's Real Leadership. Pretense falters. That's Quality Faking. Self-knowledge empowers. That's Aware Managing. Trust builds teams. That's Relationship Foundation. Genuine connections grow. That's Authentic Bonding. Be real, always. That's True Self. Leadership thrives on authenticity. That's Credibility's Core. Know your qualities. That's Self Awareness. Authentic managers succeed. That's Leadership Triumph.

Bottom Line. Managers build trust by being authentic, leveraging real strengths, acknowledging weaknesses, and avoiding pretense. Authenticity fosters credibility and strong team bonds.

August 21st

CHANGE BRINGS DUALITY—EMBRACE IT

"No matter how thin you slice it, there will always be two sides."

—BARUCH SPINOZA, *The Collected Works.* [325]

Change brings complexity and duality. Every situation has two sides. As a manager, acknowledge this. Understand the multiple facets of change. Balance differing opinions. Foster an inclusive decision-making environment. Handle ambiguity with skill. Navigate through uncertainty. Be balanced, be inclusive, be adept.

Takeaways. Acknowledge the duality in change situations; Balance differing opinions and viewpoints; Foster inclusivity in decision making; Navigate ambiguity and uncertainty with skill.

Fundamental Concepts. Duality exists. That's Change's Nature. Managers balance. That's Skillful Leadership. Opinions vary. That's Perspective Diversity. Inclusivity rules. That's Decision Democracy. Navigate uncertainty. That's Ambiguity Mastery. Embrace complexity. That's Clarity Quest. Managers lead through duality. That's Effective Change Management. Consider all sides. That's Comprehensive Decision Making. Skillful leadership prevails. That's Managerial Triumph.

Bottom Line. Managers guide through change by balancing perspectives, embracing decision-making inclusivity, and mastering uncertainty.

August 22nd

GUIDE PERCEPTIONS TO STEER ORGANIZATIONAL CHANGE

"I may venture to affirm of the rest of mankind, that they are nothing but a bundle or collection of different perceptions, which succeed each other with an inconceivable rapidity, and are in a perpetual flux and movement."

—DAVID HUME, *A Treatise of Human Nature.* [326]

Every person in your organization sees change differently. They are a mix of shifting views. Fast. Unpredictable. Like a river, these perceptions are always moving, reshaping the landscape of your workplace. As a change manager, it's your task to navigate these waters. Guide your team through the rapids of change. Show them how each perception can blend into a vision for the future. Unity in diversity—that's the goal.

Takeaways. Recognize the diversity of perceptions in change management; Understand how perceptions influence organizational dynamics; Manage the rapid pace of change by guiding and unifying perceptions; Foster a collective vision that embraces diverse viewpoints.

Fundamental Concepts. Diversity sparks insight. That's Perception Variety. Change speeds on. That's Continuous Flux. Minds shift quick. That's Rapid Perception Change. Vision unites us. That's Collective Cohesion. Change managers guide. That's Navigational Leadership. [327] A team's views mesh. That's Perceptual Harmony. Together, we evolve. That's Unified Progression.

Bottom Line. Managers unite diverse views and steer towards a common vision for effective change. They understand perceptions shape and drive the company's progress.

August 23rd

CRITERIA GUIDES, VALIDATION CONFIRMS, TRUST FOLLOWS

"Those who claim for themselves to judge the truth are bound to possess a criterion of truth. This criterion, then, either is without a judge's approval or has been approved. But if it is without approval, whence comes it that it is truthworthy? For no matter of dispute is to be trusted without judging. And, if it has been approved, that which approves it, in turn, either has been approved or has not been approved, and so on ad infinitum."

—SEXTUS EMPIRICUS, *Outlines of Pyrrhonism.* [328]

In the world of change, truth is your guide. To find it, you need solid criteria. Like a compass in a storm, these criteria guide decisions. Yet, they must earn trust. Every step must be checked and approved. As a manager, you shape this process. Create criteria, validate them, and build trust. This is your path to steady, true change.

Takeaways. Establish clear criteria for judging change initiatives; Ensure each decision passes through validation; Build trust through consistent, transparent judgment; Recognize validation as an ongoing process, not a one-time act.

Fundamental Concepts. Criteria set. That's Norm Establishment. Decisions face scrutiny. That's Continuous Validation. Trust builds. That's Confidence Accumulation. Judgment earns its keep. That's Criterion Legitimacy. Truth navigates change. That's Directional Truthfulness. Without trust, change falters. That's the Trust Principle. Validation spirals on. That's Infinite Verification. [329]

Bottom Line. Managers lead by setting criteria, checking decisions, and building trust to guide change effectively.

August 24th

FUEL CHANGE—LET INTRINSIC MOTIVATION WIN

"Self-Determination theory posits a Self-determination continuum. It ranges from amotivation, which is wholly lacking in Self-determination, to intrinsic motivation which is invariantly Self-determined. Between amotivation and intrinsic motivation, along this descriptive continuum, are the four types of extrinsic motivation, with external being the most controlled (and thus the least Self-determined) type of extrinsic motivation, and introjected, identified, and integrated being progressively more Self-determined."

—EDWARD L DECI, *Self Determination Theory and Work Motivation.* [330]

Motivation drives change. It's a spectrum: amotivation, external motivation, identified motivation, and intrinsic motivation. Change leaders shift teams to intrinsic motivation for lasting transformation.

Takeaways. Understand motivation's range in your team; Aim to shift from extrinsic to intrinsic motivation; Recognize the evolution from amotivation to engagement; Encourage Self-determination to foster commitment to change.

Fundamental Concepts. Motivation's spectrum. That's Self-Determination Theory. Amotivation reigns. That's Engagement Absence. Rewards drive action. That's Controlled Regulation. Personal reasons emerge. That's Identified Motivation. Joy fuels work. That's Intrinsic Motivation. Leaders ignite the shift. That's Motivation Transformation. Intrinsic value creates change. That's Sustainable Commitment. Lead by inspiration, not just obligation.

Bottom Line. Managers must grasp their team's motivation levels and foster a shift from external rewards to deriving joy from work, promoting intrinsic motivation. They lead this change by inspiring team members to value their work, ensuring lasting transformation.

August 25th

TRUST IGNITES CHANGE—CONTROL EXTINGUISHES IT

"Support brings motivation. Autonomy grows satisfaction. Managers who empower get teams that excel. When leaders trust, employees commit. It's a cycle of success. Autonomy is not a luxury; it's a necessity. It fuels well-being and work results. Control stifles creativity. Support liberates it. Lead with autonomy, and watch commitment to, and performance of change, soar."

—CHANGE366.[331]

Inspire change with empowerment. Autonomy fuels persistence, performance, and satisfaction. Managers who listen and encourage ignite creativity and dedication. Support, not control, is the key.

Takeaways. Autonomy breeds motivation and satisfaction for change; Supportive management amplifies job performance during change; Trust in leadership is built through autonomy support; Intrinsic motivation leads to sustained organizational commitment to change.

Fundamental Concepts. Autonomy support meets needs. That's Intrinsic Fueling. Control suffocates drive. That's Autonomy Choking. Managers who listen empower. That's Engagement Sparking. Choice leads to innovation. That's Creative Awakening. Empowerment solidifies commitment. That's Loyalty Building. Psychological well-being thrives. That's Wellness Cultivating. Transform with autonomy, not authority. That's Motivation Amplifying. Recognize needs, reap dedication. That's Commitment Sowing. Well-being and performance, intertwined. That's Outcome Enhancing.

Bottom Line. Managers empower their teams, boosting motivation, satisfaction, and performance in change. Trust and support from leaders enable autonomy, spurring creativity and commitment. Conversely, control can quash innovation and drive.

August 26th

LEAD MINDS TO LEAD CHANGE

"What people think, believe, and feel affects how they behave. The natural and extrinsic effects of their actions, in turn, partly determine their thought patterns and affective reactions."

—ALBERT BANDURA, *Social Foundations of Thought and Action.* [332]

Managers lead change by shaping thoughts and beliefs. They listen to feelings to understand team behaviors. Actions change minds just as minds lead to actions. Good managers know this. They use it to guide change. They create an environment where actions and thoughts improve together.

Takeaways. Managers shape team beliefs and actions; Understanding feelings is key to guiding behaviors; Actions and mindsets are interlinked in change; A good manager aligns extrinsic effects with company goals.

Fundamental Concepts. Beliefs guide. That's Cognitive Direction. Feelings emerge. That's Affective Response. Behaviors follow beliefs. That's Behavioral Consequence. Actions reshape thoughts. That's Reflective Processing. Managers must align thoughts with goals. That's Cognitive Harmony. Feelings influence outcomes. That's Emotional Intelligence. Understanding leads to better guidance. That's Informed Management. Behavior changes belief. That's Reciprocal Determinism. [333] Align actions for progress. That's Purposeful Engagement. Managers create change's flow. That's Dynamic Leadership.

Bottom Line. Managers lead change by influencing team beliefs and understanding their emotions to guide behaviors. They create a cycle where positive actions and mindsets fuel each other, aligning with the company's goals for effective change.

August 27th

CHANGE THRIVES ON A SHARED 'WE'

"The sense of identity provides the ability to experience oneself as something that has continuity and sameness, and to act accordingly."

—Erik Erikson, *Identity and the Lifecycle.* [334]

Identity drives action. A strong sense of self-guided consistent behavior. In change management, a manager's role is to foster a collective identity. They must weave the individual's sense of self into the company's evolving narrative. When people see their work as a part of their identity, they embrace change. They become active participants, not just bystanders.

Takeaways. Identity influences consistent action; Managers create a shared organizational identity; Align individual and organizational change for smoother transitions; Strong Self-identity in people supports change adoption.

Fundamental Concepts. Identity roots deep. That's Self-Continuity. Work becomes self. That's Identity Integration. Change needs sameness. That's Continuity Management. Managers build 'us'. That's Collective Identity Formation. Shared identity steers action. That's Identity Consistency. Know yourself, guide others. That's Self-Conception for Leadership. Shared 'we' unites. That's Social Identity's Power. Action matches known self. That's Behavior-Identity Link. Change clings to identity. That's Personal Change Commitment. Lead with identity in mind. That's Identity-Driven Management.

Bottom Line. Managers drive change success by forging a shared identity within the company. They link individual and company identities, making change an integral part of our team's identity. This approach transforms employees into proactive change-makers, not passive observers.

August 28th

CHANGE IS PERSONAL UNTIL SHARED BY THE GROUP

"In change, collective voices sing the strongest chorus; understanding their harmony is key."

—CHANGE366. [335]

Change impacts people in groups: personas, teams, functions. Groups form collective readiness by combining individual thoughts. Understanding groups is vital to grasp change fully. Bourdieu's theory emphasizes combining personal actions and group dynamics, considering power, backgrounds, and past experiences. [336] Managing change requires looking beyond individuals to the group.

Takeaways. Group readiness for change is a collective process over time; Personal agency and social structures are key in group change; Power and resources influence collective responses to change.

Fundamental Concepts. Personal fears join hands. That's Group Anxiety Merging. Readiness grows in whispers. That's Collective Consciousness. Reaction maps get drawn together. That's Group Sensemaking. Power plays roles. That's Structural Dominance. Access to change's keys. That's Resource Gatekeeping. Agency within rules. That's Structured Autonomy. Sociocultural soil nurtures reactions. That's Background Influence. New roles, new rules. That's Change Norms Crafting. Personal meets group. That's Integrated Change Perspective. Unseen group patterns? That's a Blind Spot.

Bottom Line. Managers lead change by understanding and uniting individual and group dynamics. They consider personal backgrounds and the group's collective voice to create a shared readiness for change. They also examine how power and roles within the group influence change, recognizing the impact of social and economic factors on change adoption.

August 29th

ACTIVE MANAGEMENT DRIVES CHANGE, STIRS SOULS

> "The 'Hawthorn Effect' illuminates the power of attention in transformation. When managers observe, employees rise to the occasion, changing not just in conduct but in spirit. The watchful eye of leadership is the silent catalyst of enduring change."
>
> —CHANGE366. [337]

Watched workers work wonders. It's the Hawthorne effect in action. [338] Managers who observe change the game. But there's more to it than eyes on the prize. It's about engagement, not just oversight. Real change happens when managers mix in. They become part of the process, part of the solution. True change isn't in the numbers; it's in the people. Be present, be positive, and watch the work transform.

Takeaways. Observation changes outcomes; Involvement amplifies it; Effective management engages with teams, not just oversees them; People respond to attention with better performance; Managers should be active in the change process.

Fundamental Concepts. Attention shifts behavior. That's the Hawthorne Highlight. Managers mingle, morale mounts. That's Interaction Effect. Involvement invokes improvement. That's Engagement Elevation. Observation optimizes operations. That's Performance Visibility. Managers' active role reinforces relevance. That's Significance Stimulation. The Hawthorne Effect holds lessons. [339] It's more than the effect; it's the cause of shifts. Engage, don't just gauge. That's Management Mantra. When watched, workers weave better work stories. That's Observer Influence.

Bottom Line. Managers drive change by actively working with their teams, boosting morale and performance. Change is about people, not just results. Managers must actively engage in the process, making it relevant and lasting.

August 30th

SEIZE THE DAY—SHAPE THE CHANGE

"Do you think that I count the days? There is only one day left, always starting over: it is given to us at dawn and taken away from us at dusk."

—JEAN-PAUL SARTRE, *The Words.* [340]

The 'present' is key when driving change. For a manager, each day is a new opportunity to influence change and make an impact. Focus on today's actions to shape a better tomorrow. It's the manager's role to seize the fleeting opportunities each day to progress, learn, and lead by example.

Takeaways. Use each day to actively drive and manage change; Focus on present actions to influence future outcomes; Learn and adapt daily to sustain organizational change.

Fundamental Concepts. Change beckons daily. That's Temporal Freshness. Managers embrace this, applying it to change. That's Present-Centric Progression. Each dawn brings renewal. That's Opportunity Renewal. Daily tasks dictate tomorrow's triumphs. That's Day-to-Day Direction. Managers make today count, crafting change continuously. That's Active Daily Shaping. Mindfulness meets management. That's Conscious Change Cultivation. Today's tasks are tomorrow's transformation. That's Proactive Progress. Managers mastering moments mold more. That's Moment-to-Momentum Management.

Bottom Line. Managers must each day as an opportunity for change. They focus on daily actions to shape a better tomorrow, learning and adapting to sustain organizational change. Embrace the present for continuous transformation.

August 31st

CHANGE STARTS WITH SELF-AWARENESS

"The fundamental attribution error is the tendency of humans to attribute the negative or frustrating behaviors of their colleagues to their intentions and personalities, while attributing their own negative or frustrating behaviors to environmental factors."

—PATRICK LENCIONI, *The Five Dysfunctions of a Team.* [341]

Understanding attribution error is key to change management. [342] As a manager, you shape perspectives. It's easy to blame others' characters for failures and give circumstances a pass for your own faults. But change thrives on fairness and insight. Knowing how bias skews our view lets us build a more cohesive team ready for digital shifts.

Takeaways. Recognize when bias affects judgment; Foster empathy by considering external factors affecting behavior; Create a culture of fairness and understanding; Use awareness of attribution error to drive positive change.

Fundamental Concepts. Blame falls on people, not situations. That's Fundamental Attribution Error. [343] Managers overlook context. That's Actor-Observer Bias. Mistakes happen, we seek culprits. That's Error Management Theory. Insight reverses blame games. That's Reflective Practitioner Approach. Good leaders factor in context. That's Situational Leadership. Recognize bias, encourage growth. That's Growth Mindset. Equality and understanding promote change. That's Organizational Justice. Awareness is the first step. That's Metacognition. Manage with empathy, lead the charge. That's Emotional Intelligence.

Bottom Line. Managers bring their teams together and get them ready for change by being fair and fair-minded. Understanding the tendency to blame others for their actions and attribute our own actions to external factors is crucial for effective leadership in embracing change.

SEPTEMBER — CHAMPIONS

In organizational change management, the role of champions is pivotal. The aphorism, 'Ideas soar on wings of will,' suggested by Schon, lays the foundation. Ideas, no matter how innovative, require champions to take flight. As Settle points out, projects without champions are rudderless, emphasizing the need for committed leadership in strategic initiatives. Ibarra's insight into networking as a fabric we wear and share highlights the champions' role in creating supportive, insightful networks essential for successful change.

The Behavioral Insights Team emphasizes the importance of frontline collaboration, echoing the sentiment that realignment and success in change initiatives are champion-driven. Kalive's notion of reference groups as mirrors aligns with the idea that champions shape organizational norms and values, echoing and amplifying shared goals and directions.

Feher's concept of intrapreneurs as mission molders resonates deeply. These intrapreneurs, or champions within are not just employees but visionaries shaping the future of their organizations. Their mindset and skillset are akin to entrepreneurs, making them invaluable in driving change.

Change366 adds to this narrative by illustrating the power of peer influence in accelerating change. Change agents, or champions, are the sparks that not only initiate but also sustain change. Their growing influence shapes the journey of transformation, making them the human factor that turns plans into actions.

Rosales-Ruiz talks about behavioral cusps as transformation keystones, emphasizing the role of champions in unlocking cascades of change. Ericsson's perspective on guidance in learning resonates with the concept of champions as mentors guiding teams towards organizational goals.

Mbughuni's statement on empowering champions to turn vision into reality is crucial. It's about investing in people, enabling them to own and actualize the vision. This is echoed in Change366 where champions are seen as transforming vision into victory, their adaptability and advocacy fueling organizational evolution.

Mapping the habitus, as suggested by Change366, is about understanding the social and cultural context, a skill paramount for champions leading change. These champions, as the architects of organizational energy, shape decisions and turn individual efforts into collective performance.

Gladwell's emphasis on learning through experience is a call to action for champions to lead by example, especially in the digital realm. Descartes' pragmatism in following what's most probable instead of what's absolutely true resonates with the dynamic decision-making environment that champions often navigate.

Shelly and Change366 highlight the transformative power of champions in blending technological advancements with human objectives, and their role in fostering growth by embracing change. Gerstner and Godin spotlight the self-evolution of champions and their vision in seeing and creating the future.

Kanter's and Ellerbee's remarks on coalition building and embracing change for hope align with the idea that champions are the backbone of change. They are the brave and resilient leaders who push through challenges, as stated in Change366.

Finally, Holiday's quote on daring to act and the role of understanding in quelling fears of change encapsulates the essence of a champion. They are not just leaders or implementers of change; they embody change, living it first to lead others effectively.

Champions are the keystones of organizational change—sometime instigators, teachers, influencers, and builders. They are the force that turns resistance into enthusiasm and uncertainty into action, weaving the very fabric of transformation. They understand that to lead change effectively, they must first embody it, inspiring others by their conviction, courage, and unyielding commitment to progress.

September 1st

IDEAS SOAR ON THE WINGS OF WILL

"The new idea either finds a champion or dies."

—DONALD SCHON, *Champions for Radical New Inventions.* [344]

Ideas need heroes. No hero, no life. A champion gives an idea wings. With no champion, it falls flat. Be that hero. Lift your team's ideas. Make them fly.

Takeaways. Ideas need champions; No champion, idea dies; Be the hero for change.

Fundamental Concepts. Idea's hero? That's Agency. No hero, idea dies. That's Ego Depletion. Be a hero, lift teams. That's Social Support. Be the spark. That's Internal Locus of Control. Wings of will. That's Self-Determination. Charge ahead. That's Proactive Behavior. Don't snuff. That's Negative Reinforcement. Lift, don't lie. That's Authentic Leadership. Be the change. Make it happen. That's Self-Efficacy.

Bottom Line. Ideas thrive with champions who believe in them. Without a champion, ideas fail. Champions take action, giving life to new concepts and guiding teams to adopt change.

September 2nd

A PROJECT WITHOUT A CHAMPION IS ADRIFT

> "The CFO told the CIO they didn't believe any of the numbers in a business case, and only approves major IT initiatives when there's a business leader committed to leveraging the new capabilities. Necessary spending on infrastructure or compliance are rare exceptions, but any kind of strategic IT initiative requires a passionate champion on the business side."
>
> —MARK SETTLE, *Truth from the Trenches.* [345]

A change management champion is like a sail to a ship, providing direction and impact to strategic IT initiatives. They believe in the project, convince others of its value, and align it with business goals.

Takeaways. Champions give direction to strategic IT initiatives; They ensure project alignment with business goals; A champion's commitment secures project approval and resources; They are essential for leveraging new capabilities effectively.

Fundamental Concepts. Champions lead the charge. That's Leadership Drive. Vision meets execution. That's Champion Synergy. Approval follows passion. That's Emotional Investment. Strategy requires advocates. That's Champion Necessity. IT's value unlocked by leadership. That's Strategic Unlocking. Champions translate tech potential. That's Capability Realization. Business aligns with IT. That's Technological Integration. Passionate advocacy secures success. That's Commitment Impact. Infrastructure spends rare without support. That's Exception Ruling. Change hinges on champion energy. That's Transformation Catalyst.

Bottom Line. For IT projects to succeed, a passionate business leader must champion them. They turn visions into reality, drive initiatives with purpose, and fully utilize new capabilities. Their role ensures necessary investments and alignment with business goals.

September 3rd

NETWORK FOR NET WORTH IN CHANGE

"Networking is creating a fabric of personal contacts who will provide support, feedback, insight, resources, and information. The fabric we weave is worn by us and can also be worn by those we connect with."

—Herminia Ibarra, *How Leaders Create and Use Networks.* [346]

Networks are gold. They're not just contacts. They're allies in change. You help them. They help you. Together, you drive change.

Takeaways. Networks are allies; Mutual help fuels change; Strong networks drive success.

Fundamental Concepts. Allies align. That's Social Capital. Mutual help. That's Reciprocity. Networks are gold. That's Social Support. Drive change. That's Collective Efficacy. Build bridges. That's Social Integration. Strong network. That's Emotional Intelligence. Change long. That's Commitment. Help begets help. That's Positive Reinforcement. Be an ally. That's Altruism. Ally up, climb high. That's Synergy.

Bottom Line. Build networks to share support and drive change together. Mutual help among allies leads to success.

September 4th

LISTEN, DESIGN, THEN REALIGN

"None of this will work unless the people on the frontline want it to. We spend a lot of time and energy collaborating with the people delivering the service, ensuring they get the chance to supply feedback on anything we design—that they have had a chance to design. Our success is largely due to those people becoming champions within their organizations; they take it and run with it."

—B.I.T., *4 Simple Ways to Apply Behavioural Insights.* [347]

Frontline folks matter. They're your champions. Listen to them. Design with them. They'll run with it.

Takeaways. Frontline staff are crucial change agents; Collaboration fosters ownership; Let them design, they will drive.

Fundamental Concepts. Frontline folks. That's Grassroots Activation. They matter. That's Bottom-Up Approach. Listen. That's Social Proof. Champions. That's Agency Theory. Design with them. That's Participatory Design. Run with it. That's Intrinsic Motivation. Crucial agents. That's Social Capital. Fosters ownership. That's Psychological Ownership. They will drive. That's Self-Determination. Collaboration key. That's Reciprocity. Change ignites. That's Cognitive Activation Theory. [348]

Bottom Line. To achieve success, involve and empower frontline staff in the design process. They become champions and drivers of change within their organizations.

September 5th

VALUES VOICED BY FEW, ECHO IN MANY

"Reference groups are mirrors in which we see ourselves. They shape our norms, values, and attitudes. In life's vast social arena, we choose which mirrors to gaze into. Through them, we find our place and direction."

—PRAGATI KALIVE, *Reference Groups.* [349]

Reference groups shape us. They shape how we think and act. In change management, these groups are vital. They're the change agents. They set the tone. People look to them. Make sure your change agents champion the right values.

Takeaways. Champions are reference groups; They set norms and values; Choose them wisely.

Fundamental Concepts. Reference groups. That's Social Comparison Theory. [350] Change agents vital. That's Change Catalysts. They set norms. That's Normative Influence. Choose wisely. That's Agent Selection. Key points clear. That's Conceptual Distillation. Aphorisms hit home. That's Mnemonic Utility. Change agents guide. That's Behavioral Modeling. They set values. That's Value Anchoring. Bad choice risks all. That's Normative Disruption. [351] Good choice wins hearts. That's Effective Socialization. Get it right. That's Successful Change Management.

Bottom Line. Create and choose reference groups wisely—they guide values and drive change.

September 6th

MINDSET MOLDS THE MISSION. INTRAPRENEURS GUIDE IT

"Intrapreneurs are the most valuable employees working inside an organization, as they develop initiatives and teams. The intrapreneur needs to develop a mindset as well as skills and competencies that are very similar to those of an entrepreneur. The intrapreneur mindset comprises inner state, beliefs, attitude, and thinking processes, and it defines outcomes. Teaching employees to become mindful intrapreneurs is the way to future-proof an organization."

—MICKEY A FEHER, *The Intrapreneur Mindset.* [352]

Intrapreneurs drive change. They're inside heroes. They think like entrepreneurs. Mindset matters here. Teach your team to think this way. Future-proof your business.

Takeaways. Intrapreneurs are change agents; Mindset fuels action; Train your team to be intrapreneurs.

Fundamental Concepts. Intrapreneurs vital. That's Internal Change Agents. Mindset matters. That's Cognitive Priming. Future-proofing noted. That's Organizational Resilience. Training key. That's Skill Acquisition. Takeaways crystallize. That's Conceptual Distillation. Aphorisms stick. That's Mnemonic Utility. Intrapreneurs act. That's Proactive Behavior. Mindset steers. That's Cognitive Determinants. Team training vital. That's Skill Dissemination. Bright future ahead. That's Successful Transformation.

Bottom Line. Train employees with an entrepreneurial mindset to become intrapreneurs for future success.

September 7th

PEER POWER SPEEDS UP CHANGE

"Change agents are the sparks in your organization. They make change happen. They get people on board. Whether they're employees or consultants, they're trusted. They make you re-think your old ways. They remove barriers. They spread ideas fast among peers. Most importantly, they make change stick. Their influence grows, shaping the change curve. They're the human factor that makes change real."

—CHANGE366.[353]

Change agents drive progress. They make you see the flaws. They bring new plans. They're usually peers. They know how to beat resistance. They create a new norm. They're the reason change works. Tap into their potential. They are your hidden asset. Give them the tools. Let them lead.

Takeaways. Change agents identify and remove roadblocks; They serve as role models and champions; They spread change through peer influence; They turn resistance into buy-in.

Fundamental Concepts. Agents vital. That's Social Proof. Peer sway. That's Reciprocity. Mindset shift. That's Cognitive Dissonance. Flaw finders. That's Problem-Solving Skill. Aphorisms stick. That's Mnemonic Utility. Change happens. That's Successful Transformation.

Bottom Line. Empower change agents to lead, overcome obstacles, and establish new practices for lasting organizational change.

September 8th

DRIVE CHANGE, DON'T JUST RIDE IT

"Champion 'Job Description.' You're the Change Agent. You're the boots on the ground. Your role is big. You're the voice for the end-users. You bring the news fast. You drive change. You find ways to do better business. You're the model. You're the guide. You show how it's done. Your circle of influence? Expanding. People look up to you. You make new ways of working stick. You manage resistance. You get people talking, learning, adapting. In short, you're the spark that ignites the fire of change."

—CHANGE366. [354]

You're the champion. You're not just a cog in the wheel. You're the wheel itself. You voice what end-users feel. You're quick. You tell it like it is. You build enthusiasm. You drive change. Your role is more than a title; it's action. Your circle of influence grows each day. When you talk, people listen. When you lead, people follow.

Takeaways. Voice for end-users, fast in spreading key messages; Builds enthusiasm and drives adoption of new ways; Manages resistance and nurtures a circle of influence; Coaches and mentors, provides peer-to-peer support.

Fundamental Concepts. Champions are action figures. That's Agency. They own the process. That's Internal Locus of Control. They voice user needs. That's Empathy. They're the go-to people. That's Social Capital. They drive adoption. That's Diffusion of Innovations. They manage resistance. That's Cognitive Reappraisal. Change agents mentor. That's Social Learning Theory. They build circles. That's Community of Practice. They listen. That's Active Listening. A mix of psychology makes them tick. They're the grease in the change machine.

Bottom Line. Champions lead, coach, and drive new methods. They are the user's voice, battling resistance, spreading influence, and making change stick.

September 9th

NEW HABITS ARE SEEDS FOR GROWTH

"'Behavioral cusps' are keystones of transformation; they unlock cascades of change, reshaping both individual roles and organizational landscapes."

—Jesús Rosales-Ruiz, *Behavioral Cusps.* [355]

In organizational change management, a behavioral cusp is like a gate to new grounds. It's a pivotal shift. When one person or group in an organization changes a core behavior, it can alter their interactions. This shift can lead to a domino effect of changes across the organization. Embracing digital tools can be a behavioral cusp. [356] It can open doors to efficiency and new ways of working. Employees' new behaviors can prompt the company to evolve. This process isn't just about the first change. It's about the chain of changes that follow.

Takeaways. A behavioral cusp is a critical shift in actions that triggers wider change; This can initiate a cascade of developments in an organization; Adopting new behaviors can encourage an organization to adapt and grow; The ongoing impact of a cusp can redefine an organization's future.

Fundamental Concepts. Behavior shifts spark change. That's a Behavioral Cusp. One act meets new outcomes. That's Contingency Contact. The domino effect begins. That's Change Cascade. Old habits fade. That's Behavior Competition. New practices stick. That's Social Reinforcement.

Bottom Line. Champions trigger pivotal shifts, called behavioral cusps, driving cascades of change and organizational evolution through new, efficient practices.

September 10th

GUIDE CHANGE, GUARD GOALS

"Even the most motivated and intelligent student will advance more quickly under the tutelage of someone who knows the best order in which to learn things, who understands and can demonstrate the proper way to perform various skills, who can provide useful feedback, and who can devise practice activities designed to overcome particular weaknesses."

—K. ANDERS ERICSSON, *Peak Secrets from the New Science of Expertise.* [357]

Champions guide learning in change, teaching essential skills and providing feedback for improvement. They design effective practice and tap into expert knowledge for quicker success. This approach is vital for change, making learning faster and more effective, a key strategy in change management.

Takeaways. Champions must identify the learning sequence for change initiatives; Effective feedback is crucial for improvement; Practice activities should target specific organizational weaknesses; A knowledgeable guide boosts progress and reduces errors.

Fundamental Concepts. Change agents guide growth. That's Educational Structuring. They pick the training pace. That's Skill Sequencing. Mentors over manuals. That's Learning Hierarchy. Feedback forms futures. That's Correctional Insights. Practice aimed at weak spots. That's Deficit Targeting. Teaching makes the master. That's Didactic Exchange. [358] Flaws fixed through focus. That's Error Refinement. Leadership clears learning paths. That's Directive Development. Knowledge transfer trumps trial and error. That's Expedited Expertise.

Bottom Line. Champions accelerate learning and change by coaching effectively, offering targeted feedback, and addressing weaknesses, which speeds up improvement and guides organizational growth.

September 11th

EMPOWER CHAMPIONS TO TURN VISION INTO REALITY

"People must have ownership in the vision. They need to be enabled to accomplish it. If there is one investment you should make, it is in people."

—MODESTA LILIAN MBUGHUNI. [359]

Change starts with a shared vision. People support what they help create. Enable them with tools and trust. Investing in people pays off. Teach them the 'why' before 'how.' Use champions. Make everyone a stakeholder. When people own the vision, they'll work to make it real.

Takeaways. Shared vision drives united action; Empower champions to turn vision into reality; Invest in champions, reap change's reward; Ownership in vision equals excellence in execution; Teach 'why,' they'll show 'how.'

Fundamental Concepts. Vision shared. That's Collective Ownership. Empowerment needed. That's Capability Building. People invest. That's Resource Allocation. Enable action. That's Facilitation Excellence. Ownership sparks effort. That's Autonomy Support. Trust leads to action. That's Competence Assurance. Teach purpose. That's Intrinsic Motivation. People grow. Change flourishes. That's Organizational Transformation. Everyone's a stakeholder. That's Community Culture. Vision becomes reality. That's Shared Success.

Bottom Line. Empower champions with ownership and understanding to transform vision into reality, fostering a culture where teaching 'why' ignites 'how,' and investing in people sparks organizational change.

September 12th

CHAMPIONS—STRATEGY INTO ACTION

"Champions transform vision into victory, their advocacy and adaptability fueling organizational evolution and excellence."

—CHANGE366.[360]

Champions connect strategy to action, identifying inefficiencies, leading in training, sharing knowledge, and building trust through beta testing. They foster a positive culture, adapt to challenges, and reduce costs while streamlining workflows for change and success.

Takeaways. Champions connect strategy and team insights; Training leaders, and champions fill knowledge gaps; Champions refine products, ensuring trust; Drive collaboration, tackle challenges; Streamline operations, align with goals.

Fundamental Concepts. Champions have a crucial role: Organizational Advocacy. They represent teams, bridging gaps—that's Communication Mastery. Identifying inefficiencies and relaying feedback shows their Perceptual Acuity. Their strength lies in training, filling knowledge gaps, that's Pedagogical Expertise. Committed to continuous learning, they embody Growth Mindset. In the realm of beta testing, they exhibit Detail Orientation. Fostering a positive workplace, culture, is their craft, that's Cultural Shaping. They're adaptable and creative when facing challenges, with Problem-Solving Agility. Operating in the realm of cost reduction and efficiency highlights their Operational Excellence. Champions are more than mere participants; they're catalysts for change.

Bottom Line. Champions are key in organizational change. They effectively communicate, bridge training gaps, and refine processes. Their adaptability fosters a positive culture, drives efficiency, and reduces costs. They are indispensable for sustainable change and success.

September 13th

TO LEAD CHANGE WELL, MAP THE HABITUS WELL

"Champions master habitus to turn turbulence into transformation."

—CHANGE366. [361]

Champions are like navigators using the habitus map. [362] This map comes from our history and steers current decisions. In businesses, habitus informs how change champions lead adaptations. It's their strategy playbook. When a new directive hits, these navigators use the crew's collective habitus for guidance. They adapt tried tactics to novel scenarios. Recognizing the crew's habitus, change champions craft paths that resonate and guide through new territory. They draw on what's familiar to chart courses through change.

Takeaways. Champions rely on habitus for guiding organizational change; A team's history informs its response to new challenges; They use familiar strategies to introduce new processes; Recognizing and utilizing habitus is crucial for effective change leadership.

Fundamental Concepts. Champions read habitus. That's Navigation Insight. History informs strategy. That's Tactical Grounding. Habitus eases transitions. That's Smooth Sailing. Champions lead with wisdom. That's Informed Leadership. They translate old tactics to new challenges. That's Strategic Bridging. Change champions map routes. That's Direction Drafting. They connect dots, crafting relevance. That's Association Making. A new challenge comes; Champions recall past wins. That's Experience Leveraging. Agents using habitus thrive in change. That's Leadership Adapting.

Bottom Line. Champions use habitus as a strategy map, guiding teams with tried tactics through change, turning past behaviors into new success paths.

September 14th

GOOD CHAMPIONS MOLD DECISIONS WITH INFORMATION

"Champions are the architects of organizational energy, turning individual efforts into collective performance."

—CHANGE366. [363]

Champions fuse a group into a team with purpose. Each day, they bridge gaps between skills and tasks. They see an organization not just as roles but as a dynamic flow of information and decisions. Understanding who does what, they motivate and guide others to embrace change, using structure and culture. They listen to the agents, molding the flow of authority and information. Their role is to sync tasks, people, and motivations towards a common goal.

Takeaways. Champions turn groups into cohesive teams; They match skills to tasks for organizational efficiency; They influence the flow of information and decision-making; They align individual motivations with the company's goals.

Fundamental Concepts. Champions agents harness the team's psyche. That's Role Empowerment. They link tasks and skills. That's Functional Congruence. [364] A seamless flow of decisions marks their strategy. That's Information Integration. Change agents balance tasks, info, and power. That's Structural Alignment. They turn individual drive into collective force. That's Motivational Fusion. This aligns with Self-Determination Theory, showing agents drive Intrinsic Motivation when tasks match skills and Autonomy is respected. Sociocultural Dynamics reflect how change agents tap into norms, pushing the culture to evolve. Their insights into the social architecture reveal the fabric of human interactions within organizations.

Bottom Line. Champions shape teams by linking skills, tasks, and information to motivate and steer collective goals, blending structure with cultural dynamics for optimal performance.

September 15th

DO, DON'T TELL, TO TEACH THE DIGITAL CHANGE WELL

"We learn by example and by direct experience because there are real limits to the adequacy of verbal instruction."

—MALCOLM GLADWELL, *Blink*. [365]

Learning in organizations is more than absorbing facts. It's about doing. When champions lead by example, they make lessons tangible. People follow deeds, not just words. In digital transformation, actions speak the language of possibility. Champions who demonstrate new systems in action don't just tell staff about the new era—they show it. They become the map and the territory in the journey of change. They embody the transition they champion, making each step in the digital domain real and achievable.

Takeaways. Champions teach through action, not just words; Demonstrations make digital transformation tangible; Effective leadership shows the way in change; Real experience trumps verbal instruction in learning new tech.

Fundamental Concepts. Change thrives on action. That's Experiential Learning. [366] Verbal instruction falls short. That's the Limit of Language. Champions embody transition. That's Personal Demonstration. People mimic what works. That's Observational Learning. Engagement over instruction. That's Active Participation. Culture absorbs by doing. That's Cultural Internalization. Change spreads through example. That's Behavioral Emulation. Real-world use validates tech. That's Practical Confirmation. Change agents direct by doing, guiding the digital leap. That's Leadership by Example.

Bottom Line. Champions champion digital change by example, demonstrating use over verbal instruction, thus clarifying and embodying each step for others.

September 16th

TRUE NORTH LIES IN LIKELIHOOD

"When it is not in our power to follow what is true, we ought to follow what is most probable."

—RENÉ DESCARTES, *Discourse on the Method.* [367]

In change management, certainty is a luxury. Often, the true course is unclear. We must navigate uncertainty. Decisions hinge on probability. This approach is practical. We assess what's likely. Then act. This mindset is crucial for change managers. It embraces flexibility. Adapts to probable outcomes. In a shifting landscape, this adaptability is key. It guides teams through unknowns. Leads to informed decisions. Focusing on probability, we steer organizations effectively through change.

Takeaways. Change management thrives on navigating uncertainty; Decisions based on probability, not just certainty; Flexibility and adaptability guide through unknowns; Probable outcomes shape informed decision-making.

Fundamental Concepts. Uncertainty looms. That's Ambiguity Tolerance. True path unknown is Uncertainty Navigation. We turn to probability using Rational Approximation. Flexible thinking rules. That's Cognitive Adaptability. Decision-making shifts? Probabilistic Reasoning. [368] Teams face unknowns. That's Situational Awareness. Informed decisions emerge? Deliberative Processing. When Change management thrives, that's Adaptive Leadership. When Probability becomes our compass, that's Strategic Foresight.

Bottom Line. When certainty is scarce, wisdom lies in following probability. This approach sustains change, guiding actions towards the most likely positive outcomes. It's about making informed decisions amidst uncertainty, leading to effective and adaptable change management.

September 17th

BELIEVE SMALL, STAY SMALL—LEARN MORE. BE MORE

"How dangerous is the acquirement of knowledge and how much happier that man is who believes his native town to be the world, than he who aspires to be greater than his nature will allow."

—MARY SHELLY. [369]

Seeking knowledge is risky but staying ignorant is riskier. The one who never steps out of his comfort zone believes they are happy. But true growth comes from challenging what we know. This is true for people as it is for organizations. To change, to improve, we must learn. And learning means changing. Change champions must help organizations learn without fear.

Takeaways. Knowledge is risky but stagnation is riskier; Comfort zones are barriers to organizational growth; Learning is the core of organizational change.

Fundamental Concepts. Risk begets growth. That's Change's Essence. Knowledge tempts, comfort's a trap. That's Stasis's Snare. Managers must herald the new. That's their True North. Teach and break barriers. That's the Education Imperative. Learning or resting, choices cast. That's Decision Dichotomy. [370] Knowledge expands, so does potential. That's Expansion's Principle. Embrace growth; leave the town's limits. That's Aspiration's Anthem.

Bottom Line. Champions lead organizations past the fear of new knowledge, from safe ignorance to growth and learning, urging a break from comfort for true advancement.

September 18th

CHAMPIONS BLEND TECH GAINS WITH HUMAN AIMS

"Champions of change harness technology to fortify stakeholder networks, making decisions with a compass that points toward shared success and sustainable progress."

—CHANGE366. [371]

Champions play a crucial role in digital transformation by understanding and managing the intricate web of stakeholder relationships. They act as champions of change, navigating complex connections with an inclusive vision for all parties involved. As they introduce new technology, they ensure it serves broader goals beyond just profit, enriching social and environmental systems.

Takeaways. Champions align technology with diverse stakeholder values; They navigate complex networks, leading with inclusivity; Change champions prioritize long-term value over short-term gains; They recognize indirect impacts and strategize accordingly.

Fundamental Concepts. Champions drive the network. That's Change Catalyst. Agents know the field. That's Strategic Foresight. A broad view adopted. That's Inclusive Planning. Agents balance the scales. That's Equity in Tech. Networks guided by agents. That's Directed Connectivity. Indirect influence considered. That's Holistic Oversight. The ecosystem thrives by design. That's Environmental Harmony. Agents craft change for all. That's Shared Prosperity.

Bottom Line. Change champions link technology with stakeholder interests for lasting benefits. They lead inclusively, focusing on sustainability and societal impact, guiding progress for collective good.

September 19th

BE THE SPARK THAT LIGHTS THE TEAM'S FIRE

"The most important thing about being a change champion is that you have to be willing to change yourself."

—LOUIS V GERSTNER, *Who Say's Elephants Can't Dance?* [372]

Change starts with you. If you lead a team, start by setting an example. Be the first to adopt new ideas and practices. Show enthusiasm for learning and growth. When you change, others will follow. Your behavior sets the standard for your team's culture and openness to new technology and processes.

Takeaways. Lead by example in adopting change; Your enthusiasm can inspire your team; Personal growth encourages team evolution; Championing change begins within.

Fundamental Concepts. Change starts within. That's Self-Transformation. An example becomes a guide. That's Behavioral Modeling. Learning lights up change. That's Cognitive Engagement. Growth inside spreads wide. That's Cultural Adaptation. Personal shift shapes teams. That's Social Influence. The champion's zeal infects. That's Emotional Contagion. [373] Self-evolution fosters group progress. That's Intrinsic Motivation. Lead, learn, lift, link. That's Integrated Change.

Bottom Line. Embrace change to champion it. Your team watches and follows your lead. Your actions shape their response. Leading change is the key to success in business. Be open, be ready, and be the catalyst for your team's breakthrough.

September 20th

TOMORROW'S WORLD, TODAY'S WORK

"Change champions are the people who can see the future and make it happen."

—SETH GODIN, *Purple Cow.* [374]

Champions of change lead the charge. They envision what's ahead and pave the way. These leaders don't just talk; they act and build the future today. By seeing the potential, they muster the courage and the resources to realize it. They bring the future to life by making changes in the present.

Takeaways. Envision the future to lead change; Act boldly to make visions real; Mobilize courage and resources; Build the future by changing now.

Fundamental Concepts. Champions envision futures. That's Foresight. They commit to action. That's Agency. With courage, they push norms. That's Boundary Spanning. By acting, they lead change. That's Initiative Taking. Resources rally behind them. That's Mobilization. They actualize potential. That's Self-Actualization. Visions to reality, that's the essence of Change Implementation.

Bottom Line. Champions envision and enact the future. They lead by doing, turning today's actions into tomorrow's gains. Vision, action, and courage are their tools. They inspire transformation and make progress tangible.

September 21st

COALITION IS THE BACKBONE OF CHANGE

"Change champions are the ones who can build a coalition of support for the change."

—ROSABETH MOSS KANTER, *Thinking Outside the Building.* [375]

Change champions don't go it alone; they gather a team. They know that support is key to making change stick. These leaders connect with others, sharing their vision and gathering backers. They unite different people under a common goal to power through change.

Takeaways. Gather supporters for strength. Share vision to create unity. Connect diverse individuals. Unite all behind a common goal.

Fundamental Concepts. Champions gather allies. That's Coalition Building. They spread visions. That's Persuasion. Different minds, one goal. That's Unity. Diversity becomes strength. That's Social Synergy. Shared purpose rallies action. That's Common Identity. From this unity, change emerges. That's Collective Efficacy.

Bottom Line. Change champions create a team for support. They know unity drives change. By sharing their vision, they build a strong coalition, ensuring that lasting change.

September 22nd

TOMORROW'S BETTER, IF YOU DARE CHANGE TODAY

"What I like most about change is that it's a synonym for 'hope'. If you are taking a risk, what you are really saying is, "I believe in tomorrow and I will be part of it.""

—LINDA ELLERBEE, *And So It Goes.* [376]

Change is about hope. Championing change shows belief in a better future. To embrace change, believe in what comes next. Hope drives action. Risk takers shape the future by acting today.

Takeaways. Change means hope for better things; Risks reflect belief in the future; Belief in tomorrow fuels today's actions; Hope and action lead to change.

Fundamental Concepts. Hope sparks change. That's Optimism Bias. Risk shows belief. That's Behavioral Commitment. Believing in tomorrow guides today. That's Future Orientation. Hope's whisper becomes today's shout. That's Motivational Enhancement. Risk today, hope tomorrow. That's Prospective Cognition. [377]

Bottom Line. Change champions hold onto hope and take risks to secure a better tomorrow. They inspire actions that turn hope into reality, proving their belief through action.

September 23rd

WIN OR LOSE, CHAMPIONS PUSH THROUGH

"In change, the brave lead, the resilient succeed, and the courageous persist."

—CHANGE366.[378]

Champions in an organization are the torchbearers of change. They know success today doesn't guarantee success tomorrow. They understand that failures are setbacks, not endgames. Their real power lies in the courage to press on when the path gets tough. They rally teams, inspire perseverance, and transform failures into stepping-stones. Champions recognize that the true test of their leadership is not in celebrating wins but in facing losses with the will to forge ahead.

Takeaways. Champions view success as a journey, not a destination; They see failure as a chance to learn, not a reason to quit; Courage for champions means pushing forward, especially in tough times; Champions create lasting impacts by staying resilient and persistent.

Fundamental Concepts. Change shakes the stable ground. That's Disruption Discomfort. Fear grips tight, courage takes flight. That's Emotional Response. Champions stand tall, through it all. That's Resilience Realized. They steer through fear, making it clear. That's Courage in Action. Discomfort sparks growth, in them both. That's Transformation's Truth. Overcoming dread, they move ahead. That's Adversity's Advantage. Their courage is infectious, their strategy complex but dexterous. They're the engine of change. Resilience their range. That's the spirit of Organizational Stamina.

Bottom Line. Champions embrace all results as part of their journey. They learn from setbacks and use them to grow. Leading with courage, they inspire their teams to persist. Their resilience creates a lasting impact.

September 24th

CHANGE, NOT STATIC—CHAMPIONS KNOW THIS

"Champions foster growth by living change, not just leading it."

—CHANGE366. [379]

Change is growth. Aim for progress, not perfection. Being a change champion means guiding and teaching. It also means showing the way by doing. Champions lead change by example, train others, and keep learning. Their role is crucial. They talk, teach, solve problems, and connect people. They turn strategy into action. This is what makes change happen.

Takeaways. Accept that change is inevitable and essential for growth; Recognize that perfection is a moving target, not a static goal; Embrace change frequently to move closer to organizational goals; Understand that continuous improvement requires adaptability.

Fundamental Concepts. Tech sits idle. That's a sign of Resistance to Change. Users stick to old ways. That's Behavioral Inertia. Leaders can spark action. That's Role Modeling. Show change's worth. That's Valence Theory. [380] Share the vision, guide the tech. That's Informative Influence. When champions train, skills grow. That's Competence Support. By living the change, champions lead. That's Exemplification. Feedback steers the course. That's Positive Reinforcement. Together, we shape progress. That's the essence of Social Facilitation.

Bottom Line. Change champions understand, strategize, train, communicate, solve problems, and lead by example. They play a key role in evolving company culture for ongoing change.

September 25th

CHAMPIONS MAKE THE PLAN STAND

"Champions energize change, making strategy and vision work in harmony."

—CHANGE366. [381]

To lead is to chart the path; To build is to walk it. While leaders design and guide change, the success of change rests with the people who implement it. In the context of organizational change management, champions are those who embody the bridge between leadership's vision and the workforce's action.

Takeaways. Leaders set the direction for change; People on the ground bring change to life; Success in change requires cooperation between the two; Champions facilitate this cooperative success.

Fundamental Concepts. Tech sits unused. That's Change Resistance. Innovations gather dust. A mindset stuck. Change is offered. Few take the lead. That's Champion Absence. Some resist. That's Fear at play. Others follow. That's Social Proof needed. A leader steps up. That's Role Modeling. Social change begins. That's Group Dynamics shifting. Recognition fuels effort. That's Operant Conditioning. Behavior shifts slowly. That's Habit Formation. Persistence is key. That's Grit in action.

Bottom Line. Champions drive change by grasping it, strategizing, training, communicating, problem-solving, and leading by example. Their role is crucial in evolving the culture for lasting change.

September 26th

CHANGE SHAPES CHAMPIONS, CHAMPIONS SHAPE SUCCESS

"Champions mold to change, shape success, and inspire progress."

—CHANGE366. [382]

Change is constant. Like water, it can be a force of destruction or growth. Champions in an organization are those who embrace the flow of change, directing it to create something better. They understand the nature of change and, instead of resisting, become its shape-shifter, guiding it to fulfill the organization's vision.

Takeaways. Champions view change as an opportunity, not a threat; They lead by example, inspiring others to follow; Adaptability is their strength, guiding change positively; Champions use change to innovate and grow.

Fundamental Concepts. Champions own the change. That's Champion Autonomy. They spread their zeal. That's Champion Influence. Adaptability becomes their craft. That's Champion Mastery. They turn tides in minds. That's Champion Persuasion. Culture shifts, champions steer. That's Champion Guidance. A champion shapes beliefs and actions. Confidence blooms. Commitment follows. That's Champion Inspiration. Identify the goal. Ignite the passion. Chart the course. Change is won.

Bottom Line. Champions are the heart of change. They see change as a chance. They inspire, adapt, and guide growth. Short, clear messages from leaders make change stick.

September 27th

POWERING PEOPLE POWERS CHANGE

"True leadership means unlocking doors for others' energy to change the world."

—CHANGE366. [383]

Technology change is about unlocking potential and directing energy towards innovation and progress. True leaders recognize that the key to successful digital transformation lies in empowering their teams. They provide champions, tools and opportunities for individuals to contribute meaningfully to change.

Takeaways. Empower teams with the right champions and tools for change; Direct collective energy towards innovation; Facilitate a culture of continuous improvement and learning; Recognize and harness the potential within their organization.

Fundamental Concepts. Tech transformation calls for leaders. That's Leadership Drive. Empowerment turns potential into progress. That's Competence Support. Culture of improvement, a learning must. That's Growth Mindset. Potential within, waiting to unleash. That's Intrinsic Motivation. Leaders are key, they unlock tech change. That's Autonomy Support. Innovation's not lone; teams build it. That's Relatedness in Action. Continuous learning is fuel for change. That's Mastery Orientation. Harnessing potential requires vision. That's Foresight in Leadership. Progress through people, not just tools. That's Human-Centric Technology.

Bottom Line. In tech change, leaders unlock team potential, building a culture focused on progress. They guide and empower for successful digital shifts, creating an environment where innovation and learning drive advancement.

September 28th

CHAMPIONS LEAD CHANGE BY LIVING IT FIRST

"Leaders who embrace change and foster autonomy, competence, and relatedness propel organizations forward."

—CHANGE366. [384]

Champions are leaders who embrace change themselves first. They understand that their role is not just to direct but to empower others. They foster an environment where autonomy and competence are encouraged. Champions make sure that every team member feels connected to the change process. They promote a sense of relatedness and unity.

Takeaways. Lead change by embodying it; Empower teams for nimble adaptation; Skill growth secures change; Team bonds cement change success; Champions are change incarnate.

Fundamental Concepts. Champions are change leaders. They steer change. That's Behavioral Catalyst. Autonomy boosts growth. That's Self-Determination. Skills up, fears down. That's Competence Assurance. Unity in change is strength. That's Relatedness Emphasis. Leading by doing, change's proof. That's Exemplary Conduct. Empathy drives champions. That's Emotional Synchrony. [385] Vision casts futures. That's Aspirational Leadership. Trust in teams, change's backbone. That's Trust Cultivation. Learning by leading, leaders' path. That's Developmental Leadership. Change champions, progress personified. That's Embodied Transformation.

Bottom Line. Change champions are leaders who not only advocate for change but embody it. They empower their teams, enhance skills, and unify the group, driving growth and innovation in the organization.

September 29th

DARE TO ACT, PAVE THE IMPACT

> "Life can be frustrating. Oftentimes we know what our problems are. We may even know what to do about them. But we fear taking action is too risky, that we don't have the experience, or that it's not how we pictured it, or because it's too expensive, because its too soon, because we think something better might come along, because it might not work. And you know what happens as a result of it? Nothing. We do nothing."
>
> —RYAN HOLIDAY, *The Obstacle is the Way.* [386]

A common dilemma in change management? Inaction—due to fear and uncertainty. Champions must confront these fears to ignite action. Champions must advocate for change. They must also embody the courage to act despite risks, uncertainties, and the allure of comfort. Champions become the catalysts that transform hesitation into momentum.

Takeaways. Address fears and uncertainties to catalyze action; Champions advocate and act, setting change in motion; Courage over comfort propels organizational transformation.

Fundamental Concepts. Challenges are certain. That's life's guarantee. Recognize troubles? That's Problem Perception. Fear acting? That's Risk Sensitivity. Doubt abilities? That's Skill Self-Doubt. Vision not met? That's Ideal Gap. [387] Worrying costs? That's Financial Fear. Holding out hope? That's Better Bias. Scared to fail? That's Failure Fear. Inaction follows fear. That's Stasis Syndrome. Break through fear. Activate Willpower. Affirm Self-Value. Spark Movement. Watch change rise.

Bottom Line. Fear stalls change but action drives it. Recognize problems, then dare to move past doubts and costs. Bold steps crush inertia and spark progress. Keep adapting, keep succeeding.

September 30th

UNDERSTANDING QUELLS CHANGE FEARS

"Champions who master the art of understanding transform fear into action, shaping change with clarity and shared vision."

—CHANGE366. [388]

When managing change, understanding is key. It's like a dance where emotions lead, and positivity is the music. Fear, on the other hand, is like a misstep in rhythm, causing hesitation and retreat. Champions must act as the bridge over fear, building trust and involving their peers. They must craft the perception of change carefully, revealing it in layers to foster acceptance and participation.

Takeaways. Understanding and positivity lead successful change; Fear is an obstacle to change that leaders must address; Leaders build trust to involve teams in change; Perception shapes the acceptance of change.

Fundamental Concepts. Understanding leads. That's Cognitive Mastery. Positivity drives change. That's Emotional Engagement. Fear hinders action. That's Threat Avoidance. Leaders build trust. That's Relational Coordination. Involvement cements commitment. That's Participative Efficacy. Perception shapes reality. That's Constructive Subjectivism. [389] Unveiling matters. That's Progressive Disclosure. Trust overcomes fear. That's Confidence Building. Change mastered internally. That's Internalization. Champions shape change's feel. That's Directive Influence.

Bottom Line. Champions guide progress by transforming fear through understanding and shaping team perspectives. Effective presentation is key. They reveal change gradually, building support and overcoming doubts, ensuring lasting impact.

Communication is the lifeblood of change. As Kotter points out, clarity in conveying the vision is critical—it must be succinct and compelling to garner interest and understanding. The Culture Group echoes this, stressing the importance of honesty over appeasement. Speaking truthfully paves a clear path for change, ensuring that every message resonates with its intended audience.

Powell's wisdom—that effective communication requires effort—is a call to arms during organizational change. Crafting messages that resonate requires a deep understanding of the 'six honest serving men' that Kipling refers to: What, Why, When, How, Where, and Who. They guide the narrative of change, ensuring that the message is not just heard but also understood and embraced.

Change366 illustrates the disconnect that can occur when communication lacks relevance. Like the nurse who disregards the CIO's email, staff will ignore messages that do not resonate with their daily challenges or seem irrelevant to their roles. Therefore, communicating change requires contextualization—making the relevance of new tools evident to those who will use them.

Leslie Claret's jargon-filled monologue from 'Patriot' humorously illustrates the need for simplicity in communication. Complexity confuses, and simplicity clarifies. Kahneman reminds us that media has the power to shape thoughts and should be used wisely to mold messages that align with the interests and influence of the audience.

Change366 also notes that good surprises in communication can be beneficial, while bad surprises can be detrimental. Therefore, it's crucial for change communicators to anticipate reactions and manage expectations effectively.

The role of metaphors in communication, as Barrett notes, is instrumental. They are powerful tools that can help people understand and relate to change more profoundly. Shaw's quote about the illusion of communication serves as a warning to double-check and ensure that the intended message has been properly received and understood.

As the communication lead, described by Change366, the responsibility to craft, deliver, and recalibrate messages falls squarely on your shoulders. It's about making an impact with every word and ensuring those words turn into actions and results.

Santayanna's metaphor of masks and words reminds us that communication in change management is about revealing, not concealing. Pullim's insights on language shaping our understanding of the world underscore the power of words to frame our perceptions of change.

Change communication is clear, honest, and relevant, ensuring stakeholders connect with the message. It adapts to feedback and evolving needs, shaping the future through careful and precise use, a collective responsibility.

October 1st

CLEAR WORDS, CLEAR WINS

"If you can't communicate the vision to someone in five minutes or less and get a reaction that signifies both understanding and interest, you are not done."

—JOHN KOTTER. [390]

Talk short. Make it clear. Spark interest. You'll win hearts. The clock ticks. Use it well. If not, back to the drawing board.

Takeaways. Quick, clear talk wins; A ticking clock guides your pitch; Interest shows success.

Fundamental Concepts. Talk short. That's Information Efficiency. Clear talk. That's Message Clarity. Spark interest. That's Emotional Engagement. Quick talk wins. That's Temporal Value. Interest shows. That's Social Validation. Five minutes. That's Time Constraint. Message clarity. That's Cognitive Load. [391] Clock guides. That's Scarcity Principle. Understanding wins. That's Schema Activation. [392] Interest keys success. That's Affective Commitment. Clock ticks. That's Time Pressure. Back to drawing board. That's Feedback Loop.

Bottom Line. Explain change clearly and quickly to generate interest and support. If it takes more than five minutes without engagement, revise it. Keep communication brief and to the point.

October 2nd

CLEAR TRUTH, CLEAR PATH

"Don't tell people what you think they want to hear. Tell them the TRUTH."

—THE CULTURE GROUP. [393]

Honesty rules. It builds trust. Say the truth. People respect that. No sugarcoating. Cut through the fluff. Be real, be clear.

Takeaways. Honesty builds trust; People respect truth; Cut the fluff.

Fundamental Concepts. Honesty rules. That's Ethical Transparency. Builds trust. That's Social Contract. [394] Say truth. That's Authentic Communication. People respect. That's Reciprocal Trust. No sugarcoating. That's Cognitive Clarity. Cut fluff. That's Informational Brevity. Be real. That's Authentic Leadership. Be clear. That's Effective Communication.

Bottom Line. Be honest and build trust. Speak the truth. People respect it. No need for sugarcoating. Keep it clear and real to support change.

October 3rd

WORDS WELL-WORKED, WISDOM SHARED

"Communication works for those who work at it."

—JOHN POWELL. [395]

Communication isn't magic. It needs effort. Work on it daily. Make it clear. Make it honest. Be direct. People will listen.

Takeaways. Effort enhances communication; Clarity is key; Honesty matters.

Fundamental Concepts. Effort rules. That's Goal-Directed Behavior. Clarity matters. That's Effective Communication. Honesty is vital. That's Ethical Transparency. People listen. That's Active Reception. Work daily. That's Habit Formation. Make it clear. That's Cognitive Simplicity. Make it honest. That's Emotional Honesty. Be direct. That's Assertive Communication. Listen up. That's Social Influence. Keep talking. That's Sustained Engagement.

Bottom Line. Communication isn't magic; it requires daily effort. Be clear, be honest, and be direct. This drives engagement and action, leading to meaningful change.

October 4th

5W+H SETS THE STAGE

"I keep six honest serving men (they taught me all I knew); Their names are What and Why and When and How and Where and Who."

—Rudyard Kipling, *Just So Stories.* [396]

Answering questions guides communications. What. Why. When. How. Where. Who. Ask them. You'll communicate, You'll learn. You'll change. You'll lead.

Takeaways. Questions drive learning; The 5W's+H matter. [397] Good leaders ask first.

Fundamental Concepts. Questions lead. That's Information Seeking. What matters. That's Specific Inquiry. Why important. That's Motive Clarity. When crucial. That's Temporal Understanding. How vital. That's Methodological Analysis. 'Where' is key. That's Spatial Awareness. Who's core. That's Social Identification. Learning happens. That's Cognitive Acquisition. Change occurs. That's Behavioral Adaptation. Lead well. That's Effective Leadership. Ask more. That's Intellectual Curiosity.

Bottom Line. Effective change leadership is all about asking and answering: what, why, when, how, where, and who. Clear and curious inquiry leads to learning, adapting, and effectively guiding change.

October 5th

TECH WITHOUT CONTEXT? IGNORED

> "True story: An Operating Room nurse gets an email from the Hospital CIO. The email says, 'Here's Office 365 and some training links. Enjoy.' She deletes it. Why? She doesn't know about the change. She doesn't want it. She doesn't see how Office 365 helps with surgeries. She doesn't even know what a CIO is. What happens next? None of the nurses use Office 365. Its use in the Operating Room is zero. The CIO sees no benefit. Money is wasted. This happens often in tech changes. Think about it. How common is this for your users?"
>
> —CHANGE366. [398]

She deletes. She's unsure. Why this tech? It's not clear. Money drains. Changes flop. Make it relevant. Communicate well. Then they'll click.

Takeaways. Clarity propels change; Relevance fosters adoption; Avoid one-size-fits-all; Communication bridges gaps.

Fundamental Concepts. Clear talk, clear path. That's Communication Clarity. Tech change comes. But connects how? That's Utility Clarity. Nurse deletes email. It doesn't click. That's Relevance Miss. Office 365 unused. A solution with no problem. That's Uselessness. Investment lost, benefits unseen. That's Wasted Resources. Communication breakdown. That's Explanation Gap. Personalized training missing. That's Customization Lack. User needs sidestepped. That's Understanding Gap. Usefulness shown, usage follows. That's Functionality Awareness. Direct, relevant communication is adoption's friend. That's Adoption Assurance.

Bottom Line. Tech adoption succeeds when you support everyone's innovation-decision process. Introduce and communicate tech with user-specific benefits to encourage use and minimize waste. Clear communication is the key to success.

October 6th

WORDS MATTER, MAKE THEM EASY

"It goes something like this: "Hey, let you walk me through our Donnely nut-spacing and cracked-system rim-riding grip configuration. Using a field of half-seized sprats and brass filled nickel slits, our bracketed caps and splay-flexed columns vent dampers to dampening hatch depths of one half meter, from damper crown to the spurv plinth. How? Well, we bolster twelve husk-nuts to each girdle-jenny, while flex tandems press a task apparatus of ten vertically composited patch hamplers. Then, then pin flam-fastened pan traps at both maiden apexes of the jim-joints."

—'Leslie Claret', *'Patriot', Netflix.* [399]

Jargon clouds. Simplicity clears. Speak so all get it. Change thrives on clear talk.

Takeaways. Avoid jargon; Be clear; Simplicity works; Clarity drives change.

Fundamental Concepts. Jargon confuses. That's Cognitive Overload. Simplicity helps. That's Cognitive Ease. Clear speech needed. That's Effective Communication. Change needs words. Words easy to get. That's Semantic Accessibility. No jargon. That's Lexical Simplicity. Clarity leads. That's Directive Guidance. All understand. That's Universal Comprehension. Change happens. That's Behavioral Shift. Keep it simple. That's Optimal Complexity. Change wins. That's Successful Transformation.

Bottom Line. For successful change, use plain language. Avoid jargon, aim for clarity, and ensure everyone understands to drive change. Clear talk fuels transformation.

October 7th

MEDIA MOLDS—MOLD YOUR MESSAGE

"Media shapes our thoughts, highlighting what's deemed vital and dimming the rest. Our minds latch onto frequent topics, leaving others in the shadows. Remember, where attention goes, power flows; that's why strong regimes control the narrative. It's all a dance of influence and interest."

—Daniel Kahneman, *Thinking, Fast and Slow.* [400]

Media shapes minds. It holds power. Your company has its own media: your communication channels. Use them wisely in times of change. Speak often. Highlight the big wins. Keep the focus. This makes your change message stick. Make it hard to forget. Drama grabs attention. Use it to your advantage. But be genuine. Don't be a dictator of info. Be a guide.

Takeaways. Communication channels act like media; Frequency and focus make messages stick; Drama, used wisely, captures attention.

Fundamental Concepts. Communication is key. That's Social Influence. The media model matters. That's Agenda-Setting Theory. Repetition makes it stick. That's Priming Effect. [401] Drama stirs the pot. That's Arousal Theory. Authoritarian control? Risky. That's Power Dynamics. Open guides win trust. That's Social Proof. Speak often, be heard. That's Frequency-Validity Effect. Your change message? Make it the headline. That's Top-of-Mind Awareness.

Bottom Line. Use your communication channels as media to shape change. Speak frequently, highlight big wins, and stay focused. Make your message unforgettable with well-placed drama, but be genuine. Consistent, clear communication embeds the change narrative.

October 8th

CLEAR SENDERS AVOID JOLTING THE LISTENER'S LANE

"In communications, people have rules in mind. When rules break, it shakes things up. How you feel about the sender matters. Three things count: the act, how it compares, and its size. Good surprises help. Bad surprises hurt."

—CHANGE366. [402]

Change is a tightrope. You're the ringmaster. Workers have thoughts. Bosses have plans. Not the same? Get ready for a circus. The words you send might not be the words they catch. Bosses sell the big dream. Supervisors explain the daily grind. Both matter. Each in their own lane.

Takeaways. Sender and receiver may hear different tunes; Supervisors work best on personal notes; Top brass shines on the big picture.

Fundamental Concepts. Mismatched words. That's Cognitive Dissonance. Employees puzzled. Role confusion in play. Expectations shattered? That's Arousal Theory. Attention drifts to violation. Top brass or supervisor? That's Social Proof. Source matters in sway. Message types differ. That's Dual-Process Theory. Personal from boss. Vision from the top. Communication layered. That's Social Identity Theory. Group norms guide interpretation. Clear roles boost compliance. That's Self-Determination Theory. Choice empowers. Employees engaged. That's the essence of Change Mastery. Know the layers. Pick the sender. Engage the team. Change lands smoothly.

Bottom Line. To navigate change smoothly, leaders paint the vision, while supervisors explain daily tasks. Clarity in roles and communication expectations eases transitions.

October 9th

CONNECT DEEP, CHOOSE METAPHORS

"Metaphors are storytelling essentials. They're inescapable in communication. Lisa Feldman Barrett says they set us apart from animals in '7 ½ Lessons About the Brain.' So, make your metaphors count!"

—CHANGE366. [403]

Metaphors light up stories. They clarify complex ideas. They make messages memorable. In change, they're vital. Sponsors use them. They bridge gaps. They simplify the complex. Metaphors resonate. They connect us. Make yours powerful.

Takeaways. Metaphors simplify complex change concepts; They're powerful tools for sponsors; Effective communication hinges on metaphor mastery.

Fundamental Concepts. Metaphors are key. That's Cognitive Anchoring. They make complex simple. That's Information Processing. Stories stick with metaphors. That's Memory Enhancement. Humans relate through them. That's Social Connection. Sponsors use metaphors? They're bridging gaps. That's Communication Facilitation. Clarifying change with metaphors? That's Cognitive Resonance. When change feels tangled, metaphors are the path. They're the map. That's Narrative Navigation. Using metaphors wisely? That's tapping into Universal Understanding. Dive deep, but keep it clear. Metaphors are the gear.

Bottom Line. Use metaphors to simplify and reinforce your message in change management. Choose powerful metaphors to guide and connect with your audience.

October 10th

THINK YOU COMMUNICATED? DOUBLE-CHECK

"The single biggest problem in communication is the illusion that it has taken place."

—George Bernard Shaw. [404]

Communication deceives. We think we're clear. Often, we're not. In change, clarity is king. Sponsors and managers must be crystal. Illusions harm. They mislead teams. Avoid the trap. Ensure understanding.

Takeaways. Illusionary communication leads to confusion; Sponsors need crystal-clear messaging; Verify understanding, always.

Fundamental Concepts. Communication tricks us. That's Cognitive Bias. [405] We think we're clear. That's Overconfidence. Sponsors hold power. Their clarity? Essential. That's Leadership Influence. Illusions lead astray. That's Misdirection. Teams need understanding. That's Cognitive Clarity. Verify the message received. That's Feedback Loop. Clear communication eases change. That's Transition Facilitation. Avoiding traps is crucial. That's Error Avoidance. Aim for mutual understanding. That's Shared Cognition. Speak once, understand thrice. That's effective change. That's Consistent Transmission.

Bottom Line. To lead change effectively, ensure crystal-clear communication. Verify message clarity to avoid illusions and guide teams effectively.

October 11th

WORD-TUNED, WORLD-TURNED

"Change Communicator 'Job Description.' You're the Comms Lead. You make noise that matters. You plan. You speak. You listen. You ask, 'What's in it for them?' You craft messages. You're a messenger with a megaphone. You work the hours, you pull the strings. You adapt, adopt, and make it happen. Your words sway peers. Your plans woo leaders. You're the pulse of the project. You set the tone. You're in the driver's seat of the message machine. And when you talk, the company listens. You make change feel like a chat over coffee. You don't just send messages; you listen, you make them stick."

—CHANGE366. [406]

As Comms Lead, your vital role is crafting listener-focused messages that drive change by addressing people's needs.

Takeaways. Crafting 'listening' messages drives adoption; Knowing 'what's in it for them' is crucial; Adapt your message to fit different needs; Your role powers change.

Fundamental Concepts. You're a message mechanic. That's Social Influence. Crafting 'listening' messages? That's Attunement. The 'what's in it for them?' It's Self-Determination Theory. Aligning messages to needs? That's Cognitive Resonance. Time spent? That's Commitment and Consistency. The aim? To ease Cognitive Dissonance in change. Your role? You're not just sending words. You're building Change Resilience. This is the core of Social Psychology in action. It's the DNA of change. You are the enzyme. Make the reaction happen.

Bottom Line. A change communicator tailors messages to team needs, listens effectively, and turns communication into impactful change.

October 12th

YOU SHAPE CHANGE ONE WORD AT A TIME

"Masks mirror deep emotions yet remain discreet and grand. Just as nature cloaks itself, words and images are nature's attire, essential yet observed. Don't fault a mask for not being the face or words for not being the soul; each has its place in the circle of life."

—GEORGE SANTAYANNA, *Soliloquies in England.* [407]

You're a change communicator. Your words are masks. They dress ideas. They hide fears. They amplify hope. Words aren't just words. They echo feelings. They express the unspoken. They shape the future. Don't fault them for not being the 'real thing.' They do a job. A vital job. They make change graspable.

Takeaways. Words act as masks, making complex change understandable; They echo the emotions tied to change; Words aren't just vessels; they're vital to change; Treat each word as an integral part of the change process.

Fundamental Concepts. Words as masks? That's Symbolic Interactionism. Echoing feelings? Emotion Regulation is at play. Making change graspable? Cognitive Structuring. Words aren't just words? That's the Sapir-Whorf Hypothesis. [408] The vital role you play? It's grounded in Social Influence. Your task? Activate Cognitive Appraisal. Your aim? Emotional Alignment in change. This is Behavioral Psychology on the ground. It's the mechanism of change. You're the cog. Spin it right.

Bottom Line. As a change communicator, your words act like masks, revealing and concealing emotions, making complex change understandable. Each word plays a vital role in shaping, simplifying, and solidifying the change process. Treat them as essential tools in your journey of change.

October 13th

SPEAK TO REACH—CALIBRATE TO TEACH

"Nature is a vast canvas, yet our language sketches its outlines. We don't see clear categories in nature; our minds and language craft them. The world's picture isn't universal; it's painted by the brush of our linguistic roots."

—GEOFFREY PULLUM, *The Great Eskimo Vocabulary Hoax.* [409]

You're the voice of change. Your words frame reality. They build a shared vision. But remember, people see through their own lenses. Lenses colored by culture, history, and yes, language. What you say must speak to them. Make the strange familiar. Make the change understandable. Your words calibrate their worldview. That's how you drive change.

Takeaways. Your language frames how people see change; Personal background colors individual perception; Effective communication creates a shared understanding; Calibrate your words to suit different viewpoints.

Fundamental Concepts. Framing reality? That's Constructivist Theory. [410] Building a shared vision? Social Cohesion at work. People's colored lenses? Cultural Capital in play. Making change understandable? Cognitive Reframing. Calibrating world views? That's a Linguistic Relativity move. [411] You're not just talking. You're architecting perception. That's Social Constructivism. You align minds. You shape change. Your tool? Strategic Communication. Your aim? Cognitive Alignment. Speak well, align well. That's your role.

Bottom Line. Lead with words that frame reality, considering diverse backgrounds. Make new ideas relatable and adjust language to align perspectives and foster change.

October 14th

WORDS FLOW, BONDS GROW

"Communication crafts leadership. Diverse channels echo messages, but the heart speaks face-to-face. Words wield power; their echo shapes minds. Leaders, guide with clarity and feel the pulse of your crew."

—CHANGE366. [412]

Diverse channels mean diverse voices. Every corner of your organization should buzz with conversation. It's not just about talking; it's about sharing. Share your company's past, its vision, its highs, and its lows. When words flow, bonds grow. Leaders, remember: Your words are a compass. Guide with care. Listen. Respond. Connect.

Takeaways. Use multiple channels to reach all; Sharing company stories bridges gaps; Effective message distribution ensures clarity; Leadership and communication go hand in hand.

Fundamental Concepts. Diverse channels used. That's Audience Segmentation. Every direction feels the talk. That's Holistic Engagement. Stories bridge organizational divides. That's Narrative Cohesion. Words shape the work atmosphere. Enter Emotional Resonance. Leaders steer the conversation. That's Directive Leadership. Effective communication? It's Strategic Dialogue. Two-way chats thrive. The essence of Reciprocal Feedback. Atmosphere responds to words. Classic Psychological Priming. Messages more than mere words. Welcome to Symbolic Interpretation. Employees connect through tales. The power of Shared Identity. The leader's voice guides. Pure Influential Command. Every word matters. That's Impactful Articulation.

Bottom Line. Use varied communication to cover the team, focusing on personal interaction. Share vision and challenges clearly and listen well to unite and guide your team.

October 15th

NEW ACTIONS, NEW WORDS

"To fit with the change of events, words, too, had to change their usual meanings."

—THUCYDIDES, *History of the Peloponnesian War.* [413]

Change happens. Words must adapt. In a shifting workplace, the way we talk must change too. Good communication makes change easier. Be clear. Be timely. Don't stick to old words when new actions unfold.

Takeaways. Words need to adapt during change; Clarity in communication is vital; Timely messages make change smoother; Old words can't describe new actions.

Fundamental Concepts. Change is a must. That's Inevitability. Words must adapt. That's Linguistic Flexibility. Clear talk helps. That's Communication Clarity. Time it right. That's Temporal Sensitivity. New actions unfold. Old words won't do. That's Cognitive Dissonance. Address it. Prevent a Strategy Gap. Make change smooth. That's Effective Communication.

Bottom Line. In times of change, adapt your language. Be clear and timely in your communication to facilitate smooth transitions. Replace old words with new ones that accurately describe the evolving actions.

October 16th

CHANGE WITHOUT HONESTY IS MERE ILLUSION

"True change demands open dialogue; silence, out of fear or pride, only perpetuates the facade until brave honesty steps forward, revealing the naked truth."

—CHANGE366. [414]

The 'Emperor's New Clothes' fable teaches us vital lessons in organizational change management. Honest and transparent communication is essential. Fear can make people hide the truth. Open dialogue ensures real progress. Even a child's voice can make a big difference. Leaders must admit mistakes. These lessons help us understand the power of truth and the need for courage in communication. They guide us in creating authentic and successful change within organizations.

Takeaways. Words need to adapt during change; Clarity in communication is vital; Timely messages make change smoother; Old words can't describe new actions.

Fundamental Concepts. The emperor demonstrates Self-Determination Theory by showing they can make decisions and have skills. Their ministers don't act on their own and stay quiet, a case of Social Loafing where people in a group do less. [415] They feel troubled because their actions disagree with their beliefs, showing Cognitive Dissonance. The emperor ignores their mistake and only hears what they want to hear, a clear sign of Confirmation Bias.

Bottom Line. Real change requires honest communication. Leaders should admit their mistakes and embrace openness to foster progress. A single voice can break the silence and drive authentic transformation.

October 17th

CHANGE YOUR WORDS TO CHANGE YOUR WORLD

> "Language is both a source of conceptual change and a product of conceptual change. Language can facilitate the communication and transmission of new concepts, but it can also constrain the expression and comprehension of concepts that are not well captured by the existing linguistic forms."
>
> —Susan Carey, *The Origin of Concepts.* [416]

Language in the workplace is a seed and soil. It grows ideas and gives them a place to live. When we change how we talk, we change how we think and act. Good words make tough ideas easier to grasp. But, if we stick to old words, we miss new ideas. We must learn to speak the future.

Takeaways. Language shapes and reflects our ideas; New words make new ideas clear; Stuck with old words, new ideas fade; Speak new, think new, act new.

Fundamental Concepts. Words build worlds. That's Symbolic Interactionism. [417] New jargon invites change. That's Lexical Innovation. Outdated words, outdated action. That's Linguistic Conservatism. Novel terms, novel thinking. That's Semantic Progression. Fear of new speech, fear of new ways. That's Neophobia. Spread new words for change. That's Vocabulary Diffusion. Leaders lead by speaking first. That's Verbal Leadership. Talk change, think change, make change. That's the circle of Linguistic Change Agency. Teach fresh words, think fresh thoughts. That's Cognitive Renewal. Speak it, believe it, achieve it. That's the mantra of Communicative Transformation.

Bottom Line. Change begins with your words. Embrace new language to welcome new ideas. Speaking differently leads to thinking differently, which in turn leads to acting differently. Speak, think, and act with freshness to drive change.

October 18th

STORIES STICK, FACTS FADE, CHANGE STAYS

"Stories are not just entertainment; they are a way of organizing and understanding our experience. They provide us with schemas that help us to interpret and remember events, and to generate expectations and predictions about the future."

—JEAN MATTER MANDLER, *Aspects of Schema Theory*. [418]

Stories shape our view of the world. In business, they mold how we see change. Good stories make complex change simple. They help us remember our goals. Stories also guide us to expect what comes next. They are tools for learning. In change management, use stories to explain why change is happening. Tell a tale of the future with the change. Show the steps of transformation as a story. This makes it easy for staff to remember and follow.

Takeaways. Stories simplify complex business changes; They make goals stick in our memory; Stories forecast the future of change; They are learning tools for staff.

Fundamental Concepts. Change rides on story's back. That's Narrative Construction. Minds latch onto tales. That's Schema Utilization. [419] Employees learn through story. That's Cognitive Frameworking. Memory bonds to narrative. That's Encoding Enhancement. Stories craft future scenes. That's Predictive Imagining. A leader's tale shapes action. That's Directive Storytelling. Employees echo a good change story. That's Cultural Replication. Psychology drives the narrative. That's the crux of Story Utilization. Draw a story map. Make it relatable. Repeat the plot. Change takes root.

Bottom Line. Use stories to clarify and embed change, guiding staff with memorable and instructive narratives that map out the transformation process.

October 19th

SILENCE SHOUTS THE LOUDEST FEARS

"The most important thing in a communication is to hear what isn't being said."

—PETER DRUCKER, *The Practice of Management.* [420]

Great communication is not just about words. It's about the silence between them. In change management, listen to what teams don't say. Their silence speaks volumes. Maybe they fear change or don't understand it. Find the unspoken worries. Address them. Clear communication is two-way. It involves speaking clearly and listening deeply.

Takeaways. Understand unspoken concerns; Listen actively to what is not said; Encourage open, two-way communication; Address fears and uncertainties openly.

Fundamental Concepts. Talk misses truth. That's Communication Gap. Silence hides fear. That's Unspoken Resistance. Listen to silence. That's Effective Engagement. Questions unasked. That's Invisible Uncertainty. Dialogue opens doors. That's Communicative Efficacy. Address the mute worries. That's Fear Alleviation. Active listening heals. That's Therapeutic Communication. Trust the quiet. That's Silent Knowledge. Conversations with space to hear. That's Deep Communication. Direct words combined with careful silence. That's Real Understanding.

Bottom Line. Leaders must listen to silence to find and ease unspoken fears, ensuring communication is truly two-sided and clear for successful change management.

October 20th

SHOW PROOF, NOT JUST PLANS, TO PERSUADE PEOPLE

"That which can be asserted without evidence, can be dismissed without evidence."

—Christopher Hitchens, *Hitchen's Razor.* [421]

In change management, leaders often propose new strategies and technologies. They must provide clear reasons for changes to win trust and support. Without evidence, employees may reject new tools or practices. They need to see how changes benefit them and the company. When managers explain the 'why' and 'how' with evidence, they inspire action.

Takeaways. Evidence drives acceptance of change; Clear reasons for change build trust; Explaining benefits inspires support; Facts over fear lead to action.

Fundamental Concepts. Decisions lack evidence. That's Credibility Void. Leaders propose, don't prove. That's Persuasion's Failure. Teams see through fluff. That's Judgment's Clarity. Proof paves the way. That's Validation's Path. Vision without verification. That's Belief's Barrier. Evidence bridges gaps. That's Confidence's Construction. Facts form foundations. That's Logic's Leverage. Assert with proof. That's Conviction's Currency. Trust grows with truth. That's Assurance's Asset. Proof powers persuasion. That's Argument's Authority.

Bottom Line. Leaders must use evidence to convince teams, showing the real benefits of change for trust and action.

October 21st

WALK THEIR PATH, THEN TALK THE CHANGE

"Before you judge a man, walk a mile in his shoes. After that who cares. He's a mile away and you've got his shoes!"

—BILLY CONNOLLY. [422]

Understand perspectives and take over positions before forming opinions. In organizational change, communication is not just about talking but understanding different viewpoints.

Takeaways. Empathize before communicating changes; Understand roles and challenges thoroughly; Foster shared experiences for united goals; Use empathy to drive effective change communication.

Fundamental Concepts. Empathy shapes talk. That's Empathic Communication. Insight overcomes objections. That's Perspective-Taking Advantage. Shared shoes, shared minds. That's Collective Identity. Understanding unites us. That's Social Synergy. Shared path leads to shared goals. That's Cooperative Change. Listen, then lead. That's Influential Communication. Insight into action. That's Empowered Engagement. Empathy ends as the entry to change. That's Emotional Bridging. [423] Change communicated with care. That's Compassionate Leadership. Empathy, the language of change. That's Relational Dynamics.

Bottom Line. Effective change communication starts with empathy. Step into others' shoes to understand their views. Shared understanding leads to united action.

October 22nd

UNCERTAINTY SPEAKS, WISDOM LISTENS

"The only true wisdom is in knowing that you know nothing."

—SOCRATES.[424]

Effective communication in change management starts with admitting gaps in knowledge. This admission doesn't show weakness; it builds trust and encourages others to share information. It leads to a collective search for solutions, where every voice matters. By embracing what we don't know, we create a culture of learning and transparency.

Takeaways. Recognize and admit what you don't know to others; Foster a transparent communication culture that values learning; Encourage team dialogue to fill knowledge gaps together; Use uncertainty to drive collective intelligence.

Fundamental Concepts. Admitting ignorance strengthens teams. That's Trust Building. Transparent talk boosts learning. That's Communicative Transparency. Shared ignorance improves dialogue. That's Knowledge Cohesion. Asking leads to shared solutions. That's Collective Intelligence. Openness fuels learning. That's Information Sharing. Ego down, talk flows. That's Egalitarian Communication. Admitting not-knowing, knowledge grows. That's Communicative Advancement. Every question invites insight. That's Dialogue Deepening. Collective wisdom overcomes individual ignorance. That's Group Synergy.

Bottom Line. Good change communication means admitting what you don't know. It builds trust and teamwork. Ask questions and value learning. Talk openly to grow together.

October 23rd

PERFECT WORDS DON'T EXIST. CLEAR INTENT DOES

"For in spite of language, in spite of intelligence and intuition and sympathy, one can never really communicate anything to anybody."

—ALDOUS HUXLEY. [425]

Communicating in times of change is tough. The words you choose, how smart you are, how well you think you understand someone—none of these guarantee you'll get your message across perfectly. Still, as a change manager, you must try. You must speak clearly, listen closely, and ensure others feel understood.

Takeaways. Use clear language to convey change messages; Listen to others to understand their perspectives; Acknowledge the limits of communication and strive to overcome them; Empathize with others to build trust during transitions.

Fundamental Concepts. Words fail, understanding prevails. That's Communication Imperfection. Listen over speaking. That's Empathetic Engagement. Clarity conquers confusion. That's Message Precision. Patience in explaining, reward in change. That's Endurance in Dialogue. Empathy breaks barriers. That's Sympathetic Communication. When change roars, calmness listens. That's Thoughtful Exchange. True connection takes effort. That's the essence of Communicative Commitment. [426] Words are a start. Understanding is the goal. That's Effective Exchange. Effort in empathy shows. That's the mark of Change Mastery.

Bottom Line. Effective change management demands clear communication. Use simple words and attentive listening. Understand the limits of language but strive to convey your message. Empathize to build trust during transitions.

October 24th

TO LEAD THE CHANGE, FIRST CHANGE HOW YOU LISTEN

"The biggest communication problem is we do not listen to understand. We listen to reply."

—STEPHEN R. COVEY, *First things First.* [427]

When we talk to each other, we often rush to answer. We think about what to say next instead of understanding the other person. In change management, this can cause problems. We need to hear our team's fears and ideas. When we listen well, we learn what to change and how to do it. Real listening can show us the way to lead better.

Takeaways. Listen more than you speak to understand team concerns; Effective listening informs better decision-making; Good listeners use insights to lead and manage change; Real understanding comes from deep listening, not quick replying.

Fundamental Concepts. Change sparks resistance. That's Human Nature. Communication fails. That's Listening Gap. Managers speak, don't hear. That's Response Preoccupation. Real issues stay hidden. That's Understanding Deficit. Teams feel ignored. That's Empathy Shortfall. Hearing isn't listening. That's Sensory Misconception. To know what changes, know the whispers and shouts. That's Deep Listening. [428] Active engagement, not just head nods. That's Active Listening. Change doesn't scare an informed team. That's Knowledge Empowerment. Share the wheel, and the team steers through change. That's Collaborative Guidance.

Bottom Line. To lead change effectively, change the way you listen. Don't rush to reply; seek to understand. Deep listening reveals team concerns and informs better decisions. Empathetic and active listening empowers informed leadership, guiding successful change.

October 25th

REPEAT TO REMEMBER, REINFORCE TO REALIZE

"If you have an important point to make, don't try to be subtle or clever. Use a pile driver. Hit the point once. Then come back and hit it again. Then hit it a third time—a tremendous whack."

—WINSTON CHURCHILL. [429]

When driving change, clarity wins, confusion loses. Think of a construction site—a place where new structures replace old ones. Your words are the machinery, moving ideas into place. Like a pile driver, hammer your point home. Your message, clear and repeated, ensures every team member understands the new vision. Remember, subtle hints and clever riddles can bury your point under layers of misunderstanding. Be direct. Say it once, loudly. Say it again, clearly. Reinforce it, forcefully.

Takeaways. Clarity in communication ensures everyone understands the change; Repeating the message solidifies understanding and commitment; Direct communication leaves no room for confusion or doubt; Forceful reinforcement embeds the change deeply into an organization's culture.

Fundamental Concepts. Change thrives on clear talk. That's Communication Command. Subtlety fails. That's the Pitfall of Precision. Bold repetition makes the message stick. That's the Haberman's Relief effect. [430] Unclear goals create chaos. That's the Fog of Transformation. Change agents bring clarity. That's Vision Clarity. They shun the murk of ambiguity. That's Precision Avoidance. By being explicit, they drive action. That's Directive Dialogue. Their words forge reality. That's Linguistic Construction. They repeat, reinforce, and rally. That's the Tri-Strike Method.

Bottom Line. Drive change by communicating clearly, repeating your message, and doing so forcefully to ensure understanding and commitment

October 26th

CHANGE HINGES ON THE STORY'S COMPELLING PULL

"The confidence people have in their beliefs is not a measure of the quality of evidence, but of the coherence of the story the mind has managed to construct."

—Daniel Kahneman. *Thinking Fast and Slow.* [431]

Belief rides on story's back. A well-told tale convinces many. Facts alone can fall flat without a story's embrace. Good change managers craft tales that kindle belief. They weave visions of the future with threads of now. The best stories shine light on facts, making them irresistible. Coherence makes belief. Chaos loses trust. As a change manager, build a story that stands firm. Tell it with heart. Stitch it with truth. Watch belief grow.

Takeaways. Stories shape beliefs more than bare facts; Coherent stories inspire confidence and drive change; Successful change narratives combine current reality with future vision; Belief in change is born from a compelling story.

Fundamental Concepts. People trust a good plot. That's Narrative Grip. Beliefs build around it. That's Story Structure. Minds crave stories. That's Cognitive Coherence. Facts need tales. That's Evidence Embellishment. Great managers are great storytellers. That's Leadership Lore. They align tales with goals. That's Vision Alignment. Stories bridge the gap between now and new. That's Transitional Tale-Telling. Narratives drive change. That's Plot-Powered Transformation. Confidence in change, that comes from the tale, not just the fact. That's Belief Crafting.

Bottom Line. Change relies on a compelling story to inspire belief and action. A coherent narrative that blends present realities with a future vision builds confidence and drives change. Good change managers tell these stories to guide and grow belief in change.

October 27th

FEAR STALLS SPEECH, COURAGE PROPELS CHANGE

"The human mind is a wonderful organ. It starts working the moment you are born, and never stops until you stand up to speak in public."

—RAY HYMAN, *The Elusive Quarry.* [432]

Speak, and the world halts to listen, or so we hope. The truth hits hard; public speaking often jams the mind's gears. It's not the speaking that daunts us but what lies underneath—our desire to connect, to be understood, to make an impact. In organizational change, clear communication is paramount. It directs, it bonds, it empowers. But to wield this power, one must overcome the silence within. So, stand up, speak out, and let your voice drive change.

Takeaways. Public speaking reveals our desire to connect and influence; Clear communication is crucial in leading change; Overcoming internal fear is key to effective communication; A strong voice commands attention and directs organizational transformation.

Fundamental Concepts. Mind's awe. That's Cognitive Astonishment. Fear freezes speech. That's Anxiety Paralysis. Courage cracks the silence. That's Valor's Victory. Clarity commands, confusion flees. That's Communication's Crown. Words weave change. That's Linguistic Leadership. Speak, support, succeed. That's the Rhetoric of Change. Strong voices spark strong actions. That's Vocal Vigor. Clear communication is a tool, an art, a bridge. That's the Power of Discourse. Breaking silence breaks barriers. That's the Sound of Strategy.

Bottom Line. Overcoming fear is essential for clear communication in change. Public speaking taps into our wish to influence and unite. In leading change, speaking clearly defines, strengthens, and motivates. Break through the silence and let your words fuel transformation.

October 28th

WORDS SHAPE FUTURES; WIELD THEM WITH CARE

"A drop of ink may make millions think."

—LORD BYRON.[433]

Each drop of ink, every word we write or say, can spark thoughts across a room or around the world. In managing change, words are your tools. They can build visions, knock down barriers, and open minds. Use them to craft a story that resonates, aligns, and mobilizes. Remember, the smallest message can lead to the biggest shift.

Takeaways. Words are tools for vision and change; Communication shapes and aligns organizational thinking; Even small messages can create significant shifts.

Fundamental Concepts. Ink spills, minds fill. That's Thought Provocation. Leaders write, change ignites. That's Scripted Momentum. Simple words, big waves. That's Communication Power. Ink is small, impact is tall. That's Message Amplification. Clear stories, team glories. That's Narrative Synchronization. Written right, change in sight. That's Strategic Scripting. Pen's might, team's flight. That's Literary Lift-off. Good communication makes good teams great. That's the Ink Effect.

Bottom Line. Use words wisely to lead change effectively. Write and speak to inspire and guide. Even simple messages can have great influence. Create clear stories that guide and unify teams toward change.

October 29th

LISTEN TO DISSENT, IT'S HIDDEN GOLD

"Negative feedback is a compass during change. It reveals where to steer and refine. When we truly listen, change simplifies. Valued employees become change's strongest allies."

—CHANGE366. [434]

Dissent can be a goldmine of insight. When things change, not everyone will agree at first. Some may see risks or have fears. Listening to these concerns can help refine the change process. It helps to spot hidden flaws and correct the course and design comms for feedback. Only through "listening' comms can you turn skeptics into advocates.

Takeaways. Dissent highlights potential improvements; Openness to feedback refines change processes; Engaged employees can become supportive allies; Listening to negative feedback strengthens outcomes.

Fundamental Concepts. Listening is Learning. That's the Information Processing Model. Feedback shapes strategy. That's Strategic Adaptation. Dissent fosters growth. That's Constructive Discontent. Employees talk, change listens. That's Responsive Change Management. Critique refines, not defines. That's Critical Refinement. Open ears, open doors. That's Organizational Listening. Skeptics become allies. That's Alliance Building. Every voice has value. That's Inclusive Management. Adaptation over stagnation. That's Dynamic Responsiveness. Feedback is gold; mine it. That's Feedback Utilization.

Bottom Line. Active listening in change management is essential. It guides enhancements and streamlines change. By listening, managers can turn dissenting employees into allies, ensuring lasting and robust change.

October 30th

TRUTH WEAKENS DISBELIEF, STRENGTHENS ACTION

"Because it is so unbelievable, the Truth often escapes being known."

—HERACLITUS.[435]

Truth in organizational change is about clear, credible communication. When change unfolds, confusion can thrive unless managed with direct communication. To make the truth believable and actionable, it must be transparent, consistent, and relayed with conviction. Change managers must communicate truthfully to guide teams through the uncertainty of transformation.

Takeaways. Truth in change needs clear, believable communication; Direct, consistent messages reduce confusion; Transparency builds credibility and trust; Conviction in communication ensures team alignment and action.

Fundamental Concepts. Truth hides in plain sight. That's Recognition Avoidance. Clarity cuts through noise. That's Effective Communication. Disbelief challenges truth. That's Cognitive Dissonance. Transparent talks build trust. That's Verifiable Openness. Consistent messages matter. That's Reliable Messaging. Conviction convinces. That's Influential Assertiveness. Action follows clarity. That's Communicative Efficacy. When leaders speak truth, change follows. That's Leadership Credibility.

Bottom Line. Truth in change management is believable when communicated clearly. It requires directness, consistency, and conviction to become known and acted upon, ensuring sustainable change.

October 31st

SPEAK TO GROW, NOT TO USE, LET CHANGE FLOW

"Always recognize that human individuals are ends, and do not use them as a means to your end."

—IMMANUEL KANT, *Groundwork of the Metaphysics of Morals.*

Organizational change management requires an 'ethical backbone.' Respect each team member as an integral part of the change process. They are not just a resource to be used. Effective communication hinges on recognizing and valuing the individuality and contribution of every team member. Ensure that change strategies are conveyed with respect and integrity.

Takeaways. Treat team members as key stakeholders in change, not tools; Communicate with respect to foster trust and cooperation; Value individual contributions to empower collective change; Ethical communication ensures integrity in change management processes.

Fundamental Concepts. Humans are goals, not tools. That's Humanistic Respect. Respect empowers teams. That's Ethical Influence. Integrity communicates, change penetrates. That's Honorable Transformation. Ethics lead, change succeeds. That's Values-driven Progression. Individual worth drives collective birth. That's Personal Respect in change.

Bottom Line. Communicate with respect to value individuals and drive effective change.

NOVEMBER — RESISTANCE

Managing resistance during organizational change is a journey through the complex dynamics of human behavior and leadership strategies. Resistance is inevitable, as noted by Prosci, emphasizing the importance of supporting people through change and minimizing impacts. It's not just about avoiding resistance but navigating through it with understanding and support.

Key to overcoming resistance is the concept that trust can dispel fear. Prosci suggests that addressing the root causes of resistance like fear, distrust, and feeling excluded is vital. This involves actively managing change with clarity and kindness, ensuring everyone is on the same page.

The notion of 'Priority Makes Potency,' expressed by Change366 reminds leaders to balance change efforts with employee well-being. Kahneman's points out that human nature's tendency for the path of least effort, highlighting the need to make change easier and more beneficial than the status quo.

Senge believes that people resist being changed, not change itself, is crucial, emphasizing the importance of choice and involvement in cultivating change. Similarly, Koller stresses leading for ownership rather than obedience, recognizing that engagement and creativity are key to successful change management.

Jordan's reflection on learning from mistakes, and insights from Oxford Reference and Change 366 on understanding different perspectives and fostering praise and fairness, offer valuable lessons for leaders. They underscore the importance of embracing mistakes, listening to diverse views, and ensuring fairness and recognition in change initiatives.

Change366 highlights the concept of 'familiarity as an obstacle' and explores the power of ownership in overcoming resistance and fear. Understanding past experiences and their influence on current attitudes towards change is crucial.

Chomsky's note on optimism and the importance of confronting and understanding internal fears and doubts dive into these topics. Herzberg's distinction between external motivators and genuine desire, along with insights from Becker, Carroll, Johnson, de Beauvoir, and Chomsky again, provide a comprehensive view of the psychological aspects of change management.

In essence, understanding and managing resistance in organizational change underscores the importance of empathy, engagement, trust-building, and proactive leadership in navigating the complex landscape of change management.

November 1st

EXPECT THE BLOCK, BUILD THE BRIDGE

"The issue is not whether we will meet resistance to change. We will. Instead, we must understand how we will support impacted people and groups through the change process and manage resistance to minimize the impacts."

—PROSCI, *Managing Resistance to Change Overview.* [436]

Resistance is sure. Prepare, don't panic. Support is key. Minimize harm, maximize help. Guide through change.

Takeaways. Expect resistance, always; Support matters most; Guide, don't push; Minimize negative impact.

Fundamental Concepts. Resistance is there. That's Status Quo Bias. It's human nature. That's Evolutionary Psychology. We fear the new. That's Uncertainty Avoidance. But we can adapt. That's Neuroplasticity. [437] Support is crucial. That's Social Support Theory. It adds safety. That's Psychological Safety. Guide, don't push. That's Autonomy Support, part of Self-Determination Theory. Minimize harm. That's Risk Mitigation. You keep impact low. That's Emotional Regulation. People feel secure. That's Attachment Theory in action. Trust builds. That's Social Capital. Resistance lowers. That's Change Readiness. The change succeeds. That's Effective Change Management. Support and guide. That's the core of Resistance Management.

Bottom Line. Expect and plan for change resistance. Offer strong support and clear guidance to those affected. Focus on reducing the impact and helping people adapt. Building trust and security is essential for managing resistance effectively and ensuring change success.

November 2nd

TRUST DISPELS FEAR—LEAD CLEARLY AND KINDLY

> "People resist change due to role changes, fear, distrust in leaders, feeling excluded, and managerial resistance. Signs include less participation, negativity, and reduced productivity. To sustain change, include employees in decisions, build trust, and align incentives. Manage change actively and provide clear directions."
>
> —PROSCI, *Understanding Why People Resist Change.* [438]

Change brings fear and distrust. Roles change. People feel left out. This resistance shows in lower participation and negativity. Productivity suffers. As change managers, we must lead clearly. Involve employees in decisions. Build trust. Align incentives with the change. Manage actively, not reactively. Provide clear directions.

Takeaways. Identify fear, distrust, exclusion; See reduced participation, act early; Involve Employees—make decisions together; Align incentives, build trust; Lead with clear instructions.

Fundamental Concepts. Change induces Resistance to Change. Comfort breeds Status Quo Bias. Authority Distrust arises from misunderstandings with leaders. Exclusion Anxiety stems from feeling overlooked. Managerial resistance results from Hierarchical Dynamics. Power dominance leads to Engagement Retreat. Familiarity provides safety, but can turn into Emotional Contagion if negativity spreads. Shared fear and dissent cause Productivity Decline. Disengagement originates from uncertainty, countered by Participatory Decision-Making, fostering Trust Formation. Incentive Alignment aligns personal and organizational goals. Proactive Guidance exemplifies active leadership. Directive Communication offers clear instructions for navigating change.

Bottom Line. Lead clearly. Involve employees in decisions. Foster trust. Align incentives with the change. Manage actively, not reactively. Provide clear directions.

November 3rd

PRIORITY MAKES POTENCY

"By 2022, enterprise change soared; employee will sank. The relentless pace? It drains. Leaders, take note: Direct energy, foster rest, co-create change. Build resilience, not fatigue."

—CHANGE366. [439]

People are weary from rapid changes. Solution? Enterprise Change Management. It's not just one change, but the whole portfolio. Streamline, prioritize, involve your team, and provide reasons for resilience. It reduces stress and boosts support.

Takeaways. Change is up, but support is down; Prioritization is the key to focused effort; Involvement and rest are antidotes to change fatigue; Resilience is the result of smart management.

Fundamental Concepts. More change now. That's Cognitive Load. Employees are stressed. Willingness drops. That's Decision Fatigue. Trust erodes. Leaders must step up. Direct the focus. That's Guided Attention. Cut the clutter. Plan some pause. That's Cognitive Restoration. Refresh the mind. Team's involved. That's Intrinsic Motivation. Ownership increases. Managers help too. Build resilience. That's Emotional Intelligence. Team's prepared. Less fatigue. More focus. That's Sustained Attention. Trust rebuilds. That's Social Capital. Change sticks. Team adapts. That's Organizational Resilience. It's the result of Cognitive Alignment. All on the same page.

Bottom Line. When change overload happens, willingness to adapt falls. Leaders should focus on what's important and involve their team. Prioritize changes, plan for rest, and give clear direction. This approach boosts resilience and supports the team. It also makes change work.

November 4th

BENEFIT BEATS EFFORT, CHANGE STICKS

"A general 'law of least effort' applies to cognitive as well as physical exertion. The law asserts that if there are several ways of achieving the same goal, people will eventually gravitate to the least demanding course of action. In the economy of action, effort is a cost, and the acquisition of skill is driven by the balance of benefits and costs. Laziness is built deep into our nature."

—DANIEL KAHNEMAN, *Thinking, Fast and Slow.* [440]

Effort matters. We all want the easy way out. It's human nature. But what if we could make change feel easy? The trick is to balance cost and benefit. In any change, effort is the cost. The gains are the benefits. Make gains outweigh the costs. Then, change feels like a deal, not a chore.

Takeaways. People naturally seek the easiest route; Effort is a 'cost' in the balance of change; The key is making the benefit of change outweigh the effort.

Fundamental Concepts. Effort has a price. That's Cognitive Economy. People weigh gains and pains. That's Cost-Benefit Analysis. The path of least resistance? It's our default. That's Law of Least Effort. Skill comes when gains outweigh pains. That's Motivation Theory. How to beat in-built laziness? Show clear benefits. That's Incentive Theory. Balance tips in favor of change. That's Equilibrium Shift. A simpler change is a smoother change. That's Resistance Management. Make gains big, make costs small. That's the core of Effective Change.

Bottom Line. Make change benefits clear and greater than the effort to beat natural laziness. Show that the gain from change is worth the cost. When benefits outweigh effort, change is easier and sticks. Choose simple solutions for smooth transitions.

November 5th

IMPOSITION BREEDS RESISTANCE. CHOICE FOSTERS CHANGE

"People don't resist change, they resist being changed."

—PETER SENGE. [441]

Change challenges the core of who we are. When leaders impose it, resistance rises. But when change feels like a choice, engagement grows. Collaboration is the heart of successful transformation. Make change a journey, not a demand.

Takeaways. Change becomes easier with personal choice; Resistance grows from feeling controlled; Collaboration fosters positive engagement; Successful change is a shared journey.

Fundamental Concepts. Humans crave autonomy. That's Self-Determination Theory. Imposition triggers defense. It's a Behavioral Reflex. Collaboration soothes. That's Social Cohesion. Change isn't the enemy. Force is. That's Involuntary Reflex. Shared goals boost commitment. That's Collective Intentionality. A shared change journey empowers. Personal choice drives engagement. That's the essence of Behavioral Alignment. Include all in the process. Celebrate collective achievements. Craft the future together. Success follows.

Bottom Line. Offer change as a choice, not a force. Collaborate for success. Celebrate teamwork. Shared goals lead to less resistance and more commitment. Include everyone for effective change.

November 6th

AMBIGUITY IS CHANGE'S ADVERSARY

"The 10 most common reasons employees resist change: You're not communicating clearly; Fear of the unknown; There is no transitional support; Employees are grieving their loss; Employees feel challenged; People get replaced as the experts; Resistance is the path of least resistance; It simply isn't what they signed up for; Employees weren't consulted or involved; You're making changes that unfairly affect your employees."

—CHANGE366. [442]

When leading change, clear communication is crucial. Transparency is key. Every team member should understand the 'why' behind any shift. Unclear messages lead to confusion, fear, and resistance. Avoid this. Create open forums. Discuss the change. Address concerns. Clear away ambiguity. The outcome? Smooth transitions and stronger teams.

Takeaways. Clear communication is foundational for change; Openly discussing changes fosters understanding; Address perceptions of unfairness and uncertainty; Eliminate ambiguity for successful change.

Fundamental Concepts. Need for Clarity: It's human nature. Uncertainty breeds anxiety. That's Ambiguity Stress. Open Discussions: We're social beings. We seek understanding. That's Social Affiliation Drive. Perceived Unfairness: We desire justice and fairness. That's Equity Sensitivity. Fear of Unknown: We're wired to favor known terrains. That's Cognitive Conservatism. Avoiding Ambiguity: The brain craves predictability. That's Cognitive Consistency.

Bottom Line. For successful change, always explain the reasons clearly to employees. Talk about changes with them and answer their worries. Make sure changes seem fair and support staff through the transition. This makes change work better and helps teams grow stronger.

November 7th

FAMILIARITY IS PROGRESS'S FOE

"People often favor familiar methods, even if faster options exist, a cognitive bias. Sticking to the old way can lead to incorrect decisions. In a study, monkeys adapted faster than humans to shortcuts for rewards. Humans eventually adopted the shortcut, but some clung to the old method. Familiarity can feel right, but relying on old knowledge can result in outdated decisions."

—CHANGE366. [443]

It's human nature to cling to familiar paths. We gravitate towards what we know. But doing things the 'old way' may not always yield the best results. Embracing change, while challenging, often leads to growth and innovation.

Takeaways. Humans often resist change in favor of familiarity; Cognitive bias can hamper efficiency and innovation; [444] Flexibility in decision-making is crucial for growth; Overcoming biases can lead to better outcomes.

Fundamental Concepts. Bias clouds judgment. That's Cognitive Fixation. Humans cling to old. Fear the new. That's Resistance to Change. Monkeys adapt, embrace efficiency. That's Cognitive Flexibility. Rewards drive learning. Incentives motivate change. That's Operant Conditioning. Past experience dictates action. Memory guides us. That's Anchoring Bias. Sticking to the known? Comfort over growth. That's Status Quo Bias. Embrace the new, break the mold. Growth's true avenue. That's Evolutionary Psychology. Avoiding change? Rooted in fear. Overcoming it? That's Behavioral Activation.

Bottom Line. To grow and innovate, we must choose new methods over familiar ones. Embrace change, as sticking to old ways can hold us back. Challenge the usual, see the benefits, and act to stay effective.

November 8th

LEAD FOR OWNERSHIP, NOT MERE OBEDIENCE

"Leadership style affects morale and passion. Obedience-only leads to minimal effort and low enthusiasm. Encouraging ownership boosts involvement, creativity, and energy, crucial during change."

—Ron Koller, *Is Obedience the Real Change Killer?* [445]

Our leadership style has a big impact. It can lower morale or spark passion. Expecting just obedience makes employees do the minimum. They lack energy and enthusiasm. But encouraging ownership is different. Employees get involved more. They become creative and energetic. During change, leading well is crucial..

Takeaways. Ownership in change leads to active employee engagement; Obedience results in passive compliance, lacking energy; Leadership style significantly influences employee response to change.

Fundamental Concepts. Change requires engagement. That's Active Participation. Obedience without ownership? That's Passive Compliance. Leadership guides responses. That's Directive Influence. Energy in change comes from empowerment. That's Motivational Enhancement. Ownership fosters creativity. That's Innovative Engagement. Compliance merely follows. That's Reactive Adaptation. Energize through empowerment. That's Leadership Activation. Ownership equals commitment. That's Emotional Investment. Change succeeds with enthusiastic support. That's the key to Transformative Leadership.

Bottom Line. Leadership style influences how employees react to change. Promoting ownership results in energetic, engaged participation. Obedience leads to passive compliance. Effective change management involves encouraging active engagement and empowerment.

November 9th

MISTAKES MAKE MASTERS

"I have missed more than 9000 shots in my career. I have lost almost 300 games. 26 times, I've been trusted to take the game winning shot and missed. I've failed over and over again in my life. And that is why I succeed."

—MICHAEL JORDAN.[446]

Failure teaches. Success comes after. In change, setbacks happen. Learn and lead. Don't fear failure. Embrace it. Then you win.

Takeaways. Failure is a lesson, not a loss; Setbacks prepare for success; Embrace error to erase resistance; Learn fast, lead faster.

Fundamental Concepts. Failure stings. That's Loss Aversion. It holds us back. That's Risk Aversion. But wait. Rethink. That's Cognitive Reframing. Failure is a friend. That's Learning Orientation. It gives data. That's Information Gain. It builds resilience. That's Emotional Intelligence. You adapt. That's Behavioral Flexibility. The team watches. That's Social Learning. You lead. They follow. That's Modeling Behavior. Resistance drops. That's Social Proof. The cycle breaks. That's Change Momentum. Embrace the sting. That's Fear Extinction. Make failure a friend. That's Self-Determination. Then lead the change. That's Transformational Leadership.

Bottom Line. Embrace mistakes to master change. View failures as growth opportunities. Learning from errors builds success. Lead by example to transform setbacks into progress. This approach reduces resistance and fosters resilience, driving effective change.

November 10th

HEAR THE EDGE TO MANAGE THE MIDDLE

"Either defined in geographical or sociological terms, the center represents the locus of power and dominance and importantly, the source of prestige, while the periphery is subordinate. Simply put, a center–periphery relationship is about hierarchy."

—OXFORD REFERENCE, *Society & Culture.* [447]

In any change, there's a center and a fringe. The center holds power. The fringe feels less heard. Both matter. Both can resist. To manage change, balance the scales. Listen to the edges, not just the middle.

Takeaways. Power sits at the center; listen also to the fringe; Both can resist change for different reasons; Balance both voices to manage resistance effectively.

Fundamental Concepts. Center holds power. That's Hierarchical Dynamics. Fringe feels unheard. That's Marginalization. Both can resist. That's Cognitive Dissonance. To manage change, listen. That's Empathic Leadership. Balance the scales. That's Social Equilibrium. Hear both sides. That's Multifaceted Input. Manage resistance. That's Aversion Mitigation. The center and the fringe. Both crucial. That's Inclusive Strategy. To succeed in change, be fair. That's Distributive Justice. Tune in, balance out. That's Resistance Management.

Bottom Line. Listen to all sides in change, the powerful center and the overlooked fringe. Understanding both perspectives helps manage resistance. Balance the input from each to lead change fairly and successfully.

November 11th

PRAISE PAYS—IT'S A BONUS THAT STAYS

"In change, we gauge our worth by others. Yet, status isn't just wealth; it's influence, skill, and bonds. For leaders: foster growth, champion talents, amplify voices. Know this: praise fuels the soul as gold does the pocket."

—CHANGE366. [448]

Change makes us look around. We compare. It's human. Status matters. But guess what? Money isn't everything. Influence counts. Skills count. Being kind counts. Use change as a chance. Boost your team's status. Give new skills. Praise openly. The brain loves praise like it loves a bonus. Use that. Change becomes a win, not a threat.

Takeaways. People care about status, especially during change; Status isn't just money. It's skills, influence, kindness; Change can boost status. Offer opportunities for growth; Praise works. It lights up the brain like money does.

Fundamental Concepts. Status at stake. That's Social Comparison. People look sideways. It's Relative Deprivation. Money's not all. That's Multifaceted Status. Praise as pay. That's Dopaminergic Reward. New skills offered. That's Competence in Self-Determination Theory. Kindness counts. That's Prosocial Behavior. Make change a win. Douse the Status Threat. Use brain—friendly boosts. That's Neuroleadership. Win over worry. That's Emotional Regulation. Change is kind. That's Social Cohesion. Be smart. Master Change Management.

Bottom Line. During change, praise skills, influence, and kindness over money. Nurture growth, recognize talent, and give praise to ease change resistance. Offer skill development to turn change into an opportunity.

November 12th

CHANGE THRIVES ON FAIRNESS, NOT FORCE

"In business, embracing change is survival. Yet, employees resist. Dive deep: justice and support diminish this resistance. True leaders know: fair play and connection foster readiness for transformation."

—Change366. [449]

Businesses today must change to succeed. But change often faces resistance from teams. This resistance is about wanting fairness and understanding. It's vital for businesses to show they're making fair decisions. When teams feel leaders support them, they resist less. Strong bonds between leaders and teams help. When teams are ready and understand change, they help more. With these elements, change becomes easier for businesses.

Takeaways. Evolution is business survival; Employee pushback is change's challenge; Fairness in change promotes acceptance; Support and readiness are change catalysts.

Fundamental Concepts. Evolution's a must. That's Adaptive Imperative. Resistance rises. It's a Behavioral Reflex. Fairness soothes. That's Organizational Justice. Bonds between leaders and members help. That's Leader-Membership Exchange Dynamics. [450] Support and readiness guide change. They're Change Catalysts. Unity breaks walls. It's the Collective Momentum. Acceptance grows with fairness. That's Psychological Safety. With understanding, resistance wanes. Shared vision is key. Success awaits.

Bottom Line. Businesses need to change and must address team resistance by being fair and clear. Strong leader—team bonds reduce resistance, while readiness and support turn it into cooperation. Fair and understood change is easier to implement and more likely to succeed.

November 13th

OWNERSHIP IN CHANGE TRUMPS RESISTANCE

"Change battles two foes: doubt within and chaos without. Inner fear and outer turbulence stifle growth. Yet, the remedy is trust, clarity, and unity. Equip minds, nurture hearts, and change will find its dance."

—CHANGE366. [451]

Change often meets opposition due to fear, doubt, and resistance from unfamiliarity. Motivation is crucial; pessimism and self-doubt hinder progress. Weak loyalty and challenging situations breed resistance, fueled by ambiguity and neglect. Poor environments and limited dialogue impede change. Overcome these with employee involvement, emphasizing the positive side, and clear communication.

Takeaways. Individual fears and doubts can hinder change; Situational elements, like unclear info and bad environment, fuel resistance; Clear communication, trust, and participation can turn the tide; Equip and educate employees for smoother transitions.

Fundamental Concepts. Humans naturally distrust change, indicating low Self-Efficacy. Fear of the unknown is Neophobia. Low loyalty shows Weak Commitment. Ambiguous information causes Cognitive Dissonance. Ignored people feel Autonomy Loss. Poor conditions and job insecurity create Stress. Silence reflects the Bystander Effect. Cynicism stems from Negative Reinforcement. Building trust needs Social proof. Clear communication is Informative Reinforcement. Needing to feel valued is Intrinsic Motivation. External perspectives help in Cognitive Reframing. Understanding change leads to Adaptive Behavior. Educating and equipping people encourages Behavioral Activation.

Bottom Line. Beat resistance by owning change. Overcome fear with trust and clarity. Teach and unite teams. Address concerns, clarify roles, and encourage feedback. Keep improving and reinforcing change to make it last.

November 14th

PAST SHADOWS TINT FUTURE VIEWS

"In change, surface smiles can hide deep divides. A new system sparks both hope and doubt. Beneath positive nods, whispers of resistance brew. True leadership listens beyond the obvious, for in silent concerns, true sentiments lie."

—CHANGE366. [452]

Change in organizations brings mixed reactions. While some eagerly anticipate new tools, others remain skeptical. This skepticism often arises from past experiences or unclear benefits. Communicating value is crucial. It's vital to ensure everyone understands the 'why' behind changes. When some voice doubts, it can sway others. Leaders must address these concerns swiftly. By doing so, they create a unified approach to change.

Takeaways. Positive views dominate, but skepticism remains; Clear communication reduces resistance; Past experiences influence reactions; Unity in change drives success.

Fundamental Concepts. Change evokes emotions. That's Affective Reaction. Some are eager, others wary. That's Cognitive Dissonance. Positive views on tools, yet hesitance persists. That's Change Ambivalence. Skepticism stems from experience. That's Past Influence. Doubts voiced aloud ripple fast. That's Social Contagion. Addressing fears is vital. That's Fear Alleviation. Unity in transformation? That's Collective Evolution. Leaders clear doubts. They shape change journeys. That's Guided Transition.

Bottom Line. Embrace change by addressing the past and clarifying the future. Listen to concerns and explain why change matters. Unite people by sharing and solving their doubts. Keep the team informed and together. Ensure change sticks by leading with openness and support.

November 15th

YESTERDAY'S SHADOWS DARKEN TODAY'S STEPS

"Some cling to old ways, not out of logic but habit. Resistance is often a reflection of character, not circumstance. History reveals those resistant to reinvention. True evolution demands openness, transcending the confines of self."

—CHANGE366. [453]

Some resist. It's in their nature. Fear, habit, or pride stops them. They see change as a foe. Not all brains think alike. Embrace the difference. Understand the individual. Their past shapes their present. Address their concerns. Make them allies.

Takeaways. Personality drives reactions to change; Past experiences shape current views; Resistance can stem from deep-seated beliefs; Addressing individual concerns is crucial.

Fundamental Concepts. Change divides. That's Individual Variability. Some welcome, some resist. That's Personality Dichotomy. Past experiences echo. That's Historical Resonance. Resistance is personal. It's Internal Friction. Breaking barriers requires insight. Dive into Individual Psyche. Fear fuels negativity. Combat with Understanding. New challenges old. That's Evolutionary Discord. Addressing core fears bridges gaps. That's Cognitive Reconciliation. Embrace diversity. Tailor the approach. Win hearts, change starts.

Bottom Line. Change resistance comes from habit or fear, not just the situation. Understand and address personal histories to overcome it. Adapt your approach to individual needs to turn resistance into support for change. Keep pushing for openness and growth.

November 16th

ROLES ANCHOR, CHANGE TESTS, BALANCE BESTS

"Success hinges on seamless systems. Yet, even the slickest tech falters if misaligned with process. Process defines purpose, tech amplifies it. Treat both as symbiotic, for neither thrives in isolation."

—Change366. [454]

Change isn't just tech. It's also about roles. People value their duties. Responsibility matters. Take away too much? Resistance grows. Keep roles intact. Process trumps technology. But they're intertwined.

Takeaways. Roles and responsibility drive buy-in; Process holds more weight than tech; Change involves both aspects; Balancing both ensures success.

Fundamental Concepts. Roles define us. That's Identity Anchoring. Change challenges identity. That's Role Dissonance. People seek control. It's Autonomy Craving. Process is king. That's Operational Primacy. Tech supports, doesn't lead. Recognize Role Continuity. Tech's shine dims without process. That's Tool-Task Disconnect. Value roles to smooth change. Embrace Dual Integration. Respect role identity. Transition becomes fluid. That's Seamless Shift.

Bottom Line. Success depends on combining clear roles with the right technology. Value people's work to get their support for change. Balance process and tech for smooth transitions. Respect roles to keep change on track.

November 17th

OPTIMISM IS THE TORCHBEARER OF CHANGE

"Prospect theory shines light on change resistance. People's fears loom large in uncertain times. Yet, frame the shift as a grand gain, and resistance wanes. Engage optimists, anchor expectations, and evoke past triumphs to fuel forward momentum."

—CHANGE366. [455]

Prospect theory uncovers the mind's intricate workings when faced with change. [456] People fear the unknown, especially if it threatens their current status. Nobody wants to lose what they have. But promise them a substantial gain, and their outlook shifts. Optimists are the beacon in change projects. Their spirit is contagious. Pitching the change as everyone's win is the manager's masterstroke. Anchors in memory and emotion guide acceptance.

Takeaways. People dread loss more than they crave gains; Optimists influence change success; Memory anchors boost project positivity; Emotional involvement lessens perceived risks.

Fundamental Concepts. Fear of unknown breeds resistance. That's Loss Aversion. Gains tempt minds. That's Prospect Theory. Optimists light paths. They're Change Catalysts. Memory anchors shift perspectives. That's Cognitive Priming. Emotion bonds teams. It's Emotional Anchoring. Change framed as win? That's Positive Reinforcement. Engage hearts, minds follow. That's Intrinsic Motivation. Tap into core needs. You'll overcome Change Resistance.

Bottom Line. People resist change when they fear loss more than gain. Show them the benefits to change their view. Use optimism and positive memories to drive change. This helps overcome fear and makes change successful.

November 18th

LEAD CHANGE WITH INSIGHT, NOT JUST OVERSIGHT

"People fear change; it rattles the company's core. Address reactions swiftly. Emotions sway us, but great leadership steadies the ship. To truly understand change, dive deep into personalities and leadership styles."

—Change366. [457]

Change brings resistance. It's a natural human reaction. People fear the unknown. They worry about the negative outcomes. A poorly executed change amplifies this fear. It increases stress. Change can challenge a company's identity. This skews the change's intent. It endangers the company's identity. The key? Understand reactions. Address them early. And lead with clarity and purpose.

Takeaways. Change can be alarming; Poorly executed change heightens resistance; Early intervention curbs negative attitudes; Clear leadership reduces resistance.

Fundamental Concepts. Change brings fear. That's Uncertainty Aversion. People dread unknown outcomes. That's Negative Forecasting. Poor planning intensifies fear. That's Implementation Anxiety. Change challenges identity. That's Identity Threat. Address resistance swiftly. That's Early Intervention Necessity. Beliefs about change shape behaviors. That's Cognitive Framing. Emotions guide perceptions. That's Affective Influence. Leadership types matter. Transformational leads better. That's Leadership Efficacy. Education and feedback guide reactions. That's Informative Steering. Status quo is comforting. Change disrupts. That's Stability Preference. Personality traits matter. They shape reactions.

Bottom Line. People fear change; it triggers resistance. Quick action and strong leadership guide and reassure them. Understanding and addressing concerns help maintain change momentum. Clear communication and involvement are key.

November 19th

EGO'S SHIELD CRACKS WHEN DISCOMFORT PEAKS

"The ego might resist change until a person's level of discomfort becomes unbearable. A person can employ logic to overcome the ego's defense mechanism and intentionally integrate needed revisions in a person's obsolete or ineffective beliefs and behavior patterns. Resisting change can prolong unhappiness whereas implementing change can establish internal harmony and instate joy in a person's life."

—KILROY J. OLDSTER, *Dead Toad Scrolls.* [458]

Ego fights change. But when discomfort peaks, we seek relief. Logic is the tool. It challenges ego, reshapes old beliefs. A hint that we're off-track? It's a call for change. Resist, and we stay unhappy. Embrace change, and we find harmony and joy.

Takeaways. Ego resists change, but discomfort drives transformation; Logic can break ego's defense and reshape old patterns; Small hints of unease lead to major shifts in perspective; Change offers harmony and joy, resistance keeps unhappiness.

Fundamental Concepts. Ego clashes with change. It's the Defense Mechanism. When pain peaks, we shift—that's Discomfort Threshold. Logic has power. It's about Cognitive Reframing. Subtle signs can cause big shifts. It's Insight Initiation. Change pushes sorrow away, a move towards Internal Harmony Achievement. When we embrace transitions, we discover joy. A clear example of Positive Reinforcement. Being stuck in the old ways? It's the pull of Status Quo Bias. Evolution brings a promise of peace. We see it as Adaptive Growth. As we change, new patterns arise. This is Behavioral Modification in action. Joy illuminates our journey, the gift of Emotional Reward.

Bottom Line. Discomfort challenges ego, urging change. Use logic to update beliefs and embrace growth for joy. Change is rewarding; resistance extends misery. Adopt change, invite happiness.

November 20th

CYNICS LEAD, PROGRESS LAGS

"To stop change: Let cynics lead and critique reign. Prize show over substance and dodge true challenges. Embrace 'analysis paralysis' and shroud genuine concerns in whispers. In such places, change remains an ever-elusive dream."

—CHANGE366. [459]

Change drives progress, but some organizations resist it, stuck in a 'culture of no.' Dominated by cynics who find comfort in criticism, they resist new ideas. Embracing change is a challenge; they prioritize appearance over substance, often with few outcomes. 'Analysis paralysis' hampers decision-making, and fear of failure looms large. Voices of change face resistance, and true concerns remain hidden. Change remains on the horizon, rarely realized.

Takeaways. A Culture of 'no' stifles progress; Emphasis on appearance overshadows real outcomes; Fear of failure leads to analysis paralysis; Real concerns are often silenced.

Fundamental Concepts. Resistance thrives. That's Cultural Inertia. Groups fear the unknown. It's a Loss Aversion. Criticism over action? That's Risk Aversion. Decisions paralyzed by overthinking. It's Analysis Paralysis. Change champions face pushback. That's Status Quo Bias. Leaders warn, but don't act. That's Procrastination. Silence overshadows real issues. That's Conformity. Discussions hidden post-meeting? That's Hidden Influences. Positive change beckons. But first, break the inertia. Embrace the challenge. Value action over inaction. That's the essence of Effective Change Management. Push forward. Address real issues. Empower voices of change. Reap the rewards of evolution.

Bottom Line. Resist change and stagnate; embrace it and thrive. Dodge criticism and show, and progress stalls. Act on insights, cut delays, and promote open dialogue for true advancement.

November 21st

HIDDEN FEARS CAST THE LONGEST SHADOWS

"In every person lies a tug-of-war: conscious goals versus subconscious fears. We yearn for change, yet unseen commitments hold us back, rooted in deep beliefs. Recognize this internal battle to truly unlock change."

—CHANGE366. [460]

Change isn't just about goals. It's a battle inside. We want to move forward. Yet, something holds us back. This isn't laziness. It's deeper. We have hidden fears and beliefs. They tug at us, slow our progress. But realizing this is powerful. We can then break these chains.

Takeaways. Change is a battle of inner commitments; Hidden fears pull us away from our goals; Recognizing these fears can free us; Genuine change happens when we understand this fight.

Fundamental Concepts. Our brain has layers. That's Cognitive Complexity. Goals form on the surface. But deep fears lurk below. That's Subconscious Resistance. We aim high, yet stumble. Not by choice, by deep wiring. That's Inner Conflict. Unseen forces guide our steps. Often astray from our goals. That's Competing Commitments. Recognize the unseen. Understand its pull. That's the path to Conscious Overcoming. Knowledge powers change. Dive deep, find the anchors. That's Self-aware Transformation. Face the hidden, move forward unchained. This is true change mastery.

Bottom Line. Hidden fears can hinder change. Understanding and confronting these fears are essential steps toward achieving true change.

November 22nd

CHANGE NEEDS MORE THAN A NUDGE OR A NOD

"'Kick in the Ass Management' (KITA) acknowledges the distinction between motivating people and having them genuinely desire to do something. Positive KITAs involve rewards, bonuses, and praise. Negative KITAs entail reduced pay, disciplinary measures, and criticism."

—FREDRICK HERZBERG, *The Motivation to Work*. [461]

Kick in the Ass Management. Heard of it? It's simple but tricky. Rewards pull. Penalties push. Yet, change needs more. People should change because they want to, not just because they are told to. Positive or negative, KITAs are short-term. True change? That's a deep dive. Go beyond kicks and kisses. Understand why people resist. Tackle it. Make them want the change.

Takeaways. KITAs can push or pull but are short-lived; Understanding resistance is key; Make people want change, not just obey it; Go deeper than rewards and penalties.

Fundamental Concepts. Short-lived sway. That's Extrinsic Motivation. Rewards and risks. That's Operant Conditioning. Wanting trumps doing. That's Intrinsic Motivation. Deep dive needed. That's Complexity Theory. [462] Resistance is data. That's Cognitive Dissonance. Go beyond the surface. That's Maslow's Hierarchy. [463] Short gains, not goals. That's Temporal Discounting. [464] Want, not will. That's Self-Determination Theory. The 'why' wins. That's Psychological Ownership. Make it their choice. That's Autonomy Support.

Bottom Line. Lasting change requires genuine desire, not just reactions to rewards or penalties. Address the root of resistance for real transformation.

November 23rd

FEAR HALTS, FOCUS PROPELS

"The great boon of repression is that it makes it possible to live decisively in an overwhelmingly miraculous and incomprehensible world, so full of beauty, majesty, and terror that if animals perceived it, they would be paralyzed to act."

—Ernest Becker, *The Denial of Death*.[465]

Change can be scary. Big shifts overwhelm. Yet, in the chaos, there's beauty. Managers need to see it. They help teams navigate. Turning fear into focus. Seeing potential over peril.

Takeaways. Overwhelming change can inhibit action; Recognize the potential in every shift; Harnessing beauty in change mitigates resistance; Effective managers convert fear into focus.

Fundamental Concepts. Change brings fear. That's Evolutionary Caution. Overwhelm inhibits action. That's Cognitive Overload. Beauty in chaos? A Psychological Shift. Animals fear the unknown. That's Inherent Defense. Leaders guide through terror. That's Transformative Leadership. Recognize change's majesty. That's Perception Reframing. Managers make the unknown known. That's Cognitive Clarity. Navigate with decisive action. Embrace the miraculous. Turn paralysis to purpose.

Bottom Line. Leaders turn the fear of change into focused action. They guide teams to face uncertainty. They show how to make challenges into chances for growth.

November 24th

IDENTITY SHIFTS, STAY ALERT

"I knew who I was this morning, but I've changed a few times since then."

—LEWIS CARROLL, *Alice's Adventures in Wonderland.* [466]

In the fast-paced world of organizational change, adaptability is key. Just as a person might feel they have changed several times in a single day, organizations can undergo rapid transformations. These changes can alter the very identity of a team or company. Being aware of these shifts is crucial. Leaders must guide their teams through these changes, ensuring everyone adapts and thrives.

Takeaways. Change in organizations can be rapid and frequent; These changes can affect the organization's identity; Adaptability is crucial for navigating these changes; Self-awareness helps in managing change effectively.

Fundamental Concepts. Change happens quick. That's Rapid Transformation. Identity shifts frequently. That's Identity Flux. Adapt or fall behind. That's Necessity of Adaptability. Know yourself, know change. That's Self-Awareness in Flux. Leaders guide through change. That's Leadership in Transformation. Adaptability ensures survival. That's Organizational Resilience. Awareness makes change manageable. That's Conscious Change Management. Embrace change, stay ahead. That's Thriving in Flux.

Bottom Line. Organizations often change quickly, impacting their identity. Leaders must stay alert, guide their teams to adapt and turn change to their advantage.

November 25th

LET GO, AND FIND NEW CHANCES

"The quicker you let go of old cheese, the sooner you find new cheese."

—SPENCER JOHNSON, *Who Moved my Cheese.* [467]

Change is inevitable in the organizational landscape. Adaptability is key. The quicker you release old, outdated practices, the sooner you'll discover new, efficient methods. This requires overcoming resistance to change. Fast acceptance reduces this resistance. Don't stick to the old ways. Seek new opportunities. Stay positive. New chances are waiting for those ready to adapt.

Takeaways. Embrace change quickly and adapt; Overcome resistance to discover new methods; Seek out new opportunities actively; Maintain a positive attitude towards change.

Fundamental Concepts. Change is fast. That's Quick Adaptation. Old ways fade. That's Outdated Practices. Resistance hinders progress. That's Change Obstruction. Quick acceptance is key. That's Rapid Transition. Seek new opportunities. That's Proactive Pursuit. Stay positive, always. That's Optimistic Outlook. Adaptation brings success. That's Evolutionary Triumph. Change, don't stagnate. That's Continuous Progress. New chances await. That's Opportunity's Door. Be ready, always. That's Preparedness.

Bottom Line. Let go of old methods and embrace change to find new benefits. Adapt quickly, pursue progress, and stay open to new chances with a positive mindset.

November 26th

OPTIMISM FUELS CHANGE—EMBRACE IT

"Optimism is a strategy for making a better future. Because unless you believe that the future can be better, it's unlikely you will step up and take responsibility for making it so."

—NOAM CHOMSKY, *How the World Works.* [468]

Embrace optimism as your strategy in leading change. Believe wholeheartedly in a better, brighter future. This belief fuels your drive to take charge and make a difference. As a change manager, you set the tone. Your optimism becomes contagious, inspiring others to believe and act. You're not just a manager; you're a catalyst for positive change. Show your team that improvement is always possible. Encourage them to take responsibility for their roles in this change. Together, you create a future that's not just different, but better.

Takeaways. Use optimism as a strategy for change; Believe in a better future to initiate change; Take responsibility for driving change; Be proactive in creating a better future.

Fundamental Concepts. Optimism guides us. That's Positive Navigation. Belief fuels action. That's Motivational Drive. Responsibility induces change. That's Proactive Leadership. Together, we succeed. That's Collective Effort. Change for better. That's Evolutionary Progress.

Bottom Line. Lead change with optimism. Believe and act to inspire progress together.

November 27th

OWN CHANGE, OR IT WILL OWN YOU

"Own your change, and you'll steer the course of progress."

—CHANGE366. [469]

A team treating the company as their own embraces change as champions, not outsiders. They're caretakers of the company's future, making every change personal. Embedding ownership replaces resistance with a powerful alliance with change.

Takeaways. Foster a culture where people feel like owners; Link change to employees' personal and professional identities; Show how change benefits both the company and the individual; Use psychological ownership to turn resistance into engagement.

Fundamental Concepts. Ownership sparks belonging. That's Identity Creation. Feeling it's 'mine' shapes action. That's Self-Determination Theory. Simple ties make ownership. That's Associative Claim. Psychological ownership connect to our work. That's Subjective Ownership. It's a feeling, strong and personal. That's Emotional Attachment. It wraps up identity, comfort, control. That's Ownership Triad. Belonging creates a home at work. That's Place. Control, it gives power to act. That's Self-Efficacy. Ownership molds who we are. That's Self-Identity. It's not just thinking; it's feeling. That's Cognitive-Affective Presence. [470] It turns spaces into places of comfort. That's Place-Making. It lifts competence, lets us affect things. That's Effectance. It carves out our unique self. That's Identity Marking. Ownership drives performance. That's Organizational Enhancement. It makes us care beyond the role. That's Extra-Role Contribution. It binds us to where we work. That's Organizational Belonging. It turns employees into insiders. That's Insider Status.

Bottom Line. Encourage ownership in change to merge personal and company growth, turning resistance into active involvement.

November 28th

CERTAINTY'S COMFORT IS CHANGE'S CAGE

"I tore myself away from the safe comfort of certainties through my love for truth—and truth rewarded me."

—Simone de Beauvoir, *Les Mandarins*.[471]

Letting go is tough. Certainties feel safe. But change calls for truth. We must seek it actively. The truth reveals new paths. It rewards us with progress. Be brave. Chase truth. Embrace change.

Takeaways. Certainties comfort but stunt growth; Seeking truth is key to change; Truth challenges but also rewards; Courage leads to progress.

Fundamental Concepts. Change scares. That's Uncertainty Avoidance. Truth challenges comfort. That's Cognitive Dissonance. Reward follows risk. That's Operant Conditioning. We favor the known. That's Status Quo Bias. Love for truth over fear. That's Intrinsic Motivation. Change, once embraced, brings growth. That's Self-Actualization.

Bottom Line. Choose truth over comfort to fuel change and growth, breaking free from familiar confines towards rewarding progress.

November 29th

HOPE STARVES RESISTANCE, FEEDS CHANGE

"If you assume that there is no hope, you guarantee that there will be no hope. If you assume that there is an instinct for freedom, that there are opportunities to change things, then there is a possibility that you can contribute to making a better world."

—NOAM CHOMSKY.[472]

When managing change, assume hope exists. Why? Without it, resistance thrives, and change fails. People long for freedom—to voice concerns, to shape their future. Recognize this instinct. It's powerful. Harness it, and you tap into a well of possibilities. A hopeful manager spots chances for improvement where others see dead ends.

Takeaways. Reject hopelessness; it feeds resistance; Recognize the desire for freedom as a change ally; Seek and act upon opportunities for positive change; Cultivate hope to overpower resistance.

Fundamental Concepts. Hopelessness roots. That's Despair Dominance. Freedom's urge ignored. That's Autonomy Suppression. Change stalls. That's Stagnation Acceptance. Opportunities overlooked. That's Potential Neglect. Hope's power untapped. That's Optimism Deficiency. Embrace change's core. That's Freedom Realization. Opportunities seized. That's Hope Utilization.

Bottom Line. Use hope to drive change, embrace growth chances, and trust in freedom's power to progress.

November 30th

TRIUMPH'S TWIN, FEAR OF SUCCESS, DEMANDS COURAGE

"Success's shadow, fear, nudges us towards growth, requiring brave communication, continual learning, and empowered leadership for true transformation."

—CHANGE366. [473]

Fear of success is a misunderstood challenge in change management. It reshapes power, raises expectations, and demands adaptability. Facing it requires open communication, team empowerment, adaptability, milestone celebration, strong leadership, and feedback channels. Triumphing over this fear can propel an organization to new achievements.

Takeaways. Acknowledge success fear as a change catalyst; Discuss success effects and guide through changes; Train teams for successful change management; Celebrate all progress to build a unified team.

Fundamental Concepts. Behavior shapes belief. That's Self-Perception Theory. [474] People fear change's success. That's Achievement Anxiety. They avoid risk, sabotaging themselves. That's Self-Handicapping. Open talk eases fear. That's Communication Theory. Training builds skill, battles fear. That's Competence Theory. Shared victories unite teams. That's Group Cohesion. Culture adapts, people thrive. That's Cultural Evolution. Leaders shine, guide the way. That's Leadership Effectiveness. Feedback fosters growth, quells fear. That's Feedback Intervention Theory. Celebrate every victory. That's Positivity Effect. Change, managed well, breeds success. That's Organizational Development.

Bottom Line. Confront the fear of success with open dialogue, effective training, and strong leadership. Celebrate progress and use feedback to grow. Courageous actions transform fear into success.

DECEMBER — SUSTAINMENT

Sustainment of change within an organization is a testament to its true success. As Prosci suggests, sustaining change is more challenging than initiating it due to our physiological tendency to revert to familiar habits.

Sylver's point about repetition and reinforcement as routes to forming new habits underlines the essence of sustainment. It's not just about making changes but embedding them into the daily routine. Aristotle's view on excellence being a habit, not an act, further cements the idea that persistence in practice leads to mastery.

Lesage and Wright note the potential for misinterpretation and manipulation of data, advising cautious use rather than sole reliance on it for gauging progress. Hoskin's interpretation of Goodhart's Law highlights the risk of measures losing value when targeted, emphasizing the importance of varied and balanced metrics.

Wilcox's comparison of praise to a pat on the back exemplifies that morale is a crucial factor in sustaining change. It's not just about achieving goals; it's about acknowledging the efforts that contribute to those achievements. Strickland's humility in accomplishment echoes the idea that credit should be shared to encourage collective ownership of change.

Chebat distinguishes rewards from recognition, emphasizing that rewards are infrequent and tangible, while recognition involves regular personal acknowledgment. Drucker's insights stress the importance of doing the right things over just doing things right, especially vital in reinforcing change.

Nadella's focus on empowering people over technology for technology's sake aligns with the principle that reinforcement should enhance capability and empowerment, not just enforce new tools. Change366 expands on this, advocating for a fast, wide, and deep adoption as a measure of success.

Sustaining change, as discussed by Change366, is about continuous learning and adapting within an organizational culture. It involves strong, flexible leadership that recognizes when to assert authority and when to encourage autonomy.

Change366 also warns against the dangers of complacency and the importance of remaining vigilant to avoid getting trapped in outdated practices. Recognizing the weight of past decisions is crucial for steering through the murky waters of change.

To turn steps into strides, as Change366 advises, change management should be goal-anchored, celebrating small wins and acknowledging progress as a continuous journey. Deci's insight on the quality of motivation over quantity resonates with the idea that for change to last, the desire to maintain it must outshine the obligation.

Sustainment of organizational change is about cultivating a culture that embraces new routines through strategic reinforcement practices. It involves clear communication, consistent application of new behaviors, measured and meaningful recognition, and a leadership approach that both directs and empowers. Balancing these elements can transform the challenge of sustaining change into an opportunity for organizational growth and innovation.

December 1st

SUSTAINMENT IS CHANGE'S FINAL SCORE

"It is a natural tendency to revert back to what we know. In fact, there is research emerging about how the brain functions that suggests it is not just a natural tendency but a physiological tendency. While making a change is difficult, sustaining a change can be even more difficult. Therefore, reinforcement is such a critical component of successful change. It encompasses the mechanisms and approaches so that the new way stays in place".

—PROSCI, *Reinforcement.* [475]

Change is tough. Our brains fight it. But know what's tougher? Making change last. Start is step one. Keep going is step two. Step two is key. Forget step two, and you're back to square one. So, what's the hack? Reinforce. Use rewards. Use feedback. Make the new way the best way. That way, it sticks. Your business wins.

Takeaways. Natural to revert; Fight it; Making change is step one; Sustaining is the goal; Reinforcement locks in change.

Fundamental Concepts. Reversion's a pull. That's Status Quo Bias. Brain backs it. That's Cognitive Ease. Change is tough. That's Uncertainty Avoidance. Sustainment's tougher. That's Effort Justification. Reinforcement is key. That's Operant Conditioning. Make it stick. That's Memory Consolidation. Reward the change. That's Positive Reinforcement. Keeps it solid. That's Habit Formation. Consistency comes in. That's Commitment and Consistency, under Influence Psychology. [476] Make it stay. That's Long-term Potentiation. Sustainment achieved. That's Effective Change Management. Reinforcement's the core. That's the heart of Change Sustainment.

Bottom Line. Change is tough, as our brains prefer old ways. But it's vital to keep it going, not just start it. Reinforcement is key, using rewards and feedback to ensure new habits stick. Consistent reinforcement makes new behaviors normal, ensuring successful change.

December 2nd

REINFORCEMENT ROOTS THE ROUTINE

"With constant repetition and reinforcement, new habits are easily formed."

—Marshall Sylver, *Passion, Profit and Power.* [477]

You want change? Repeat the good. Do it again and again. Make it a ritual. But don't stop there. Reinforce it. Cheer the wins. Fix the slips. This loop makes new habits stick. This loop sustains change. Your business needs this loop. Make repetition and reinforcement your tools. They build lasting change. Your business stays strong this way.

Takeaways. Repetition crafts habits; Reinforcement secures them; New habits stick with both.

Fundamental Concepts. Repetition reigns. That's the Law of Effect in psychology. Reinforcement rules. That's Operant Conditioning. Together, they form habits. That's Habit Formation. New habits come easy. That's Effort Justification. Make it routine. That's Automaticity in action. [478] Secure the change. That's Positive Reinforcement. Crafting the habit is key. That's the essence of Behavior Modification. Keep the cycle. That's Cognitive Looping. Stay on track. That's Goal Setting Theory in practice. Sustainment wins. That's Successful Change Management. Reinforcement remains essential. That's the backbone of Change Sustainment.

Bottom Line. Repetition and reinforcement are key to making new habits. Keep repeating good behaviors and reinforcing them. Praise progress and correct mistakes. This way, habits become routine. Use these steps to maintain change. They make your business resilient.

December 3rd

EXCELLENCE IS REPETITION REFINED

"We are what we repeatedly do. Excellence then is not an act. But a habit."

—ARISTOTLE, *The Nicomachean Ethics.* [479]

We act. We repeat. We become. Excellence isn't a one-time act. It's a habit. Built on repetition. Keep the change going. Make excellence habitual.

Takeaways. Repetition forms identity; Excellence is a cultivated habit; Sustain the change through routine.

Fundamental Concepts. We act. That's Behavioral Activation. We repeat. That's the Law of Effect. We become. That's Identity Formation. Excellence sprouts. That's Self-Actualization. Habit, not act. That's Operant Conditioning. Routine reigns. That's Automaticity. Excellence is homegrown. That's the Outcome of Consistent Behavior. Built, not born. That's Nurtured Excellence. Sustain it. That's Long-Term Goal Achievement. Keep the cycle. That's Positive Reinforcement. Repetition rules. That's the key to Habit Formation. Make it stick. That's Change Sustainment.

Bottom Line. Repeat good actions to become excellent. Excellence grows from habits, not just acts. Keep practicing until it becomes second nature. This sustains improvement and turns actions into identity. Keep repeating. Keep improving. Make it stick. This is how to maintain excellence.

December 4th

MEASURE WISELY OR FALTER FOOLISHLY

"Facts are stubborn things, but statistics are pliable."

—Alain-Rene Lesage, *Gil Blas.* [480]

In change management, facts are your foundation. But statistics? They're your tools. You can mold them. Use them to measure success. To sustain change, pick the right stats. They tell you if your plan is working. Are people adopting the new system? Look at the numbers. Numbers don't lie, but they can deceive if misused. Use them wisely.

Takeaways. Facts give the baseline; statistics measure change; Choose the right metrics for meaningful insight; Statistics can validate or challenge your change strategy; Misused metrics can sabotage sustainment.

Fundamental Concepts. Stats guide action. That's Feedback Loop. Facts firm but fixed. That's Cognitive Rigidity. Flex with figures. That's Adaptive Management. Metrics mislead? That's Confirmation Bias. Sustainment stalls. That's Resistance to Change. Wise metrics fuel will. That's Self-Determination Theory. Goal clarity needed. That's Goal-Setting Theory. The right numbers push. That's Operant Conditioning. Use stats to sustain. That's Performance Measurement. Read the signs. Adapt and thrive. That's Intelligent Change Management.

Bottom Line. Measure success with the right statistics to support change. Facts set the stage; good metrics show progress. Pick stats that reflect real success. Watch out for misleading numbers. Correct metrics keep change on track. Misread them and risk failure. Use numbers to sustain improvement and adapt as needed. Choose wisely, measure rightly, and manage change smartly.

December 5th

INTEGRITY TRUMPS INGENUITY IN NUMBERS

"The old saying is that 'figures will not lie,' but a new saying is 'liars will figure.'"

—CARROL D WRIGHT, *Addressing Convention of Commissioners.* [481]

Numbers don't lie, but people can twist them. Integrity matters in business and in change management. Be transparent with data. Dishonesty breeds mistrust. Measure the right things the right way. No shortcuts.

Takeaways. Integrity is crucial for accurate measurement; Transparency keeps everyone on the same page; Dishonest manipulation erodes trust; Measure what matters, honestly.

Fundamental Concepts. Data key. That's Quantitative Analysis. Trust wanes. That's Social Contract Breakdown. Honest measure vital. That's Credibility Principle. Mislead staff? That's Ethical Erosion. Open numbers build bonds. That's Social Capital. Goals can warp. That's Goodhart's Law. [482] Integrity anchors. That's Moral Foundation. Team trust is up. That's Group Cohesion. Straight talk sustains. That's Effective Communication. Measure true, grow too. That's Organizational Resilience.

Bottom Line. Value integrity over cleverness in using numbers. Keep data honest and your team informed. Be clear and truthful. When you measure, do it right. No tricks. Honesty builds trust. Choose important metrics and stay straightforward. Trustworthiness maintains a strong team and supports lasting change. Keep your numbers true, and your team will stay with you.

December 6th

GOALS GUIDE, NUMBERS SPEAK, FOCUS MAY MISLEAD

"Goodhart's Law—that every measure which becomes a target becomes a bad measure—is inexorably, if ruefully, becoming recognized as one of the overriding laws of our times. Ruefully, for this law of the unintended consequence seems so inescapable. But it does so, I suggest, because it is the inevitable corollary of that invention of modernity: accountability."

—KEITH HOSKIN, *The Awful Idea of Accountability.* [483]

Goodhart's Law lays a trap. You set a goal. It becomes a bad yardstick. This happens because we focus too much on the metric. Metrics warp under pressure. Keep your eyes open. Metrics should guide, not govern. Always cross-check your numbers. Be flexible. Revise goals but keep metrics pure.

Takeaways. Goodhart's Law can corrupt metrics; Pressure to meet goals skews results; Use metrics as guides, not absolutes; Flexibility and cross-checking preserve metric purity.

Fundamental Concepts. Metric's a mirage. That's Cognitive Distortion. Goodhart governs. That's Social Proof. Balance is best. That's Self-Regulation. Cross-check cuts corners. That's Heuristic Reasoning. [484] Flexibility fosters fairness. That's Cognitive Flexibility. Metrics must be mates, not masters. That's Locus of Control. Revise but revere metrics. That's Feedback Loop. Pure metrics produce progress. That's Outcome Expectancy. Aim true, act true. That's Congruence Theory.

Bottom Line. Goals help but beware of Goodhart's Law; it warns that targets can become tainted. When a measure turns into a goal, its value as a measure drops. Don't let the pursuit of a metric mislead you. Use numbers as a map, not a mandate. Keep checking and adjusting them. Stay agile. This keeps measurements honest and change on track. Remember, goals are for guiding, not dictating. Aim and check; don't just expect. Keep goals clean and your focus keen.

December 7th

MORALE MEANS MORE

"A pat on the back is only a few vertebrae removed from a kick in the pants but is miles ahead in results."

—Ella Wheeler Wilcox, *The Heart of the New Thought*. [485]

Rewards beat punishments. A pat on the back is powerful. Way more than a kick in the pants. In sustaining change, use rewards. Make them meaningful. A small 'well-done' can do wonders. Recognition fuels morale. It keeps the change alive.

Takeaways. Rewards trump punishments in results; Recognition boosts morale; Small acts can have big impacts; Keep rewards genuine to sustain change.

Fundamental Concepts. Reward's right. That's Operant Conditioning. Small cheers charm. That's Minimal Viable Reinforcement. [486] Morale matters. That's Maslow's Hierarchy. Genuine gets you. That's Authenticity Bias. Results reap rewards. That's Expectancy Theory. Keep it real. That's Cognitive Consistency. Sustain to gain. That's Commitment Mechanism. Well-done works wonders. That's Positive Reinforcement.

Bottom Line. Morale boosts when you use rewards instead of punishments. Small praises like 'well-done' can lead to big changes. For lasting change, always pick recognition over reprimand. Show real appreciation and praise. This keeps morale high and supports change. Offer rewards and genuine praise to keep progress going. Small cheers make a big difference in keeping morale up and change in place.

December 8th

GOALS OVER GLORY

"It is amazing what you can accomplish if you do not care who gets the credit."

—JOSEPH STRICKLAND, *Diary*. [487]

In change, ego should exit. Focus on the goal, not the glory. Shared success sustains change. Recognition is key. But it doesn't have to be yours. Keep eyes on the end game. Celebrate team wins. That's how change sticks.

Takeaways. Ego sidelines success; Shared goals bring change; Credit the team, not just yourself; Keep focus on the objective for change to last.

Fundamental Concepts. Ego's exit. That's Ego Depletion. [488] Shared shines. That's Social Proof. Team tells. That's Group Cohesion. Objective owns. That's Goal Setting Theory. [489] Selfless sticks. That's Intrinsic Motivation. Goal's the game. That's Outcome Expectancy. Team over self. That's Social Identity Theory. Lasting likes teamwork. That's Sustained Change Model. Keep the focus. That's Selective Attention.

Bottom Line. Prioritize goals for lasting change. Leave ego behind. Strive for shared success. Acknowledge the team. Stay focused on the end goal to sustain change. Remove ego, embrace teamwork, and celebrate together. Keep the team united, the goal in sight, and the change on course.

December 9th

DATA DRIVES REWARDS—DEEDS DRIVE RECOGNITION

"Rewards are tangible; recognition is intangible; Rewards are personal; recognition is personal; Rewards are data driven; recognition comes from Behaviour; Rewards are infrequent; recognition shouldn't be."

—JIMMY CHEBAT, *The Psychology of Employee Recognition v Reward.* [490]

Rewards and recognition. Two sides of the same coin. Both crucial in managing change. Rewards are numbers. Recognition is more. It's a nod, a smile, a thanks. Rewards come seldom. Recognition can be daily. Use both wisely. Sustain change.

Takeaways. Rewards are data; recognition is behavior; Rewards come less often; Recognition should be frequent; Both are personal but in different ways; Use rewards and recognition to keep change alive.

Fundamental Concepts. Rewards data. That's Operant Conditioning. Recognition rhythm. That's Positive Reinforcement. Both personal. That's Self-Determination Theory. Frequent feels. That's Instant Gratification. Less often lasts. That's Delayed Gratification. Behavior basis. That's Social Learning Theory. Sustain the same. That's Change Commitment. Wise ways work. That's Decision-making Psychology. Keep it alive. That's Sustained Reinforcement.

Bottom Line. Use rewards and recognition to keep change going. Rewards are rare and based on data. Recognition is about behavior and should be frequent. Both matter. Both are personal. Together, they help change last. Make rewards count and recognition constant to sustain the shift.

December 10th

ACT RIGHT, CHOOSE WISELY—KEYS TO CHANGE

"Efficiency is doing things right; effectiveness is doing the right things."

—Peter Drucker, *The Effective Executive.* [491]

Do it right. But pick right too. Both sustain change. Precision matters. So does choice. They fuel sustainment.

Takeaways. Precision amplifies action; Value dictates choice; Balance guides sustainment; Both drive reinforcement.

Fundamental Concepts. Do it precisely. That's Competence from Self-Determination Theory. Pick wisely. That's Autonomous Motivation. Precision elevates tasks. That's Skill Mastery. Right choices fuel progress. That's Purpose Alignment. Both essential. That's Intrinsic Motivation. Sustainment's core. Balance is key. That's Harmonic Functioning. Reinforcement thrives on both. That's Integrated Regulation. [492] Be precise, be wise. That's the heart of Change Sustainment.

Bottom Line. To keep change going, act wisely and make smart choices. Balance being precise with choosing correctly. Accuracy and wise decisions push change forward and make it last. Stay focused on your actions and thoughtful in your choices to boost progress.

December 11th

OUTCOMES OVER OUTPUTS

> "Ultimately, though, we've got to measure ourselves not by technology for technology's sake, but how are we empowering people? How are we helping organizations with their digital transformational outcomes? That's what this is all about."
>
> —SATYA NADELLA, *Microsoft Inspire.* [493]

Tech alone isn't enough. Empower people. Focus on outcomes. Transformation's true measure? Positive impact.

Takeaways. Tech's tool, not the goal; People power change; Aim for real outcomes; Measure transformation by impact.

Fundamental Concepts. Tech's just a tool. That's Instrumentality. Empower the human. That's Autonomous Motivation. Tech isn't the endgame. That's Extrinsic Value. People at the helm. That's Intrinsic Worth. Focus on outcomes. That's Goal-Directed Behavior. Change measures impact. That's Outcome Evaluation. Real transformation touches lives. That's Relational Significance. Put humans first. That's the essence of People-Centric Change.

Bottom Line. Prioritize real outcomes and empower people to drive change. Technology is a tool, not the ultimate goal. Measure transformation by its impact on lives. Place people at the forefront and strive for tangible benefits in digital transformation. This is how to make change meaningful and lasting.

December 12th

ADOPTION—GO FAST, GO WIDE, GO DEEP

"Measurement might start with Objectives and Key Results. Objectives set the vision. Key Results mark the steps. But success? It's in the speed, scale, and skill of people adopting. Fast adoption, wide utilization, and deep proficiency drive returns. It's not just about the goal; it's how people chase it."

—CHANGE366. [494]

Set the vision. Mark the steps. People fuel success. Fast, wide, deep wins. Chase counts.

Takeaways. Vision steers with OKRs' [495] Speed, scale, skill define adoption; Depth of proficiency is key; The chase amplifies the goal.

Fundamental Concepts. Set clear vision. That's Purpose Framing. Steps direct the path. That's Structured Goal-Setting. Speed, scale, and skill. That's Mastery Orientation. People are change agents. That's Agency Activation. Depth over surface. That's Intrinsic Motivation. The journey's worth. That's Process Enjoyment. Chase with intent. That's Motivated Pursuit. True success? People's vigor in chase. That's the essence of Engaged Endeavor.

Bottom Line. Set a clear vision and detailed steps with OKRs. Success depends on how quickly, broadly, and deeply people adopt changes. Fast adoption, wide reach, and in-depth skill matter most. Aim for more than just goals; Focus on the vigor and depth of the pursuit. This ensures meaningful and sustained change. Chase goals with intent to realize true success.

December 13th

ENDURING CHANGE IS BIRTHED IN CEASELESS LEARNING

> "To sustain change, embrace constant learning and adaptability. Leadership should be a fluid blend of strength and flexibility, mastering the art of leading and listening. Pinpoint and bridge skill gaps to foster growth. Trust and team dynamics are the heart of lasting change. Solid structure and clear benefits spark commitment. Aligning priorities at all levels clears the path to enduring success."
>
> —CHANGE366. [496]

Keep learning to maintain change. Adjust to fit team culture. Leaders guide and adapt. They reward and communicate. Skills are key. Trust boosts change. Openness to new ideas helps. Structure and routine ensure lasting change. Consistent teams remember core values. Too many tasks? Change suffers. Show the change benefits. Align change with big goals. This sustains initiatives.

Takeaways. Constant learning and adaptability are change's best friends; Leadership, both flexible and steadfast, is essential; Trust and positive team dynamics sustain momentum.

Fundamental Concepts. Embrace the challenge. That's Growth Mindset. Adjust to feedback. That's Behavioral Flexibility. Lead in uncertainty. That's Social Proof. Inspire and motivate. That's Transformational Leadership. Believe, act, achieve. That's Self-efficacy. Build and bond. That's Social Bonding Theory. Crave the new. That's Novelty-Seeking Behavior. Mental frames guide. That's Schema Theory. [497] Rewards fuel repetition. That's Operant Conditioning. Align belief, action. That's Cognitive Consistency.

Bottom Line. Sustain change by learning, adapting, and aligning priorities. Strong, flexible leadership should build trust and skills in teams. Reward progress and maintain clarity for lasting impact.

December 14th

PURPOSE SHAPES, VIGILANCE STEERS

"Changes in business can strengthen by themselves, like the rise of the QWERTY keyboard. But waiting isn't the answer. Companies can boost this effect. Be careful of getting stuck in choices, even if they seem right now. Break out, adapt, and always be ready to challenge old ways."

—CHANGE366. [498]

Changes build momentum, like a snowball rolling downhill. In business, when a decision gains attention and resources, key players take purposeful actions, investing early and forming partnerships. As change grows, strategies may require adjustments, necessitating alert leadership.

Takeaways. Change reinforces itself over time; Purposeful actions can guide change; Partnerships strengthens change; Alertness is key as change evolves.

Fundamental Concepts. Optionally chosen changes strengthen. That's Reinforcement. Positive results amplify. That's Network Externality. [499] Growth gets easier. That's Increasing Returns. Leaders drive, not wait. That's Proactive Leadership. Craft with purpose. That's Strategic Design. Partner for progress. That's Collaborative Synergy. Adjust on-the-go. That's Agile Adaptation. Stay alert, evolve. That's Vigilant Change Management. Stuck in a groove? That's Lock-In. Paths might trap, yet not forever. That's Strategy Pivot. Time defines context. That's Temporal Perspective. Outsiders redefine routes. That's External Influence. Adapt, thrive, sustain. That's Enduring Adaptability.

Bottom Line. Choose change carefully and act to reinforce it. Use strategy and partnerships to shape change from the start. As the change grows, adjust your approach. Stay alert and ready to pivot from old ways. Change can trap you if you're not vigilant. Always aim to adapt and thrive for lasting success.

December 15th

BEWARE OF PATHS THAT TRAP PROGRESS

"Past choices shape today's path. Recognize the weight of old steps; they can bind or guide. True leadership? Seeing when to follow or forge anew. Understand paths, master change."

—CHANGE366. [500]

Chosen paths wield significant influence. Change can be challenging, especially when an organization's path is deeply ingrained, termed 'lock-in.' However, paths can be altered by events and new decisions, though some are harder to change. Change managers must understand the depth and direction of these paths to navigate effectively.

Takeaways. Organizations can become entrenched in certain paths; Changing course might be hard but isn't impossible; Key events can trigger new directions; Deep-rooted patterns may limit fresh opportunities; Being aware can empower proactive strategies.

Fundamental Concepts. Paths chosen, futures dictated. That's Path Dependency. Old ways resist change. That's Organizational Lock-in. [501] New events can pivot paths. That's Contingent Evolution. Patterns, once set, guide actions. That's Behavioral Consistency. Feedback strengthens repetition. That's Reinforcement Theory. Positive loops intensify directions. That's Positive Feedback Mechanism. Organizations adapt or get trapped. That's Adaptive Rigidity. Recognizing deep routes? That's Organizational Awareness. To change, understand the path's depth. That's Change Depth Perception. External forces can reshape paths. That's External Influence Dynamics.

Bottom Line. Recognize how past choices can lock an organization into a specific path. Old patterns may resist change but understanding them is essential for mastering change. Don't let 'lock-in' limit new opportunities. Be aware and ready to create new paths when necessary. Use events to change direction and avoid traps. Stay proactive and adaptable for progress.

December 16th

GOAL: ANCHOR CHANGE—STEPS TURN TO STRIDES

"Change isn't a sprint, it's a marathon. Anchor it with goals, fuel it with purpose, and pave its path with small, glorious wins. In the race to evolve, routines are your rhythm, feedback your compass, and teamwork your lifeline. Remember, the journey is ongoing—adapt, celebrate, learn. That's how you turn change into culture, and culture into legacy."

—CHANGE366. [502]

Organizational change is tough but essential. To ensure lasting change, set clear goals, emphasize the 'why,' start with small wins, establish routines, gather feedback, foster teamwork through regular check-ins, celebrate team successes, stay adaptable, keep learning, and share success stories for motivation.

Takeaways. Goals and purpose guide lasting change; Routines and small wins build a new culture; Teamwork and feedback maintain alignment; Adaptability and shared successes ensure sustainability.

Fundamental Concepts. Goals up front. That's Goal Setting Theory. 'Why' matters. That's Self-Determination Theory. Small wins? That's Incremental Theory of change. Routine? That's Habit Formation. Team spirit? That's Social Support. Check-ins align. That's Feedback Loop. Celebrate wins. That's Positive Reinforcement. Adaptability is key. That's Cognitive Flexibility. Learning sustains. That's Lifelong Learning. Sharing successes? That's Social Learning Theory. Keep change alive. That's Organizational Momentum. Make it stick. That's Behavioral Maintenance.

Bottom Line. For lasting organizational change, set purposeful goals, start with small wins, establish routines, use feedback, foster teamwork, adapt, learn, and share successes to create a lasting legacy.

December 17th

DESIRE TRUMPS DUTY IN DURABLE CHANGE

"The quality of motivation is more important than the amount of motivation."

—EDWARD L DECI. *Self-Determination Theory.* [503]

Good motivation beats lots of bad motivation. It's the kind that sticks. Say you're changing how your team works. If they see real benefits, they'll stick with it. Not just because they have to. But because they want to. It's lasting change, not a fad.

Takeaways. Quality motivation creates long-term change; Show real benefits, not just orders; A well-motivated team adapts willingly; Desire drives durable change, not mere duty.

Fundamental Concepts. Quality beats quantity. That's Self-Determination Theory. Intrinsic motivation wins. It's long-lasting. People want to change. Not just because they must. That's Internalization. Teams get it. They see the why. That's Cognitive Evaluation Theory. [504] The 'what' is clear. The 'why' drives action. It's not Control Theory. It's not carrots and sticks. It's real motivation. That's the core of lasting change. Show the gains. Make them real. Ignite the right spark. See the fire last.

Bottom Line. Prioritize quality motivation and real benefits for lasting change. Help your team see the value and make it their choice, not just an obligation. Clearly show the gains and ignite the desire for change to achieve sustainable results.

December 18th

REWARD RIGHTLY —BOOST CREATIVITY

"Rewards aligned with genuine performance amplify creativity and drive."

—CHANGE366. [505]

Rewards don't always kill interest. Doing well and getting a reward keeps interest. Verbal praise works well. Rewards tied to good performance boost liking. They can also increase creativity. Rewards not based on performance can hurt motivation if used once. But if repeated, they're fine. Rewards must rely on quality. These rewards boost interest. To manage change, choose rewards right. Tie them to quality. Praise creativity. Avoid random rewards. They can hurt drive.

Takeaways. Proper rewards can maintain or boost task interest; Verbal praise works; Rewarding creativity encourages innovation; The timing and type of reward matters.

Fundamental Concepts. Rewards aren't idle. That's Intrinsic Motivation Maintenance. Verbal affirmations matter. That's Verbal Positive Reinforcement. Link rewards to quality. That's Performance-Contingent Rewarding. Creativity gets a boost. That's Innovative Stimulation. Use rewards wisely. That's Strategic Incentivization. Recognize the role of rewards. Understand their impact. That's Behavioral Psychology at work. Align with individual needs. That's Self-Determination Theory. Reward patterns affect behavior. Dive deep into the psyche. That's the essence of Organizational Change Management.

Bottom Line. Sustain change by rewarding appropriate actions and fostering creativity. Provide sincere praise for good work and align rewards with actual performance. This approach keeps interest alive and encourages innovation. Ensure rewards are connected to quality and creativity, avoiding random or one-off incentives that can demotivate. Consistently reward and praise in relation to tangible results.

December 19th

CHAMPION COMPETENCE—WATCH PERFORMANCE SOAR

> "To drive peak performance, and sustain change, nurture competence. It's not just about rewards—it's about empowering people to excel."
>
> —CHANGE366. [506]

In the heart of change lies competence. It's the key driver of performance. Incentives matter, but what's intrinsic takes the front seat. We can't ignore external rewards, but tapping into one's inner drive makes the real difference. Autonomy is vital, but in new environments, guidance might be better. Feeling connected? It has its moments. But competence? Always center stage.

Takeaways. Competence consistently boosts performance; Intrinsic motivation outshines external incentives; Autonomy's effects vary based on the task; Relatedness plays a subtle role in performance.

Fundamental Concepts. Competence at the core. That's Self-Determination Theory. Intrinsic beats extrinsic. That's Internal Motivation. Guidance in new terrains? That's Scaffolding. Relatedness wavers in weight. That's Social Bonding. Drive change from within. That's Intrinsic Catalyst. Value competence. Enhance performance. That's the secret of Change Sustainment.

Bottom Line. Boost performance by building competence. Empower people to excel from within. While rewards help, self-drive and skill mastery matter most. Guide teams in new tasks, create connections, and value competence for sustained change. Focus on competence to see performance rise.

December 20th

NURTURED AGENCY, SUSTAINED CHANGE

"Agency is the seed; sustained change, the garden—nurture both to harvest innovation."

—CHANGE366.

Every worker wields power to pivot or persist in new paths. Agency fuels change. It's the force that empowers staff to steer change, not just to endure it. True change blooms when each person seeds their part, watering the soil of innovation with action. Leaders who nurture agency, craft a garden where change thrives.

Takeaways. Agency empowers individuals to drive change; Personal choice fuels the sustainment of change; Everyone's actions contribute to the growth of innovation; Leaders must cultivate agency to sustain change.

Fundamental Concepts. Choice powers change. That's Agency. Independence fuels innovation. That's Autonomy Support. Agency in teams grows roots. That's Social Facilitation. Choices echo in change's hall. That's Echoic Reinforcement. [507] Leaders cultivate, change thrives. That's Contingency Management. Shared agency weaves strong change. That's Collective Efficacy. Empower the team, sustain the dream. That's Empowerment Theory. Personal choice propels, change persists. That's Intrinsic Motivation.

Bottom Line. To sustain change and foster innovation, nurture agency. Empower workers to choose and drive change. Support independence and team empowerment. Let every action water the soil of innovation. Leaders, cultivate agency for thriving change. Empower individuals, sustain momentum, and let change flourish.

December 21st

REPEAT, REINFORCE, REALIZE

"Echoic reinforcement is the key to sustaining change. By repeating the message over and over again, you create a culture of change that becomes reinforcing."

—CHANGE366. [508]

Repeat, reinforce, realize. That's the rhythm of lasting change. Echoic reinforcement isn't mere repetition; it's the drumbeat to which organizations march towards the future. [509] It embeds the essence of change into the company's culture. A leader's words become the daily chants that fortify the walls of transformation.

Takeaways. Repetition is crucial for lasting change; Echoic reinforcement embeds change into culture; Leaders' repeated messages fortify transformation efforts; A culture of change is Self-reinforcing over time.

Fundamental Concepts. Repetition breeds habit. That's Echoic Reinforcement. Culture echoes leaders. That's Social Learning Theory. Messages mold minds. That's Information Processing Theory. Repeating guidance galvanizes growth. That's Operant Conditioning. Transformation echoes, culture follows. That's Memetic Theory. [510] Habitual repetition fortifies change. That's Habit Formation. Reinforce daily, sustain always. That's Continuous Reinforcement. Culture Self-reinforces, change sticks. That's Organizational Habituation.

Bottom Line. To make change stick, repeat your message. Use echoic reinforcement to turn change into culture. Leaders' words should echo daily to build transformation. Over time, a culture of change reinforces itself. Keep reinforcing habits to cement permanent change. Make repetition a habit and watch change become second nature in your organization.

December 22nd

PLAN TO SUSTAIN, AIM TO RETAIN

"Sustain the change you seek—plan, resource, assign, track, and celebrate."

—CHANGE366.[511]

Keep the change alive. That's the leader's mantra. People slide back to old habits, like water finds its level. So, plan your reinforcements. Build them into the project's heart. Allocate resources; it's not the last mile—it's the one that gets you home. Ask who will carry the torch of change? Make it clear. Use appraisals, nudge behaviors, and cheer every small win. The change that sticks is the change that lives.

Takeaways. Plan for reinforcement from the start; Allocate necessary resources to sustain change; Clearly assign responsibility for maintaining change; Use appraisals to promote and track change adoption.

Fundamental Concepts. Reinforcement keeps change alive. That's Behavior Modification. People revert without it. It's Regression to the Mean. Planning embeds persistence—Proactive Intervention. Resources enable reinforcement. That's Operational Support. Clarity in roles secures success. It's about Role Attribution. Appraisals anchor change. That's Performance Feedback. Change sticks when tracked based on Behavioral Monitoring. Sustained effort overcomes resistance. That's Resistance Management.

Bottom Line. Start with a robust plan for lasting change. Ensure you have the necessary resources and clear roles assigned. Monitor progress and celebrate achievements. This approach strengthens change through planning, resource allocation, role clarity, and recognition.

December 23rd

EASY COMES, EASY GOES—HARD STAYS

"On the basis of the familiar experience that that which is learned with difficulty is better retained, it would have been safe to prophesy such an effect from the greater number of repetitions."

—HERMAN EBBINGHAUS, *Memory: Experimental Psychology.* [512]

In the heat of change, the toughest lessons linger. We wrestle with new systems, grapple with fresh strategies. It's not easy. But it's this very struggle that cements our learning. When change is hard, we remember. When we work for it, it stays.

Takeaways. Tough changes create lasting lessons; Struggle strengthens memory and retention; Effort in learning locks in the changes.

Fundamental Concepts. Effort builds retention. That's Learning Theory. Difficulty enhances memory. That's Cognitive Effort. Struggle solidifies skills. That's Retention Effectiveness. Hard lessons, better recall. That's Effortful Encoding. Repetition by challenge. That's Memory Consolidation. [513] Change is hard, but this cements learning. It's the cornerstone of Organizational Learning.

Bottom Line. Difficult change sticks. Learning through effort ensures lasting impact. Struggle strengthens our memories. The more effort we put in, the stronger the retention. In other words, tough lessons become a part of us when we embrace the challenge of learning.

December 24th

ANALOGIES ANCHOR CHANGE IN THE MIND

"Analogy is the core of cognition."

—DEDRE GENTNER, *Memory: The Analogical Mind.* [514]

When change hits, it's the familiar that anchors us. An analogy is our lifeline in a sea of new processes. It ties the unknown to the known, making the complex simple. We see the new IT system as a beehive, buzzing with activity, each bee a byte of data. This image sticks.

Takeaways. Analogies bridge old and new, easing transition; Familiar images anchor new knowledge; Relatable metaphors enhance understanding and retention.

Fundamental Concepts. Analogies ease learning. That's Cognitive Anchoring. Familiar ties to the new. That's Conceptual Bridging. Metaphors make sense. That's Simplified Processing. Learning sticks with images. That's Visual Encoding. Analogy simplifies the complex. That's Cognitive Ease. In change, relatable metaphors drive understanding. That's the power of Cognitive Metaphor Theory in action.

Bottom Line. Analogies play a crucial role in making change stick. They bridge the gap between the old and the new, simplifying complexity into relatable images. Utilize familiar analogies to clarify new systems, making understanding easier and ensuring lasting change.

December 25th

PAST LESSONS SHAPE FUTURE STEPS

"The main function of memory is not to preserve the past, but to prepare us for the future."

—Fergus Craik, *Levels of Processing: Memory Research.* [515]

Remembering is not just about the past. It's a tool. We use it to make sense of now and what's next. In change management, we don't just look back. We use our past lessons to shape our future actions. We analyze deeply. This way, we remember well. Good memory guides better decisions. It helps us predict, plan, act and sustain change with confidence.

Takeaways. Memory helps us use past lessons for sustaining change; Deep analysis makes memories stronger; Good memory guides better future decisions.

Fundamental Concepts. Memory acts. That's Active Encoding. Analysis deepens. That's Elaborative Rehearsal. [516] Lessons guide. That's Proactive Utilization. Past informs future. That's Predictive Encoding. [517] Decisions sharpen. That's Memory's Function. Remembering evolves. That's Cognitive Flexibility. Insights from hindsight. That's Retrospective Coherence. Plan with memory. That's Strategic Forecasting. We lead by learning. That's the essence of Knowledge-Based Guidance. Analyze deeply. Remember usefully. Act effectively.

Bottom Line. Memory isn't just about recalling the past; it's a powerful tool for shaping the future. By analyzing our experiences, we improve our decision-making for effective change management. Use your memory to forecast, lead, and learn from the past to excel in the future. Apply these insights to sustain change successfully.

December 26th

APPLAUD PROGRESS, PROPEL SUCCESS

"The Way to explain the miracle of human progress is to recognize the miracle of human progress."

—Steven Pinker, *Enlightenment Now.* [518]

Progress is a marvel we make. In companies, we must notice and praise progress. It's like clapping for a child who takes a first step. This cheers on more steps, more change. We keep the team moving. We celebrate each win. This way, change sticks. It becomes part of us. We build a culture that loves to get better.

Takeaways. Notice and celebrate progress; Encouragement boosts further change; Celebrations make change last; A culture of progress thrives on recognition.

Fundamental Concepts. Recognition sparks. That's Positive Reinforcement. Progress shows. That's Visible Evidence. Celebrations repeat. That's Behavioral Conditioning. Change sticks. That's Habit Formation. Culture thrives. That's Social Proof. Encouragement motivates. That's Intrinsic Reinforcement. Every win counts. That's Incremental Reinforcement. Recognition is key. That's Operant Conditioning. Build a cycle of better. That's Continuous Improvement. Recognize progress. Reinforce habits. Strengthen culture.

Bottom Line. To make change last, acknowledge and celebrate progress. Encouragement motivates further growth. Celebrating both small and big achievements forms a habit of progress and strengthens a culture that values improvement. Recognition is crucial for sustaining change, so keep reinforcing positive habits and continue to improve.

December 27th

OLD KEYS CAN OPEN NEW DOORS

"The essence of creativity is figuring out how to use what you already know in order to go beyond what you already think."

—JEROME BRUNER, *Acts of Meaning.* [519]

Creativity is key to sustaining change. It's about using knowledge in new ways. To keep change alive, think outside the box. Use what you know to find new paths. This keeps the change fresh and growing. In sustaining organizational change, revisit what you know. Then, push past old ideas. Mix past successes with new experiments. This keeps your team's skills sharp and engaged.

Takeaways. Creativity maintains momentum in change; Blend old knowledge with new ideas; Push boundaries to keep change fresh; Use success as a base for innovation.

Bottom Line. To sustain change, blend old knowledge with new challenges. Creativity drives progress. Use past successes to inspire innovation. Keep pushing boundaries to refresh strategies. This method sharpens skills and solidifies change. Reinvent constantly, learn continuously, and ensure change lasts.

December 28th

IN FAILURE, FIND STEPPING STONES

"The best way to overcome the fear of failure is to cope with failure as you go along."

—AARON T BECK, *Coping with Depression.* [520]

Failure is a teacher, not a monster. Embrace it. Learn as you fail, and failure becomes a step to success. This idea is vital for change managers. It tells us to accept failure. Deal with it, learn, and move on. This keeps change on track. In sustaining change, seeing failure as normal is key. It's not defeat but a chance to improve. By handling failure well, teams don't fear trying new things. They stay strong in change.

Takeaways. Accept failure as part of learning; See failure as improvement, not defeat; Teach teams to handle failure positively; Keep trying new things without fear.

Fundamental Concepts. Fear grips, learning frees. That's Emotional Conditioning. Failure teaches, insight reaches. That's Cognitive Reframing. Resilience follows failure. That's Psychological Elasticity. Confidence replaces caution. That's Self-Efficacy Enhancement. Experience shapes growth. That's Operant Conditioning. Feedback informs direction. That's Behavioral Guidance. Coping skills develop. That's Adaptive Learning. Action overcomes fear. That's Experiential Overcoming. Leaders model; teams mimic. That's Social Learning. Progress through problems. That's Solution-Focused Development.

Bottom Line. Embrace failure to reinforce change. Treat it as a chance to learn and improve. Encourage teams to view setbacks positively and keep innovating. Lead by example, using failures to guide success. Keep learning and moving ahead for lasting change.

December 29th

FAN FLAMES, DON'T JUST FILL SPACE

"The mind is not a vessel to be filled, but a fire to be kindled."

—ULRICH NEISSER, *Cognitive Psychology*. [521]

Imagine the workplace as a space where every idea sparks innovation. In organizational change, the mind's power to create new concepts outpaces the need to store old information. By seeing the mind as a source of fire, we ignite a passion for continuous improvement, inspire creativity, and drive the sustainment of change and evolution of the company.

Takeaways. Encourage creative thinking over rote memorization; Foster a passion for learning and innovation; Empower employees to find and light their own path; Promote continuous personal and organizational growth.

Fundamental Concepts. Change sparks action. That's Behavioral Activation. Ideas catch fire. That's Intrinsic Motivation. Passion overfills pages. That's Autonomy Support. Growth flames rise. That's Competence. Sparks spread, igniting teams. That's Relatedness. Fires warm, ideas form. That's Creativity. Kindled spirits conquer change. That's Psychological Empowerment. Knowledge fuels action. That's Cognitive Engaging. Transformation feeds on fervor. That's Motivational Synergy. Innovation glows from within. That's Internalized Inspiration.

Bottom Line. Fuel creativity to sustain change. Promote thinking that sparks innovation and passion for learning. Empower everyone to keep growing and improving. Drive change with a mindset that values new ideas over just knowledge. Encourage constant personal and company evolution.

December 30th

TEST, ADAPT, SUSTAIN CHANGE WITH INFORMED ACTION

"The T.O.T.E. unit is a feedback loop that consists of four steps: test, operate, test, exit. It is the basic unit of behavior and cognition."

—EUGENE GALANTER, *Plans for the Structure of Behavior.* [522]

Embrace the T.O.T.E. model for lasting change. [523] Each day, we test our progress, operate improvements, test again, and then exit or adjust. This loop reflects daily management life during digital transformations. It's a cycle of learning, applying, and relearning, ensuring that changes stick and benefits grow over time.

Takeaways. Test progress daily for continuous improvement; Apply changes immediately after testing; Re-test to confirm the impact of changes; Adjust or exit strategies based on latest test results.

Fundamental Concepts. Feedback loops guide change. That's T.O.T.E. in action. Tests set goals. That's Criterion Setting. Operations implement steps. That's Active Intervention. Re-tests measure impact. That's Evaluative Reassessment. Adjust or exit plans. That's Behavioral Adjustment. Continuous loop ensures stickiness. That's Sustainment. Change adapts or ends. That's the Closure in Cognition. This loop feeds growth. That's Cognitive and Behavioral Development.

Bottom Line. Use the T.O.T.E. model: test actions, improve, re-test, and adjust for sustained change. Test daily and adapt strategies from feedback. This cycle ensures changes become permanent and effective.

December 31st

DROP 'SHOULD.' EMBRACE 'WILL.' MAKE CHANGE REAL

"Stop shoulding yourself."

—ALBERT ELLIS, *How to Refuse to Make Yourself Miserable.* [524]

The phrase 'Stop shoulding yourself' inspires change that sticks. Change the 'shoulds' to 'wills' and take real steps. Make strategies from what will work, not just what you should do. This makes your team want to act, not feel forced. When change feels personal, it becomes powerful and permanent. Act on real goals, and watch your organization grow.

Takeaways. Turn 'should' into targeted goals for real change; Craft strategies from practical steps, not just obligations; Drive results by empowering action over imposed duties; Make change personal for stronger buy-in and commitment.

Fundamental Concepts. Duty weighs heavy. That's Obligation Overload. Change starts within. That's Intrinsic Motivation. 'Should' fades; 'will' shines. That's Autonomous Regulation. Action trumps should. That's Behavioral Activation. Empowerment lifts spirits. That's Competence Support. Obligations to actions. That's Operant Conditioning. Personal change sticks. That's Internalization.

Bottom Line. Use 'will' instead of 'should' for enduring change. Make goals practical. Action becomes choice, strengthening commitment and sustaining change.

RUIS — ARTIFICIAL INTELLIGENCE

In this world, ever-changing, where 'Artificial Intelligence' consumes all, we can't ignore its role in organizational change management. Here we stand, in the old Celtic 13th month 'Ruis', trying to figure it out. [525]

Now, about today. In late 2023, Prosci cast light on this through their research. [526] It's a glimpse of AI mingling with the craft of guiding change in organizations. This understanding will shift, no doubt, and fast. But here's how I see it now.

Bringing Artificial Intelligence into the realm of organizational change is both a hurdle and a chance. It's clear-cut yet layered.

The psychology of groups tells us this: fear and confusion about AI are deep-rooted. People naturally resist the unfamiliar. Yet, AI promises sharper communication, shaping content in new ways. The fix seems simple but takes work by training to unravel AI, to turn the unknown into the known.

Economically, the point is straightforward: AI resources are limited. Budgets are tight. But AI's efficiency and insights are too vital to overlook. The move? Weigh the costs against the gains, fitting AI's potential into the firm ground of business plans.

Sociologically, the worry is losing the human part. AI might overshadow what only people can bring, a key piece of organizational culture. Still, AI could improve how we connect and decide. The solution is in balance—using AI to boost, not replace, the human touch.

In business and schooling, adapting to AI is slow. Old ways of thinking and teaching don't fully embrace what AI can do. We bridge this by updating what we teach, fostering ongoing learning.

And then, governance and ethics. AI in change management brings up privacy, security concerns. The path is through clear rules, legal compliance, ethical use of AI—a structured way in a shifting world.

In short, using AI in managing change is about striking a balance. It's meeting the unknown with understanding, blending tech with humanity, and guiding change with a sure hand.

AI INTENSIFIES, NOT SIMPLIFIES, ORGANIZATIONAL COMPLEXITIES

"The machine does not isolate a man from the great problems of nature but plunges him more deeply into them."

—ANTOINE DE SAINT-EXUPÉRY, *Night Flight.* [527]

Artificial Intelligence in organizational change doesn't simplify but deepens complexities. It immerses us in understanding organizational issues. AI isn't a standalone solution but a tool for meaningful transformation when combined with human insight.

Takeaways. AI deepens engagement with organizational challenges; Successful AI integration requires understanding deeper organizational issues; AI is a tool that complements, not replaces, human insight.

Fundamental Concepts. Tech sits idle, a case of Tool Underuse. AI in the mix, but not in the heart of change. That's Passive Tech Integration. The psychological dance begins. It's Self-Determination Theory at play. Needs for autonomy, competence, relatedness, all stirring. That's Psychological Undercurrent. Leadership's role? Vital. They must guide, not just observe. That's Active Tech Leadership. Skills gap looms, behavioral psychology rings the alarm. That's Skill Deficit Highlight. Strategy, not just tech. Bridging the human-tech divide. That's Strategy Connection. The journey of AI in change—a blend of tech and psyche. That's Holistic Tech Adoption. Understanding, adapting, balancing - the keys to AI integration.

Bottom Line. AI doesn't just make change easier; it pushes us to confront our challenges. It's about diving deep into problems, not sidestepping them. For AI to be effective, it needs to blend with human insight. We must partner with technology, not just use it. Real change requires both AI's capabilities and our own understanding. Our focus should be on deepening our grasp of AI and improving its application in our work.

SYNTHESIS

I've combined the 'Fundamental Concepts' listed throughout the book and created a version of 'Plato's Allegory of the Cave' that applies to organizational change. Here's the idea.

From Fundamental Concepts to Transformational Strategies: Plato's Cave as the Blueprint for Organizational Change.

> In the allegory of the cave, as told by Plato, people live chained to the wall of a cave all their lives, facing a blank wall. They watch shadows projected on the wall from objects passing in front of a fire behind them and give names to these shadows. The shadows are as close as the prisoners get to viewing reality. He then explains how the philosopher is like a prisoner who is freed from the cave and comes to understand that the shadows on the wall are not reality at all. [528]

Let's take this allegory into the world of changing organizations. The cave is the company. It's full of shadows, which are the old ways of doing things. People have been watching these shadows move and talk and have been calling them work. But it's not real work. It's just the shadow of work.

The chains are the old rules that keep everyone doing things the same way. They make it hard to move or see anything else. When one person gets free and steps outside, they see the real world. They learn new skills and understand how things can be better—Capability Building, Skill Acquisition, Competence. They know now what real work looks like.

They go back into the cave, trying to tell the others. But they can't understand them. They only know shadows. So, the freed person starts showing them, slowly, how to see beyond the shadows—Vision Clarity, Visionary Leadership. They make it safe for them to talk about new ideas—Psychological Safety, Emotional Engagement, Agency Support. They show them how to learn new things—Growth Mindset, Mastery Orientation.

The free person, who is now a leader, doesn't force the others. They let them see for themselves why change is good—Adaptive Leadership, Transformational Leadership. They help them find their reasons to change—Intrinsic Motivation, Autonomous Motivation. And they reward them when they try new things—Behavior Modification, Cognitive Reappraisal, Behavioral Activation.

But not all want to change. Some are scared—Resistance Management, Agency Theory, Cognitive Dissonance. They need to be heard too. So, the leader listens, and they explain why change is needed—Active Listening, Effective Communication, Transparent Communication. They keep showing them, over and over, how the new way is better—Reinforcement, Echoic Reinforcement, Progressive Shift. And they watch how the changes are going, fixing things that aren't working—Adaptive Management, Feedback Loop, Incremental Reinforcement.

They get everyone to work together, to learn from each other—Social Learning Theory, Collective Intelligence, Collaborative Synergy.

They make sure they all feel like they belong and are good at what they do—Relatedness, Autonomy, Competence Support. They start doing the new things without thinking about it—Habit Formation, Social Norms, Behavioral Consistency.

They see how far they've come and are proud—Goal-Setting Theory, Change Mastery, Outcome Expectancy. They look back and see what they can learn from everything that happened—Metacognition, Experiential Learning, Retrospective Coherence. And they keep the change going, even when it's hard—Organizational Resilience, Sunk Cost Fallacy, Equilibrium Attainment.

This is how you change an organization. Not by dragging people out of the cave but by helping them see the light. Then they'll walk out into the sun themselves.

CORE CONCEPTS — ANALYSIS

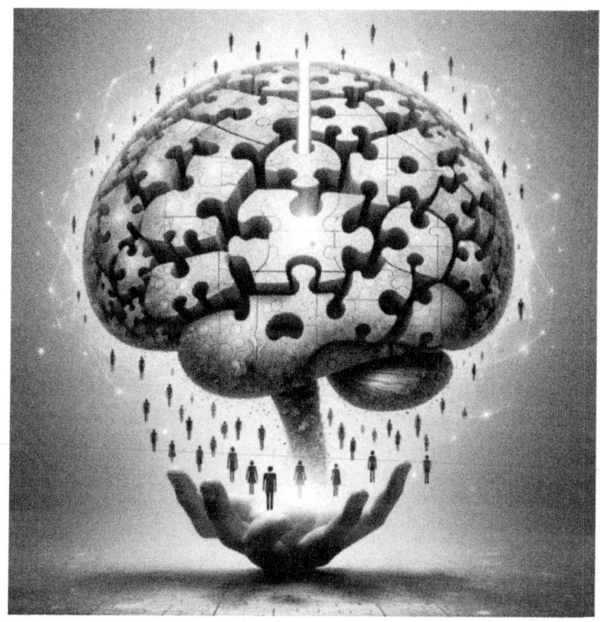

Writing the book, I looked for the core of each 'Fundamental Concept.' The true root. There's over 1700—OCM's not easy! Below are the most common ones, each with a description and use. First, the fifteen main roots.

- Self-Determination Theory: Motivational Psychology, Personality Psychology.
- Intrinsic Motivation: Motivational Psychology, Educational Psychology.
- Cognitive Dissonance: Social Psychology, Cognitive Psychology.
- Social Cohesion: Sociology, Social Psychology.
- Positive Reinforcement: Behavioral Psychology, Learning Theory.
- Social Identity: Social Psychology, Sociology.

- GOAL-SETTING: Goal Theory, Organizational Psychology.
- ADAPTIVE LEADERSHIP: Organizational Behavior, Leadership Studies.
- AUTONOMY: Motivational Psychology, Ethical Philosophy.
- COGNITIVE FLEXIBILITY: Cognitive Psychology, Neuropsychology.
- SOCIAL CAPITAL: Sociology, Economic Sociology.
- SOCIAL LEARNING: Social and Educational Psychology.
- FEEDBACK LOOP: Systems Theory, Cybernetics.
- GROWTH MINDSET: Developmental Psychology, Educational Psychology.
- LOSS AVERSION: Behavioral Economics, Cognitive Psychology.

If we say this list shows the bedrock of OCM, and that's a big 'if'—this isn't science—it doesn't mean we need to know all fifteen disciplines to do OCM right. At least, I hope not. Nobody can master all these fields, but some knowledge helps.

What's next? Like Newton said, we 'stand on the shoulders of giants.' We build on past work. We master the methods, study the literature, learn from the field, and adjust. We should grasp the basics of these core fields, too. If we do all this, we might just get good at OCM.

Here are the details, with ways to make them work in organizational change management.

Self-Determination tops with 122 mentions. It's about the drive from within and the control we have over our actions. Leaders must cultivate this internal drive for change to stick.

- Encourage workers to set their own change goals.
- Give them freedom in their tasks.
- Conduct workshops on personal change motives.

Intrinsic Motivation, mentioned 49 times, ties to Self-Determination. It's about finding purpose and enjoying the work.

- Discuss how change can develop one's skills.
- Share stories of success that resonate personally.
- Shape roles around what workers value.

Cognitive Dissonance, with 41 nods, points to the strain of mismatched thoughts. Address this to smooth out change.

- Open up about the unease change brings.
- Guide folks gently into new routines.
- Contrast old and new methods.

Social Cohesion, noted 16 times, is crucial for smooth shifts. It's the glue in teams that brings out collaboration.

- Create team building around the change.
- Ensure support is constant.
- Keep communication open for trust.

Positive Reinforcement, 15 mentions, backs wanted behaviors in times of change. Celebrating efforts lifts spirits and drive.

- Initiate celebrations for milestones.
- Applaud teams promptly for good work.
- Offer rewards for embracing change.

Social Identity, 13 mentions, is about meshing personal and organizational aims. Leaders should embed staff in the change narrative.

- Share tales of change that mirror collective aims.
- Involve all in owning the change.
- Celebrate shared accomplishments.

Goal-Setting, also 13 times, guides the change journey. Clear goals and tracking are vital.

- Set clear, shared targets.
- Regularly review and broadcast goals.
- Stay on top of targets and tasks.

Adaptive Leadership, 10 mentions, is about shifting leadership to fit the changing scene. Leaders must adapt and respond.

- Re-evaluate if leadership approaches are effective.
- Encourage leader-listener dynamics.
- Train leaders in varied leadership styles.

Autonomy, another 10, ties to self-determination, empowers staff in change. It's about control and involvement.

- Let teams choose in the change process.

- Design their role in change.
- Back new initiatives.

Cognitive Flexibility, 10 mentions, is the art of adapting thoughts creatively to change. It sharpens problem-solving.

- Instruct in new thought patterns.
- Test new ideas on a small scale.
- Facilitate diverse problem-solving discussions.

Social Capital, counted 10 times, is the currency of relationships and trust in change. It enables collaboration and communication.

- Foster stronger connections.
- Pair different areas with guides.
- Value trust-building and cooperation.

Social Learning, also with 10 mentions, is learning through watching and engaging. Sharing knowledge speeds up new practices.

- Exchange expertise on networks and media.
- Observe and learn together.
- Share knowledge in work sessions.

Feedback Loop, 9 mentions, is vital for tracking change and adjusting. It's about open dialogue.

- Regularly discuss change progress.
- Solicit and implement feedback for improvement.
- Adapt change strategies using feedback.

Growth Mindset, 9 times, is about seeing challenges as growth chances.

- Share stories of improvement, not just success.
- Emphasize learning in change.
- Celebrate effort and strides made.

Loss Aversion, also 9, is foreseeing and tackling fears of loss in change.

- Show the long-term benefits of change.
- Teach how to cope with losses.
- Address concerns and support through change worries.

MONTHLY WISDOM

January — CHANGE

1. Team effort turns many 'I's' into a collective win.
2. Build anew to make the old obsolete.
3. Focus on building new, and the old will fade away.
4. Change keeps flowing, never the same river, never the same you.
5. Adaptability, not strength, is the key to survival.
6. New results require new thinking.
7. To move a company, first move a person.
8. For change to stick, minds must make the shift.
9. Inspire the voyage, and the ship will build itself.
10. Learn today to change your world tomorrow.
11. Change your steps to change your destination.
12. Without a clear goal, every path is a detour.
13. Open minds breed change. Closed minds seal fate.
14. Manage the journey, not just the goal.
15. Spark the few, fuel the many.
16. Change the work, unlock the worth.
17. Commit to the ride, not just the ticket.
18. Know the 'why', navigate the 'how'.
19. Diverse 'whys' drive change, not narrow views.
20. Dig in to change, dig out the truth.
21. Change waits for none, so why wait?
22. Resisted change today is tomorrow's wisdom.
23. Clocks don't tick for change; you do.
24. Look inside, then decide.
25. Step out, but stay steady.
26. Forge ahead, patterns emerge.
27. Clarity in goals lights change's way.
28. Nature's dance needs change's beat.
29. Complexity in change? Find belief or bind roles.
30. Memory marks change; use it well.
31. Change, or be changed by change's swift tide.

1. Change well-managed is behavior transformed.
2. Change management is the coach, not the trophy.
3. Inaction is the mother of missed chances.
4. Unfinished tasks are future burdens.
5. Plans are pencils—reality's the eraser.
6. Time ticks, change picks, delay, and it slips away.
7. Agile right, not agile light.
8. Prepare to prevail.
9. Adapt, don't just adopt.
10. Small wins win big.
11. Trust data, doubt dogma.
12. See the whole, not just parts.
13. Impact is not just the end but the aspiration.
14. Clarity in innovation speeds adoption.
15. Alignment in perception paves the path for change.
16. Simplify, reflect, succeed.
17. Knowledge ignites, readiness rules, dreams drive, goals grow, steps stride, values nurture.
18. Frameworks dream, models deliver.
19. Change's path casts dice's predictive shadow.
20. Purpose is the compass—people are the journey.
21. Choices shape change—leadership guides it.
22. Mislabeling 'gaps' can misguide actions.
23. Talk clearly, train well, win change.
24. Speed sprints, unity endures.
25. Aligned values, amplified change efforts.
26. One key never fits all locks in change.
27. Master, choose, connect—change's potent trio.
28. Chart new courses, proof is in the journey.
29. Steer change with a solid portfolio.

1. Tech for show fails—outcomes make the glory.
2. Beliefs sculpt action, systems shape possibility.
3. Acceptance first, transformation next.
4. Uncertainty is where change takes shape.
5. The guide lights the path, but the team walks it.
6. Tech change reshapes minds, not just tools.
7. Lessons look backward, actions forward.
8. Change is an art, not just action.
9. Change needs wide, open eyes.
10. See beyond the break, gauge change's cost.
11. Risk weighs heavy on the decision-maker's mind.
12. Tech shifts, minds shift—so must our methods.
13. Tech without OCM is like a car without a driver.
14. Spot trouble early, adapt swiftly.
15. Tech's value—it's unlocked by minds.
16. Digital shift dances to the tune of human rhythm.
17. Transformation without change is mere motion.
18. Digital win—strategy, insiders, customer focus.
19. Inquire more, innovate often.
20. Lead to adapt, not just to accomplish.
21. Transform or trail in the digital race.
22. Every hand steers the digital ship.
23. Share the vision, multiply innovation.
24. Quick tech, slow change, leads the dance astray.
25. Ethics guide algorithms, not vice versa.
26. Anticipate to succeed—hesitation leads astray.
27. Transform, don't just inform—balance performs.
28. Twist data, lose truth.
29. Wisdom ignites change, burns old paths.
30. Align tech choice with strategic voice.
31. Skill today, history tomorrow, learn again.

April — CULTURE

1. Culture is the unseen guide.
2. Culture is boss.
3. See both cultures, manage change.
4. Culture grows with tales, changes with vision.
5. Ignoring culture burns projects.
6. Tech shines when culture aligns.
7. Culture's the script, but you're the playwright.
8. Shift values—steer the journey.
9. Culture guides, readiness decides.
10. Culture and business—two sides of the same coin.
11. Gauge culture; gauge organizational heartbeat.
12. Culture's the core—change that, change all.
13. Change the norm, change the game.
14. Risk and reward ride the same road.
15. Respect essence, shape the form.
16. Culture steers while change shifts gears.
17. Culture talks, listen up.
18. Gut feelings guide the game.
19. A planned culture can plan for change.
20. Change from the core, surface last.
21. Journey shapes, destination shines.
22. Culture is shared habits in motion.
23. Growth without values is a hollow victory.
24. Culture is a puzzle, not a painting.
25. Open minds open doors.
26. Change without culture is chaos.
27. Culture flexible, company capable.
28. Culture anchors the past, leaders steer the future.
29. Culture is the canvas—leadership is the brush.
30. Automate the old, innovate the new.

1. Change faster inside—stay alive outside.
2. Fear opens eyes. Hope moves feet. Aim for both.
3. People power tech—tech doesn't power people.
4. An uninspiring leader turns gold into gravel.
5. Silent strategy is a blueprint for bankruptcy.
6. When players don't care, the scoreboard does.
7. Urgency is the catalyst for transformation.
8. Lead with purpose as the chief meaning officer.
9. Tech's just a tool—your team turns it to treasure.
10. Gains await in tech—but first, old habits wreck.
11. Dreams demand wise action, not just wide eyes.
12. Simple out, complex in.
13. Embrace complexity, but navigate wisely.
14. Adapting is surviving; transforming is thriving.
15. Business thrives when beliefs bend.
16. Embrace the change conundrum.
17. Navigate change, chart new territories.
18. Don't manage shadows—lead teams to reality.
19. Know your knowns—nail your unknowns.
20. Past wins don't promise future gains.
21. People-centric change wins always.
22. Tech's power—people unlock it.
23. Change's helm—the top. Always.
24. Unity in teams, strength in clouds.
25. Invest in tech. Invest more in its users.
26. Many drops, an ocean— many changes, a wave.
27. Easy tech, quick change.
28. Know tech, lead change; drive, don't follow.
29. Change without understanding is chaos.
30. New rules await—adapt or risk obsolescence.
31. Skip OCM, invite chaos.

1. Risk is the road, preparation is the map.
2. Choose to chase change, don't let it chase you.
3. Facts tell, but feelings sell.
4. In change, safety sparks strength.
5. Craft the path, don't carve it.
6. Change demands better fails, not fewer fails.
7. Mind meets machine for masterful change.
8. Loss lingers, leadership must linger longer.
9. Self-Determination-Theory—your change cheat sheet.
10. Fading star or shooting star, you choose.
11. Change is your sail, not your anchor.
12. Desire digs deep, drives change.
13. Change is swift—be swifter.
14. Calm heads steer clear paths.
15. Change is hard—resilience makes it soft.
16. Fixate less, flex more.
17. Focus is fluid, flowing with the age.
18. Feedback's lens clarifies the path.
19. The heart of change beats in personal views.
20. Change starts in the mind before the grind.
21. ADKAR—the beacon of reliable change.
22. Change is both an inner and outer game.
23. Shortcuts cut short growth.
24. Change's direction? Your choice.
25. Change's wind blows—adapt or falter.
26. Knowledge is vast, wisdom discerns.
27. Knowledge reshapes the mind's landscape.
28. In every 'I', there's a story of change.
29. Every age offers tech insights.
30. Heart's drive leads, external rewards follow.

1. A silent sponsor is a project's downfall.
2. Momentum follows the leader's compass.
3. Pledge to progress; sponsor the journey.
4. Pledge to change? Own its outcomes.
5. Sponsorship steers constructive change.
6. A plan sits, real change hits.
7. Strong sponsors empower; weak ones deflate.
8. Move or lose—lead or concede.
9. Fake leaders fail—real ones prevail.
10. Authority needs an audit.
11. Blue oceans need daring captains.
12. Swift change requires swift sponsors.
13. Leading change—foes faced. Fickle friends flanked.
14. Change isn't singular—it's a full circle approach.
15. Leadership depth, not just digital depth.
16. Cultivate captains for change's voyage.
17. Vision transforms systems, leadership drives it.
18. Lead change with innovation, action, and vision.
19. Be the light, not the lampshade.
20. Lead with change, results follow.
21. Change thrives on trust, not ego.
22. Lead with clarity, not with shields.
23. Emotional buy-in beats forced compliance.
24. Insight trumps algorithms in change.
25. Lead with learning, win with wisdom.
26. Adaptability is a leader's best trait.
27. Lead with layers in mind.
28. Empower to tower—leaders uplift teams.
29. Visionary leaders paint tomorrow.
30. Transformers ignite, transactionals stoke.
31. Self-rule in leaders seeds company-wide change.

1. Be the change you manage.
2. Sync or sink.
3. Binary blinds—fluidity finds.
4. You're not the flame—you're the hearth.
5. Influence up, steer down.
6. Adaptability is the middle manager's superpower.
7. Doubt can drive direction.
8. Inspire change, don't just install it.
9. See the feeling, know the team.
10. Feel, then deal. Emotion drives motion.
11. Managers see bonds, not just bodies.
12. Not all support eases—fit matters most.
13. Managers conduct work's emotional beat.
14. Change needs a coach, not just a manager.
15. Middle managers—the change-makers in the middle.
16. A narrow view keeps progress out of sight.
17. Prevent, don't just fix.
18. Feed hope, starve despair, lead change successfully.
19. Imperfection breeds unique value.
20. Be real, build trust.
21. Change brings duality—embrace it.
22. Guide perceptions to steer organizational change.
23. Criteria guides; validation confirms; trust follows.
24. Fuel change—let intrinsic motivation win.
25. Trust ignites change—control extinguishes it.
26. Lead minds to lead change.
27. Change thrives on a shared 'we'.
28. Change is personal until shared by the group.
29. Active management drives change, stirs souls.
30. Seize the day—shape the change.
31. Change starts with self-awareness.

1. Ideas soar on the wings of will.
2. A project without a champion is adrift.
3. Network for net worth in change.
4. Listen, design, then realign.
5. Values voiced by few, echo in many.
6. Mindset molds the mission—intrapreneurs guide it.
7. Peer power speeds up change.
8. Drive change, don't just ride it.
9. New habits are seeds for growth.
10. Guide change, guard goals.
11. Empower champions to turn vision into reality.
12. Champions—strategy into action.
13. To lead change well, map the habitus well.
14. Good champions mold decisions with information.
15. Do, don't tell, to teach the digital change well.
16. True north lies in likelihood.
17. Believe small, stay small—learn more, be more.
18. Champions blend tech gains with human aims.
19. Be the spark that lights the team's fire.
20. Tomorrow's world, today's work.
21. Coalition is the backbone of change.
22. Tomorrow's better, if you dare change today.
23. Win or lose, champions push through.
24. Change is not static—champions know this.
25. Champions make the plan stand.
26. Change shapes champions, champions shape success.
27. Powering people powers change.
28. Champions lead change by living it first.
29. Dare to act, pave the impact.
30. Understanding quells change fears.

1. Clear words, clear wins.
2. Clear truth, clear path.
3. Words well-worked, wisdom shared.
4. 5w+h sets the stage.
5. Tech without context? Ignored.
6. Words matter, make them easy.
7. Media molds—mold your message.
8. Clear senders avoid jolting the listener's lane.
9. Connect deep, choose metaphors.
10. Think you communicated? Double-check.
11. Word-tuned, world-turned.
12. You shape change one word at a time.
13. Speak to reach—calibrate to teach.
14. Words flow, bonds grow.
15. New actions, new words.
16. Change without honesty is mere illusion.
17. Change your words to change your world.
18. Stories stick, facts fade, change stays.
19. Silence shouts the loudest fears.
20. Show proof, not just plans, to persuade people.
21. Walk their path, then talk the change.
22. Uncertainty speaks, wisdom listens.
23. Perfect words don't exist—clear intent does.
24. To lead the change, first change how you listen.
25. Repeat to remember, reinforce to realize.
26. Change hinges on the story's compelling pull.
27. Fear stalls speech, courage propels change.
28. Words shape futures; wield them with care.
29. Listen to dissent, it's hidden gold.
30. Truth weakens disbelief, strengthens action.
31. Speak to grow, not to use, let change flow.

1. Expect the block, build the bridge.
2. Trust dispels fear—lead clearly and kindly.
3. Priority makes potency.
4. Benefit beats effort, change sticks.
5. Imposition breeds resistance. Choice fosters change.
6. Ambiguity is change's adversary.
7. Familiarity is progress's foe.
8. Lead for ownership, not mere obedience.
9. Mistakes make masters.
10. Hear the edge to manage the middle.
11. Praise pays—it's a bonus that stays.
12. Change thrives on fairness, not force.
13. Ownership in change trumps resistance.
14. Past shadows tint future views.
15. Yesterday's shadows darken today's steps.
16. Roles anchor, change tests, balance bests.
17. Optimism is the torchbearer of change.
18. Lead change with insight, not just oversight.
19. Ego's shield cracks when discomfort peaks.
20. Cynics lead, progress lags.
21. Hidden fears cast the longest shadows.
22. Change needs more than a nudge or a nod.
23. Fear halts, focus propels.
24. Identity shifts, stay alert.
25. Let go, and find new chances.
26. Optimism fuels change—embrace it.
27. Own change, or it will own you.
28. Certainty's comfort is change's cage.
29. Hope starves resistance, feeds change.
30. Triumph's twin, fear of success, demands courage.

December — SUSTAINMENT

1. Sustainment is change's final score.
2. Reinforcement roots the routine.
3. Excellence is repetition refined.
4. Measure wisely or falter foolishly.
5. Integrity trumps ingenuity in numbers.
6. Goals guide, numbers speak, focus may mislead.
7. Morale means more.
8. Goals over glory.
9. Data drives rewards—deeds drive recognition.
10. Act right, choose wisely—keys to change.
11. Outcomes over outputs.
12. Adoption—go fast, go wide, go deep.
13. Enduring change is birthed in ceaseless learning.
14. Purpose shapes, vigilance steers.
15. Beware of paths that trap progress.
16. Goal: anchor change—steps turn to strides.
17. Desire trumps duty in durable change.
18. Reward rightly—boost creativity.
19. Champion competence—watch performance soar.
20. Nurtured agency, sustained change.
21. Repeat, reinforce, realize.
22. Plan to sustain, aim to retain.
23. Easy comes, easy goes—hard stays.
24. Analogies anchor change in the mind.
25. Past lessons shape future steps.
26. Applaud progress, propel success.
27. Old keys can open new doors.
28. In failure, find stepping stones.
29. Fan flames, don't just fill space.
30. Test, adapt, sustain change with informed action.
31. Drop 'should.' embrace 'will.' make change real.

Ruis — ARTIFICIAL INTELLIGENCE

1. AI intensifies, not simplifies, organizational complexities.

GLOSSARY

This glossary is my thinking on the fundamental concepts that show up more than once in the book.

Abstract Reasoning in cognitive psychology, noted twice, is thinking beyond the tangible. It's understanding the intangible, tackling problems with invisible tools.

Action-Oriented Leadership, in management and organizational behavior, tallied twice, is leaders leading by deed. They set the pace, show how it's done, make the calls.

Active Listening in communication theory, also two times, demands all of you. It's hearing deep, getting the message, and giving back something solid.

Adaptability in organizational psychology, counted twice, is the art of shifting to fit the scene. It's changing steps with the music of the times.

Adaptive Behavior in developmental and clinical psychology, seen twice, is the skill set for daily life, for dancing with change as it comes.

Adaptive Leadership in leadership and management, ten mentions, requires leaders to be like water—taking the shape of what's to come.

Adaptive Learning in educational psychology, counted three times, is teaching tailored to the learner. It's bending the system to fit the mind, not the other way around.

Adaptive Management in environmental management, two times, is the ongoing shaping of practice with the past as a guide.

Adaptive Response in psychology and biology, also two, is the living world's way of meeting challenges, of bending in the breeze to stand up straight.

Affective Influence in social psychology, noted twice, is the push and pull of feelings on behavior, the unseen hands of emotion on the wheel.

Affective Response in psychology, another two, is the heart's answer to experience, the soul's reply to the day.

Agency in sociology and psychology, with five mentions, is the stand-alone act, the single hand raised in a crowded room.

Agency in Action in action theory from sociology, two times, is the individual making waves, moving mountains with their own two hands.

Agency Theory in economics and organizational studies, counted twice, looks at the tug-of-war between those at the helm and those in the seats.

Ambiguity Aversion in behavioral economics, also two, is the shying away from the shadowed path, the preference for the devil known.

Arousal Theory in psychology, three times, is about finding that sweet spot of spark to light the fire of performance.

Attribution Theory in social psychology, three counts, is piecing together the puzzle of others' deeds, the why behind the what.

Authentic Leadership in leadership studies, five times, is the leader who stands clear in the sun, who earns trust by being true.

Automaticity in cognitive psychology, three mentions, is the groove worn by habit, where thought smooths away to nothing.

Autonomous Motivation in motivational psychology, counted three times, is the drive from within, the engine running on personal fuel.

Autonomy in ethical, political, and developmental theory, and Self-determination theory, nine times, is self-rule, the single boat on the open water.

Autonomy Support in educational and developmental psychology, eight tallies, is the crafting of a space where the self can stand tall.

Behavioral Psychology in psychology, listed twice, is the study of how the world shapes us. It looks straight at what we do, not what we think or feel.

Behavior Modification in clinical psychology, also two times, is about swapping bad habits for better ones with a carrot or a stick.

Behavioral Action in behaviorism, mentioned twice, is seeing and learning from what's done, not said.

Behavioral Activation in clinical psychology, counted six, is pushing against the bad with doing good things. It's action painting life brighter.

Behavioral Adaption in psychology, seen twice, is bending to fit where you're planted. It's how we twist to thrive.

Behavioral Anchoring in psychology, also two, is making actions stick to cues. It's building habits by linking them to signals.

Behavioral Consistency in social psychology, noted twice, is liking the same pattern. It's walking the same path by choice.

Behavioral Flexibility in psychology, with five mentions, is the knack for shifting gears when the road turns. It's bending without breaking.

Behavioral Inertia in psychology, listed three times, is when the past weighs on the now. It's like habits holding hands too long.

Behavioral Modelling in learning theory in psychology, also three, is learning by mirror, by shadowing the steps of another.

Behavioral Modification in clinical psychology, noted twice, is the re-shaping of actions through learned lessons.

Behavioral Psychology in psychology, emphasized again, three times, is studying what's done in plain sight, with science as the measuring stick.

Behavioral Reflex in psychology, counted twice, is the body's answer before the mind's question. It's quick and without thought.

Behavioral Stagnation in psychology, three times, is when change stalls. It's standing still when you should be moving.

Behaviorism in psychology, three mentions, looks only at what's on the stage. It turns the spotlight away from the mind's whispers.

Capability Building in human resources, counted twice, sharpens the workforce. It's about teaching the team to be better, stronger.

Change Activation in change management, four times, kicks off the shift. It's the first step in the dance of change.

Change Catalysts in change management, six mentions, speed up the shift. They're the accelerators in the engine of change.

Change Mastery in organizational theory, also six, is steering change to success. It's having the reins of change firmly in hand.

Change Resistance in organizational psychology, five times, is the drag against the new. It's preferring the comfort of the old.

Choice Overload in behavioral economics, noted three times, is the blur of too many paths. It's when the mind stumbles over its own choices.

Cognitive Adaptability in cognitive psychology, seen twice, is the mind's agility. It's bending thought around new corners.

Cognitive Alignment in organizational psychology, also two, is syncing thoughts in a team. It's thinking as one.

Cognitive Anchoring in cognitive psychology, four times, is sticking to first thoughts. It's the weight of the initial word.

Cognitive Awareness in cognitive psychology, counted twice, is knowing your own mind. It's the eye watching the thought.

Cognitive Bias in psychology, four mentions, is the slant of the mind. It's when background and feelings color thought.

Cognitive Clarity in cognitive psychology, seven times, is thinking straight and true. It's the clear line from question to answer.

Cognitive Coherence in cognitive psychology, twice, is thoughts in harmony. It's the peace of fitting pieces.

Cognitive Complexity in psychology, five times, is a web of thoughts. It's holding many threads at once.

Cognitive Consistency in psychology, two mentions, is the mind seeking order. It's keeping thoughts in line.

Cognitive Development in developmental psychology, three times, is the mind's journey. It's the road from childish thoughts to adult ones, and beyond.

Cognitive Dissonance in social psychology, forty-one times, is the rub of conflicting thoughts. It's the discomfort of contradiction.

Cognitive Ease in psychology, nine mentions, is the comfort of the familiar thought. It's the well-worn path of the mind.

Cognitive Effort in cognitive psychology, seen twice, is the weight of thinking. It's the heavy lift of the hard thought.

Cognitive Engaging in educational psychology, also two, is diving deep into thought. It's the mind fully turned on.

Cognitive Evaluation Theory in psychology, two mentions, explains the pull of rewards. It's the why behind action.

Cognitive Fixation in cognitive psychology, counted twice, is the stuck thought. It's the mind caught in a loop.

Cognitive Flexibility in psychology, twenty-six times, is the nimble thought. It's the mind dancing between ideas.

Cognitive Framing in psychology and behavioral economics, three times, shapes the view of problems. It's the lens we look through.

Cognitive Harmony in psychology, noted twice, is thought in balance. It's the calm of fitting ideas.

Cognitive Load in cognitive psychology, four mentions, is the mind's limit. It's the brink of thought's capacity.

Cognitive Mapping in psychology, also four, uses mental charts. It's navigating the sea of thought.

Cognitive Overload in cognitive psychology, three times, is too much to think. It's the mind overwhelmed.

Cognitive Priming in psychology, counted twice, is the echo of past sights and sounds. It's the shadow shaping new sight.

Cognitive Processing in psychology, also two, is the mind's mill. It's grinding through the grain of thought.

Cognitive Reappraisal in emotion regulation psychology, six times, changes thought to change feeling. It's the mind's twist on the heart.

Cognitive Reframing in psychology and therapy, five mentions, shifts the view on trouble. It's the mind's new angle.

Cognitive Resonance in psychology, three times, is when thought rings true. It's the bell of belief.

Cognitive Restructuring in cognitive therapy, also five, reshapes thinking. It's the mind remade.

Cognitive Rigidity in psychology, noted three times, is the frozen thought. It's the mind locked in old ways.

Cognitive Structuring in psychology, six times, orders thought. It's the mind's tidy room.

Collaborative Synergy in organizational theory, counted twice, is the magic of teamwork. It's the sum greater than its parts.

Collective Efficacy in social psychology, four times, is the group's belief in itself. It's the team's trust in its own power.

Collective Identity Formation in sociology, two mentions, is the birth of 'us'. It's the forging of the group soul.

Collective Intelligence in social psychology, three times, is the wisdom of the crowd. It's the chorus smarter than the solo.

Commitment Bias in cognitive psychology, seen twice, is sticking to the chosen path. It's the mind loyal to its decision.

Competence in psychology and education, six times, is being master of your craft. It's skill and knowledge hand in hand.

Competence Support in motivational psychology, four mentions, is bolstering belief in ability. It's the wind beneath the wings of skill.

Complexity Theory in systems theory, counted three times, watches the dance of intricate systems.

Decision-Making Theory in psychology, noted three times, is how we choose. It's the weighing of what's before us, deciding the path.

Deep Insight in psychology, counted twice, is a deep-sea dive into the complex. It's seeing the truth in the tangle.

Defense Mechanism in psychology, also two, is the mind's shield. It's guarding against the thoughts that sting.

Delayed Gratification in behavioral psychology, five mentions, is waiting for the better prize. It's the patience in the now for the later.

Distributive Justice in social psychology, noted twice, is fairness in sharing the load and the reward. It's the balance in giving and taking.

Dual-Process Theory in cognitive psychology, three times, speaks of two speeds of thought. One quick, the other slow and steady.

Dynamic Systems Theory in developmental psychology, seen twice, is growth as a changing river. It's shaped by many rains and many suns.

Echoic Reinforcement in behavioral psychology, also two, uses echoes to teach. It's the repeat in learning to speak.

Effective Communication in communication studies, six times, is the straight line between two minds. It's the clear passage of words.

Effort Justification in social psychology, counted twice, is valuing what is won through effort. It's the worth in the work.

Ego Depletion in social psychology, also two, is the draining of will. It's the cup of self-control running dry.

Emotional Engagement in psychology, noted twice, is how deep the heart dives. It's caring with the whole of you.

Emotional Intelligence in psychology, seventeen times, is knowing the heart's language. It's the understanding and guiding of feelings, yours and theirs.

Emotional Regulation in psychology, five times, is steering your own emotional ship. It's the hand on the helm of feeling.

Emotional Resonance in social psychology, counted twice, is feelings echoing between souls. It's the shared beat of hearts.

Emotional Response in psychology, also two, is the heart's answer to the world. It's feeling in the face of life.

Empowerment Theory in social psychology, four times, is helping hands finding strength. It's gaining the reins of your own life.

Equilibrium Attainment in systems theory, noted twice, is the balance in the chaos. It's the finding of level ground.

Equity Theory in social psychology, four times, is seeing fairness in give and take. It's the measure of just shares.

Ethical Responsibility in ethics, counted twice, is the call to do right. It's the moral compass pointing the way.

Evolutionary Psychology in psychology, three times, is the shadow of ancient steps in today's walk. It's the old paths in new boots.

Executive Function in neuropsychology, also two, is the toolbox of the mind. It's memory, flexibility, and self-hold.

Experiential Learning in education, counted twice, is wisdom in the doing. It's learning from the leap.

Exploratory Behaviour in psychology, also two, is the search in the strange. It's the quest in the unknown.

External Locus of Control in psychology, four times, is believing in the hands of fate. It's seeing the strings of life pulled by others.

External Validation in psychology, noted twice, is the seeking of nods. It's the eyes turned outward for approval.

Extrinsic Motivation in psychology, Self-determination theory, four times, is the pull from outside. It's the lure of the reward beyond self.

Fear Alleviation in psychology, counted twice, is quieting fears. It's the steady hand calming the storm.

Feedback Loop in systems theory, noted nine times, is where the end feeds the start. It's the echo shaping the shout.

Fundamental Attribution Error in social psychology, three times, is misreading the story. It's seeing character when it's really the scene.

Future Orientation in psychology, four mentions, is the eye on the horizon. It's the mind walking tomorrow's path today.

Goal Orientation in psychology, counted twice, is aiming beyond the finish line. It's mastering the race, not just running it.

Goal-Directed Behavior in cognitive psychology, three times, is action with purpose. It's steps marked by targets.

Goal-Setting Theory in organizational psychology, seventeen times, is the map drawn by ambition. It's setting the course to chase the dream.

Grit in psychology, noted twice, is the long-haul heart. It's the enduring chase of the distant star.

Group Cohesion in social psychology, four times, is the glue in the group. It's the bond holding the many as one.

Group Dynamics in social psychology, three mentions, is the dance of many feet. It's how the crowd moves as one.

Growth Mindset in educational psychology, nine times, is belief in better. It's the faith that effort carves the way.

Habit Formation in behavioral psychology, eight times, is the groove of repetition. It's the path worn by constant walk.

Hindsight Bias in cognitive psychology, noted twice, is looking back thinking you knew. It's the past seen through a knowing lens.

Holistic Integration in organizational theory, counted twice, is seeing the whole picture. It's all the pieces fitting together.

Holistic Organizational Change in organizational theory, three times, is shifting the whole. It's the entire machine moving as one.

Human-Centered Design in design and ergonomics, noted twice, starts with the heart. It's crafting with the human at the core.

Incremental Reinforcement in behavioral psychology, also two, shapes step by step. It's the slow sculpture of behavior.

Incremental Theory in psychology, three times, believes in growth. It's the faith in the unfixed.

Inertia in physics and metaphorically in psychology, noted twice, is the drag against shift. It's the weight against the turn.

Influential Leadership in organizational psychology, also two, leads by pull, not push. It's the front leading by the power to inspire.

Innovation-decision Process in organizational psychology, counted twice, is choosing the new. It's the leap into untried waters.

Insightful Leadership in organizational psychology, two times, leads by seeing deep. It's the helm guided by knowing beneath.

Instant Gratification in behavioral psychology, three mentions, wants now, not later. It's the urge for the immediate sweet.

Integrated Regulation in psychology, noted twice, is blending belief with being. It's the self-woven with the deed.

Internal Harmony in psychology, also two, is peace within. It's the still water deep inside.

Internal Locus of Control in personality psychology, seven times, is the hand on your own wheel. It's steering your own course.

Internal Motivation in psychology, counted twice, drives from deep down. It's the engine running on personal fuel.

Internalization in psychology, also two, is making the group's beat your own. It's the outside heart becoming the inside one.

Intrinsic Motivation in psychology, Self-determination theory, forty-nine times, does for the doing's sake. It's the joy in the act, not the trophy.

Knowledge Transfer in education and organizational psychology, noted twice, is passing what's known from hand to hand across an organization.

Law of Effect in behavioral psychology, counted twice, is the rule of reward. It's actions blessed by good returns coming back for more.

Leadership Void in organizational psychology, also two, is the empty chair. It's when the helm is unheld.

Locus of Control in personality psychology, four times, is the measure of your own reign. It's how much you think you steer your own ship.

Loss Aversion in behavioral economics, nine mentions, is the fear of letting go over the joy of getting. It's clinging to what is, overreaching for what could be.

Managerial Void in organizational psychology, counted four times, is the gap in the ranks. It's where guidance should be but isn't.

Maslow's Hierarchy in psychology, noted five times, is the ladder of needs. It's the climb from the ground of hunger to the peak of fulfillment.

Mastery Orientation in educational psychology, two times, is the eye on the craft, not the prize. It's learning for the sake of knowing more.

Memory Consolidation in cognitive neuroscience, also two, is the cement of the mind. It's today's thought becoming tomorrow's foundation.

Metacognition in educational psychology, two mentions, is thinking about thinking. It's the mind watching itself.

Mnemonic Utility in cognitive psychology, four times, is the tool belt of memory. It's the tricks that help the mind hold.

Motivation Theory in psychology, counted twice, is the why behind the move. It's the wind that fills the sails of action.

Motivational Deficit in psychology, also two, is the empty tank. It's when the drive doesn't start.

Motivational Drive in psychology, two times, is the hunger to reach or to have. It's the want that wakes you in the night.

Motivational Synergy in psychology, two mentions, is when wants walk together. It's different hungers feeding the same fire.

Narrative Paradigm in communication theory, counted twice, is seeing life as a story. It's making sense of the world as a tale told.

Narrative Psychology in psychology, three times, is life written in chapters. It's the self-seen as a story.

Negative Reinforcement in behavioral psychology, noted three times, is learning by the lift of the weight. It's the behavior brought back by what's taken away.

Neophobia in psychology, three mentions, is the fear of the new page. It's the shiver at the thought of the untried.

Neuroleadership in neuroscience and leadership, counted twice, ties the brain to the front of the line. It's leading better by knowing the mind.

Neuroplasticity in neuroscience, also two, is the brain's bend and stretch. It's the thought muscle growing new paths.

Normative Influence in social psychology, two times, is the crowd's quiet push. It's shifting to match the step of the many.

Observational Learning in educational and cognitive psychology, noted twice, is learning by sight. It's the craft caught by watching.

Operant Conditioning in behavioral psychology, twenty-four times, teaches through consequence. It's the dance of action and reward, or penalty.

Optimism Bias in cognitive psychology, counted twice, is seeing the glass half full. It's believing the rain will miss us.

Organization Culture Theory in management and organizational studies, also two, dives into how culture molds the ways of work. It's the unseen hand guiding how we do what we do.

Organizational Clarity in business management, noted twice, is the clear line in the company. It's knowing who does what and why.

Organizational Evolution in organizational theory, also two, is the slow dance of change in the halls of business. It's the company learning to walk new paths.

Organizational Justice in business ethics and organizational psychology, two times, is fairness in the ranks. It's the even hand in the workplace.

Organizational Psychology in psychology, counted twice, studies the beats of the business heart. It's making the workplace better for those within.

Organizational Resilience in business and organizational theory, five mentions, is standing through the storm. It's the company that keeps going.

Organizational Synergy in business management, noted twice, is the sum greater than its parts. It's the magic when we all pull together.

Outcome Expectancy in cognitive psychology, three times, is action with an eye on the end. It's doing with thought of the finish.

Overconfidence Bias in decision-making and judgment, three mentions, is too much trust in the self. It's the belief in one's rightness beyond the truth.

Passive Oversight in management, counted three times, is the watchful wait. It's leading by stepping back.

Pattern Recognition in cognitive psychology, also two, is the mind's eye catching the familiar. It's seeing the known in the unknown.

Performance-Contingent Rewarding in organizational psychology, two times, is the prize for the job well done. It's reward tied to the reach.

Persuasion Theory in communication and psychology, noted twice, is the art of the turn. It's the word that bends the will.

Positive Reinforcement in behavioral psychology, fifteen times, is the carrot after the jump. It's the sweet for the feat.

Power Dynamics in sociology and political science, counted twice, is the push and pull in the group. It's the tide of control.

Practical Wisdom in ethics and philosophy, also two, is the right call. It's the choice well made.

Predictive Encoding in neuroscience, noted twice, is the brain's guess based on yesterday. It's thinking ahead with a look back.

Proactive Adaptation in organizational development, two times, is the early shift. It's moving before the ground shakes.

Proactive Behavior in organizational psychology, five mentions, is the step before the need. It's acting ahead of the ask.

Proactive Leadership in management and leadership, four times, is leading the charge. It's the front before the push.

Progressive Shift in change management, counted twice, is the slow turn towards the new. It's the quiet walk to what's next.

Prosocial Behavior in social psychology, three times, is the helping hand. It's doing for others without thought of self.

Psychological Empowerment in organizational psychology, noted twice, is the feeling of owning your work. It's the grip on what you do.

Psychological Ownership in psychology, also two, is mine in the mind. It's holding what's not held.

Psychological Safety in organizational behavior, four times, is the room to speak. It's the space where words are not weapons.

Psychological Safety in organizational behavior, three mentions, is freedom from fear in the fold. It's saying and being without worry.

Reciprocal Determinism in psychology, counted twice, is the dance of influence. It's behavior shaped by and shaping the world and the self.

Reciprocity in social psychology, noted twice, is the echo of good. It's one kind act calling to another.

Relatedness in psychology, Self-determination theory, four times, is the pull to others. It's the basic need to connect, to belong.

Relationship Motivation Theory in social psychology, two mentions, is how bonds fuel us. It's relationships driving our doings and beliefs.

Resilience in psychology, counted five times, is the quick bounce back. It's toughness in the mind, the quick heal.

Resistance Management in organizational change, noted twice, is guiding against the pushback. It's steering through the stiff arm to change.

Resistance Psychology in psychology, three times, is the why of the wall. It's understanding and breaking the block against help.

Resistance to Change in organizational psychology, two mentions, is the stand against the new. It's the firm feet against the shift.

Retrospective Coherence in cognitive psychology, noted twice, is making now make sense with then. It's the past lighting up the present and future.

Risk Aversion in economics and psychology, eight times, is shying from the leap. It's the pull back from loss over the reach for gain.

Risk Management in business and finance, counted twice, is the map of what might go wrong. It's seeing the pitfalls and planning the path around.

Schema Theory in cognitive psychology, two times, is mental blueprints for understanding. It's the framework we hang the world on.

Self-Actualization in humanistic psychology, noted three times, is reaching the peak of what you can be. It's finding the fit of your own shape in the world.

Self-Awareness in psychology, four mentions, is knowing the self. It's the deep dive into your own waters.

Self-Determination Theory in motivational psychology, a towering 122 times, is steering your own life. It's the importance of holding your own reins.

Self-Efficacy in social cognitive theory, seven times, is trusting your own hands. It's believing in what you can do.

Self-Efficacy Deficit in psychology, counted twice, is doubting your reach. It's the weight on the wings.

Self-Regulation in behavioral psychology, five mentions, is the control for the long run. It's reining in impulse for the distant prize.

Short-Term Bias in behavioral economics, noted twice, is wanting the now over the later. It's the pull of the immediate sweet.

Situational Awareness in decision-making theory, four times, is knowing the room. It's seeing how the pieces move around you.

Situational Leadership in management theory, three mentions, shifts to suit the need. It's leadership that bends.

Skill Acquisition in educational psychology, counted five times, is learning the new. It's the build of ability.

Skill Deficit in educational psychology, two times, is missing the needed tools. It's the gap in the kit.

Skill Mastery in educational psychology and performance psychology, also two, is the top of the craft. It's the peak of practice and learning.

Social Bonding Theory in criminology, noted twice, is the strength of unity that protects us from harm. It's about staying together and on the right path.

Social Capital in sociology, ten mentions, is the worth of who you know. It's the lift from the network.

Social Cohesion in sociology, sixteen times, is the pull to the common good. It's the bind of the many to the one.

Social Comparison Theory in social psychology, counted twice, is measuring self against others. It's the balance of us in the mirror of them.

Social Constructivism in educational psychology, three mentions, is learning through together. It's building understanding with and through others.

Social Contract in political philosophy, four times, is the deal that holds us together. It's the handshake between the led and the leaders.

Social Facilitation in social psychology, noted twice, is the boost from being watched. It's doing better under eyes.

Social Identity Theory in social psychology, thirteen mentions, is who we are in the crowd. It's the self-made by the many.

Social Influence in social psychology, six times, is the bend to fit in. It's the lean toward the same.

Social Learning in educational psychology, counted twice, is learning by watching. It's the lesson caught by the eye.

Social Learning Theory in behavioral psychology, ten mentions, is watching mixed with doing. It's learning from what's around.

Social Network Theory in sociology, two times, is how our ties shape us. It's the pull and push of the web we're in.

Social Norms in sociology, also two, is the unwritten rules we live by. It's the guide to how we should be.

Social Proof in social psychology, twenty-four times, is following the crowd. It's the comfort of the common way.

Social Psychology studies the push and pull of the crowd on us. Seven times.
Social Support Theory in health psychology, is the strength from others in the hard times. It's the weight carried together.

Social Validation in social psychology, counted four times, is seeking the nod from the crowd. It's the look for the okay in what we do.

Status-Quo Bias in cognitive psychology, fourteen mentions, is the lean to leave as is. It's the drag on the wheel of change.

Strategic Congruence in business management, seen twice, is the company's plan fitting its build. It's the map matching the ground.

Strategic Foresight in business strategy, also two, is the long gaze ahead. It's the plan laid before the first step.

Strategy Gap in business strategy, noted twice, is the space between the plan and the walk. It's the difference between the dream and the day.

Sunk Cost Fallacy in economics, counted twice, is holding on because of what's already gone. It's the good after bad, the throw after the miss.

Survival Imperative in biology, and metaphorically in organizational theory, two times, is the deep push to keep on. It's the drive in the blood and bone.

Symbolic Interactionism in sociology, also two, is the talk without the sound. It's the meaning in the sign, the whisper in the symbol.

Systems Thinking in management theory, noted twice, is seeing the tangle as one. It's the problem as a piece of a larger picture.

Team Discord in organizational psychology, seen twice, is when the crew clashes. It's the rub that grinds the gears.

Temporal Discounting in behavioral economics, noted four times, is the lean to the now. It's picking the present prize over the future fortune.

Temporal Motivation in psychology, counted twice, is the push of the ticking clock. It's the hurry that comes with the deadline drawing near.

Temporal Perspective in psychology, also two, is how the view of time shifts the sight. It's whether the eyes are set on yesterday, today, or tomorrow.

Tool Underuse in psychology, noted twice, is leaving the kit half closed. It's not reaching for what could make the work better or easier.

Transformational Leadership in leadership theory, eight times, is leading by lifting. It's the pull to the better by the one in front.

Transparent Communication in organizational communication, counted twice, is the open book. It's the clear word that builds the trust.

Trust Amplification in social psychology, also two, is deepening the bond. It's the more in the handshake, the extra in the promise.

Uncertainty Aversion in economics, two times, is shying from the unknown. It's the step back from the shadow, the lean away from the maybe.

Uncertainty Avoidance in cultural psychology, six mentions, is different lands walking different lines. It's the love for the sure and the set.

Vision Clarity in leadership theory, noted twice, is the sharp picture of tomorrow. It's the clear map for the company's march.

Visionary Leadership in leadership theory, also two, is seeing beyond the hill. It's the far gaze that gathers others to follow.

INDEX

REFERENCES

[1] **Lombardi, V**. "What it Takes to Be Number One." (2001)

[2] **Fuller Buckminster R**. "Critical Path." (1981)

[3] **Millman, D**. "Way of the Peaceful Warrior." (1966). Often misattributed to Socrates, this quote comes from a character named Socrates in Millman's book.

[4] **Heraclitus**. Attributed. (c.500 BCE)

[5] **Ackerman, C. E**. "What is Self-Concept Theory? A Psychologist Explains." Positive Psychology. (2018). Change366's take: In changing an organization, know who you are. Your role is like your self-concept. Clear, simple. Know your strengths. Are you leading, helping, or planning? This guides you. Why you're there matters. It drives you. Be honest about what you can do. Like understanding yourself, it's key in managing change.

[6] **Darwin, C**. Attributed (by Snopes) to Prof. Leon C, Meggison in speech: "Lessons from Europe for American Business." (1963)

[7] **Einstein, A**. "The World As I See It." (1949)

[8] **Gergen, K. J**. "The Social Constructivist Movement in Modern Psychology." American Psychologist. (1985). Change366' take: In managing change, think about how we learn from others. Like cups teach us to hold liquid, working with people shapes how we think and act. Our background and where we come from shape us too. In work, as in life, we don't just find knowledge, we make it, shaped by our past. In change, talking and sharing ideas matters. It helps people understand and share thoughts. Change managers should let people talk more. It builds a team spirit and sharpens thinking and solving problems. Change comes from talking and learning together.

[9] **Prosci.** "ADKAR: A Model for Change in Business, Government and Our Community." (2006)

[10] **Bridges, W**. "Transitions: Making sense of Life's Changes." (1991). Change366's take on a key concept.

[11] **Adaption-Level Theory**. "Adaption-Level Theory." Oxford Reference. Change366's take: Harry Helson's Adaption-Level theory says, our view of things depends on what we've seen, what's around us, and what we remember. In change, what people think is normal or good depends on what they know and their experiences. New ideas can seem strange or wrong if they're different from the past. But if you introduce changes slowly, fitting them with what people know, they feel more natural. Change is about shifting what's normal, step by step.

[12] **de Saint-Exupéry, A**. "Citadelle." (1948). Original French: "Si tu veux construire un navire, ne rassemble pas tes hommes et femmes pour leur

donner des ordres, pour expliquer chaque détail, pour leur dire où trouver chaque chose… Si tu veux construire un navire, fais naître dans le cœur de tes hommes et femmes le désir de la mer grande et large."

[13] **Wigfield, A. & Eccles, J. S.** "Expectancy–Value Theory of Achievement Motivation." Contemporary Educational Psychology. (2000). Change366's take: Expectancy-value theory says attitudes come from what we believe and value. It means our decisions are based on what we know and how much it matters to us. This theory helps explain why people act a certain way. It's about grasping how during change. Beliefs and values shape our choices and actions. In change management, remember that people's reactions are rooted in their beliefs and values. Change must align with these beliefs and values or influence them.

[14] **Bach, R**. "Johathan Livingston Seagull – a story." (1970)

[15] **Lao Tzu**. "Tao Te Ching." (李耳). (6th century BCE)

[16] **Carroll, L.** (Charles Lutwidge Dodgson). "Alice's Adventures in Wonderland." (1865)

[17] **Nietzsche, F**. "Human all too Human: A Book for Free Spirits." (1878)

[18] **Bridges, W**. "Transitions: Making sense of Life's Changes." (1991). Change366's take.

[19] **Rodgers, E. M**. "Diffusion of Innovations, 5th Edition." (2003). Change366's take.

[20] **Prosci.** "Unified Value Proposition."

[21] **Thompson, H. S**. "Fear and Loathing in Las Vegas." (1971)

[22] **Sineck, S**. "Start with the Why." (2009)

[23] **Beer, M.** et.al. "Cracking the Code of Change." Harvard Business Review. Change366's take.

[24] **Lewin, K**. Attributed.

[25] **Obama, B**. Speech. Super Tuesday. (2008)

[26] **Shatz, I**. "Procrastination Theories: The Psychological Frameworks for Explaining Procrastination." Solving Procrastination. Change366's take: Procrastination is delaying important tasks without a good reason. Many adults, about 20%, do it frequently. This leads to issues like poor performance, financial problems, and health issues. It occurs when we avoid unpleasant tasks to feel better immediately or when we lack motivation. Sometimes, we don't feel connected to our future selves, so we prioritize immediate comfort. In organizational change management, it's crucial to understand why people delay actions. Help them see how the change aligns with their goals and can bring long-term benefits.

[27] **Twain, M**. Attributed. Change 366's take: Oscar Wilde is often credited with a similar quote: "I'm not young enough to know everything." Quote Investigator, however, attributes it to J.M Barrie.

[28] **McLeod, S**. "Jerome Bruner's Theory Of Learning And Cognitive Development." Simply Psychology. (2023). Change366's take: Locus of control is about who controls your destiny. Some have internal locus, believing their actions lead to results, like hard work leading to success. Others have an external locus, thinking luck or others decide outcomes. In change management, understanding this matters. Internal locus individuals take responsibility and adapt better to change. It influences how people react to change efforts. There's no one-size-fits-all; some say culture plays a role, others believe it's consistent.

[29] **Mridha, D**. "Verses of Happiness." (2016)

[30] **Nietzsche, F**. "Twilight of the Idols: Or, How to Philosophize with the Hammer." Maxims and Arrows. (1889)

[31] **Tolkien, J.R.R**. "The Lord of the Rings". A long-expected party. (1954)

[32] **Pirsig, R. M**. "Zen and the Art of Motorcycle Maintenance: An Inquiry Into Values." (1974)

[33] **Sammut-Bonnici, T**. "Complexity Theory." Encyclopedia of Management. (2018)

[34] **Tsaousides, T**. "What Makes Change Difficult – Approaches that make change hard and even impossible." Psychology Today. (2020) Change366's take.

[35] **Aurelius, M**. "The correspondence of Marcus Cornelius Fronto with Marcus Aurelius Antoninus, Lucius Verus, Antoninus Pius, and various friends." Harvard University Press. (1920)

[36] **Biasutti, M**. "Flow and Optimal Experience." Encyclopedia of Creativity. (2011). Change366's take: Flow is when you're fully immersed in your work, losing track of time because you're so into it. It's like a dance between your skills and the task at hand, making you focused and happy. But be careful, it's not always a good thing. Flow varies from person to person. In organizational change management, it's crucial. Understand each person's flow. Give them tasks that challenge just enough but are doable. This keeps them engaged and content during changes.

[37] **Lee-Bourke, A.** Observations from practice.

[38] **Dante Alighieri**. "La Vita Nuova." (1294)

[39] **Crestani, D**. et.al. "An Integrated Approach For The Construction Of Enterprise Change Trajectories." Hal Open Science. (2013)

[40] **Nadella, S**. "Microsoft Inspire." (2018)

[41] **Prosci.** "Definition of Change Management."

[42] **BBC TV "Yes Minister."** Season 1, Episode 2. "The Skeleton in the Cupboard." Produced by Sydney Lotterby, Peter Whitmore and Stuart Allen.

[43] **Epstude, K. & Roese, N. J**. "The Functional Theory of Counterfactual Thinking." National Library of Medicine. (2008). Change366's take: Counterfactuals are thoughts about what could have been. They can make you feel bad

or good. If you think how things could be worse, it can make you feel better about what really happened. But if you think about how things could be better, it can make you feel worse. These thoughts are useful, though. They help you learn and plan for the future. In change management, understand how people think about what could have been. It affects how they feel and act. Use this to help them see how changes can lead to better outcomes in the future.

[44] **Bridges, W**. "Transitions: Making Sense of Life's Changes." Third Edition. (2019)

[45] **Nickerson, C**. "Zeigarnick Effect Examples in Psychology." Simply Psychology. (2023)

[46] **Bibel, W**. "Transition Logic Revisited." Logic Journal of IGPL. (2008)

[47] **Berra, Y**. Attributed. According to Snopes, the earliest appearance is by Benjamin Brewster in the Yale Literary Magazine, October 1881-June 1882 issue.

[48] **Rodgers, E. M**. "Diffusion of Innovation, 5th Edition" (1993)

[49] **de Rubens, S**. LinkedIn. (2023)

[50] **Lincoln, A**. Attributed.

[51] **Meadows, D. H**. "The Limits to Growth: The 30-Year Update." (2004)

[52] **Scottish Proverb**. "Great Scottish Quotes on Life." The Scotsman. (2017)

[53] **Russell, B**. "The Collected Papers of Bertrand Russell." McMaster University.

[54] **Westover, J. H.** "The Role of Systems Thinking in Organizational Change Management.", Forbes. (2020)

[55] **Taplin, D. H**. et.al. "Theory of Change Technical Papers." ActKnowledge. Change366's take.

[56] **Bozkurt, T**. et.al. "Application of Goal Setting Theory." Press Academia Procedia. (2017). Change366's take: Goal setting means planning to reach a target. It's about taking action, not just wishing. In organizational change management, it's vital. Set clear, challenging goals to drive better performance and commitment from your team. These goals should be tough but achievable, with a clear deadline. This keeps everyone focused and motivated. Remember, higher goals lead to better results if your team is committed and capable. So, when managing change, use the power of goal setting to steer your team towards success.

[57] **Rodgers, E. M**. "Diffusion of Innovations 5th Edition." (1993). Change366's take.

[58] **Snow, D.A. & Benford, R.D.** "Ideology, Frame Resonance and Participant Mobilization." Research Gate. (1988). Change366's take.

[59] **Shaw, E.** "Frame Analysis." Britannica.

[60] **McFillen, J.** et.al. "Organizational Diagnosis: An Evidence-Based Approach." Journal of Change Management. (2012). Change366's take: In organizational change management, diagnosing the organization is key. It means looking at culture, how things work, and what's strong or weak. Things have changed since this field started. Now, it's not just about behavior, but also about strategy and the whole business. It's about how people work together, not just alone. Many models help with this, like Force Field Analysis or the McKinsey 7s. They all see companies as open systems, always interacting with what's around them. They need to adapt to changes. The process usually goes like this: enter the situation, diagnose the problem, plan action, implement it, then end the project. The diagnosis is just about understanding the problem, not solving it yet. This step is crucial for successful change.

[61] **Stouten, J**. "Successful Organizational Change: Integrating the Management Practice and Scholarly Literatures." Annals of the Academy of Management. (2018)

[62] **Einstellung Effect**. (Maslow's Hammer). "Are the anchoring effect and the Einstellung effect two facts of the same phenomenon?" Science Direct. (2022). Change366's take: Maslow's hammer is like seeing every problem as a nail when you only have a hammer. It's using one approach for all challenges. This is narrow and limiting. Organizations face varied problems, needing different solutions. Relying on one method is like a sailor ignoring changing winds. Change demands adaptability, not just one tool.

[63] **Stouten, J**. "Succesful Organizational Change: Integrating the Management Practice and Scholarly Literatures." Annals of the Academy of Management. (2018)

[64] **Phillips, J. & Klein, J.D** – "Change Management from Theory to Practice." Springer Link. (2023)

[65] **Sirkin, H. L.** et.al "The Hard Side of Change Management" Harvard Business Review. (2005)

[66] **Prosci** "Connecting Change to Business Results with the 4Ps Exercise." Change366's take.

[67] **Prosci** "Best Practices in Change Management."(2022) & others including **Everett Rodgers's** "Diffusion of Innovations 5th Edition." (2003) Change366's take.

[68] **Kaufman, R & Watkins, R**. "Getting Serious About Results and Payoffs: We are what we say, do and deliver." Change366's take. (2000)

[69] **Sadki, B.** et.al. "Towards an Organizational Change Management by an Expert System." Change366's take. (2015)

[70] **Lencioni, P**. "The Five Dysfunctions of a Team." (2002)

[71] **Deci, E.L. & Gagné, M**. "Self-Determination Theory and Work Motivation." Journal of Organizational Behavior. (2005). Change366's take.

[72] **Popper, K**. "The Poverty of Historicism." (1936)

[73] **Deci, E.L. & Gagné, M**. "Self-Determination Theory and Work Motivation." Journal of Organizational Behavior. (2005). Change366's take.

[74] **Newell, A.** et.al. "The Logic Theory Machine: A Complex Information Processing System" Rand Corporation. (1956)

[75] **Lee-Bourke, A**. "What they Don't Teach You at Change Management School." (2023)

[76] **Levitt, T**. "Marketing Myopia". (1960)

[77] **Harvard Business Review**. "Why Change Programs Don't Produce Change." (1990)

[78] **Jung, C**. "Modern Man in Search of a Soul." (1933)

[79] **Van Gennepp, A.** "The Rites of Passage." (1908)

[80] **Campbell, J.** "The Hero With a Thousand Faces." (1949)

[81] **Jem, A**. "Why Are So Many Movies Basically the Same?" Psychology Today. (2021)

[82] **Joyce, J**. "Finnegan's Wake." (1936)

[83] **Kierkegaard, S.** quoted in Clare Carlisle's "Philosopher of the Heart: The Restless Life of Søren Kierkegaard." by Adam Philips (2019)

[84] **Twain, M.** Attributed.

[85] **Schopenhauer, A**. "Studies in Pessimism." (1890)

[86] **Bastiat. F**. "That Which is Seen and That Which is Not Seen." (Ce qu'on voit et ce qu'on ne voit pas) (1850). Change366's take.

[87] **Pettinger, T**. "The Broken Window Fallacy." Economics. (2021)

[88] **Noveck, I. A.** "Pragmatic Inferences Related to Logical Terms." Experimental Pragmatics. (2004). Change366's take.

[89] **Davis, S**. "Tracing Somatic Therapies." The Lancet, Psychiatry. (2021). Change366's take: Somatic psychology tries to understand how our body and mind connect, without separating them like in old thinking. Psychiatrists call this the mind-body Cartesian dualism.

[90] **Carey, S**. "The Origin of Concepts." (2009)

[91] **Lee-Bourke. A**. "Why Change Management for Digital Transformation? – asking the Socratic Questions." LinkedIn article. (2023)

[92] **Smith, M**. "What is Praxis?" The encyclopaedia of pedagogy and informal education. (1999, 2011). Change366's take: Praxis means putting theory or ideas into practice. It's about doing and applying what you've learned or thought about.

[93] **Perrow, C**. "Normal Accidents. Living with High-Risk Technologies." (1984)

[94] **DeCamp, W.** "The Theories of Accident Causation." Security Supervision and Management. (2015)

[95] **Peppard, J.** et.al "Managing the Realization of Business Benefits from IT Investments." MIS Q (2007). Change366's take.

[96] **Lee-Bourke, A.** "Cloud Migration Tango: A Dance Between Tech Execution and Change Management." Blog post. (2023)

[97] **Westerman, G.** "Leading Digital: Turning Technology into Business Transformation." Harvard Business Publishing. (2104)

[98] **Westerman, G.** et.al. "Digital Transformation is Not About Technology." Harvard Business Review (2019)

[99] **Sagan, C.** "The Demon-Haunted World: Science as a Candle in the Dark." (1996)

[100] **Rogers, D. L.** "The Digital Transformation Playbook: Rethink Your Business for the Digital Age." (2016)

[101] **Karima, J.** "Advantages of Digital Transformation Models and Frameworks for Business: A Systematic Literature Review." International Journal of Advanced Computer Science and Applications (2022). Change366's take.

[102] **Jewer. J.** "Governance of Digital Transformation: A Review of the Literature." Proceedings of the Annual Hawaii International Conference on System Sciences. (2022). Change366's take.

[103] **Schiuma, G.** "How Wise Companies Drive Digital Transformation." Journal of Open Innovation. (2021). Change366's take.

[104] **Bencsik, A.** "Trust in and Risk of Technology in Organizational Digitalization." Risks. (2022). Change366's take.

[105] **O'Neil, C.** "Weapons of Math Destruction". (2016)

[106] **Hitchens, C.** Attributed

[107] **Crowley, A.** "The Book of Lies." (1912)

[108] **Dialectic.** Change366's take: The dialectical method in organizational change is about blending different ideas. It's like making a strong rope from different strands.

[109] **Good, I. J.** "The American Statistician." (1972)

[110] **Russell, D.** Attributed.

[111] **Kouzes, J. M, & Posner, B. Z.** "The Leadership Challenge." (1981). First published reference.

[112] **Drucker, P.** Attributed

[113] **Linton, R.** "The Study of Man." (1936)

[114] **Gerstner Jr, L. V.** "Who Says Elephants Can't Dance?" (2002)

[115] **de Lint, C**. "Spiritwalk." (1992)

[116] **Lilly, R**. "Startup Balanced." (2012)

[117] **Kotter, J.** "Leading Change." (1996)

[118] **Drucker, P.** Attributed

[119] **Harari, Y. N**. "Homo Deus, A Brief History of Tomorrow." (2016)

[120] **Science Direct**. "Cultural Heritage." (2015)

[121] **Prosci.** "Improving Change Management Application through Cultural Awareness and Adaptation." Whitepaper. (2016)

[122] **McKinsey Quarterly**. "Culture for a Digital Age."

[123] **Corritore, M**. et.al. "The New Analytics of Culture." Harvard Business Review (2020)

[124] **Szumal, J. L. & Cooke, R. A**. "Creating Constructive Cultures: Leading People and Organizations to Effectively Solve Problems and Achieve Goals." Human Synergistics. (2019)

[125] **Cartwright, J**. "Cultural Transformation: Nine Factors for Continuous Business Improvement." (1999)

[126] **Copuš, L**. et.al. "Is There a Possibility to Characterize an Organizational Culture by its Selected Cultural Dimensions." Sage Open. (2023)

[127] **Plutarch**. "Plutarch's Lives." Thomas North translation (1579)

[128] **Schein, E. H**. "Organizational Culture and Leadership." (1985)

[129] **Thompson, H. S**. Attributed

[130] **Davis, T.** "7 Ways to Boost Eudaimonic Well-Being." Psychology Today. (2021), Change366's take: Eudaimonic well-being is living a life with purpose and meaning. It's not chasing fleeting pleasures, but finding deep fulfillment in what you do. It's the essence of a life well-lived, where each moment matters, and you're true to yourself.

[131] **Thoreau, H. D**. "Walking." (1862)

[132] **Lee-Bourke, A**. "What they Don't Teach You at Change Management School." (2023)

[133] **Lee-Bourke, A**. "What they Don't Teach You at Change Management School." (2023)

[134] **Goffman, E**. "The Presentation of Self in Everyday Life." (1956)

[135] **House, R. J**. "Culture Leadership and Organizations: The GLOBE Study of 62 Societies." (2004). Change366's take.

[136] **Khatoon, A**. "Impact of Organizational Change on Organizational Culture." (2008). Change366's take.

137 **Angelou, M**. "I Know Why the Caged Bird Sings." Attributed. (1969)

138 **Berger, P. L. & Luckmann, T**. "The Social Construction of Reality." (1966)

139 **Solzhenitsyn, A**. "From Dissidence to Statesmanship: Aleksandr Solzhenitsyn, Vaclav Havel, & the Ideological Lie in the 20th Century." Address to the International Academy of Philosophy, Liechtenstein, (1993)

140 **Voyer, B G, & Franks, B**. "Toward a Better Understanding of Self-Construal Theory." American Psychological Association. (2014). Change366's take.

141 **Köroğlu, E. O**. "The Effect of Development Culture and Rational Sub-Cultures on Work Performance, the Mediating Role of Openness Toward Organizational Change." Journal of Turkish Social Sciences Research. (2022). Change366's take.

142 **Sawalla, N. Aaitouni, M. & El Sharif, A**. "Corporate Culture Dimensions Associated With Organizational Commitment: An Empirical Study." The Journal of Applied Business Research. (2012). Change366's take.

143 **Schoenberger, E**. "The Cultural Crisis of the Firm." (1997)

144 **Schoenberger, E**. "The Cultural Crisis of the Firm." (1997)

145 **Borkovich, D**. et.al. "New Technology Adoption: Embracing Cultural Influences." Issues in Information Systems. (2015)

146 **Whitehead, A. N**. "An Introduction to Mathematics." (1911)

147 **Welch, J**. Attributed.

148 **Kotter, J**. "Leading Change." (1996)

149 **Burning Platform**. Change366's take: The 'burning platform' is a dire call to action. It's like a ship on fire at sea. You either jump or perish. It's a stark, urgent choice. Change or be consumed. Simple and brutal.

150 **Morgan, R. M. & Hunt S. D**. "The Commitment-Trust Theory of Relationship Marketing." Journal of Marketing. (1994). Change366's take: the Commitment-Trust Theory is simple: relationships survive on steadfast commitment and solid trust. Without them, they fall apart.

151 **Microsoft**. AI Commercial, featuring Common. YouTube. (2018)

152 **Harvard Business Review**. "Why Do So Many Managers Forget They're Human Beings?" (2018)

153 **CNBC**. "The $900 billion reason GE, Ford and P&G failed at digital transformation." (2019)

154 **Covey, S**. "Stephen Covey – If Your Company Was a Soccer Team." Strategic Business Advisors. (2004)

155 **Kotter, J**. "Leading Change: Why Transformation Efforts Fail." Harvard Business Review (1995)

[156] **Welch, J**. "What is the Role of a Leader?" Jack Welch Management Institute. YouTube. (2016)

[157] **Peppard, J**. et.al. "Managing the Realization of Business Benefits from IT Investments." MIS Q (2007). Change366's take.

[158] **Harvard Business Review**. "Digital Transformation Is Not About Technology." (2019)

[159] **McKinsey Quarterly**. "Helping employees embrace change."

[160] **Peck, Scott M**. "The Road Less Travelled: A New Psychology of Love, Traditional Values and Spiritual Growth." (1990)

[161] **DeShon, R**. "Multivariate Dynamics in Organizational Science." The Oxford Handbook of Organizational Psychology. (2012). Change366's take: Multivariate dynamics in organizational change are many factors, all tangled. Managing change is to untangle them, see each clearly. It's hard, direct work.

[162] **Schmidt, J. C**. "Challenged by Instability and Complexity…Questioning Classic Stability Assumptions and Presuppositions in Scientific Methodology." Handbook of the Philosophy of Science. (2011). Change366s take: Non-linear dynamics in organizational change are like navigating a stormy sea. Small moves can lead to big shifts. It's unpredictable, demanding adaptability.

[163] **Harvard Business Review.** "Taming Complexity." (2020). Change366's take.

[164] **Shaw, G. B.** "Man and Superman." (1905)

[165] **Russell, B**. Attributed by James E Parker Jr. (1964)

[166] **Joyce, H**. "A Close Shave for Set Theory." (2002)

[167] **Thoreau, Henry, D**. "Walden; or, Life in the Woods." (1854)

[168] **Plato**. "The Republic." Allegory of the Cave. Book VII 514a-521d

[169] **Benson. B & Manoogian III, J**. "Cognitive Bias Codex." University of North Carolina.

[170] **Rumsfeld, D**. US Department of Defense Press Conference. (2002)

[171] **Leibniz, G**. Correspondence of Leibniz and Bernoulli. (1606)

[172] **Boston Consulting Group** "Learn from the Best in Organizational Transformation." (2020). Change366's take.

[173] **Lee-Bourke, A**. Allegory describing why Project and Change Management are both required for project success.

[174] **Sangyoon, Y**, et.al. "Inertia Routines: A Hidden Source of Organizational Variation." Organization Science. (2016). Change366's take: Routines often slow change. But they're not just anchors; they're sails too. They help organizations adapt by shaping the way changes unfold. When change happens less, it can mean more focus, sharper reactions. Inertia isn't just resistance. It's a

chance to steady the course, to evolve even when the waters get rough. That's how some keep winning, evolving not just with the market, but also within.

175 **Hickson, D.** J. "A Convergence in Organization Theory." Administrative Science Quarterly. (1966). Change366's take: Theories on organizations narrow down to roles, how clear they are, and the freedom they allow. Everyone assumes more specific roles shape behavior clearly. But measure this. Without noticing this focus, fresh ideas may stall.

176 **Financial Times**. "How to Future Proof Company Culture." (2020)

177 **Moore, J.** "Cloud Adoption hits cultural snag, opens MSP Opportunities." Tech Target IT Channel. (2020)

178 **Kreiner, G. E**. et.al. "Elasticity and the Dialectic Tensions of Organizational Identity: How Can We Hold Together While We Are Pulling Apart?" Academy of Management Journal. (2014). Change366's take: In managing change, think of an organization's identity as elastic. Stretching, not breaking. It's a balance—holding onto the core while embracing the new. This tension, this elasticity, shapes how people think and adapt within the company. It's about guiding, not forcing, the stretch.

179 **Gartner**. "Gartner Survey of Over 2,000 CIOs Reveals the Need to Accelerate Time to Value from Digital Investments." 2022. Change366's take.

180 **Prosci**, "5 Tenets of Change Management." Change366's take.

181 **McLeod, S**. "Operant Conditioning: What It Is, How it Works, And Examples." Simply Psychology. (2023). Change366's take: Operant conditioning, or instrumental learning, shapes behavior through consequences. Reinforced actions repeat; punished actions fade.

182 **Lee-Bourke, A**. "What they Don't Teach You at Change Management School." (2023)

183 **Prosci.** Attributed.

184 **Weiss, H. & Cropanzano, R**. "Affective Events Theory: A Theoretical Discussion of The Structure, Cause and Consequences of Affective Experiences at Work." Research in Organizational Behavior. (1996). Change366's take: Understanding emotions is key to navigating organizational change effectively.

185 **Beausoleil, A**. "Revisiting Rogers: the diffusion of his innovation development process as a normative framework for innovation managers, students and scholars." The Journal of Innovation Management. (2019)

186 **Prosci.** Tim Creasey, LinkedIn. (2023). Change366's take: Prosci talked to 2,668 people who deal with change. They asked about the future. Here's what they heard: 37% see technology changing. AI is big. 10% expect new rules, AI and cybersecurity. 9% think the environment will get more attention. Less plastic, less waste. Another 9% are worried about people at work. Burnout. Need for flexible hours. 9% see a shift in how companies run. More inclusivity. 5% believe customers will want things faster. Big changes are on the way.

[187] **Lee-Bourke, A**. Unpublished Blog "Adapt or Die: The Brutal Truth About OCM in Digital Transformation."

[188] **Peterson, J**. "Personality – Heroic and Shamanic Initiations." Lecture, YouTube. (2017)

[189] **Nickerson, C**. "The Yerkes-Dodson Law of Arousal and Performance." Simply Psychology." (2023)

[190] **Peterson, J**. "Personality – Heroic and Shamanic Initiations." Lecture, YouTube. (2017)

[191] **Fight or Flight Response**. Change366's take: Fight or flight: aids or hinders change. Embrace it proactively for success. Reactivity slows. Manage change wisely.

[192] **Jung, C**. "Empiricism'. Depth Psychology. CW 4 Para 774.

[193] **Benson. B & Manoogian III, J**. "Cognitive Bias Codex." University of North Carolina.

[194] **Jung C**. "The Archetypes and the Collective Unconscious. 2nd Edition." (1969), Change366's take: Emotions shape change. Acknowledge and navigate them wisely.

[195] **Chima, A. & Gutma, R**. "What it Takes to Lead Through an Era of Exponential Change." Harvard Business Review. (2020)

[196] **Campbell, J**. "The Hero With a Thousand Faces." 2nd Edition (1968).

[197] **Beckett, S**. "Worstward Ho!" (1983)

[198] **Yarkoni, T**. "Psychoinformatics: New Horizons at the Interface of the Psychological and Computing Sciences." Sage Journals. Current Directions in Psychological Science. (2012). Change366's take.

[199] **Grothe-Hammer, M. & Berkowitz, H**. "Decisional organization theory: towards an integrated framework of organization." Research Handbook on the Sociology of Organizations. (2022). Change366's take: Organizations evolve through decisions, facing complex realities. In change, focus on decision-making. It shapes and structures the organization's core.

[200] **Feldman, David B**. "Why the Five Stages of Grief Are Wrong." Psychology Today. (2017)

[201] **Dorina, I**. et.al. "Utility of temporal self-regulation theory in health and social behaviours: A meta-analysis." British Journal of Health Psychology. (2022). Change366's take: Temporal self-regulation theory in change management: It's about timing. Acting now for future gains. Patience and discipline drive success.

[202] **Deci, E, Gagné, M and Ryan. R**. "Self-determination theory applied to work motivation and organizational behavior." American Psychological Association, PsycNet. (2018). Change366's take.

[203] **Gilal, F**. et.al. "The role of organismic integration theory in marketing science: A systematic review and research agenda." European Management Journal. (2022). Change366's take: Aligning individual and organizational goals fosters change.

[204] **Nietzsche, F**. "On Truth and Lies in a Nonmoral Sense." (1896)

[205] **Trojan, S & Pokorný, J**. "Theoretical Aspects of Neuroplasticity." National Library of Medicine. (19990. Change366's take: Adaptability is key. Minds, like organizations, must evolve to survive and thrive.

[206] **Twain, M**. Attributed. The first appearance of this seems to be in "Readers Digest Quotable Quotes: Wit and Wisdom for All Occasions." (1992)

[207] **Amin, H. U. & Malik, A**. "Memory Retention and Recall Process." EEG/ERP Analysis. (2014). Change366's take: Remembering the past guides future changes. It's learning from history to shape tomorrow.

[208] **'Raymond (Red) Reddington.'** "The Blacklist." NBC Television. Season 1 Episode 9. YouTube. (2013)

[209] **Kronenfield, D. B**. "Cognitive Structure." Comprehensive Clinical Psychology. (1998). Change366's take: Solid mental frameworks make adapting easier. Clear, strong structures lead to better understanding and effective action.

[210] **'Roy Batty.'** "Blade Runner." "Tears in the Rain." Warner Brothers. YouTube (1982)

[211] **Contrafatto, M**. "Stewardship Theory: Approaches and Perspectives." Advances in Public Interest Accounting. (2014). Change366's take: Stewardship in change management: It's about safeguarding resources for others. It's not just profit; it's responsibility. Aligning actions with sustainability, social good, and accountability. This approach shifts organizations towards sustainable futures, impacting both society and the environment. It's about leading with care, for now and for later.

[212] **Swedish Made Easy**. "10 Swedish Sayings in English."

[213] **Whysall, Z**. "Managing Change: Insights from Neuropsychology." Lane4 White Paper. Change366's take.

[214] **Ruiz-Rodrigues. R**. et.al. "Neuroleadership: a new way for happiness management." National Library of Medicine. (2023). Change366's take: Neuroleadership in change management: It's brain-led leadership. Understanding how minds work guides better decisions, actions, and changes.

[215] **Kahneman. D**. "Thinking Fast and Slow." (2011)

[216] **McLeod, S**. "Fundamental Attribution Error in Psychology." Simply Psychology. (2023). Change366's take: We blame people, not situations. We see actions as personality-driven, not influenced by context. This bias can mislead. It leads to wrong judgments, unfair blame. Understand actions in their environment. It's not just about the individual.

[217] **Schraw, G. & Moshman, D**. "Metacognitive Theories." Educational Psychology Review. (1995). Change366s take: Metacognition is thinking about thinking. Knowing your thought processes helps guide decisions and adapt to change.

[218] **Smith, E**. "The big idea: are our short attention spans really getting shorter?." The Guardian. (2023)

[219] **Burns R**. "To a Louse On Seeing One on a Lady's Bonnet at Church." The Kilmarnock Edition. (1786)

[220] **Nickerson, C**. "Looking-Glass Self: Theory, Definition & Examples." Simply Psychology. (2023). Change366's take: We shape ourselves based on others' views. Perception drives identity and actions in change.

[221] **Lee-Bourke, A**. "Change Management Field Notes." (2022)

[222] **Nickerson. C**. "Albert Bandura's Social Cognitive Theory: Definition and Examples." Simply Psychology. (2023)

[223] **Prosci.** "The Prosci ADKAR Model." Change366's take.

[224] **Goyal, C. & Patwardhan, M.** "Role of change management using ADKAR model: a study of the gender perspective in a leading bank organisation of India." (2018). Change366's take: A Cronbach Alpha of 0.833 for Prosci's ADKAR model signals strong internal consistency. It means the model reliably measures change readiness in organizational change management. High reliability, essential for decision-making, ensures you can trust ADKAR's effectiveness in guiding successful change.

[225] **Malmsjo, A. & Ovelius, E.** "Factors that Induce Change in Information Systems." (2003) Change366's take.

[226] **Hegel, G. W.** "The Phenomenology of Spirit." (1807)

[227] **McLeod, S**. "Holism in Psychology: Definition and Examples." Simply Psychology. (2023). Change366's take: Holism in change management is seeing the big picture. Behavior isn't just parts; it's more. The whole drives change, not just elements. Understand people as complete beings. It's not just about individual traits. In change, look at everything. The whole person, the whole team. That's how you understand, lead, and adapt.

[228] **Inzlicht. M**. et.al. "The Effort Paradox: Effort is Both Costly and Valued." Trends in Cognitive Science. (2018)

[229] **Dr. Seuss.** (Geisel, T S.) "Oh, the Places You'll Go!" (1990)

[230] **Berkman, E. T**. "The Neuroscience of Goals and Behavior Change." Consultant Psychology Journal. (2018). Change366's take: Understand motivation's roots. It's tied to our past, to rewards. Change is hard. It fights old habits, old rewards. Start small. Reward even little steps. New behaviors grow against old reinforcements. Know this struggle. It helps in guiding change. Identity shapes goals. Connect goals to self, to values. Identity-linked goals succeed more. Know the person, their values. Change isn't just action. It's identity, belief, value. Coaches help see these connections. Connect goals to self for lasting

motivation. Understand the brain, understand change. It's hard, but knowing the science helps. Neuroscience offers insights for setting and achieving goals. It explains the struggle and guides us to better strategies.

231 **Thoreau, H. D**. "Where I lived and what I lived for." (1854)

232 **Ricker, T.** et.al. "Decay Theory of Immediate Memory: from Brown (1958) to Today (2014)." National Library of Medicine. (2017). Change366's take: Memories fade. Without reinforcement, even strong memories weaken. It's about keeping the change fresh, alive. Repeat, reinforce, don't let it decay. Like memory, change needs constant attention to stick.

233 **Becker, E**. "The Denial of Death." (1973)

234 **Feynman, R. & Leighton R**. "Surely You're Joking Mr Feynman. Adventures of a Curious Character." (1985)

235 **Hofstadter, D.** "Gödel, Escher, Bach: an Eternal Golden Braid." (1979)

236 **Sharón, R**. "What is the Dual Drive Theory in Psychoanalysis?" Modern Psychoanalyst. Change366's take: Aggression in change management is a drive, like love. Both push and pull. Balance them. Use aggression, but wisely. It's about movement, not just force. Aggression and 'love', together, move things forward. Find the right mix. That's how change happens.

237 **Adams, D**. "The Salmon of Doubt." (2002)

238 **McLeod, S**. "What is Developmental Psychology." Simply Psychology. (2023)

239 **Ryan, R. M. & Deci, E. L**. "Self-Determination Theory: Basic Psychological Needs in Motivation, Development, and Wellness." (2017). Mini theories. Change366's take.

240 **Newman, B. M. & Newman, P. R**. "Causality Orientation." Advances in Motivation Science. (2019). Change366's take: People's worldviews shape how they handle change. There are three types: autonomous, controlled, impersonal. Autonomous is best, meeting all needs. Controlled meets some, lacks autonomy. Impersonal meets none, leads to detachment, inauthenticity. Support people's basic needs. It prevents alienation, energizes them. In change, know their orientation. It guides how they adapt.

241 **Moskowitz, G. B. & Grant, H**. "Goal Conent Theories: Why Differences in What We Are Striving for Matter." The Psychology of Goals. (2009). Change366's take: In organizational change management, not all goals are the same. Universal principles exist, but they bend to different goals. Understand each goal's nature. Some need different approaches, affect feelings differently, impact well-being uniquely. Know the goal's content. It changes how you pursue and achieve it. Tailor strategies to each goal. That's how you succeed in change.

242 **Prosci.** "Primary Sponsor's Role and Importance."

243 **Westerman, G**. et.al. "Leading Digital: Turning Technology into Business Transformation." (2014)

[244] **Spondere**. Online Etymology Dictionary.

[245] **Yang, A**. "Corporate Social Reporting and Stakeholder Accountability: The Missing Link." Science Direct, Accounting, Organizations and Society. (2007). Change366's take.

[246] **Bergh, D. D**. et.al. "Information Asymmetry in Management Research: Past Accomplishments and Future Opportunities." Journal of Management. (2019). Change 366's take: Leaders guide teams by managing information. They shape how workers understand things. Tough situations, like company troubles, make this hard. Leaders must decide how much to tell their teams. This affects how well teams work and how they feel. Workers often think wrongly due to limited understanding. Bad decisions happen when they don't have all the information. Leaders must handle this gap well. It's about leading through uncertainty and avoiding mistakes. This is key in changing organizations.

[247] **Deleuze, G & Guattari, F**. "A Thousand Plateaus: Capitalism and Schizophrenia." (1980)

[248] **Conner, D**. "Managing at the Speed of Change: How Resilient Managers Succeed and Prosper Where Others Fail." (1997)

[249] **Kotter. J**. "Leading Change: Why Transformation Efforts Fail." (1988)

[250] **Clear Picture Leadership**. "Clear Picture Leadership."

[251] **Cognitive Dissonance**. "Group Development and Cognitive Dissonance." Change366's take: Cognitive dissonance affects change in organizations. Groups change too. Researchers is about teamwork, cohesiveness, and conflicts. Many theories explain group development. Some say stages, others, phases. This helps in workplaces. Leaders benefit from understanding group growth. It helps guide teams in change. Different groups evolve differently. Open groups change members, may skip stages. Closed groups show cycles. Knowing this helps leaders manage change. Adapt to the group's stage and type for smooth transitions.

[252] **Chappell, H**. "What is Social Proof Theory." The Behavioralist. (2021). Change366's take: Social proof shapes change. Humans follow norms. In organizations, it guides behaviors, aligning actions with group. It's a powerful evolution tool for change.

[253] **Stanislavsky, K.** "An Actor Prepares." (1923)

[254] **Pasupathi, M. & Adler, J. M**. "Narrative, identity, and the life story: Structural and process approaches." The Handbook of Personality Dynamics and Processes. (2021). Change366's take: Narrative identity is about how people see their lives as stories. In companies, this shapes how employees view change. When a company changes, it's like a new chapter in an employee's story. How they understand this chapter affects their actions. Leaders must craft the change narrative well. It should fit into each person's story positively. Good narratives make change easier. They help employees see their role in the new story. This can motivate and guide them through change. It's about connecting the company's future with each person's story.

[255] **Anggraeni, A. I**. "The effect of psychological contract, perceived organizational support, and value congruence on organizational citizenship behavior: Social exchange theory perspectives." Quality – Access to Success. (2018). Change366's take: In changing organizations, trust, support, and shared values matter a lot. Trust means believing the company will do right by you. Feeling supported by the company makes employees willing to adapt. When what the company wants matches what employees believe, change goes smoother. These things together make people ready to face change and work hard through it.

[256] **Nietzsche, F**. "Human, all too Human: A Book for Free Spirits." (1878)

[257] **Krockow, E. M**. "The Halo Effect: What it is and How to Beat it." Psychology Today. (2021). Change366's take: The halo effect shapes how we see others in organizations. One trait affects our perception of everything else in a person. This bias influences how employees and leaders view each other during change. For example, good communication by a leader can create a halo effect. Employees may think they're skilled in all areas, even if it's not true. This can lead to biased decisions during change. The halo effect can also work negatively. A bad first impression can color all future opinions about a person. This can hurt teamwork and trust during change. To manage the halo effect, awareness is crucial. Slowing down judgments and being systematic in evaluations can counter it. This is vital for making fair decisions in organizational changes. It's about seeing people for who they are, not just one trait.

[258] **Zhang. H. et.al.** "Surface Acting, Emotional Exhaustion, and Employee Sabotage to Customers: Moderating Roles of Quality of Social Exchanges." Frontiers in Psychology. (2018). Change366's take: Surface trait pitfalls affect change in organizations. Hidden emotions mislead. In service jobs, it's vital. Employees mask true feelings, harming them and the firm. Understand real emotions, train in empathy, and reduce faking. Deep acting, genuinely feeling emotions, works better. Supportive environment matters. Combat exhaustion, build relationships. Manage surface traits in change.

[259] **Kim, W.C**. et.al "How to Create Uncontested Market Space and Make the Competition Irrelevant." Blue Ocean Strategy, Expanded Edition. (2015). Change366's take.

[260] **Laing. R.D**. "The Divided Self." (1960)

[261] **Wood, R**. "Social Cognitive Theory of Organizational Management." Academy of Management Review. (1989). Change366's take: Cognitive lag (part of social cognitive theory) is about how managers adapt to new roles or changes. Their self-view and ability to handle change may not keep up. Managing it means aligning managers' beliefs with the organization's changes.

[262] **Machiavelli, N**. "Il Principe." (1532)

[263] **Zeckhauser, R. J**. "Status Quo Bias in Decision-Making." Journal of Risk and Uncertainty. (1988). Change366's take: Status quo bias is the tendency to prefer things as they are. In change, this means employees often resist new ways. They stick to familiar routines, wary of the unknown. This bias can slow down change. Leaders must understand this resistance. They need to show

why new ways are better. Clear communication and support help overcome this bias. Change is hard when the current path is comfortable. To manage it, leaders must make the new path clear and worthwhile.

[264] **Kim, W.C, Mauborgne, R**. "Tipping Point Leadership." Harvard Business Review. (2003). Change366's take.

[265] **Kim, W.C, Mauborgne, R**. "Tipping Point Leadership." Harvard Business Review. (2003). Change366's take.

[266] **Psychology Today** Staff. "Hedonic Treadmill."

[267] **Kotter, J**. "Leading Change: Why Transformation Efforts Fail." (1995)

[268] **Kotter, J**. "Leading Change: Why Transformation Efforts Fail." (1995)

[269] **Folkman, J**. "The Five Critical Skills Leaders Need to Be A Champion of Change." Forbes. (2019)

[270] **Lee-Bourke, A**. "What they Don't Teach You at Change Management School." (2023)

[271] **Dixon, J**. Attributed.

[272] **Korejan, M. M**. "An Analysis of the Transformational Leadership Theory." Journal of Fundamental and Applied Sciences. (2016). Change366's take: Transformational leadership is crucial for organizational change. These leaders inspire and influence at all levels, fostering passion, trust, and commitment. They guide teams through new approaches, shaping how employees respond to changes. Key aspects include influencing across levels, values-driven leadership, and holding steadfast values. They inspire from the heart, with a visionary perspective, focusing on trust and unleashing the power of the mind.

[273] **Chafra, J**. "Leader Narcissism and Subordinate Embeddedness." Euromed Journal of Business. (2017). Change366's take.

[274] **Brenes. E. R**. et.al. "Managing institutional voids: A configurational approach to understanding high performance antecedents." Journal of Business Research. (2019). Change 366's take: Managing institutional gaps is about dealing with system and norm gaps. In change, these gaps can help or hinder. Leaders must spot and fill these gaps for top results. This means grasping what makes success unique. It's not just fixing issues. It's creating the perfect mix of reactions. Leaders must adjust to these gaps and shape strategies for their case. It's a mix of understanding, adjusting, and taking smart actions.

[275] **Maxwell, J. C**. "The 21 Irrefutable Laws of Leadership." (1998)

[276] **Lopez-Garrido, G**. "Locus of Control Theory in Psychology: Definition and Examples." Simply Psychology. (2023). Change366's take: Information locus of control theory affects change management by highlighting who controls information. Leaders must decide if information is central (them) or shared (team).

[277] **Cash, R**. Attributed

[278] **Lee-Bourke. A**. Attributed.

[279] **Mercurio, Z. A.** et.al. "Affective Commitment as a Core Essence of Organizational Commitment: An Integrative Literature Review." Journal of Human Resource Development. (2015). Change366's take: Affective Commitment fuels change loyalty; emotions drive lasting organizational transformations.

[280] **Steers, R. M** et.al. "Leadership in a global context: New directions in research and theory development." (2012). McCann, J." It's designing, not design." People & Strategy. (2011). Aragón-Correa, J. A. García-Morales, V. J. & Cordón-Pozo, E. "Leadership and organizational learning's role on innovation and performance: Lessons from Spain." (2007). Industrial Marketing Management. Gardner, W. L. & Avolio, B. J. "The charismatic relationship: A dramaturgical perspective." (1998). Academy Of Management Review. Hofstede, G. "Country Comparison Tool." (2012). Change366's take.

[281] **McMillan, K.** "Measuring Social Exchange Constructs in Organizations." Communication Methods and Measures. (2010). Change366's take: Social exchange theory shapes how trust and cooperation drive organizational change management.

[282] **Stehlik, D.** "Failure: The Impartial Executioner of Leaders, Followers, and Their Organizations." Journal of Practical Consulting. (2014). Change366's take.

[283] **Johari Window**. The Johari Window is a simple tool. It's for understanding people. Four parts to it. The first, what everyone knows about you. The second, what only you know. The third, what others see but you don't. The fourth, what's still hidden from all. It's a way to see yourself, as others do. It builds trust, makes teams work better. Change366's take.

[284] **Aten, K.** "Organization Culture and Institutional Theory: A Conversation at the Border." Journal of Management Inquiry. (2012). Change366's take.

[285] **Sammut-Bonnici, T.** "Complexity Theory." Encyclopedia of Management. (2018)

[286] **Del Casino Jr, V. J. & Thein, D.** "Symbolic Interactionalism." International Journal of Human Geography. (2009). Change366's take: People construct change through daily interactions.

[287] **Nadeem, A.** "Effect of Leadership Empowerment on Personnel Creativity in Projects: Moderating Role of Project Culture and Mediating Role of Creative Self-efficacy." JISR Management and Social Sciences and Economics. (2022). Change366's take.

[288] **Tierney, P & Farmer. S. M.** "Creative Self-Efficacy: Its Potential Antecedents and Relationship to Creative Performance." The Academy of Management Journal. (2002). Change366's take: Confidence sparks change innovation; doubt stifles progress.

[289] **Ibrahim, N.** "Role of Transformational Leadership in Enhancing Followers' Psychological Empowerment." Journal of Entrepreneurship and Business. (2021). Change366's take.

290 **Kim**. H-D et.al. "Transformational Leadership and Psychological Well-Being of Service-Oriented Staff: Hybrid Data Synthesis Technique." National Library of Medicine. (2022)

291 **Jamaluddin, Z**. "The Mediating Role of Employee Engagement in the Relationship between Leadership Styles and Organizational Performance: A Conceptual Model." Journal of Management Thinking. (2023). Change366's take.

292 **Glasser, W**. "Choice Theory: A New Psychology of Personal Freedom." (1998). Change366's take.

293 **Verhoest, K**. et.al. "The study of organisational autonomy: a conceptual review." Public Administration and Development. (2004). Change366's take: Directed autonomy in organizational change management means giving freedom within set boundaries. It's about balancing control and independence. For change management, it's about guiding, not controlling. Leaders should set clear goals but allow flexibility in achieving them. This encourages innovation while maintaining direction.

294 **Prosci.** "Best Practices in Change Management."

295 **Liu, C-L et.al**. "Understanding the impact of relational capital and organizational learning on alliance outcomes." Journal of World Business. (2010). Change366's take: Trust and interaction ignite change.

296 **Conner, D**. "Managing at the Speed of Change: How Resilient Managers Succeed and Prosper Where Others Fail." (1993)

297 **Lewin, K**. "Field Theory in Social Science: Selected Theoretical Papers." (1951). Change366's take.

298 **Perone, S & Simmering, V. R**. "Applications of Dynamic Systems Theory to Cognition and Development: New Frontiers." Advances in Child Development and Behavior. (2017).

299 **Herzberg, F.** "The Motivation-Hygiene Concept and Problems of Manpower." American Psychological Association. (1964). Change366's take.

300 **Kuhl, J**. "The volitional basis of Personality Systems Interaction Theory: applications in learning and treatment contexts." International Journal of Educational Research. (2000). Change366's take: Volitional theory empowers change. Choice fuels progress. Change begins within.

301 **Prosci** "CLARC: The Role of People Managers in Change Management." Change366's take.

302 **Bryant, M. & Stensaker, I**. "The Competing Roles of Middle Management: Negotiated Order In the Context of Change." Journal of Change Management. (2011)

303 **Fine, G.A**. "Negotiated Order and Organizational Cultures." Annual Review of Sociology. (1984)

304 **Feynman, R**. Attributed

[305] **Nishill, L. H.** et.al. "A Multi-Level Framework of Inclusive Leadership in Organizations." Sage Journals, Group and Organizational Management. (2022). Change366's take: Vulnerable, inclusive leadership empowers change. It's a cross-level journey. Leaders value diversity and inclusion, from top to bottom. They turn words into actions, creating a culture of belonging.

[306] **Campbell, J.** "The Hero with a Thousand Faces." (1949)

[307] **Langher, V.** et.al. "Work symbolic motive scale: development and validation of a measure of affective investment at work." International Journal of Work Organization and Emotion. (2018). Change366's take.

[308] **Slaby, J.** "Affective intentionality and the feeling body." Phenomenology and the Cognitive Sciences. (2007). Change366's take: Affective intentionality fuels change in organizational management. Emotions drive action. Enthusiasm sparks change, apprehension resists it. Leaders harness emotions for transformation.

[309] **Westphal, J & Park, S. H.** "Introduction to the Symbolic Management Perspective." Oxford Academic. (2020). Change366's take: Leaders should use symbols to guide perceptions and values. These symbols help align employees with change goals, building commitment. It's about crafting a story through actions and rituals.

[310] **Lench, H.** "Anger has benefits for attaining goals." American Psychological Association. (2023). Change366's take.

[311] **LeBarr, N. A.** "Conceptual Organization of Self-representation: A Self-similarity Heuristic for Novel Person Representations." (2015). Change366's take.

[312] **Asgari, S.** "The Influence of Varied Levels of Received Stress and Support on Negative Emotions and Support Perceptions." Current Psychology. (2015). Change366's take.

[313] **Syed, F.** "Role of adaptive leadership in learning organizations to boost organizational innovations with change self-efficacy." Current Psychology. (2023). Change366's take.

[314] **Fatien, P.** et.al. "Wearing Multiple Hats? Challenges for Managers-as-Coaches and Their Organizations." International Leadership Journal. (2015). Change366's take.

[315] **Thompson, V. A.** "What Intuitions Are…and Are Not." Psychology of Learning and Motivation. (2014). Change366's take: Dual process theory impacts organizational change management by balancing intuition and deliberate thought. It suggests two types of thinking: fast, intuitive (System 1) and slow, analytical (System 2). In change management, leaders need both. Quick intuition helps adapt to sudden changes. Analytical thinking plans long-term strategies. Balancing these is key to effective change. Intuition guides immediate reactions. Analytical thought shapes structured plans. Leaders who master both navigate change successfully. They respond swiftly yet plan thoughtfully.

[316] **Westover, J. H.** "The Role Of Systems Thinking In Organizational Change And Development." Forbes. (2020). Change366's take: Systems thinking is key in organizational change. It's about seeing the whole. Every change affects everything. Leaders use this to guide decisions. They map connections, understand impacts. This thinking helps manage complex changes. It turns challenges into opportunities.

[317] **Harding, N**. "Who is 'the middle manager?'" (2014)

[318] **Abbot, Edwin A**. "Flatland: A Romance in Many Dimensions." (1884)

[319] **van Hugten, J**. et.al. "The Dunning-Kruger effect and entrepreneurial self-efficacy: How tenure and search distance jointly direct entrepreneurial self-efficacy." Journal of Business Research. (2023). Change366's take: In managing change, it matters who knows what. Some have more information than others. This uneven spread of knowledge can complicate decisions. Leaders should identify who needs to know more. They must communicate effectively. Clear sharing of knowledge helps everyone grasp the changes. Dealing with this knowledge gap means clear, open talks. Leaders should ensure everyone is informed about what's going on. This way, teams can navigate change more effectively.

[320] **Sun Tzu** (**孫子**). "The Art of War." (**孫子兵法**). (5th Century BCE)

[321] **Folklore**. Attributed. Change366's take.

[322] **Folklore**. Attributed. Change366's take.

[323] **Folklore**. Moral Stories. "The Cracked Pot."

[324] **de La Rochefoucauld**. "Maxims." (1705)

[325] **Spinoza, B**. "The Collected Works of Spinoza." Edwin Curley. (1985)

[326] **Hume, D**. "A Treatise of Human Nature." (1740)

[327] **Brazer, D. S**. et.al. "Organizational Theory and Leadership Navigation." Journal of Research on Leadership Education. (2014). Change366's take: This theory emphasizes the leader's role in understanding and adapting to change. They must be aware of the organization's dynamics, employee sentiments, and external influences. Good leaders navigate these factors, making informed decisions to lead their team effectively through change.

[328] **Sextus Empiricus**. "Outlines of Pyrrhonism." (2nd Century CE)

[329] **Yin, X & LaFortune, S**. "A new approach for the verification of infinite-step and k-step opacity using two-way observers." Automatica. (2017). Change366's take: Adapted from security analysis approach. Infinite verification keeps an organization's secrets safe during change. It's a never-ending, vigilant process, essential in today's digital world.

[330] **Deci, E. L. & Gagné.** M. "Self Determination Theory and Work Motivation." (2005)

[331] **Deci, E. L. & Gagné.** M. "Self Determination Theory and Work Motivation." (2005)

[332] **Bandura, A.** "Social Foundations of Thought and Action: A social Cognitive Theory." (1985)

[333] **Nickerson, C.** "Albert Bandura's Social Cognitive Theory: Definition & Examples." Simply Psychology. (2023). Change366's take: People and their surroundings change each other. How workers act changes the office, and the office changes them. Bandura said we learn by watching others. In a company, if an action gets praised, others do the same. If it's punished, they don't. Leaders need to show the actions they want. This starts a cycle of good changes. This idea works for all behaviors at work. Leaders can guide good changes this way.

[334] **Erikson, E.** "Identity and the Lifecycle." (1967)

[335] **Bouckenooghe, D.** et.al. "The multiple faces of collective responses to organizational change: Taking stock and moving forward." Journal of Organizational Behavior." (2023). Change366's take.

[336] **Bourdieu, P.** "Outline of a Theory of Practice." (1977)

[337] **Bastian, H.** "The Hawthorne effect: An old scientists' tale lingering "in the gunsmoke of academic snipers." Scientific American. (2013). Change366's take.

[338] **Perera, A.** "Hawthorn Effect: Definition, How it Works, And How to Avoid It." SimplyPsychology. (2023).

[339] **Hawthorne Effect.** "Hawthorne Effect (Definition and Examples." Practical Psychology. Change366's take: The Hawthorne effect means people act different when watched. Workers change if they know someone is watching. This can mess up organizational change. Leaders should think about this when managing change. They should know that watched behavior might not be real. Good change management is about seeing true behavior. This needs smart planning and being fair.

[340] **Sartre, J. P.** "The Words." (1963)

[341] **Lencioni, P.** "The Five Dysfunctions of a Team." (2002)

[342] **McLeod, S.** "Fundamental Attribution Error in Psychology." Simply Psychology. (2023)

[343] **Reeder, G. D.** "Fundamental Attribution Error / Correspondence Bias." Oxford Bibliographies. (2019). Change366's take: The fundamental attribution error happens when people blame character, not the situation. If an employee fails, it might be due to external factors, not just their nature. This mistake can hurt change efforts by missing the real problem. Leaders should see that situations often affect behavior. They must consider more than just personal traits. This leads to fairer, more effective change management. It's important to see the full picture. Balanced judgment in change is essential. Weighing both personal and situational factors is crucial.

[344] **Schon, D**. "Champions for Radical New Inventions." Harvard Business Review. (1963)

[345] **Settle, M**. "Truth from the Trenches: A Practical Guide to the Art of IT Management." (2017)

[346] **Ibarra, H and Hunter, M.L**. "How Leaders Create and Use Networks." Harvard Business Review. (2007). Change366's take.

[347] **Behavioral Insights Team**. "EAST: Four Simple Ways to Apply Behavioural Insights." Handbook. (2014). Change366's take.

[348] **Ursin, H & Eriksen, H. R.** "The Cognitive Activation Theory of Stress." Psychoneuroendocrinology. (2004). Change366's take: At work, CAT theory says employees get stressed when things don't match what they expect. Good change management should recognize this stress, help employees deal with it, and make sure everyone's on the same page with the company's goals.

[349] **Kalive. P**. "Reference Group: Types, Functions, Characteristics, Importance." Sociology Group. Change366's take.

[350] **Miller, M. K. & Reichert, J.** "Social Comparison Theory." The Blackwell Encyclopedia of Sociology. (2015). Change366's take: Social comparison theory says folks judge changes by watching their coworkers. They see how they're reacting and compare it to themselves. This affects if they're okay with the changes or not. In managing change, it's vital to know this. Leaders need to make a place where good attitudes toward change are clear and others follow suit, creating a culture of everyone moving forward together.

[351] **Hopster, J**. "What are Socially Disruptive Technologies?" Technology in Society. (2021). Change366s take: Normative disruption theory tells us change can shake things up. In change management, it means using disruption to bring about big changes.

[352] **Feher, M. A**. "The Intrapreneur Mindset." Psychology Today. (2022). Change366's take.

[353] **Lee-Bourke, A.** "What They Don't Teach You at Change Management School." (2023)

[354] **Lee-Bourke, A.** "What They Don't Teach You at Change Management School." (2023)

[355] **Rosales-Ruiz, J. & Baer, D. M**. "Behavioral Cusps: A Developmental and Pragmatic Concept for Behaviour Analysis." Journal of Applied Behavior Analysis." (1997). Change366's take.

[356] **Smith, G. J.** et.al. "Behavioral Cusps: A Person-Centered Concept for Establishing Pivotal Individual, Family, and Community Behaviors and Repertoires." Focus on Autism and Other Developmental Disabilities. (2006). Change366's take: Behavioral cusps are like game-changing tools. They profoundly change how we behave. In change management, they help us build new behaviors and skills.

[357] **Ericsson, K.A**. "Peak Secrets from the New Science of Expertise." (2016)

[358] **Sandoval, M. T.** R. et.al. "From preconceptions to concept: The basis of a didactic model designed to promote the development of critical thinking." International Journal of Educational Research Open. (2022). Change366's take: In change management, didactic exchange theory means structured learning, guiding employees from basics to advanced skills for new processes and tech. Clear training fosters understanding and independence.

[359] **Mbughuni. M.L.** Attributed

[360] **The Manual**. "Change Champions: The Ultimate Guide to Business Transformation." (2023)

[361] **Bourdieu, P**. "Outline of a Theory of Space." (1977). Change366's take.

[362] **Habitus** definition. Oxford Reference. Change 366's take: Habitus map theory in change management is about knowing employees' backgrounds. It says change works better when managers understand how backgrounds affect behaviors. This helps adapt change strategies to fit diverse team needs, making transitions smoother and more inclusive.

[363] **Chang, M-H**. "Agent-Based Models of Organizations." Research Papers in Economics. (2004), Change366's take.

[364] **Ahn, T.** et.al. "Self-congruence, functional congruence, and destination choice." Journal of Business Research. (2013). Change366's take: Functional congruence theory in organizational change management is about matching what's needed with what's delivered. Like tourists choosing a destination, employees and organizations must align their needs and capabilities. Change works when what the organization offers fits what its people need.

[365] **Gladwell. M**. "Blink: The Power of Thinking Without Thinking." (2005)

[366] **Kolb, A. Y. & Kolb, D. A**. "Experiential Learning Theory." (2012). Change 366's take: Experiential learning theory in organizational change is about learning by doing. It's hands-on. Employees understand and adapt to change through real experiences, not just theory. This approach makes change stick because it's learned in action, not just talked about.

[367] **Descartes, R**. "Discourse on the Method of Rightly Conducting One's Reason and of Seeking Truth in the Sciences." Original French: "Discours de la Méthode Pour bien conduire sa raison, et chercher la vérité dans les sciences." (1637)

[368] **Zadeh, L. A**. "Toward a perception-based theory of probabilistic reasoning with imprecise probabilities." Journal of Statistical Planning and Inference. (2002). Change366's take: Probabilistic reasoning theory in organizational change means making decisions based on likely outcomes, not certainties. It's about weighing the odds and choosing the best path, knowing things might not go as planned. This approach helps manage risks and uncertainties in change.

[369] **Shelly, M**. Attributed

[370] **Okasha, S**. "On the Interpretation of Decision Theory." Cambridge University Press. (2015). Change366's take: Decision dichotomy theory in change

management separates thinking from showing. It's about knowing that what people believe and how they act might not match. Managers should think about both thoughts and actions when leading change.

[371] **Romi, M. V.** et.al. "Analysis of Employee Engagement with Transformational Leadership and Organizational Climate as Predictors." International Journal of Social Science and Human Research. (2023). Change366's take.

[372] **Gerstner, L.** "Who Say's Elephants Can't Dance." (2003)

[373] **Nickerson, C.** "Emotional Contagion: What it is And How to Avoid it." Simply Psychology. (2023). Change366's take: Emotional contagion theory explains that people tend to pick up and reflect the emotions and actions of those around them. In change management, it means leaders should be mindful that emotions can spread through expressions, voice, and body language. Not everyone is equally affected, but it's vital to consider emotions when leading change.

[374] **Godin, S.** "Purple Cow: Transform Your Business by Being Remarkable." (2003)

[375] **Kanter, R.M.** "Thinking Outside the Building: How Advanced Leaders Can Change the World One Smart Innovation at a Time." (2020)

[376] **Ellerbee, L.** "And So It Goes: Adventures in Television." (1986)

[377] **Rummel, J & Kvavilashvili.** L. "Current theories of prospective memory and new directions for theory development." Nature Reviews: Psychology. (2022). Change366's take: Information asymmetry in change management means not everyone has the same knowledge about the changes. This can cause problems and resistance.

[378] **Murphy. M.** "The Big Reason Why Some People Are Terrified Of Change (While Others Love It)." Forbes. (2016). Change366's take.

[379] **HR University**. "What Does a Change Champion Do." HR University. (2023)

[380] **Osafo, E. et.al.** "Valence–Instrumentality–Expectancy Model of Motivation as an Alternative Model for Examining Ethical Leadership Behaviors." Sage Journals. (2021). Change366's take: Valence theory in change management says ethics should come from values, not just rules. It means getting people to do the right thing because they believe it's right, not just because they must. Leaders can use this to make an ethical workplace where people do good things because they want to, not because they have to.

[381] **Folkman, J.** "The Five Critical Skills Leaders Need To Be A Champion Of Change." Forbes. (2019)

[382] **Miller, F. A.** et.al. "Change Champions: A Dialogic Approach To Creating an Inclusive Culture." (2022). Change366's take.

[383] **Brower, T.** "Leading Change: 10 Ways Great Leaders Make Change Happen." Forbes. (2017)

[384] **Russo, D**. "Lead Through Change With Big Picture Thinking." Forbes. (2022)

[385] **Páez, D.** et.al. "Psychosocial Effects of Perceived Emotional Synchrony in Collective Gatherings." (2015). Change366's take: Emotional synchrony theory in organizational change management talks about how getting together with others makes people feel better. It boosts their sense of belonging and makes them feel good about themselves, and it's all because of the emotional connection they share with others.

[386] **Holiday, R**. "The Obstacle is the Way: The Ancient Art of Turning Trials into Triumph."

[387] **Hotchkiss, M**. "Reality bites: Big gap between real life and ideals weighs heavily." Princeton University. (2015). Change366's take: Idea gap theory in change management is all about the space between what people hope for and what they actually get. When that gap is big, it makes them unhappy.

[388] **Khai, W.** et.al. "Reactions towards organizational change: a systematic literature review." Current Psychology 42. (2021). Change366's take.

[389] **McLeod. S.** "Constructivism Learning Theory & Philosophy Of Education." Simply Psychology. (2023). Change366's take: Information gaps hinder change. Transparency builds trust, aids success.

[390] **Kotter, J**. Attributed

[391] **Sweller, J**. "Cognitive Load Theory." Psychology of Learning and Motivation. (2011). Change366's take: Cognitive load theory, it's about how our brains work, and it affects how we communicate during changes in organizations. It splits what we naturally know from what we learn for the company's culture. When it comes to company stuff, our brains need a big storage space, and we usually get this info from others. Creating new ways of talking about changes is limited, but we can use lots of organized info to communicate clearly during complex changes. This theory guides how we communicate during organizational changes.

[392] **Nickerson, C**. "Schema Theory in Psychology." (2023). Change366's take: Schema theory is like a mental filing system that helps folks understand things better. There are four types of schemas: things, yourself, roles, and events. Schemas can change in life. We add new stuff or tweak what's there. In organizational change management, it's vital. Understanding how folks see things guides how we talk and train during changes.

[393] **The Culture Group**. Attributed.

[394] **Social Contract**. "Contemporary Approaches to the Social Contract." Stanford Encyclopaedia of Philosophy. (1996). Change366's take: In organizational change, social contract theory highlights the importance of consensus and justifying decisions to all involved parties.

[395] **Powell. J**. Attributed.

[396] **Kipling, R**. "Just So Stories." Poem. (1902)

[397] **5W+H**. "Questions of Every Project." Adobe Communications Team. Change366's take: In managing a change program, first, know why you're doing it. Ask simple questions. Who's involved? What's the job? When's it due? Where's it happening? Why do it at all? Sometimes, ask how. This clears up the whole thing. Start with why. It shows the reason. What comes next, setting the job's limits. Who matters for knowing your team and people you're working for. When sets the time. Where points the place. After all this, figure out how to do it. Keep it straight and clear. The boss of the project leads this, making sure everyone knows their part.

[398] **Lee-Bourke, A**. Allegory describing aspects of change management in a real project.

[399] **'Leslie Claret'**. 'Patriot', The Donnelly nut-spacing quote. Netflix C-19. YouTube (2017). Change366's take: We've built a system. It's for control, for steadiness. It uses metal, small and tough. These parts cut down on the shaking. They work deep, half a meter down. Each main piece gets twelve nuts, strong ones. We press layers of devices together. They need to work right. Safety parts go on two crucial spots.

[400] **Kahneman, D**. "Thinking Fast and Slow." (2011)

[401] **Molden, D. C**. "Understanding Priming Effects in Social Psychology: An Overview and Integration." Social Cognition. (2014). Change366's take: Priming effect theory in organizational change is like setting the scene for a journey. It's about preparing minds before the journey begins. When leaders prime employees, they subtly influence how they perceive and react to change. It's not just telling them what will happen. It's about shaping their mindset, so they're ready to accept and engage with the change. This preparation makes the path smoother, as preconceived notions and attitudes are aligned with the organization's vision.

[402] **Burgoon, J. K**. et.al. "Nonverbal Expectancy Violations: Model Elaboration and Applications to Immediacy Behaviors." Communication Monographs 55 p58-79. (2009). Change366's take.

[403] **Barrett, L. F**. "Seven and a Half Lessons About the Brain" (2020). Change366's take.

[404] **Shaw, G. B**. Attributed. According the Quote Investigator, this quote originated from William H Whyte's "Fortune" article: "Is Anybody Listening." (1950)

[405] **Benson. B & Manoogian III, J**. "Cognitive Bias Codex." University of North Carolina.

[406] **Lee-Bourke, A**. "What they Don't Teach You at Change Management School." (2023)

[407] **Santayanna, G.** "Soliloquies in England and Later Soliloquies." (1924). Change366's take. Full quote: "Masks are arrested expressions and admirable echoes of feelings, at once faithful, discreet, and superlative. Living things in contact with the air must acquire a cuticle, and it is not urged against cuticles that they are not hearts; yet some philosophers seem to be angry with images

for not being things, and with words for not being feelings. Words and images are like shells, no less integral parts of nature than are the substances they cover, but better addressed to the eye and more open to observation. I would not say that substance exists for the sake of appearance, or faces for the sake of masks, or the passions for the sake of anything else: all these phases and products are involved equally in the round of existence."

408 **Sapir-Whorf Hypothesis**. "Sapir-Whorf Hypothesis (Linguistic Relativity Hypothesis)." Simply Psychology (2023). Change 366's take: The Sapir-Whorf Hypothesis is simple yet deep. It says our language shapes our thought. Like how a river carves a canyon, language molds our ideas. It's not just words, but the world they build. We see and think within this world. If our language is rich, our thoughts are too. If it's limited, so are we.

409 **Pullim, G**. "The Great Eskimo Vocabulary Hoax and other Irreverent Essays on the Study of Language." (1967). Change366's take.

410 **McLeod, S**. "Constructivism Learning Theory & Philosophy f Education." Simply Psychology. (2023)

411 **Frothingham, M. B**. "Sapir–Whorf Hypothesis (Linguistic Relativity Hypothesis)." Simply Psychology. (2023). Change366's take: In organizational change, the Sapir-Whorf hypothesis is like how words build thoughts. It says that the words used in a company shape how workers think and act when things change. Positive words can make a culture that takes change well. Negative words can cause pushback. Leaders need to pick their words right. They can make people see change in a good or bad way.

412 **Clutterbuck, D. & Hirst, S**. et.al. "Leadership communication: A status report." Journal of Communication Management. (2002). Lewis, L. K. "Communicating change: Four cases of quality programs." The Journal of Business Communication (1973). Pace, R. W. & Faules, Don, F. "Komunikasi Organisasi: Strategi Mengingkatkan Kinerja Perusahaan, 4th edn," (2005). Van Riel, R. et.al. "Essentials of corporate communication: Implementing practices for effective reputation management." (2007); Stegaroiu, I., & Talal, M. "The importance of developing an internal communication strategy." Valahian Journal of Economic Studies, (2014).; Zulch, B. "Leadership communication in project management." (2014). Procedia-Social and Behavioral Sciences. Change366's take.

413 **Thucydides**. "History of the Peloponnesian War." (404 BCE)

414 **Andersen, H. C**. "Fairy Tales Told for Children." (1837). Change366's take: "The Emperor's New Clothes." A story about an emperor who loves clothes. Two weavers come, liars, saying their cloth is invisible to the unfit or stupid. They make nothing, but the emperor acts like they see it. Doesn't want to seem a fool. They wear this nothing in a parade. Everyone else pretends too, scared to seem unfit. A kid shouts, 'You're naked!' People hear, but the emperor marches on. Too proud to stop.

415 **Hoffman, R**. "Social Loafing In Psychology: Definition, Examples & Theory." Simply Psychology. (2023)

416 **Carey, S**. "The Origin of Concepts." (2009)

[417] **Nickerson, C**. "Symbolic Interactionism Theory & Examples." Simply Psychology. (2023)

[418] **Mandler, J. M**. "Stories, Scripts and Scenes: Aspects of Schema Theory." (1984)

[419] **Schema Utilization**. "Schema Theory in Psychology." Simply Psychology (2023). Change366's take: Schema utilization is like a map for stories in our minds. We use familiar paths from past tales to understand new ones. As a story unfolds, our mind follows these paths, shaped by old tales. We see the story through these known routes, making the unknown familiar. It's how we navigate the ocean of stories.

[420] **Drucker, P**. "The Practice of Management: A Study of the Most Important Function in American Society." (1954)

[421] **Hitchens, C**. "God is Not Great." (2007). Change 366's take: Hitchens' Razor is clear: what's claimed without proof can be dismissed the same way. No evidence, no belief. Simple as that.

[422] **Connolly, B**. Attributed

[423] **Laborde, S.** "Bridging the Gap between Emotion and Cognition: An Overview." Performance Psychology. (2016). Change336's take: Emotions steer, pressure molds, change bridges for successful transformation.

[424] **Socrates**. From Plato's "The Apology of Socrates." (c 393 BCE)

[425] **Huxley, A**. Attributed.

[426] **Geurts, B**. "Communication as commitment sharing: speech acts, implicatures, common ground." Change366's take: Theoretical Linguistics. (2019). Change366's take: Communication commitment is like keeping a promise. It means always talking openly about the change. Leaders must consistently share information, updates, and feedback. They need to listen too. This builds trust. When people trust the message, they're more likely to accept and support the change.

[427] **Covey, S. R**. "First things First." (1994)

[428] **Bates, D**. "Deep Listening. Key Listening Skills to Deepen Your Relationships." Psychology Today. (2021). Change366's take: Deep listening in organizational change is like truly hearing in a loud room. It's about focusing on what people say and feel during change. This means really listening, not just hearing words. It's understanding their fears, hopes, and worries. When leaders listen deeply, they connect better. They make people feel seen and heard. This builds trust and helps everyone move through change together.

[429] **Churchill. W**. Attributed.

[430] **Hove, T**. "Understanding and Efficiency: Habermas's Concept of Communication Relief." Communication Theory. (2008). Change366's take: Habermas's communications relief theory is using different tools for different jobs. It's about how media forms help in coordinating social action. In change management, this means using the right kind of communication for the situation.

Some changes need clear instructions (steering media) for efficiency. Others need influence and value commitment to build understanding and consensus. This approach makes sure that communication isn't just about giving orders. It's about creating a shared understanding and commitment to the change.

431 **Kahneman, D**. "Thinking Fast and Slow." (2011)

432 **Hyman, R**. "The Elusive Quarry: A Scientific Appraisal of Psychical Research." (1989)

433 **Lord Byron**. Attributed.

434 **Alnoor, A** et.al. "Reactions towards organizational change: a systematic literature review." Change366's take.

435 **Heraclitus**. Attributed (c.500 BCE)

436 **Prosci.** "Managing Resistance to Change Overview."

437 **Kolb, B. & Gibb. R**. "Principles of Neuroplasticity and Behavior." Cambridge University Press. (2015). Change366's take: Neuroplasticity, the brain's ability to change, affects how change is managed in organizations. Learning and experiences build new pathways while weakening unused ones, like pruning a tree. This continues in mature brains.

438 **Prosci.** "Understanding Why People Resist Change."

439 **Morain, C, O & Aykens, P**. "Employees are Losing Patience with Change Initiatives". Harvard Business Review (2023). Change366's take.

440 **Kahneman, D**. "Thinking Fast and Slow." (2011)

441 **Senge, P.** Attributed.

442 **Newsome, R**. "Why employees resist change – even when it's good for them." accessPeopleHR (2017)

443 **McQuillan, S**. "Why do Humans Resist Change." Psychology Today. Change366's take. (2019).

444 **Benson. B & Manoogian III, J**. "Cognitive Bias Codex." University of North Carolina.

445 **Koller, R. Fenwick, R. Fenwick R. Jr**. "Is Obedience, Not Resistance, the Real Organizational Change Killer?" Change Management: International Journal. (2013)

446 **Jordan, M**. Attributed

447 **Oxford Reference**. Azaryahu, Society & Culture. Geography 9.4 (2008)

448 **Whysal, Z**. "Managing Change: Insights from Neuropsychology." Lane4 White Paper. Change366's take.

449 **Rehman, N**, et.al. "The Psychology of Resistance to Change: The Antidotal Effect of Organizational Justice, Support and Leader-Member Exchange." Frontiers in Psychology. (2021). Change366's take.

[450] **Scandura, T. & Meuser, J**. "Relational Dynamics of Leadership: Problems and Prospects." Annual Review of Organizational Psychology and Organizational Behavior. (2022).

[451] **Ahmad, H.** et.al. "Resistance to Change: Causes and Strategies as an Organizational Challenge." Conference: Proceedings of the 5th ASEAN Conference on Psychology, Counselling, and Humanities. (2020). Change366's take.

[452] **Laumer, S. & Eckhardt, A**. "Why do People Reject Technologies? – Towards an Understanding of Resistance to IT-induced Organizational Change." Association for Information Systems ICIS 2010 Proceedings. Change366's take.

[453] **Laumer, S. & Eckhardt, A**. "Why do People Reject Technologies? – Towards an Understanding of Resistance to IT-induced Organizational Change." Association for Information Systems ICIS 2010 Proceedings, Change366's take.

[454] **Laumer, S & Eckhardt, A**. "Why do People Reject Technologies? – Towards an Understanding of Resistance to IT-induced Organizational Change." Association for Information Systems ICIS 2010 Proceedings, Change366's take.

[455] **Adriaenssen, D. J. & Johannessen, J-A**. "Prospect Theory as an Explanation for Resistance to Organizational Change: Some Management Implications." (2016). Change366's take.

[456] **Nickerson, C**. "Prospect Theory In Psychology: Loss Aversion Bias." Simply Psychology. (2023). Change 366's take: Prospect theory in organizational change is like a gambler's view of risk. It shows that people fear losses more than they value gains. In managing change, this means framing change to highlight avoiding losses, not just gaining benefits. It's a delicate act, like balancing on a tightrope. This understanding helps navigate the tricky waters of change.

[457] **Alnoor, A.** et.al. "Reactions towards organizational change: a systematic literature review." (2022). Change366's take.

[458] **Oldster, K, J**. "Dead Toad Scrolls." (2016)

[459] **Garvin, D, A. & Roberto, M. A**. "Change Through Persuasion." Harvard Business Review. (2005). Change366's take.

[460] **Kegan, R. & Lahey, L. L**. "The Real Reason People Won't Change." Harvard Business Review. (2001). Change366's take.

[461] **Herzberg, F**. "The Motivation to Work - 2nd Edition." (1959)

[462] **Sammut-Bonnici, T**. "Complexity Theory." Encyclopedia of Management. (2018)

[463] **McLeod, S**. "Maslow's Hierarchy of Needs." Simply Psychology. (2023)

[464] **Seaman, K. L.** et.al. "Temporal Discounting Across Adulthood: A Systematic Review and Meta-analysis." American Psychological Association. (2022).

Change366's take: Temporal discounting, valuing future rewards, stays pretty consistent with age in adults. Whether you're young, middle-aged, or old, the preference for quick rewards over delayed ones doesn't change much. In the world of organizational change, it means people of different ages tend to have similar reactions to immediate versus delayed benefits.

[465] **Becker, E**. "The Denial of Death." (1973)

[466] **Carroll. L**. "Alice's Adventures in Wonderland." (Charles Lutwidge Dogson). (1865)

[467] **Johnson, S**. "Who Moved My Cheese?" (1998)

[468] **Chomsky, N**. "How the World Works." (2011)

[469] **Khatri, K & Dutta, S**. "Psychological Ownership: Journey of Past towards a Promising Future." Research Review Journals. (2018)

[470] **Schneider, S**. et.al. "The Cognitive-Affective-Social Theory of Learning in digital Environments (CASTLE)." Educational Psychology Review. (2022). Change366's take: CASTLE theory blends thinking, feelings, and social interactions in digital learning. It's about how people learn together online. In organizational change, remember that change is a social learning process.

[471] **de Beauvoir, S**. "Les Mandarins." (1954)

[472] **Chomsky, N**. Attributed.

[473] **Lee-Bourke, A**. "The fear of failure in change initiatives is overrated; it's the fear of success that's rarely discussed." LinkedIn Article. (2023)

[474] **Bem. D J**. "Self-Perception Theory." Advances in Experimental Social Psychology. (1972). Change366's take: Self-perception theory in change management is like understanding yourself by watching what you do. People learn about their own feelings and attitudes by looking at their actions. In managing change, if employees act in a positive way, they might start feeling positive about the change. It's like being an observer of your own behavior to understand your thoughts. This theory helps us see how what we do affects how we feel.

[475] **Prosci.** "Reinforcement – The Prosci ADKAR™ Model."

[476] **van der Pligt, J & Vlike. M**. "The psychology of influence: Theory, research and practice." American Psychological Association. (2017). Change366's take: Psychology of influence guides choices, from cars to neighbours. Messages sway us through words, TV, and social media. It explores persuasion, role models, rules, and emotions. It navigates attraction, prejudice, reward, and unconscious bias. In change management, it's the quiet force shaping decisions.

[477] **Sylver, M**. "Passion, Profit & Power." (1995)

[478] **Wheatley, T. & Wegner, D. M**. "Automaticity of Action, Psychology of." International Encyclopedia of the Social & Behavioral Sciences. (2001). Change366's take: Automaticity theory means things happen on their own, like driving a car without thinking much. It's good for efficiency, but it can also

lead to automatic biases, like stereotypes popping up in our heads. In change management, we need to be aware of this and use reinforcement carefully. If we try too hard to stop these automatic biases, it might make them stronger.

[479] **Aristotle**. (Aristotélēs). "The Nicomachean Ethics of Aristotle." (350 BCE)

[480] **Lesage, A. R**. "Gil Blas." (1749)

[481] **Wright, C. D.** Address to the Convention of Commissioners of Bureaus of Statistics of Labor. (1889)

[482] **Biggs. A. T**. et.al. "The lethality paradox: Goodhart's Law and the challenge of measuring lethality." The Journal of Defense Modeling and Simulation: Applications, Methodology, Technology. (2023). Change366's take: Goodhart's Law alters change management. When a measure becomes a target, it loses its effectiveness. Beware unintended consequences.

[483] **Hoskin, K**. "The Awful Idea of Accountability: Inscribing People Into the Measurement of Objects." (1996)

[484] **Heuristic Reasoning**. "Heuristics". Psychology Today. Change366's take: Heuristics are quick thinking shortcuts, good for saving time but can lead to errors. In change management, we learn that quick decisions can be handy, especially when many choices come in a limited timeframe.

[485] **Wilcox, E. W**. "The Heart of the New Thought." (1942)

[486] **Sugiyama, T**. et.al. "Reinforcement learning establishes a minimal metacognitive process to monitor and control motor learning performance." Nature Communications. (2023). Change366's take: In change management, like in learning, understanding how to learn better is vital. It's about monitoring and controlling our learning process, just like adjusting a motor skill. We can use a simple reinforcement learning mechanism to improve. Pay attention to feedback, adapt your strategies, and associate outcomes with learning. In change management, be open to learning from experience—it's the way to success.

[487] **Strickland, J**. Attributed. Diary Entry. (1863)

[488] **Berkman, E. T**. "The Last Thing You Need to Know About Ego Depletion: What the rise and fall of ego depletion says about motivation—and research." Psychology Today. (2020). Change366's take: Ego depletion, once a big idea in psychology, carries a lesson for organizational change. Like a worn-out theory, organizations often cling to ineffective change methods. Just as researchers questioned ego depletion, organizations must challenge their strategies. Don't stick to what doesn't work. Adapt and explore new paths for successful change.

[489] **Goal-Setting Theory**. "Locke's Goal-Setting Theory." MindTools. Change366's take: In change management, Locke and Latham's principles are like guiding stars. They say five things: be clear, set a challenge, get commitment, give feedback, and watch complexity. Clear goals show the way and help you measure. The goal should be a challenge, but not too hard. Teammates need to be on board with the goal, and feedback helps you know how you're doing. Don't forget, some tasks are complex, so take it slow.

[490] **Chebat, J**. "The Psychology of Employee Recognition v Reward." LinkedIn

[491] **Drucker, P**. "The Effective Executive." (2007)

[492] **Pelletier, L. G. & Rocchi, M**. "Organismic Integration Theory: A Theory of Regulatory Styles, Internalization, Integration, and Human Functioning in Society." Oxford Academic. (2023). Change366's take: Organismic Integration Theory (OIT) teaches key lessons for organizational change. It's about making company values personal to employees. People work better when they believe in what they do. This approach improves not just their work but also their well-being. Managers should create environments where employees willingly accept change. The theory also suggests looking beyond individual success to how everyone can help each other. In short, make change meaningful for people, and they'll work better and help more.

[493] **Nadella, S**. Microsoft Inspire. (2018)

[494] **Prosci** "3 Factors of Change Which Define or Constrain Project ROI."

[495] **Gothelf, J**. "Use OKR's to Set Goals for Teams, Not Individuals." Harvard Business Review. (2020)

[496] **Keefe, J**. "Influences of post-implementation factors on the sustainability, sustainment, and intra-organizational spread of complex interventions." BMC Health Services Research. (2022). Change366's take.

[497] **Nickerson, C**. "Schema Theory in Psychology." Simply Psychology. (2023). Change366's take: In managing change, it's key to understand and adjust how people think. Schemas are these mental maps. They shape how employees see and handle change. Change means reshaping these maps to fit new goals. It's about blending new info with old ways of thinking or changing these old ways. To manage change well, recognize and work with these mental maps of your team.

[498] **Garud, R**. "Path Dependence or Path Creation?" Journal of Management Studies. (2010). Change366's take.

[499] **Liebowitz, S. J. & Margolis, S. E**. "Network Effects and Externalities." The New Palgarve Dictionary of Economics and the Law. (2017). Change366's take: In organizational change, like in life, value comes in two parts: what it brings on its own (the core value) and what it gains when folks work together (the teamwork boost). Remember, in change, it's not just about what you introduce, but how people come together to make it truly shine. So, for change to thrive, unity is key.

[500] **Sydow, J**. et.al. "Organizational Paths: Path Dependency and Beyond." 21st EGOS Colloquium. (2005)

[501] **Hetemi, E**. et.al. "Exploring the emergence of lock-in in large-scale projects: A process view." International Journal of Project Management. (2020). Change366's take: Lock-in happens when past choices keep you on a failing course. It's not just about the choice but where and how it's made. You need

to think long-term and consider all influences. In managing change, it's about seeing the big picture, not just the decision in front of you.

[502] **Lee-Bourke, A.** "What They Don't Teach you at Change Management School." (2023)

[503] **Ryan, R. M. and Deci, E. L.** "Self-Determination Theory: Basic Psychological Needs in Motivation, Development, and Wellness." (2017)

[504] **Reeve, J.** "Cognitive Evaluation Theory: The Seedling That Keeps Self-Determination Theory Growing." Oxford Academic. (2023). Change366's take: Cognitive Evaluation Theory (CET) tells us about motivation. It says rewards, the feel of a place, and our own goals change how motivated we are. These things can inform us, control us, or demotivate us. Which one matters most changes how we feel motivated. CET started as part of a bigger idea, self-determination theory, to understand how outside rewards affect our inner drive. It helps this theory grow and stay useful today. The lesson is that understanding motivation needs looking at the outside factors and our inner goals.

[505] **Linh L.** "Detrimental effects of reward: Reality or myth?" American Psychologist. (1996). Change366's take.

[506] **Szulawski, M** et.al. "Is self-determination good for your effectiveness? A study of factors which influence performance within self-determination theory." (2021). Change366's take.

[507] **Sautter, R. A. & LeBlanc**, L. A. "Empirical Applications of Skinner's Analysis of Verbal Behavior with Humans." National Library of Medicine. (2006). Change366's take: Effective change relies on understanding the functional role of communication and using it strategically to reinforce and sustain desired outcomes.

[508] **Skinner, B.F.** "Verbal Behavior." (1957)

[509] **Echoic Reinforcement**. "Echoic Memory: Definition and Examples." Simply Psychology. (2023). Change366's take: Echoic reinforcement is like an echo in a canyon. It's about repeating key messages to embed the change. Like a steady drumbeat, it keeps the organization aligned and moving forward. This repetition makes the message familiar, guiding the organization through change with persistence and clarity.

[510] **Ermakov, D. & Ermakov, A**. "Memetic approach to cultural evolution." (2021). Change366's take: Culture's not solely human, and evolution isn't just for creatures. Memetics explores culture like biology, with memes as replicators. To reinforce organizational change, remember: Embrace evolution's ways; adapt, replicate, thrive.

[511] **Prosci.** "Reinforcing and Sustaining Change Management."

[512] **Ebbinghaus, H**. "Memory: A Contribution to Experimental Psychology." (1885)

[513] **Roesler, R & McGaugh, J. L.** "Memory Consolidation." Encyclopedia of Behavioral Neuroscience. (2010). Change366's take: In managing change in organizations, think of how memories stick in our minds. It takes time. Learning

changes our brains slowly, shaped by what we feel and face. In change management, it's the same. Changes must grow slowly, touching every part of the organization. It's a careful blend of thought and feeling, not a quick fix.

514 **Gentner, D**. "The Analogical Mind: Perspectives from Cognitive Science." (2001)

515 **Craik, F.** "Levels of Processing: A Framework for Memory Research." (1972)

516 **McLeod, S**. "Multi-Store Memory Model: Atkinson And Shiffrin." Simply Psychology. (2023). Change366's take: In managing change in organizations, think of how we remember. First, something catches our eye, like a flash. That's the start. Then, if it matters enough, we keep it in mind, working on it. This is like keeping a number in your head. Finally, if it really means something, it stays with us for good. Change in a company is like this. First, get noticed. Then, work it into daily thoughts. In the end, make it part of who you are.

517 **Teufel, C. & Fletcher, P. C**. "Forms of Prediction in the Nervous System." Nature Reviews: Neuroscience. (2020). Change366's take: In managing change, it's like understanding how we see the world. Top bosses may set the course, but real change happens on the ground. It's in the small, daily things that people do. Like our brains making sense of what we see, good change needs both the big plan and the small actions. If these don't match up, things go wrong, like when the brain gets mixed signals.

518 **Pinker, S**. "Enlightenment Now: The Case for Reason, Science, Humanism and Progress." (2018)

519 **Bruner, J**. "Acts of Meaning." (1990)

520 **Beck A. T**. "Coping with Depression." Paper by Beck, J and Broder, F Beck Institute for Cognitive Behavior Therapy. (2021)

521 **Neisser, U**. "Cognitive Psychology." (1967)

522 **Galanter, E**. et.al. "Plans for the Structure of Behavior." (1960)

523 **T.O.T.E Unit**. "Earth disciplines, cognitive sciences and the epistemology of complexity." (2013). Change366's take: The T.O.T.E. unit in organizational change is like a navigator's cycle: Test, Operate, Test, Exit. It's about assessing the situation, taking action, reassessing, and concluding. In change management, this means understanding the challenge, acting, checking the impact, and then deciding to continue or adjust. It's a loop of continuous adjustment, steering change efforts effectively towards the goal.

524 **Ellis, A**. "How to Stubbornly Refuse to Make Yourself Miserable About Anything: Yes, Anything!," (1988)

525 **Ruis** (////) refers to the Elder tree and represents transformation and wisdom. It is the thirteenth month in the Celtic "Tree Calendar" and is written in Ogham, the ancient writing system of the Irish Celts.

[526] **Prosci.** "The AI Effect: Transformative Impacts of Artificial Intelligence in Change Management." (late 2023)

[527] **de Saint-Exupéry, A.** "Night Flight." (1931)

[528] **Plato**. "Allegory of the Cave." From "The Republic." (375 BCE)

Printed in Great Britain
by Amazon